ExamSim

Experience accurate, simulated exams on your own computer with interactive ExamSim software. This computer-based test engine offers knowledge and scenario-based questions modeled after the real exam questions and exam review tools that show you where you went wrong and why. ExamSim also allows you to mark questions for further review and provides a score report that shows your overall performance on the exam.

Knowledge-based questions present challenging material in a multiple-choice format. Answer treatments not only explain why the correct options are right, they also tell you why the incorrect answers are wrong.

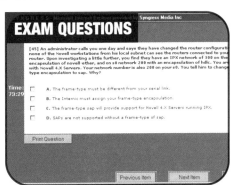

Scenario-based questions challenge your ability to analyze and address complex, real-world case studies. Some exam questions also include exhibits, just like the real exam.

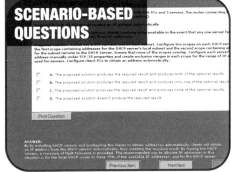

Additional CD-ROM Features

Complete hyperlinked **e-book** for easy information access and self-paced study.

System Requirements:

A PC running Microsoft® Internet Explorer version 5 or higher

The **Score Report** provides an overall assessment of your exam performance as well as performance history.

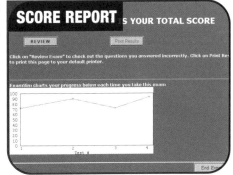

MCDBA SQL Server™ 2000 Database Design Study Guide

(Exam 70-229)

MCDBA SQL Server™ 2000 Database Design Study Guide

(Exam 70-229)

Jeffrey Bane

Anil Desai

Craig Robinson

Osborne McGraw-Hill

New York Chicago San Francisco Lisbon London Madrid
Mexico City Milan New Delhi San Juan Seoul Singapore Sydney Toronto

Osborne/**McGraw-Hill**
2600 Tenth Street
Berkeley, California 94710
U.S.A.

To arrange bulk purchase discounts for sales promotions, premiums, or fund-raisers, please contact Osborne/**McGraw-Hill** at the above address. For information on translations or book distributors outside the U.S.A., please see the International Contact Information page immediately following the index of this book.

MCDBA SQL Server™ 2000 Database Design Study Guide (Exam 70-229)

1234567890 DOC DOC 01987654321

Book p/n 0-07-212693-0 and CD p/n 0-07-212692-2
parts of
ISBN 0-07-212694-9

Publisher
Brandon A. Nordin

Vice President &
Associate Publisher
Scott Rogers

Editorial Director
Gareth Hancock

Associate Acquisitions Editor
Timothy Green

Project Editor
Jennifer Malnick

Acquisitions Coordinator
Jessica Wilson

Technical Editor
Kevin Martin, Dejan Sunderic

Copy Editor
Dennis Weaver

Proofreader
Linda Medoff

Indexer
Claire Splan

Computer Designer
Apollo Publishing Service

Series Design
Roberta Steele

This book was published with Corel VENTURA™ Publisher.

From Global Knowledge

At Global Knowledge we strive to support the multiplicity of learning styles required by our students to achieve success as technical professionals. In this series of books, it is our intention to offer the reader a valuable tool for successful completion of the MCSE and MCDBA Certification exams.

As the world's largest IT training company, Global Knowledge is uniquely positioned to offer these books. The expertise gained each year from providing instructor-led training to hundreds of thousands of students worldwide has been captured in book form to enhance your learning experience. We hope that the quality of these books demonstrates our commitment to your lifelong learning success. Whether you choose to learn through the written word, computer-based training, Web delivery, or instructor-led training, Global Knowledge is committed to providing you the very best in each of those categories. For those of you who know Global Knowledge, or those of you who have just found us for the first time, our goal is to be your lifelong competency partner.

Thank you for the opportunity to serve you. We look forward to serving your needs again in the future.

Warmest regards,

Duncan Anderson
President and Chief Executive Officer, Global Knowledge

The Global Knowledge Advantage

Global Knowledge has a global delivery system for its products and services. The company has 28 subsidiaries, and offers its programs through a total of 60+ locations. No other vendor can provide consistent services across a geographic area this large. Global Knowledge is the largest independent information technology education provider, offering programs on a variety of platforms. This enables our multi-platform and multi-national customers to obtain all of their programs from a single vendor. The company has developed the unique Competus™ Framework software tool and methodology which can quickly reconfigure courseware to the proficiency level of a student on an interactive basis. Combined with self-paced and on-line programs, this technology can reduce the time required for training by prescribing content in only the deficient skills areas. The company has fully automated every aspect of the education process, from registration and follow-up, to "just-in-time" production of courseware. Global Knowledge Network through its Enterprise Services Consultancy, can customize programs and products to suit the needs of an individual customer.

Global Knowledge Classroom Education Programs

The backbone of our delivery options is classroom-based education. Our modern, well-equipped facilities staffed with the finest instructors offer programs in a wide variety of information technology topics, many of which lead to professional certifications.

Custom Learning Solutions

This delivery option has been created for companies and governments that value customized learning solutions. For them, our consultancy-based approach of developing targeted education solutions is most effective at helping them meet specific objectives.

Self-Paced and Multimedia Products

This delivery option offers self-paced program titles in interactive CD-ROM, videotape and audio tape programs. In addition, we offer custom development of interactive multimedia courseware to customers and partners. Call us at 1-888-427-4228.

Electronic Delivery of Training

Our network-based training service delivers efficient competency-based, interactive training via the World Wide Web and organizational intranets. This leading-edge delivery option provides a custom learning path and "just-in-time" training for maximum convenience to students.

ARG

American Research Group (ARG), a wholly-owned subsidiary of Global Knowledge, one of the largest worldwide training partners of Cisco Systems, offers a wide range of internetworking, LAN/WAN, Bay Networks, FORE Systems, IBM, and UNIX courses. ARG offers hands on network training in both instructor-led classes and self-paced PC-based training.

Global Knowledge Courses Available

Network Fundamentals

- Understanding Computer Networks
- Telecommunications Fundamentals I
- Telecommunications Fundamentals II
- Understanding Networking Fundamentals
- Implementing Computer Telephony Integration
- Introduction to Voice Over IP
- Introduction to Wide Area Networking
- Cabling Voice and Data Networks
- Introduction to LAN/WAN protocols
- Virtual Private Networks
- ATM Essentials

Network Security & Management

- Troubleshooting TCP/IP Networks
- Network Management
- Network Troubleshooting
- IP Address Management
- Network Security Administration
- Web Security
- Implementing UNIX Security
- Managing Cisco Network Security
- Windows NT 4.0 Security

IT Professional Skills

- Project Management for IT Professionals
- Advanced Project Management for IT Professionals
- Survival Skills for the New IT Manager
- Making IT Teams Work

LAN/WAN Internetworking

- Frame Relay Internetworking
- Implementing T1/T3 Services
- Understanding Digital Subscriber Line (xDSL)
- Internetworking with Routers and Switches
- Advanced Routing and Switching
- Multi-Layer Switching and Wire-Speed Routing
- Internetworking with TCP/IP
- ATM Internetworking
- OSPF Design and Configuration
- Border Gateway Protocol (BGP) Configuration

Authorized Vendor Training

Cisco Systems

- Introduction to Cisco Router Configuration
- Advanced Cisco Router Configuration
- Installation and Maintenance of Cisco Routers
- Cisco Internetwork Troubleshooting
- Cisco Internetwork Design
- Cisco Routers and LAN Switches
- Catalyst 5000 Series Configuration
- Cisco LAN Switch Configuration
- Managing Cisco Switched Internetworks
- Configuring, Monitoring, and Troubleshooting Dial-Up Services
- Cisco AS5200 Installation and Configuration
- Cisco Campus ATM Solutions

Bay Networks

- Bay Networks Accelerated Router Configuration
- Bay Networks Advanced IP Routing
- Bay Networks Hub Connectivity
- Bay Networks Accelar 1xxx Installation and Basic Configuration
- Bay Networks Centillion Switching

FORE Systems

- FORE ATM Enterprise Core Products
- FORE ATM Enterprise Edge Products
- FORE ATM Theory
- FORE LAN Certification

Operating Systems & Programming

Microsoft

- Introduction to Windows NT
- Microsoft Networking Essentials
- Windows NT 4.0 Workstation
- Windows NT 4.0 Server
- Advanced Windows NT 4.0 Server
- Windows NT Networking with TCP/IP
- Introduction to Microsoft Web Tools
- Windows NT Troubleshooting
- Windows Registry Configuration

UNIX

- UNIX Level I
- UNIX Level II
- Essentials of UNIX and NT Integration

Programming

- Introduction to JavaScript
- Java Programming
- PERL Programming
- Advanced PERL with CGI for the Web

Web Site Management & Development

- Building a Web Site
- Web Site Management and Performance
- Web Development Fundamentals

High Speed Networking

- Essentials of Wide Area Networking
- Integrating ISDN
- Fiber Optic Network Design
- Fiber Optic Network Installation
- Migrating to High Performance Ethernet

DIGITAL UNIX

- UNIX Utilities and Commands
- DIGITAL UNIX v4.0 System Administration
- DIGITAL UNIX v4.0 (TCP/IP) Network Management
- AdvFS, LSM, and RAID Configuration and Management
- DIGITAL UNIX TruCluster Software Configuration and Management
- UNIX Shell Programming Featuring Kornshell
- DIGITAL UNIX v4.0 Security Management
- DIGITAL UNIX v4.0 Performance Management
- DIGITAL UNIX v4.0 Intervals Overview

DIGITAL OpenVMS

- OpenVMS Skills for Users
- OpenVMS System and Network Node Management I
- OpenVMS System and Network Node Management II
- OpenVMS System and Network Node Management III
- OpenVMS System and Network Node Operations
- OpenVMS for Programmers
- OpenVMS System Troubleshooting for Systems Managers
- Configuring and Managing Complex VMScluster Systems
- Utilizing OpenVMS Features from C
- OpenVMS Performance Management
- Managing DEC TCP/IP Services for OpenVMS
- Programming in C

Hardware Courses

- AlphaServer 1000/1000A Installation, Configuration and Maintenance
- AlphaServer 2100 Server Maintenance
- AlphaServer 4100, Troubleshooting Techniques and Problem Solving

ABOUT THE AUTHORS

Jeffrey Bane, MCSE, MCDBA, is an independent database consultant in southwest Florida. He has architected several high-profile e-commerce and cooperate databases, as well as written for SQL Server magazine numerous times. He specializes in E-business, SQL Server, and XML. He may be contacted at Jeff.Bane@TeamAllaire.com.

Anil Desai, MCSE, MCSD, MCDBA, is a Technical Architect for QuickArrow, Inc., in Austin, TX. Anil is the author of several technical books, including: *SQL Server 2000 Backup and Recovery* (Osborne / McGraw-Hill), *Windows 2000 Directory Services Administration Exam Guide: Exam 70-217* (Sybex), and *Windows NT Network Management: Reducing Total Cost of Ownership* (New Riders Press). He has made dozens of conference presentations at national events and is also a contributor to national magazines. For more information, please see http://home.austin.rr.com/akdesai or contact him at anil@austin.rr.com.

Craig Robinson is a Senior Database Developer for QuickArrow, Inc., in Austin, Texas. He has worked with Microsoft SQL Server and Oracle databases as a designer and developer for the past six years while consulting and working for small startups.

ACKNOWLEDGMENTS

We would like to thank the following people:

- Richard Kristof of Global Knowledge for championing the series and providing access to some great people and information.

- All the incredibly hard-working folks at Osborne/McGraw-Hill: Brandon Nordin, Scott Rogers, Gareth Hancock, Tim Green, and Jessica Wilson for their help in launching a great series and being solid team players.

- Jeffrey Bane would like to thank his wife and family for putting up with the long hours involved in the writing of this book, as well as noted Cold Fusion developer Hal Helms for encouraging him to start writing so many years back. Knowledge should be shared.

- Anil Desai would like to thank his wife, Monica, for her patience and support in the writing of this book, and the staff at QuickArrow, Inc., for being a great group of people to work with.

- Craig Robinson would like to thank his lovely wife, Mary, for her support and patience, as well as Phil Gingras, David Barnes, and Jennie Hoff for allowing him the opportunity to begin working with databases so many years ago.

CONTENTS AT A GLANCE

CONTENTS

PREFACE

If you're reading this right now, there's a good chance that you're already aware of the importance of relational databases in today's technical and business environment. We're also willing to bet that many readers have had at least a little experience with Microsoft SQL Server 2000. Microsoft has released this exam to test the capabilities of those who design and implement databases using its flagship relational database server platform. In some ways, this exam is an update of the SQL Server 7.0 exams. In others, however, the focus and attention to new features make it a different type of challenge.

This book covers information that will help you thoroughly prepare for taking a challenging exam. In all areas of the book, we've made sure to include details wherever relevant, and to explain difficult concepts as clearly and concisely as possible. Wherever possible, we've included real-world information and details that you should focus on for passing the live exam.

Microsoft's Exam Preparation Guide for this test lists many challenging objectives and skill requirements. Rest assured, however, that with adequate knowledge and practice, passing the exam should be a very attainable goal.

In This Book

This book is organized in such a way as to serve as an in-depth review for Microsoft *Exam 70-229: Designing and Implementing Databases with Microsoft® SQL Server™ 2000 Enterprise Edition.* This exam is designed to test the knowledge and capabilities of those IT professionals who work with SQL Server 2000 in a development role.

This book has been designed to present many topics related to SQL Server 2000 in an organized and through fashion. Each chapter covers a major aspect of the exam, and should answer several questions. First, we'll present background about why a particular topic or feature of SQL Server 2000 is relevant. It has become increasingly important for technical professionals, especially those who work with applications and database systems, to understand how technical solutions can fit business challenges. With this information in mind, each chapter drills down into the technical details of designing and implementing SQL Server 2000 databases, focusing on useful features. In-depth information about various commands and procedures is presented to ensure that you become proficient with SQL Server 2000's many features.

Of course, this information isn't just presented for the sake of knowledge. The emphasis throughout this book is to prepare you for Exam 70-229. You'll see this in the various Scenarios and Solutions, On the Job, From the Classroom, and Exam Watch notes. Overall, we feel that this book will serve as an excellent foundation in your preparation for the test, as well as for your general database-related skills. Happy reading, and good luck on the exam and your career!

On the CD

The CD-ROM contains the CertTrainer software. CertTrainer comes complete with ExamSim, Skill Assessment tests, and the e-book (electronic version of the book). CertTrainer is easy to install on any Windows 98/NT/2000/XP computer and must be installed to access these features. You may, however, browse the e-book direct from the CD without installation. For more information on the CD-ROM, please see Appendix A.

In Every Chapter

We've created a set of chapter components that call your attention to important items, reinforce important points, and provide helpful exam-taking hints. Take a look at what you'll find in every chapter:

- Every chapter begins with the **Certification Objectives**—what you need to know in order to pass the section on the exam dealing with the chapter topic. The Objective headings identify the objectives within the chapter, so you'll always know an objective when you see it!

- **Exam Watch** notes call attention to information about, and potential pitfalls in, the exam. These helpful hints are written by authors who have taken the exams and received their certification—who better to tell you what to worry about? They know what you're about to go through!

- Practice Exercises are interspersed throughout the chapters. These are step-by-step exercises that allow you to get the hands-on experience you need in order to pass the exams. They help you master skills that are likely to be an area of   focus on the exam. Don't just read through the exercises; they are hands-on practice that you should be comfortable completing. Learning by doing is an effective way to increase your competency with a product. The practical exercises will be very helpful for any simulation exercises you may encounter on the MCSE Migrating from Windows NT 4.0 to Windows 2000 exam.

on the
job

■ **On The Job** notes describe the issues that come up most often in real-world settings. They provide a valuable perspective on certification- and product-related topics. They point out common mistakes and address questions that have arisen from on the job discussions and experience.

■ **From The Classroom** sidebars describe the issues that come up most often in the training classroom setting. These sidebars highlight some of the most common and confusing problems that students encounter when taking a live Windows 2000 training course. You can get a leg up on those difficult to understand subjects by focusing extra attention on these sidebars.

■ **Scenario and Solutions** sections lay out potential problems and solutions in a quick-to-read format.

SCENARIO & SOLUTION

You want to measure the overall performance of your server, including CPU and memory utilization.	Use Performance Monitor and add the appropriate objects and counters. You can also create logs of performance activity for longer-term analysis.
You want to find the worst-performing queries in your application.	Use SQL Profiler to monitor for the worst-performing queries.
You want to be notified whenever there is a large number of locks on your database server.	Use SQL Server Alerts to configure a threshold and the methods in which the SQL Agent should notify you should the number of locks exceed the threshold.
You want to find out why a specific query is taking a long time to execute.	Use the graphical execution plan in Query Analyzer to find out which steps are taking the most time to complete.

■ The **Certification Summary** is a succinct review of the chapter and a restatement of salient points regarding the exam.

✓ ■ The **Two-Minute Drill** at the end of every chapter is a checklist of the main points of the chapter. It can be used for last-minute review.

Q&A
- The **Self Test** offers questions similar to those found on the certification exams. The answers to these questions, as well as explanations of the answers, can be found at the end of each chapter. By taking the Self Test after completing each chapter, you'll reinforce what you've learned from that chapter while becoming familiar with the structure of the exam questions.

- The **Lab Question** at the end of the Self Test section offers a unique and challenging question format that requires the reader to understand multiple chapter concepts to answer correctly. These questions are more complex and more comprehensive than the other questions, as they test your ability to take all the knowledge you have gained from reading the chapter and apply it to complicated, real-world situations. These questions are aimed to be more difficult than what you will find on the exam. If you can answer these questions, you have proven that you know the subject!

Some Pointers

When it comes to working with relational databases, the more practice and review you have, the better prepared you will be for the exam. In many of the concepts that we'll present in this book, you'll find that practice makes perfect!

Once you've finished reading this book, set aside some time to do a thorough review. You might want to return to the book several times and make use of all the methods it offers for reviewing the material.

1. *Re-read all the Two-Minute Drills*, or have someone quiz you. You also can use the drills as a way to do a quick cram before the exam. You might want to make some flash cards out of 3 × 5 index cards that have the Two-Minute Drill material on them. Be sure to review any of the points that you don't feel you thoroughly understand.

2. *Re-read all the Exam Watch notes.* Remember that these notes are written by authors who have taken the exam and passed. They know what you should expect—and what you should be on the lookout for.

3. *Review all the S&S sections* for quick problem solving and for preparing for the scenario-based test questions.

4. *Re-take the Self Tests.* Taking the tests right after you've read the chapter is a good idea, because the questions help reinforce what you've just learned.

However, it's an even better idea to go back later and do all the questions in the book in one sitting. Pretend that you're taking the live exam. (When you go through the questions the first time, you should mark your answers on a separate piece of paper. That way, you can run through the questions as many times as you need to until you feel comfortable with the material.)

5. *Complete the Exercises.* Did you do the exercises when you read through each chapter? If not, do them! These exercises are designed to cover exam topics, and there's no better way to get to know this material than by practicing. Be sure you understand why you are performing each step in each exercise. If there is something you are not clear on, re-read that section in the chapter.

INTRODUCTION

S QL Server 2000 can form the core of any business application, and the design and implementation of relational databases is an important concept for all IT professionals. Therefore, it should come as no surprise to you that Exam 70-229: *Designing and Implementing Databases with Microsoft SQL Server 2000 Enterprise Edition* can count as part of various Microsoft's premier certifications. In this section, we'll look at the requirements for the MCDBA certification (where Exam 70-229 is a core requirements), and for the MCSE and MCSD certifications (where Exam 70-229 is an elective).

Note: All of the information contained in this section was current to the time of the writing of this book. As Microsoft reserves the right to change, revise and update certification exam details, be sure to visit www.microsoft.com/trainingandservices for the most recent information before you take an exam.

MCDBA Certification

The Microsoft Certified Database Administrator (MCDBA) certification is designed for IT professionals and developers that focus on the design, implementation, administration and optimization of SQL Server 2000. Following are the requirements to obtain the MCDBA certification from Microsoft.

Microsoft Windows 2000 MCDBA Track

3 Core Exams Required:		
Candidates Who Have Not Already Passed 3 Windows NT 4.0 Exams	OR	Candidates Who Have Passed 3 Windows NT 4.0 Exams (Exams 70-067, 70-068, and 70-073)
Exam 70-215: Installing, Configuring and Administering Microsoft Windows 2000 Server		*Exam 70-240: Microsoft Windows 2000 Accelerated Exam for MCPs Certified on Microsoft Windows NT 4.0
PLUS - All Candidates - Both of the Following Exams are Required:		

Exam 70-028: Administering Microsoft SQL Server 7.0 OR Exam 70-228: Installing, Configuring, and Administering Microsoft SQL Server 2000 Enterprise Edition		
Exam 70-029: Designing and Implementing Databases with Microsoft SQL Server 7.0 OR Exam 70-229: Designing and Implementing Databases with Microsoft SQL Server 2000 Enterprise Edition		
PLUS - All Candidates - I Elective Exam Required:		
Candidates Who Have Not Already Passed 3 Windows NT 4.0 Exams	**OR**	Candidates Who Have Passed 3 Windows NT 4.0 Exams (Exams 70-067, 70-068, and 70-073)
Exam 70-216: Implementing and Administering a Microsoft Windows 2000 Network Infrastructure		*Exam 70-240: Microsoft Windows 2000 Accelerated Exam for MCPs Certified on Microsoft Windows NT 4.0
Exam 70-015: Designing and Implementing Distributed Applications with Microsoft Visual C++ 6.0		
Exam 70-019: Designing and Implementing Data Warehouses with Microsoft SQL Server 7.0		
Exam 70-087: Implementing and Supporting Microsoft Internet Information Server 4.0 (This exam has retired. Please see the "**Retirement of Exams**" notice.)		
Exam 70-155: Designing and Implementing Distributed Applications with Microsoft Visual FoxPro 6.0		
Exam 70-175: Designing and Implementing Distributed Applications with Microsoft Visual Basic 6.0		
Candidates who pass accelerated Exam 70-240 (and have also passed the three Windows NT 4.0 exams as a prerequisite) will receive credit for it as both a core exam and an elective exam in the MCDBA track. Generally, an exam that can be used as either a core or an elective counts only once toward a certification. Exam 70-240 in the MCDBA track is an exception.		

Note: At the time of this writing, Microsoft also offers a Windows NT 4.0 certification track for its premier certifications. However, this track will be retired at the end of 2001, and Microsoft is urging all new candidates to pursue the Windows 2000 track. Therefore, we have not included details related to the Windows NT 4.0 track. For details, see the Microsoft Training and Services Web site (www.microsoft.com/trainingandservices).

MCSE Certification

The Microsoft Certified Systems Engineer (MCSE) is Microsoft's premier certification for IT professionals who work with Windows 2000 and the Active

Directory. Exam 70-229 serves as an elective for this certification. A complete list of other electives is updated often and is available on the Microsoft Training and Services Web site. The following table lists the requirements to obtain the MCSE certification from Microsoft.

Microsoft Windows 2000 MCSE Track

Core Exams		
For candidates who have not already passed Windows NT 4.0 exams, all 4 of the following core exams are required:	OR	Candidates who have passed 3 Windows NT 4.0 exams (Exams 70-067, 70-068, and 70-073) instead of the 4 core exams at left may take the following:
Exam 70-210: Installing, Configuring and Administering Microsoft Windows 2000 Professional		Exam 70-240: Microsoft Windows 2000 Accelerated Exam for MCPs Certified on Microsoft Windows NT 4.0. (This accelerated, intensive exam, which will be available June 30, 2000, through December 31, 2001, covers the core competencies of exams 70-210, 70-215, 70-216, and 70-217.)
Exam 70-215: Installing, Configuring and Administering Microsoft Windows 2000 Server		
Exam 70-216: Implementing and Administering a Microsoft Windows 2000 Network Infrastructure		
Exam 70-217: Implementing and Administering a Microsoft Windows 2000 Directory Services Infrastructure		
PLUS - All Candidates – 1 of the Following Core Exams Required:		
*Exam 70-219: Designing a Microsoft Windows 2000 Directory Services Infrastructure		
*Exam 70-220: Designing Security for a Microsoft Windows 2000 Network		
*Exam 70-221: Designing a Microsoft Windows 2000 Network Infrastructure		
*Exam 70-226: Designing Highly Available Web Solutions with Microsoft Windows 2000 Server Technologies		

Elective Exams (Choose 2)

Candidates are required to pass any two elective exams. (Selected third-party credentials that focus on interoperability with Windows 2000 will be accepted as an alternative to one elective exam. Acceptable credentials have not yet been determined. We are evaluating potential third-party credentials and will list acceptable credentials on this page when they are selected.)

MCSD Certification

The Microsoft Certified Solutions Developer (MCSD) is Microsoft's premier certification for developers that work with Microsoft developer products. The focus is on the design and implementation of various types of business applications. Exam 70-229 serves as an elective for this certification. A complete list of other electives is updated often and is available on the Microsoft Training and Services Web site. The following table lists the requirements to obtain the MCSD certification from Microsoft.

MCSD Track

Core Exams (3 required)
Desktop Applications Development (1 required)
*Exam 70-016: Designing and Implementing Desktop Applications with Microsoft Visual C++ 6.0
*Exam 70-156: Designing and Implementing Desktop Applications with Microsoft Visual FoxPro 6.0
*Exam 70-176: Designing and Implementing Desktop Applications with Microsoft Visual Basic 6.0
Distributed Applications Development (1 required)
*Exam 70-015: Designing and Implementing Distributed Applications with Microsoft Visual C++ 6.0
*Exam 70-155: Designing and Implementing Distributed Applications with Microsoft Visual FoxPro 6.0
*Exam 70-175: Designing and Implementing Distributed Applications with Microsoft Visual Basic 6.0
Solution Architecture (required)
Exam 70-100: Analyzing Requirements and Defining Solution Architectures
Elective Exams (1 required): See Web site
* Core exams that can also be used as elective exams can only be counted once toward a certification. In other words, if a candidate receives credit for an exam as a core in one track, the candidate will not receive credit for that same exam as an elective in the same track.

How to Take a Microsoft Certification Exam

If you have taken a Microsoft Certification exam before, we have some good news and some bad news. The good news is that the new testing formats will be a true measure of your ability and knowledge. Microsoft has "raised the bar" for its Windows 2000 certification exams, including the SQL Server 2000 exams. If you are an expert in the Windows 2000 operating system, and can troubleshoot and engineer efficient, cost effective solutions using SQL 2000, you will have no difficulty with the new exam.

The bad news is that if you have used resources such as "brain-dumps," boot-camps, or exam-specific practice tests as your only method of test preparation, you will undoubtedly fail your exams. The new MCDBA exams will test your knowledge, and your ability to apply that knowledge in more sophisticated and accurate ways than was expected for the SQL 7 exams.

In the new certification exams, Microsoft may use a variety of testing formats that include product simulations, adaptive testing, drag-and-drop matching, and possibly even fill-in-the-blank questions (also called "free response" questions). While Exam 70-229 is not likely to include most of these format options, Microsoft recommends that test takers familiarize themselves with all the possible options. The test-taking process will measure the examinee's fundamental knowledge of SQL Server 2000 rather than the ability to memorize a few facts and then answer a few simple multiple-choice questions.

In addition, the pool of questions for each exam will significantly increase. The greater number of questions combined with the adaptive testing techniques will enhance the validity and security of the certification process.

We will begin by looking at the purpose, focus, and structure of Microsoft certification tests, and examine the effect that these factors have on the kinds of questions you will face on your certification exams. We will define the structure of exam questions and investigate some common formats. Next, we will present a strategy for answering these questions. Finally, we will give some specific guidelines on what you should do on the day of your test.

Why Vendor Certification?

The Microsoft Certified Professional program, like the certification programs from Cisco, Novell, Oracle, and other software vendors, is maintained for the ultimate purpose of increasing the corporation's profits. A successful vendor certification program accomplishes this goal by helping to create a pool of experts in a company's software and by "branding" these experts so companies using the software can identify them.

We know that vendor certification has become increasingly popular in the last few years because it helps employers find qualified workers and because it helps software vendors like Microsoft sell their products. But why vendor certification rather than a more traditional approach, like a college degree in computer science? A college education is a broadening and enriching experience, but a degree in computer science does not prepare students for most jobs in the IT industry.

A common truism in our business states, "If you are out of the IT industry for three years and want to return, you have to start over." The problem, of course, is *timeliness;* if a first-year student learns about a specific computer program, it probably will no longer be in wide use when he or she graduates. Although some colleges are trying to integrate Microsoft certification into their curriculum, the problem is not really a flaw in higher education, but a characteristic of the IT industry. Computer software is changing so rapidly that a four-year college just can't keep up.

A marked characteristic of the Microsoft certification program is an emphasis on performing specific job tasks rather than merely gathering knowledge. It may come as a shock, but most potential employers do not care how much you know about the theory of operating systems, networking, or database design. As one IT manager put it, "I don't really care what my employees know about the theory of our network. We don't need someone to sit at a desk and think about it. We need people who can actually do something to make it work better."

You should not think that this attitude is some kind of anti-intellectual revolt against "book learning." Knowledge is a necessary prerequisite, but it is not enough. More than one company has hired a computer science graduate as a network administrator, only to learn that the new employee has no idea how to add users, assign permissions, or perform the other day-to-day tasks necessary to maintain a network. This brings us to the second major characteristic of Microsoft certification that affects the questions you must be prepared to answer. In addition to timeliness, Microsoft certification is also job-task oriented.

The timeliness of Microsoft's certification program is obvious and is inherent in the fact that you will be tested on current versions of software in wide use today. The job-task orientation of Microsoft certification is almost as obvious, but testing real-world job skills using a computer-based test is not easy.

Computerized Testing

Considering the popularity of Microsoft certification, and the fact that certification candidates are spread around the world, the only practical way to administer tests for the certification program is through Sylvan Prometric or Vue testing centers, which operate internationally. Sylvan Prometric and Vue provide proctor testing services for Microsoft, Oracle, Novell, Lotus, and the A+ computer technician certification. Although the IT industry accounts for much of Sylvan's revenue, the company provides services for a number of other businesses and organizations, such as FAA pre-flight pilot tests. Historically, several hundred questions were developed for a new Microsoft certification exam. The SQL Server 2000 MCSE and MCDBA exam pool contained hundreds of new questions. Microsoft is aware that many new MCSE and MCDBA candidates have been able to access information on test questions via the Internet or other resources. The company is very concerned about maintaining the MCSE and MCDBA as "premium" certifications. The significant increase in the number of test questions, together with stronger enforcement of the NDA (non-disclosure agreement) will ensure that a higher standard for certification is attained.

Microsoft treats the test-building process very seriously. Test questions are first reviewed by a number of subject matter experts for technical accuracy and then are presented in a beta test. Taking the beta test may require several hours, due to the large number of questions. After a few weeks, Microsoft Certification uses the statistical feedback from Sylvan to check the performance of the beta questions. The beta test group for the Windows 2000 certification series included MCTs, MCSEs, and members of Microsoft's rapid deployment partners groups. Because the exams will be normalized based on this population, you can be sure that the passing scores will be difficult to achieve without detailed product knowledge.

Questions are discarded if most test takers get them right (too easy) or wrong (too difficult) and a number of other statistical measures are taken of each question. Although the scope of our discussion precludes a rigorous treatment of question analysis, you should be aware that Microsoft and other vendors spend a great deal of time and effort making sure their exam questions are valid. The questions that survive statistical analysis form the pool of questions for the final certification exam.

Test Structure

The questions in a Microsoft certification exam may not be equally weighted. From what we can tell at the present time, different questions are given a value based on the level of difficulty. You will get more credit for getting a difficult question correct than for getting an easy question correct. Because the questions are weighted differently, and because the exams may use the adaptive method of computerized testing, your score may not bear any relationship to how many questions you answered correctly.

Microsoft has implemented *adaptive* testing. Microsoft intends to convert all of its conventional exams into the adaptive format once enough data has been gathered on a particular pool of test takers. Some exams may only be offered in the conventional format if the pool of test takers is too small to gather accurate statistical data. At the time of this publication, exam 70-229 is being offered in the conventional format.

When an adaptive test begins, the candidate is first given a level-three question. If it is answered correctly, a question from the next higher level is presented, and an incorrect response results in a question from the next lower level. When 15 to 20 questions have been answered in this manner, the scoring algorithm is able to predict, with a high degree of statistical certainty, whether the candidate would pass or fail if all the questions in the form were answered. When the required degree of certainty is attained, the test ends and the candidate receives a pass/fail grade.

Adaptive testing has some definite advantages for everyone involved in the certification process. Adaptive tests allow Sylvan Prometric or Vue to deliver more tests with the same resources, as certification candidates often are in and out in 30 minutes or less. For candidates, the "fatigue factor" is reduced due to the shortened testing time. For Microsoft, adaptive testing means that fewer test questions are exposed to each candidate, and this can enhance the security, and therefore the overall validity, of certification tests.

One possible problem you may have with adaptive testing is that you are not allowed to mark and revisit questions. Since the adaptive algorithm is interactive, and all questions but the first are selected on the basis of your response to the previous question, it is not possible to skip a particular question or change an answer. See the Microsoft Training and Services Web site for more information about Microsoft's position on adaptive testing.

Question Types

Computerized test questions can be presented in a number of ways. Some of the possible formats are used on Microsoft certification exam and some are not.

True/False

We are all familiar with True/False questions, but because of the inherent 50 percent chance of guessing the correct answer, you will not see questions of this type on Microsoft certification exams.

Multiple Choice

The majority of Microsoft certification questions are in the multiple-choice format, with either a single correct answer or multiple correct answers. One interesting variation on multiple-choice questions with multiple correct answers is whether or not the candidate is told how many answers are correct.

EXAMPLE:
Which two files can be altered to configure the MS-DOS environment?
(Choose two.)

Or

Which files can be altered to configure the MS-DOS environment?
(Choose all that apply.)

You may see both variations on Microsoft certification exams, but the trend seems to be toward the first type, where candidates are told explicitly how many answers are correct. Questions of the "choose all that apply" variety are more difficult and can be merely confusing.

Graphical Questions

One or more graphical elements are sometimes used as exhibits to help present or clarify an exam question. These elements may take the form of a network diagram, pictures of networking components, or screen shots from the software on which you are being tested. It is often easier to present the concepts required for a complex performance-based scenario with a graphic than with words.

Drag and Drop

There could also be several "drag and drop" questions on the 70-229 exam. See www.microsoft.com for a more detailed explanation of the "drag and drop" question type.

Knowledge-Based and Performance-Based Questions

Microsoft Certification develops a blueprint for each Microsoft certification exam with input from subject matter experts. This blueprint defines the content areas and objectives for each test, and each test question is created to test a specific objective. The basic information from the examination blueprint can be found on Microsoft's Web site in the Exam Prep Guide for each test.

Psychometricians (psychologists who specialize in designing and analyzing tests) categorize test questions as knowledge-based or performance-based. As the names imply, knowledge-based questions are designed to test knowledge, while performance-based questions are designed to test performance.

Some objectives demand a knowledge-based question. For example, objectives that use verbs like *list* and *identify* tend to test only what you know, not what you can do.

EXAMPLE:
Objective: Identify the MS-DOS configuration files.
Which two files can be altered to configure the MS-DOS environment? (Choose two.)

    A. COMMAND.COM

    B. AUTOEXEC.BAT

    C. IO.SYS

    D. CONFIG.SYS
       Correct answers: B and **D**

Other objectives use action verbs like *install, configure,* and *troubleshoot* to define job tasks. These objectives can often be tested with either a knowledge-based question or a performance-based question.

EXAMPLE:
Objective: Configure an MS-DOS installation appropriately using the PATH statement in AUTOEXEC.BAT.

A knowledge-based question might be:
What is the correct syntax to set a path to the D: directory in AUTOEXEC.BAT?

A. SET PATH EQUAL TO D:

B. PATH D:

C. SETPATH D:

D. D:EQUALS PATH
Correct answer: B

A performance-based question might be:
Your company uses several DOS accounting applications that access a group of common utility programs. What is the best strategy for configuring the computers in the accounting department so that the accounting applications will always be able to access the utility programs?

A. Store all the utilities on a single floppy disk and make a copy of the disk for each computer in the accounting department.

B. Copy all the utilities to a directory on the C: drive of each computer in the accounting department and add a PATH statement pointing to this directory in the AUTOEXEC.BAT files.

C. Copy all the utilities to all application directories on each computer in the accounting department.

D. Place all the utilities in the C: directory on each computer, because the C: directory is automatically included in the PATH statement when AUTOEXEC.BAT is executed.
Correct answer: B

Even in this simple example, the superiority of the performance-based question is obvious. Whereas the knowledge-based question asks for a single fact, the performance-based question presents a real-life situation and requires that you make a decision based on this scenario. Thus, performance-based questions give more bang (validity) for the test author's buck (individual question).

Testing Job Performance

We have said that Microsoft certification focuses on timeliness and the ability to perform job tasks. We have also introduced the concept of performance-based questions, but even performance-based multiple-choice questions do not really measure performance. Another strategy is needed to test job skills.

Given unlimited resources, it is not difficult to test job skills. In an ideal world, Microsoft would fly MCP candidates to Redmond, place them in a controlled environment with a team of experts, and ask them to plan, install, maintain, and troubleshoot a Windows network or Exchange server. In a few days at most, the experts could reach a valid decision as to whether each candidate should or should not be granted MCDBA or MCSE status. Needless to say, this is not likely to happen.

Closer to reality, another way to test performance is by using the actual software and creating a testing program to present tasks and automatically grade a candidate's performance when the tasks are completed. This *cooperative* approach would be practical in some testing situations, but the same test that is presented to MCP candidates in Boston must also be available in Bahrain and Botswana. The most workable solution for measuring performance in today's testing environment is a *simulation* program. When the program is launched during a test, the candidate sees a simulation of the actual software that looks, and behaves, just like the real thing. When the testing software presents a task, the simulation program is launched and the candidate performs the required task. The testing software then grades the candidate's performance on the required task and moves to the next question. Simulation questions provide many advantages over other testing methodologies, and simulations are expected to become increasingly important in the Microsoft certification program. For example, studies have shown that there is a very high correlation between the ability to perform simulated tasks on a computer-based test and the ability to perform the actual job tasks. Thus, simulations enhance the validity of the certification process.

Another truly wonderful benefit of simulations is in the area of test security. It is just not possible to cheat on a simulation question. In fact, you will be told exactly what tasks you are expected to perform on the test. How can a certification candidate cheat? By learning to perform the tasks? What a concept!

Study Strategies

There are appropriate ways to study for the different types of questions you will see on a Microsoft certification exam.

Knowledge-Based Questions

Knowledge-based questions require that you memorize facts. There are hundreds of facts inherent in every content area of every Microsoft certification exam. There are several keys to memorizing facts:

- **Repetition** The more times your brain is exposed to a fact, the more likely you are to remember it.

- **Association** Connecting facts within a logical framework makes them easier to remember.

- **Motor Association** It is often easier to remember something if you write it down or perform some other physical act, like clicking on a practice test answer.

We have said that the emphasis of Microsoft certification is job performance, and that there are very few knowledge-based questions on Microsoft certification exams. Why should you waste a lot of time learning filenames, IP address formulas, and other minutiae? Read on.

Performance-Based Questions

Most of the questions you will face on a Microsoft certification exam are performance-based scenario questions. We have discussed the superiority of these questions over simple knowledge-based questions, but you should remember that the job task orientation of Microsoft certification extends the knowledge you need to pass the exams; it does not replace this knowledge. Therefore, the first step in preparing for scenario questions is to absorb as many facts relating to the exam content areas as you can. In other words, go back to the previous section and follow the steps to prepare for an exam composed of knowledge-based questions.

The second step is to familiarize yourself with the format of the questions you are likely to see on the exam. You can do this by answering the questions in this study guide, by using Microsoft assessment tests, or by using practice tests on the included CD-ROM. The day of your test is not the time to be surprised by the construction of Microsoft exam questions.

At best, performance-based scenario questions really do test certification candidates at a higher cognitive level than knowledge-based questions. At worst, these questions can test your reading comprehension and test-taking ability rather than your ability to use Microsoft products. Be sure to get in the habit of reading the question carefully to determine what is being asked.

The third step in preparing for Microsoft scenario questions is to adopt the following attitude: Multiple-choice questions aren't really performance-based. It is all a cruel lie. These scenario questions are just knowledge-based questions with a story wrapped around them.

To answer a scenario question, you have to sift through the story to the underlying facts of the situation and apply your knowledge to determine the correct answer. This may sound silly at first, but the process we go through in solving real-life problems is quite similar. The key concept is that every scenario question (and every real-life problem) has a fact at its center, and if we can identify that fact, we can answer the question.

Signing Up

Signing up to take a Microsoft certification exam is easy. Sylvan Prometric or Vue operators in each country can schedule tests at any testing center. There are, however, a few things you should know:

1. If you call Sylvan Prometric or Vue during a busy time, get a cup of coffee first, because you may be in for a long wait. The exam providers do an excellent job, but everyone in the world seems to want to sign up for a test on Monday morning.

2. You will need your social security number or some other unique identifier to sign up for a test, so have it at hand.

3. Pay for your test by credit card if at all possible. This makes things easier, and you can even schedule tests for the same day you call, if space is available at your local testing center.

4. Know the number and title of the test you want to take before you call. This is not essential, and the Sylvan operators will help you if they can. Having this information in advance, however, speeds up and improves the accuracy of the registration process.

Taking the Test

Teachers have always told you not to try to cram for exams because it does no good. If you are faced with a knowledge-based test requiring only that you regurgitate facts, cramming can mean the difference between passing and failing. This is not the case, however, with Microsoft certification exams. If you don't know it the night before, don't bother to stay up and cram.

Instead, create a schedule and stick to it. Plan your study time carefully, and do not schedule your test until you think you are ready to succeed. Follow these guidelines on the day of your exam:

1. Get a good night's sleep. The scenario questions you will face on a Microsoft certification exam require a clear head.

2. Remember to take two forms of identification—at least one with a picture. A driver's license with your picture and social security or credit card is acceptable.

3. Leave home in time to arrive at your testing center a few minutes early. It is not a good idea to feel rushed as you begin your exam.

4. Do not spend too much time on any one question. You cannot mark and revisit questions on an adaptive test, so you must do your best on each question as you go.

5. If you do not know the answer to a question, try to eliminate the obviously wrong answers and guess from the rest. If you can eliminate two out of four options, you have a 50 percent chance of guessing the correct answer.

6. For scenario questions, follow the steps we outlined earlier. Read the question carefully and try to identify the facts at the center of the story.

Finally, we would advise anyone attempting to earn Microsoft MCDBA and MCSE certification to adopt a philosophical attitude. The Windows 2000 MCSE will be the most difficult MCSE ever to be offered. The questions will be at a higher cognitive level than seen on all previous MCSE exams. Therefore, even if you are the kind of person who never fails a test, you are likely to fail at least one Windows 2000 certification test somewhere along the way. Do not get discouraged. Microsoft wants to ensure the value of your certification. Moreover, it will attempt to do so by keeping the standard as high as possible. If Microsoft certification were easy to obtain, more people would have it, and it would not be so respected and so valuable to your future in the IT industry.

1

An Overview of
SQL Server 2000

CERTIFICATION OBJECTIVES

Providing an overview of the features
and architecture of SQL Server 2000

Q&A   Self Test

The goal of this chapter is to provide an introduction and an overview of the features in SQL Server 2000. The content of this chapter will provide a brief introduction to the types of information you'll need to know for the exam, but it will not explore them in detail. Therefore, you should refer to the chapters that cover these topics in-depth for details on the exam objectives. For now, don't worry about memorizing every detail—you'll be exposed to the information that's important for the exam in later chapters.

Relational database systems deal with some issues that are very different from those affecting operating systems. The fundamental purpose of these machines is to store and provide data to many users quickly. They must do this while maintaining the integrity of the data they contain.

In many ways, dealing with relational database systems is a very different task when compared to working with other types of information technology systems. There are two main areas of responsibility for database systems. Microsoft (and others in the industry) often divides these goals into two main areas. The first is database administration. This task is related to managing and maintaining database servers and includes such topics as managing backups and recovery, setting up new databases, etc. Database development, on the other hand, focuses more on the creation of objects within databases and the implementation of a database structure that meets business requirements. There is considerable overlap in the tasks, however. For example, performance optimization is vital both for database administrators and for database designers and implementers.

exam
⊕atch

Although Microsoft's focus for Exam 70-229 is to test your ability to design and implement a database, it is helpful to be familiar with database administration concepts as well. As you work with SQL Server 2000, be sure you have a basic overview of the types of tasks that are required to build and maintain databases.

Realizing that manageability is an important concern for RDBMSs, Microsoft has gone to great lengths to ensure that SQL Server 2000 is easy to administer, even for novice users. By using the simple interface of Enterprise Manager, the most common tasks are just a few clicks away. But, if you're new to working with relational databases, don't let the simple interface fool you—there are several very important considerations that you should take into account before you work with a platform like SQL Server 2000.

In this chapter, we'll cover an overview of the major features of SQL Server 2000, with an emphasis on the types of information that are relevant to SQL Server database designers and implementers. The goal of this chapter is to provide an overview of the architecture of SQL Server 2000, and to provide a solid foundation for the other concepts covered in later chapters. The goal of this chapter is not to teach you about the specific details on which you'll be tested in Microsoft's exam. Instead, it is to familiarize you with working with SQL Server.

This chapter has been designed to be useful for many different types of readers. Whether or not you're familiar with SQL Server, I urge you to read the contents of this chapter before continuing on to the portions of the book that dive into the details of database implementation. And, if you're new to SQL Server, you'll probably find this chapter filled with a lot of new and useful information.

In this chapter, we'll start with some of the basic concepts related to database servers. You'll first read about the types of objects that make up a typical database. This is vital to understanding the content that follows. We'll also briefly cover other topics, such as the overall network and database architecture, and information from a developer's point of view. Let's begin by looking at what makes up a relational database server.

Understanding Relational Databases

All too often, technical people focus on finding the solution to a problem. However, they sometimes forget to see the big picture. When it comes to databases, it's important to first understand the reasons for having a database server. And, no, it's not just to keep you on your toes! Before moving into the specifics of SQL Server, it's worth taking some time to examine the fundamental concepts on which databases are designed and the problems they're designed to solve.

Whether or not you've had experience with database management, this section should prove useful. For those who are new to the field, this section will answer some questions about why database servers seem to be so complicated, and will provide a sound introduction to important data management issues. For old-timers, it may serve as a reminder of why we deal with such things as security, managing user access, and various types of database objects. Even if you're a database veteran, you'll probably still find it useful to review some basic issues that you may have already taken for granted.

At its most basic level, a database is simply a repository for information. This data storage space is responsible for maintaining data in an organized fashion, and then making this data available to users and applications that need it. Managing issues such as security, concurrency, and transactions is the responsibility of the database server engine. We'll get to these topics later in this chapter. First, though, we should examine the objects and relationships that make up a database.

There are many different database platforms on the market today, and each uses slightly different terminology. For example a "database instance" in the Oracle world is quite different from a "database" on SQL Server. Although the underlying concepts are the same, keep in mind that differences exist. I'll make notes where relevant, but the terminology I'll use throughout this book pertains mainly to the Microsoft SQL Server world.

exam
ⓦatch
Remember that when you're taking the SQL Server 2000 Design Exam, Microsoft will be testing you on concepts in the way that they apply to SQL Server 2000. If you've worked with other database platforms, be sure you understand how these concepts are treated in Microsoft's database solution.

Database Objects

Before diving too far into the technical guts of a relational database management system (RDBMS), let's look at the common types of database *objects* they support. These are the structures related to data with which users interact. The purpose of a database server is to store and manage data in an organized fashion. The goal is to be able to easily store and retrieve data. Database objects supported in SQL Server 2000 are described next.

Tables

The fundamental unit of data storage in a relational database is the table. Tables store information in rows. Each row, in turn, contains values for one or more columns that specify related information about a single data item. Tables are the structures in which actual information resides. Tables generally refer to a single logical entity. For example, I might create a table called "Employees". Within the Employees table, I might have rows that include information related to each employee (for example, "First Name", "Last Name", etc.). Of course, I can have many rows, each of which represents one instance of the entity that the table describes (in this case, an employee). Table 1-1 provides an example of the structure of a simple database table.

In SQL Server, tables are built within a database (which, in turn, resides on a datafile). We'll look at the actual storage concepts related to table data later in this chapter. For now, know that the majority of user-related database functions will involve the use of information stored in tables in one way or another.

Views

A *view* is a database object that actually *refers* to data stored in one or more tables. Views are database objects that are defined by SQL queries (which we'll cover later). They specify which information is to be returned to a user. Users interact with views in the same way that they interact with tables. However, views do not actually store data; instead, they retrieve relational information from tables, as illustrated in Figure 1-1. In this example, the view pulls information from a single table that contains customer order information. Although the table tracks the quantity and unit price information, users might be more interested in the total amount of the line item in an order. The view provides this information. A simple example of the view definition might be as follows:

```
CREATE VIEW OrderTotals
AS
SELECT      o.Name, o.Quantity * o.Price as [Total Amount]
FROM        CustomerOrder o
```

exam
ⓦatch

Remember that views don't actually store any data (although you can use them in much the same way that you use tables). Therefore, views have a minimal impact on the size of a database.

Views are used in several types of scenarios and can be very helpful in managing information. One benefit is in regard to security. You can create a view of a table that allows users to see only a subset of the information stored in one or more tables. This is useful, for example, if you have an Employees table that contains sensitive information.

TABLE 1-1	Employee Number	First Name	Middle Initial	Last Name	Department	Phone Extension
A Sample Table Containing Information About Employees	1	Anil	K	Desai	Engineering	0937
	2	Jane		User	Marketing	1554

	ID	Name	Quantity	Price
	1	Unit 1	1	$1.53
	2	Unit 2	12	$12.01
	3	Unit A7	5	$9.37
Table	4	Item 05	12	$0.73
	5	Item 12	18	$0.22
	6	Misc 01	37	$17.01

	Name	Total Amount
	Unit 1	$1.53
	Unit 2	$144.12
View	Unit A7	$46.85
	Misc 01	$629.37

You might create a view that allows users to query against all information except salary information. Furthermore, you might choose to restrict permissions on the underlying database itself and assign permissions to the view only. Additionally, views are useful for encapsulating business logic. By storing commonly used queries as views, you can reduce the chance that a developer will make an error in retrieving data. Views can even refer to other views, although this practice can sometimes make it difficult to debug any problems that crop up. Overall, though, views enable you to simplify administration, increase manageability, and improve security.

Indexes

Indexes are database objects that store a subset of a table's columns. They are used to speed data searches by minimizing the amount of information that must be searched by SQL Server. This works in much the same way as you might use the index of this book. Instead of flipping through all of the pages to find what you're looking for, you could look for simple keywords in the index. When you find those words, you're referred to a page number that contains the detailed information. Clearly, searching through the index is much quicker than searching through the entire book page by page (although, as with a database, both would work).

Indexes are used to reduce the amount of time it takes SQL Server to find the information a user requests. For example, suppose you often run queries that search for employees based on their last names. However, your database table for employee information actually contains much more information (for example, address, manager's name, and job title). If an index is placed on the First Name and Last Name columns of this table, SQL Server will not have to search through all the information in the table to gain this information. Instead, it will search the index (in this case, a list of all of the last names) and then go to the pertinent rows for the remainder of the data. A query that refers only to indexed columns is often called a *covered query*. If details on those rows are required, the index will point to the appropriate data storage areas.

SQL Server 2000 supports two types of indexes: clustered and nonclustered. Clustered indexes involve the physical ordering of items in a database. This means that related information is physically stored together on the hard disk. By default, SQL Server automatically creates a clustered index on the primary key (described later) when a table is created. Since this type determines the actual order in which pages are stored on the disk, a table can have only one clustered index. Clustered indexes increase performance most when you will be returning an ordered subset of information. For example, if I frequently perform queries that require a range of part numbers (for example, part # 150055–part #150116), access will be much quicker with a clustered index, since these values are physically stored near each other on the disk, and thus will require fewer I/O operations to retrieve. However, in databases that are used mainly for transaction information (such as a sales order entry system), clustered indexes can actually decrease performance.

Nonclustered indexes, in contrast, are separate structures that store a subset of the information in a table, but do not affect the physical storage of data on the disk. A table may have many nonclustered indexes. These indexes actually store *links* to the information in the covered columns, to speed searches. We'll look more closely at indexes, and their effects on performance, in Chapter 6. For now, however, understand that the proper use of indexes can dramatically improve SQL Server performance, especially for very large or very active databases.

Stored Procedures

Stored procedures are simply named collections of Transact-SQL statements or transactions that are stored within a database as an object. They contain procedural code that can be executed on demand. There are several benefits to using stored procedures vs. performing the same queries manually. Perhaps the most important benefit is the dramatic speed increase that stored procedures can cause. Stored procedures execute much more quickly than the same statements that execute on an ad hoc basis. The main reason for this performance increase is that the SQL Server 2000 database engine stores a predetermined optimal data recovery plan in cache memory. This is also one reason that you will get a much quicker response time from a query the second time you run it (provided that the data pages haven't yet expired from the cache due to other activities).

There are also security benefits to using stored procedures. Like views, stored procedures can be used to hide from users the underlying database objects that are being affected. This helps you restrict the actions that users can perform directly on database objects, and prevents you from having to rely on (and manage) complicated permissions structures. It also allows for better management of underlying table structures. For example, if you want to change an employee's address information in several tables at once, you can create a single stored procedure that will make sure that all the necessary operations are carried out. Additionally, stored procedures can call other stored procedures, allowing the development of modularly coded business rules and SQL statements.

Triggers

In some cases, you'll want to take some action every time data in a table is accessed or modified. *Triggers* allow you to automatically fire a SQL statement whenever users execute commands that access a table. The statement can then execute one or more SQL statements that modify data or perform validity checks on the operation. For example, a trigger may be used to automatically delete all employee timesheet data whenever an employee is deleted from the database. The trigger can access both "before" and "after" images of the data when it is executed. Optionally, SQL Server 2000 triggers can call other triggers to form a cascading effect (although care must be taken to avoid recursive loops).

Functions

Database administrators and designers are familiar with using functions that are built into SQL Server. For example, the GetDate() function can be used to retrieve the current date and time on the server. And, aggregate functions such as SUM, AVG, and COUNT can be used to calculate meaningful values from data. In SQL Server 2000, database administrators also have the ability to create their own custom functions. These functions might perform common tasks based on business logic.

For example, a certain financial application might often perform some calculations on a customer's salary to determine the amount of a potential loan. A database administrator could create a custom function that performs this task. The following query shows how a function called CalcCustomerLoanAmount() can be used:

```
SELECT Salary, CalcCustomerLoanAmount(Salary) as MaximumLoan
FROM   Customers
WHERE LastName = 'Smith' and FirstName = 'Bob'
```

The result would include the desired information using the custom function. Note that the use of custom functions can sometimes dramatically decrease performance. If designed correctly and used sparingly, however, functions are a great way to expand the tools in a database developer's bag of tricks.

Defaults, Rules, and Constraints

Although triggers are a good solution for executing tasks based on user actions, it's often simpler to place restrictions on the types of information that are acceptable in a column of data. SQL Server provides several different types of *constraints*:

- **NOT NULL**   A value must be specific for this column.

- **CHECK**   The values supplied must meet the criteria specified in the constraint. A database developer can define a CHECK constraint to ensure that an entered integer is an even, positive value.

- **UNIQUE**   No values in this column may be duplicates of another. This might be used, for example, in an employee information table to prevent duplicate employee numbers from being entered.

- **PRIMARY KEY**   Defines which column or columns uniquely identify each row in the database. No two rows can have the same values for the primary key.

- **FOREIGN KEY**   Enforces data integrity between tables by creating a reference for specific types of information.

We'll discuss the PRIMARY KEY and FOREIGN KEY constraints in later sections. CHECK constraints are place limitations on the types of information that can be stored in a specific column of data. For example, I might want to restrict the value in a phone number column to a 10-digit format (with no dashes or other characters). A constraint can ensure that information is entered in numeric format. If the information does not meet the criteria, an error is returned to the user. Constraints can be placed on one or more columns and can be quite complex.

Defaults are settings placed on a table that specify which values should be used if none are specified. This is commonly used in situations in which the database assumes that values are set to False unless otherwise specified.

Rules function similarly to constraints but have the added benefit of existing as database objects. In contrast to constraints—which are defined as part of a column's definition—rules can be *bound* or *unbound* to columns. This allows the flexibility of disabling a rule without losing its definition. However, only one rule may apply to a column's definition. Rules are provided mainly for backward compatibility with SQL Server applications. Microsoft recommends that, wherever possible, CHECK constraints be used instead of rules.

Domain, Entity, and Referential Integrity

It is possible to create a database in which all the information stored in tables is completely unstructured and unrelated. This would lead to many problems, however, as is often learned by those who do not take the time to adequately plan the structure of their databases. Generally, different pieces of information stored in your database objects relate to each other in some way. A commonly used example is that of a sales database. Each sale might be tied to a customer, but the actual information about the customer (including shipping address and purchase history) might be stored in other tables. In this case, there is a clear relationship between the two tables that must be kept intact. Additionally, business rules might require that each customer has a unique customer number that should never be reused.

Integrity constraints are created to ensure that these relationships are maintained in a consistent manner. There are three major types of integrity that database designers must keep in mind:

- **Domain integrity**   Ensures that values stored within a column are consistent and in accordance with business rules. Domain integrity can be based on constraints such as UNIQUE and CHECK constraints that specify what values are acceptable for each column.

- **Entity integrity**   Refers to information stored in rows (remember that each row in a table stores information about one entity of the type that the table describes). This type of constraint makes sure that the information stored in rows within a table is unique and follows any other business rules that are specified. For example, each row must contain the same number of columns (although some values may be left blank).

- **Referential integrity** Applies across tables and ensures that information between these objects is consistent. Referential integrity includes relationships between tables. The actual columns that match between the tables are known as foreign keys and primary keys. Referential integrity ensures that related information remains consistent. It solves, for example, the problem we mentioned initially—ensuring that only valid customers are used for all orders placed in the database and avoiding the problem of "orphan rows." Orphans might occur, for example, when a customer row is deleted from the database, but the customer still has orders. In this case, the orders are orphans, since their parent row (the customer information) no longer exists. When it comes time to fulfill the orders, users will find that they do not have enough information.

Figure 1-2 illustrates the three main types of database integrity.

FIGURE 1-2

Comparing various types of database integrity

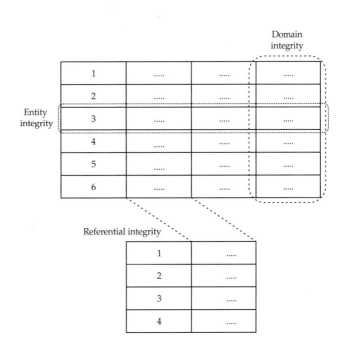

Structured Query Language

So far, we have talked about how data is stored in relational databases. We have not, however, discussed the important details related to retrieving and modifying data. The Structured Query Language (SQL, often pronounced "sequel") is the primary method used for obtaining information from an RDBMS. It is defined by the American National Standards Institute (ANSI) under several versions (often named after the year in which the standard was defined). For example, a commonly supported standard is called ANSI SQL-92. There are four main SQL Data Manipulation Language (DML) commands:

- **SELECT** Returns information from one or more database tables.
- **INSERT** Adds a new row to a table.
- **UPDATE** Modifies information in an existing row.
- **DELETE** Removes one or more rows from a table.

FIGURE I-3

Viewing the results of a SQL SELECT statement in Query Analyzer

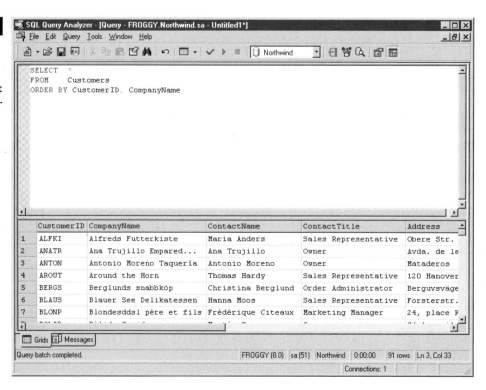

Figure 1-3 shows the results of a basic SQL SELECT statement executed in SQL Query Analyzer. For more information about SQL query syntax, see Chapter 5; and for more information about using the various features of Query Analyzer, see Chapter 6.

Batches and Transactions

SQL commands are often executed in groups of related commands. A *batch* is a group of related commands. When you run queries in SQL Query Analyzer (a process that we'll cover in a later section), the commands are implicitly sent as batch statements. Certain types of statements are not permitted within the same batch, so you can use the GO command to separate them.

Transactions are SQL commands that are not necessarily related, but must execute in an all-or-nothing fashion. Let's look at a common real-world example of a transaction. Assume that you want to carry out a financial transaction between two different banks. The basic operation should subtract money from user A's account and add the money to user B's account. For obvious reasons, you wouldn't want one of those transactions to occur without the other (or you will have made someone either very happy or very upset). To avoid this potential problem, you could combine both operations into a single transaction. In case an error occurred during the transaction (for example, one of the two servers was unavailable), neither of the two transactions would be performed.

Another example in applications is when you're updating information such as a customer's address. You wouldn't want an operation to update information regarding his or her street address without also updating the ZIP code. Again, this is a perfect place for a transaction.

Transactions must pass the "ACID" test, having all four of the following properties:

- **Atomicity** Each transaction is represented by a single all-or-nothing operation: either all steps are carried out or the entire process is aborted.

- **Consistency** No data changes should violate the structure and design of the database.

- **Independence** Transactions are not aware that other transactions are being run at the same time.

- **Durability** If an error occurs during the processing of a transaction, partial transactions should be reversed.

Distributed Transactions

In most environments, data is stored in more than one data repository. It is often necessary to run transactions that run across multiple databases and platforms. The other data repositories you are trying to access might be as unique as a Microsoft Access database or an Excel spreadsheet, but could also be another RDBMS, such as an Oracle or Sybase server. SQL Server 2000 supports the use of *linked servers,* which allow users to enter queries that refer to objects stored on other machines. DBAs can also specify whether the statements will execute on the SQL Server or on the remote data repository. In this way, users can access information stored in various locations transparently.

SQL Server Architecture

With the release of SQL Server 2000, Microsoft has further improved upon the usability and architectural enhancements it introduced with SQL Server 7.0. Users of versions of SQL Server prior to 7.0 noticed that there were significant improvements in scalability, performance, reliability, and ease of administration. SQL Server 2000 continues these enhancements by including even more new features.

One of Microsoft's foremost goals for the SQL Server platform is for it to be accepted into higher-end businesses and into enterprise-level data centers. Microsoft has made many inroads in this area against several other well-known competitors (including Oracle, and IBM's DB2). Recently, Microsoft demonstrated record-breaking cost vs. performance results in the industry-standard Transaction Processing Council (TPC)-D Benchmark suite. (For more information about the TPC benchmarks, see www.tpc.org.) These results help prove the scalability and performance that SQL Server is able to provide.

SQL Server also has many other advantages over competing platforms. Veteran DBAs and casual database users alike will appreciate the ease of management offered in SQL Server 2000. The updated visual tools (such as Enterprise Manager and Query Analyzer) make managing complex operations very simple for the end user. They also provide an intuitive method for performing common tasks that would otherwise require cracking open user guides (something that we know many users never consider!).

Now that we have a solid understanding of basic relational database concepts, it's time to look at how SQL Server 2000 is designed "under the hood." If you're new to Microsoft's premier database server platform, you'll likely find that it offers many new features that greatly help in the areas of administration, security, scalability, reliability, and performance. That's a tall order, however! Users of previous versions of SQL

Server will see a marked improvement in performance and in the ease of management of the product. This allows developers and DBAs to focus on more important tasks, such as managing applications. Let's start by looking at the various editions of SQL Server 2000, and then move on to examine the architecture of the product itself.

Editions of SQL Server 2000

The SQL Server 2000 platform has been designed to run in many different environments. Microsoft has gone to great lengths to ensure that the same code base is used, regardless, in all versions of the product, from the desktop platform to enterprise-level servers. There are several versions of SQL Server 2000, as listed in Table 1-2.

on the
()ob

Choosing the edition of SQL Server 2000 is very important in the real world. First, there can be a huge cost difference between the various versions, and licensing costs can range from a few hundred dollars to tens of thousands of dollars. Fortunately, Microsoft has been conscious of the fact that developers and users will want compatibility between the various editions of SQL Server 2000. However, be sure you fully understand what your business needs are before you invest in a database server platform.

In most environments, servers will be installed with the Standard Server product. Desktop users (such as sales staff) who require their data "to go" will likely benefit from installing the Desktop Edition. On the other end of the spectrum, large installations of SQL Server will benefit from the enhanced scalability and reliability features of the Enterprise Edition. Fortunately, all three are installed, administered, and managed similarly, thus providing end users, developers and high-end database administrators a similar console with which to work.

SQL Server Services

There are several different ways in which SQL Server can be run. On the Windows 95/98/ME platforms, SQL Server runs as an application. That is, it is launched and managed under a specific user process. If necessary, you can use SQL Server the same way in Windows NT/2000; however, it's far more likely that you'll want the program to run as a service independent of user context. This allows SQL Server to continue running *whether or not there is a user logged on to the system.* In Windows

TABLE 1-2 A Comparison of the Various Editions of SQL Server 2000 and Their Features

Edition/Version	Operating Systems Supported	Licensing Options	Notes
Desktop	Windows 95/98/ME Windows NT 4 Workstation Windows 2000 Professional	Can be installed for no additional charge if users have named SQL Server Client Access Licenses	Has limited replication and DTS capabilities; decreased memory requirements
Standard Server	Windows NT 4 Server Windows 2000 Server Microsoft Small Business Server (10GB database size limit) Microsoft BackOffice Server	Per seat or per user	Includes Microsoft English Query and OLAP Services
Enterprise	Windows NT Server, Enterprise Edition Windows 2000 Advanced Server Windows 2000 Datacenter Server	Per seat or per user	Supports clustering and very large memory and additional Analysis Services features
64-bit	64-bit versions of Windows 2000	Extremely high performance due to support for newer processor and server architectures	
Windows CE Edition	Windows Consumer Edition (CE) 2.11 or later PocketPC Other embedded systems (based on OEM support)	Designed as a storage engine for use with handheld and portable devices	Optimized for working in low-memory situations
Developer Edition	All 32-bit Windows-based operating systems	Version of SQL Server Enterprise Edition designed for development and testing purposes	
Desktop Engine	All 32-bit Windows-based operating systems	Designed for use by only a few users and can be embedded in applications	Replaces Microsoft Data Engine (MSDE); no licensing fees for small applications

NT/2000, SQL Server 2000 is generally run as a set of services. These system processes remain running and able to respond to requests on the operating system, regardless of *whether or not a user is logged on.* The specific services that are available in SQL Server 2000 are listed in Table 1-3.

on the Job

At the time of this writing, Microsoft had not yet released its Windows XP and Windows .Net Server products. It is expected, however, that SQL Server 2000 will be fully supported on these platforms.

You may not need to install, or routinely use, all of the services listed in Table 1-3. In addition to being run as a service, SQL Server can be run as an application from the command line for special situations. The SQLSERVER command can be followed by an –m switch to start the database in single-user mode, or an –f switch to start with a minimum fail-safe configuration. Both options can be helpful in database maintenance and/or troubleshooting. Keep in mind that you cannot start, stop, or pause SQL Server by using the Services Control Panel applet if you started it from the command line, because this process is not running as a service. For more details related to starting SQL Server 2000 from the command line, see the SQL Server Books Online.

With SQL Server 2000, Microsoft has introduced the ability to run multiple independent instances of the database server on the same machine. This is useful for improving security, for performing testing, and in development environments. Figure 1-4 shows an example of the dialog box that allows you to install additional instances of SQL Server 2000. This is accessed by simply rerunning the SQL Server 2000 Setup process.

Furthermore, the default instance of SQL Server on any machine may be either a SQL Server 2000 instance or an instance of SQL Server 7.0. Named instances may run SQL Server 2000. This provides excellent flexibility for environments that are attempting to upgrade but must run both versions during the transition.

Microsoft supports upgrading SQL Server 6.5 or later databases to SQL Server 2000. This procedure is easily performed using the SQL Server Upgrade Wizard, which can be accessed by clicking Start | Microsoft SQL Server – Switch | SQL Server Upgrade Wizard (see Figure 1-5).

TABLE 1-3 The Various Services That Are a Part of SQL Server 2000

Service	Executable Name	Service Name	Function	Notes
SQL Server Service	Sqlservr.exe	MSSQLServer	The main database server engine	Can be started either as a service or from the command line; this is the main instance of Microsoft SQL Server 2000 on a machine
SQL Server Service—named instances	Sqlservr.exe	MSSQL$InstanceName	Additional instances of SQL Server that reside on the same machine	Can be accessed by referring to the machine name and the instance name (for example, "Server1/Instance1")
SQL Server Agent	SQLAgent.exe	SQLServerAgent	Used for executing scheduled jobs	Account must have access to other machines to perform remote jobs
SQL Server Agent for named instances	SQLAgent.exe	SQLAgent$InstanceName	Used for executing jobs for named instances	Account must have access to other machines to perform remote jobs
MS Distributed Transaction Coordinator (MSDTC)	Msdtc.exe	MSDTC	Allows for processing and monitoring real-time transactions involving remote servers	
Full-Text Search	Mssearch.exe	MSSearch	Allows users to perform searches of TEXT column types	
Microsoft English Query	Mseq.exe		Allows end users to perform SQL queries in plain English	Installed separately after SQL Server is installed
Microsoft OLAP Services	Msmdsrv.exe	MSSQLServerOlapService	Allows for complex data analysis using data cubes	Installed separately after SQL Server is installed

FIGURE 1-4

Installing a new
instance of SQL
Server 2000

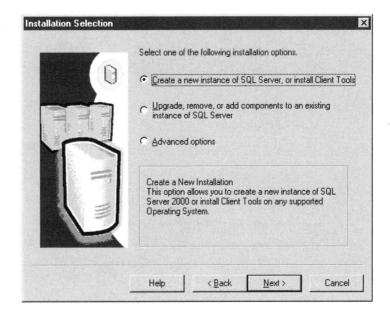

FIGURE 1-5

Using the SQL
Server Upgrade
Wizard

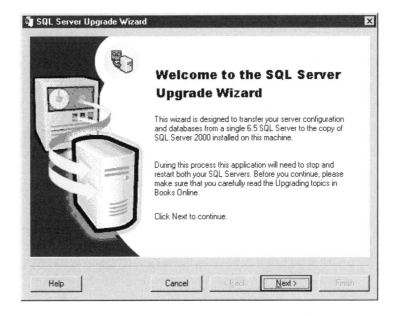

Data Storage Architecture

When it comes to designing a database server platform, there are several main concerns:

- **Reliability**   Features of the database server platform that protect against data loss or corruption and allow for dependable access from clients.

- **Availability (uptime)**   A measure of the stability of a database server based on the amount of time its services are available to end users. Availability is often measured in a percentage of uptime (for example 99.999 percent, often referred to as "five nines").

- **Scalability**   The ability of a database server platform to take advantage of faster or additional hardware and other resources.

- **Performance**   The overall efficiency of the database server at fulfilling data modification and retrieval based on business requirements.

The demands on data storage have risen exponentially in recent years. Therefore, a robust system for storing tables containing potentially billions of rows is necessary. SQL Server stores information in standard operating system files that have a special format optimized for storing relational information. At the most basic level, these files are made up of *pages*. Pages store the actual data that makes up the rows of tables and indexes. A database page is exactly 8,192 bytes in length (including 96 bytes that are used for the header). Rows cannot span pages; therefore, the maximum size a row may have is 8,060 bytes, not including overhead (with the exception of text and image datatypes, which are stored on special page types apart from the rest of the row's data). There are various types of pages for the different types of data they can contain (for example, there are different page types for tables and for indexes).

To make disk access more efficient, SQL Server allocates space in *extents*. An extent is made up of eight pages, and, therefore, it is 64K in length. Extents may contain different types of pages, if necessary. SQL Server datafiles can be stored on file allocation table (FAT) and Windows NT File System (NTFS) partition types. The only requirement is that file system compression cannot be enabled for the datafiles.

The good news is that you won't have to worry about much of this when you're working with SQL Server 2000. The architecture of the product makes the creation, maintenance, and administration of datafiles easier by allowing dynamic file allocation. Database files can be set to automatically grow and shrink as needed.

Files and Filegroups

In SQL Server 2000, the term *database* refers to a logical structure containing a set of related objects. Unlike other RDBMSs, SQL Server allows objects within a database to be owned by different users, and allows the existence of many databases on the same server. In the simplest configuration, a database has one file for data and one file for a transaction log (as described in the next section).

A SQL Server database is made up of at least one datafile (which is called the *primary datafile,* and has a default extension of .mdf) and exactly one transaction log file (which has an extension of .ldf). However, much more complex configurations are available. To spread data across multiple devices, you can choose to add one or more *secondary datafiles.* These datafiles can then contain specific database objects. This is a very powerful feature that allows you to specify exactly where information is stored. Spreading information across different drives can increase performance. For example, if you have two very active tables on your system, you may choose to place each on different drives (by creating separate datafiles). Administering files can become complicated if you have multiple files. Also, the amount of data that must be backed up can become quite large. For this reason, you can group files into logical structures called *filegroups.* SQL Server hides much of the complexity of managing datafiles, because they can be dynamically resized as needed.

The Transaction Log

When a user executes a SQL query that modifies information on the database server, the actual changes are first written to a file called the *transaction log.* Pages that have been written to the transaction log but have not yet been committed to the physical file are known as *dirty pages.* The information is temporarily held in this file until a *checkpoint* occurs. At this time, the data is actually recorded in the actual database files themselves. The transaction log provides many benefits to database users:

- ■ **Increasing performance by acting as a caching device**   Instead of writing each transaction to the datafiles individually, the server can wait until several changes are ready to be written, and then combine the changes into fewer write operations.

- ■ **Ensuring data consistency**   If an operation begins and then later aborts (due to a hardware failure, or when it reaches a ROLLBACK TRANSACTION statement), all of the operations associated with this transaction can be rolled back.

■ **Providing a "snapshot" of the database at a specific point in time** When it comes to working with many transactions that may be running at the same time, it's important for the queries to be working on a fixed set of data. For example, consider the case of a query that begins modifying 100 rows of data in separate steps. If another user attempts to make a change to some of the information at the same time, it might interfere with the logic of the query. In a case like this, the transaction log can provide a "snapshot" of the database at a specific point in time.

Figure 1-6 shows how the transaction log is used.

The transaction log cannot be disabled in SQL Server 2000, although you can choose to make it effectively useless by choosing specific database recovery model options for a database (see Books Online for a detailed description of recovery models). Certain options inactivate portions of the transaction log as soon as they are committed to disk. A major benefit of the transaction log is that it allows you to perform a point-in-time recovery (so you can roll back a database to the point in time just before an accidental modification was made).

Backup and Recovery Architecture

As you have probably guessed, Microsoft has made several major improvements to backup and recovery features in SQL Server 2000. Here is a brief, high-level overview:

■ **Recovery models** New in SQL Server 2000 is the ability to define a recovery model for each database. There are three main options: Simple (no logging), Normal (restore to point-in-time; largest log size), and Bulk Logged (some operations are not logged). Each offers a unique balance between recoverability of database information and performance.

■ **Fast differential backup** Differential backups store only the data pages that have been modified since the last full database backup. In SQL Server 7.0,

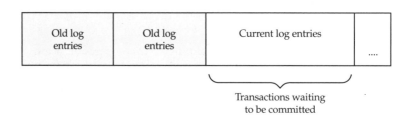

FIGURE 1-6

A logical overview of the transaction log

differential backups used up less disk space when compared to full backups, but they still required a scan of the entire database during a backup operation (thereby reducing performance). In SQL Server 2000, an entire scan of the database is no longer required. Since only the modified pages are scanned, differential backups for large databases can be performed in much less time.

- **Copy Database Wizard** SQL Server 2000 includes a new wizard that is called the Copy Database Wizard. The purpose of this tool is to copy databases between instances of SQL Server 2000, including all of the objects within a database. The wizard also has the ability to upgrade SQL Server 7.0 databases to SQL Server 2000. We'll cover the Copy Database Wizard in greater detail in Chapter 7.

- **Snapshot backups** For mission-critical applications, keeping data synchronized between servers is extremely important. SQL Server 2000 supports the redundancy of data (for fault tolerance and performance reasons) through the use of snapshot backups. This feature is primarily designed for use by Original Equipment Manufacturers (OEMs) on systems that are designed to make use of this functionality.

- **Standby server support** Log-shipping (copying of the transaction log to another server) is a common technique that can be used in most relational database server platforms. Before SQL Server 2000 this method was supported, but it was generally a painstaking process to implement and administer. In the latest version of SQL Server, the graphical administration tools can be used to implement a standby server through the use of log-shipping.

- **Logical log marks (vs. point-in-time)** The ability to restore to a point in time using transaction log backups is extremely useful—if you know the time when the failure occurred. In SQL Server 2000, database users and applications can create a logical log mark that uses a specific identifier before beginning transactions. Should the need to perform a point-in-time recovery arise, the database can be restored up to one of these logical log marks.

All of these enhancements make the tedious task of managing backup and recovery operations much more flexible and manageable.

New Features in SQL Server 2000

With SQL Server 2000, Microsoft has included many new enhancements that affect the functionality of the product. Although some of the features will be useful to all users of SQL Server (like the enhanced Enterprise Manager and Query Analyzer applications), others are less evident. Let's look at a quick overview of some of the changes to SQL Server "under the hood."

Support for Extensible Markup Language (XML)

XML is one of those technologies that is often cited by industry analysts and technical professionals as a revolutionary change. The underlying idea behind XML is to provide a standard, flexible mechanism for data interchange between applications, servers, and companies. The standard offers developers and users many advantages, including the ability to simply define and use a standard XML-based schema. Web developers, for example, can take advantage of XML technology to perform communications between different Web servers, some of which may be operated by other companies.

Although it will take time for the industry to fully take advantage of the features and capabilities of XML, many vendors and products are embracing it as a standard for data interchange. Microsoft is no exception, and SQL Server 2000 was designed to provide rich XML functionality. SQL Server 200 supports XML through the use of the FOR XML clause in standard SQL queries. Now, database users can simply execute a query with this clause to return data in an XML format. For example, the following query (run against the Northwind sample database)

```
SELECT        CustomerID, CompanyName, ContactName, ContactTitle, Country
FROM   Customers
WHERE CustomerID = 'WILMK'
FOR XML AUTO
```

produces the following output:

```
XML_F52E2B61-18A1-11d1-B105-00805F49916B
----------------------------------------
<Customers CustomerID="WILMK" CompanyName="Wilman Kala"
ContactName="Matti Karttunen" ContactTitle="Owner/Marketing Assistant"
Country="Finland"/>
```

In addition to allowing the creation of XML-formatted result sets, database developers can also take advantage of the OPENXML built-in system function for reading data from XML files. Together, these features provide a good foundation for two-way relational-to-XML data transfers.

Materialized Views

A standard view is essentially a data retrieval query (usually a simple SELECT statement that may join several tables together to obtain useful information). A materialized view has the same purpose, but it is a database object that physically stores the results of a query to disk. Now, when queries require the information specific in the view, the query optimizer can quickly obtain the results from the materialized view instead of from the tables it references. Furthermore, the view can be indexed to further improve the performance of certain queries without reducing the performance of others ("overindexing"). Although this could have been done through the creation of tables (for example through "denormalization" of the schema), it would be up to database designers to create triggers and stored procedures to keep the data in these extra tables up-to-date. Materialized views handle this tedious and error-prone task automatically.

The use of materialized views can produce a dramatic improvement in the speed of certain types of queries. Of course, the trade-off is the additional disk space that is required to store the data that makes up the views, and the system overhead that's required to maintain the views.

FROM THE CLASSROOM

Indexing Views in SQL Server 2000

When conducting interviews of technical professionals that claim they have database experience, I usually start with a simple question: "What is a view?" If they get that right, I move on to something slightly more difficult: "Where is the data for a view stored?" Those that really understand how a view works will answer that the data is stored in the underlying tables that are referred to by the view. The question that often makes people think, however, is "Can a view be indexed?" In previous versions of SQL Server, views could not be indexed because they did not store any data (the purpose of indexing is to speed the retrieval of information from disk). However, that has changed in SQL Server 2000. Be sure that you understand that materialized views are an advanced feature in SQL Server 2000, and that this feature is not available on all database platforms.

—*Anil Desai, MCSE, MCDBA, MCSD*

Partitioned Views

A simple fact for most databases is that they will grow over time—sometimes at an exponential rate. Data has a tenacious tendency to accumulate as businesses grow! Although all of the data is important, some of it might be required to be more available than other portions. For example, consider a company that has stored 15 years of sales order data. Clearly, all of the information is useful (for historical reporting and comparisons). However, the most important data is probably that generated within the last five years. Assuming all of the data is stored within one database table, the existence of all of this excess data can greatly decrease performance by bogging down queries.

One potential solution is to horizontally partition the data. In this method, certain subsets of data are moved to other tables, databases, and/or servers (see Figure 1-7). This group of servers is often referred to as a "federation" of servers because they all work together to share the load for a single data repository. To simplify the process of accessing data across these partitions (for example, when a manager requests information that spans 10 years), partitioned views can be used. The query can be executed against the view, and the query optimizer will automatically access the required tables for information.

SQL Server 2000 also supports "vertical" partitioning. In this situation, a portion of a table—for example, a commonly used column—might be broken out into another table (see Figure 1-8). Again, partitioned views can be used to simplify access to the

FIGURE 1-7

Horizontal database partitioning

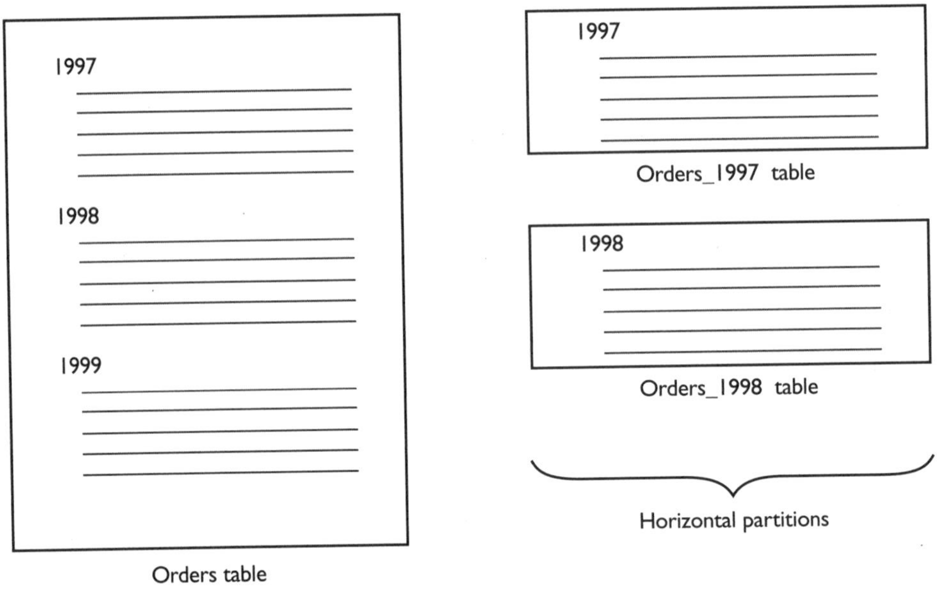

Orders table

Orders_1997 table

Orders_1998 table

Horizontal partitions

data. Overall, partitioned views can increase performance and decrease administration for medium- to large-sized databases.

Address Windowing Extensions (AWE)

Just a few short years ago, it seemed to be a distant dream that database servers would support many gigabytes of memory. Database administrators knew that adding additional memory to servers could provide dramatic improvements in performance. Now, however, larger amounts of RAM are often used to fulfill performance requirements. Coupled with the dramatic overall decrease in the price of memory modules (and improvements in manufacturing technology), systems with many gigabytes of RAM are not uncommon.

By default, the Windows NT/2000 operating systems support a memory address space of up to 4GB. Of this amount, up to 3GB can be physical RAM (the rest must be virtual memory provided by a swap file). With SQL Server 2000, however, a new

FIGURE 1-8   Vertical database partitioning

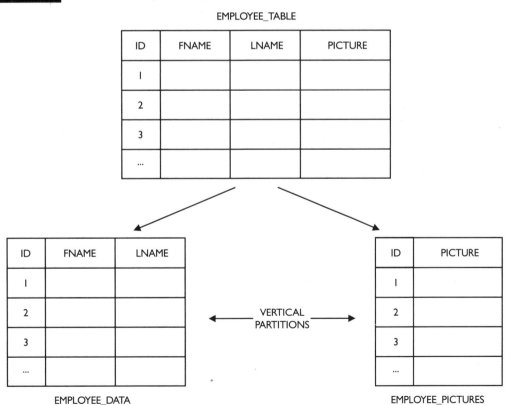

technology called Address Windowing Extensions (AWE) allows a database server platform to access up to 64GB of usable memory. This architecture is optimized for large database servers with many CPUs and can dramatically improve performance in high-performance systems. AWE is available with the Enterprise Edition of SQL Server 2000, running on Windows 2000 Advanced Server or Windows 2000 DataCenter Server.

Integration with the Active Directory

Microsoft designed the Active Directory to serve as a single repository for managing information about a network environment. Commonly stored objects include users, groups, computers, and organizational units (OUs). By using the Active Directory, users and system administrators can quickly and easily search for specific types of resources (for example, a color printer located in a specific building) throughout the entire environment. So, why not extend this functionality to apply to database servers as well?

Installations of SQL Server 2000 can be made available as objects within the Active Directory. The SQL Server 2000 object can include information about the databases stored on a specific server and other information about its configuration. With this information stored within the Active Directory, users can easily search for specific information. For example, I might want to find all of the SQL Server 2000 machines that host a copy of the Customers database. Using the Active Directory search functionality, this can be easily accomplished (see Figure 1-9).

Support for Multiple Database Versions

In an ideal world, all of our database servers would be magically upgraded to the latest version of database platform as soon as it was released (assuming this is what we wanted to do). In the real world, however, it can take months or even years of testing before a migration to a new version is possible. To ease the migration to newer versions of SQL Server, SQL Server 2000 allows for backward compatibility. Each database can use one of the compatibility levels shown in Table 1-4.

	SQL Server Version	Backward-Compatibility Setting
TABLE 1-4 Database Compatibility Levels Supported by SQL Server	Microsoft SQL Server 2000	Database compatibility level 80
	Microsoft SQL Server 7	Database compatibility level 70
	Microsoft SQL Server 6.5	Database compatibility level 65
	Microsoft SQL Server 6.0	Database compatibility level 60

FIGURE 1-9

Searching the
Active Directory
for SQL Server
replication
information

FIGURE 1-10

Changing
the database
compatibility level

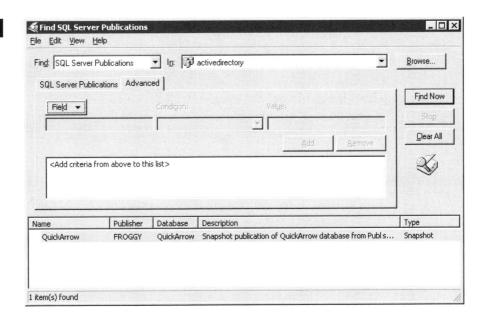

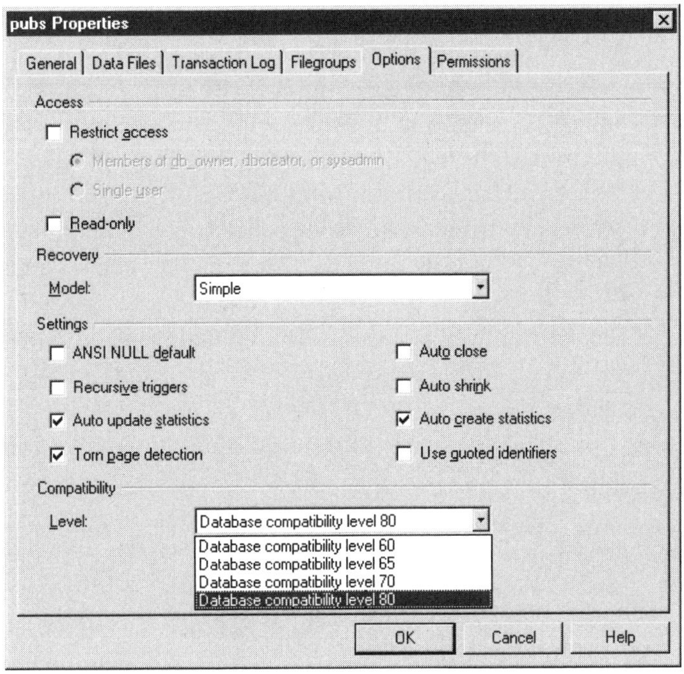

The options in Table 1-4 are extremely helpful when testing the migration of SQL-based code between versions of SQL Server. Better yet, the compatibility modes can be changed several times, even while the database is running. Note, however, that if a database is running in a backward compatible mode, users will not be able to take full advantage of all of the features of SQL Server 2000.

The database compatibility level can be easily changed within Enterprise Manager by viewing the properties of a database (see Figure 1-10).

The Transact-SQL Language

As mentioned previously, the standard language used for RDBMS communication is SQL. Microsoft's implementation of the SQL language is based on the ANSI-SQL92 standard and is called Transact-SQL (unofficially abbreviated T-SQL). This includes the standard syntax for SELECT, UPDATE, INSERT, and DELETE statements (which we covered earlier in this chapter). In addition, Transact-SQL contains many additional commands and functions that are not provided for in the ANSI specifications. It is important to note that although ANSI-SQL92 is a "standard," support for various types of commands are not necessarily consistent between platforms. For example, the supported syntax for specific JOIN statements in Oracle is not compatible with the syntax used in SQL Server.

Although users can use any standard query application that can connect to SQL Server, it is increasingly common for database developers to write programs that encapsulate the queries and process information for users. Increasingly common are Web-based applications in which a Web server or "middleware" is responsible for performing the actual database queries that obtain information as needed. Connectivity between applications and SQL Server can use various standards, such as Open Database Connectivity (ODBC), ActiveX Data Objects (ADO), and Object Linking and Embedding for Databases (OLEDB). Information about using the Transact-SQL language and the various data access components is available from SQL Server Books Online.

Dealing with database objects can be quite challenging due to the complexity of some of the commands involved. SQL Server 2000 provides built-in procedures that can be used for performing common functions and compiling information about databases and the objects that they contain. In addition to these stored procedures, built-in views can be used to query information stored within the system tables. Let's look at some commonly used stored procedures and information schema views.

TABLE 1-5	System Procedure	Purpose	Example
A Sample of Commonly Used SQL Server 2000 Stored Procedures	sp_configure	Server configuration options, which can be modified with this procedure (certain changes to these options require use of the RECONFIGURE command)	sp_configure 'user connections', 35
	sp_depends	Dependencies of database objects (for example, all the tables to which a view refers)	sp_depends myview
	sp_help	Information about a database object	sp_help mydatabase
	sp_helpdb	The size and options used for a database	sp_helpdb mydatabase
	sp_helptext	Help information regarding database objects such as triggers, views, and stored procedures	sp_helptext trigger1
	sp_lock	Current locks on database objects	sp_lock
	sp_monitor	Current database statistics	sp_monitor
	sp_spaceused	Space used by a database table or the database itself	sp_spaceused mytable
	sp_who	Current database connections	sp_who

System Stored Procedures

SQL Server 2000 includes many system-stored procedures that can be used for tasks such as managing security and working with database objects. Table 1-5 provides an example of a few commonly used commands. This by no means is a complete list. However, it does show some useful ways to obtain information about database and server configuration.

Figure 1-11 provides examples of the types of information you can obtain using a system-stored procedure.

Information Schema Views

Information schema views are built-in database views that can be queried against. Unlike stored procedures, these views return relational output that can be processed in the same

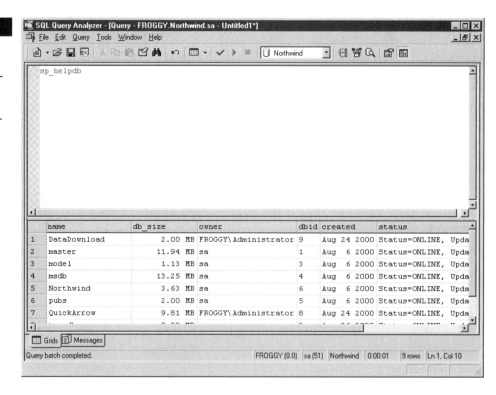

way as other query results. You can execute a SELECT statement against these values. Here's an example that returns the names of all the tables stored in a database:

```
Select * from information_schema.tables
```

Information Schema View	Information Returned
Columns	A list of all columns in all accessible tables and views
Referential_Constraints	Information about primary-key and foreign-key relationships
Schemata	Information about all the databases on the current server
Table_Privileges	Security permissions on the tables within a database
Tables	A list of all tables and views in the database
Views	Information about the specified view

Table 1-6 lists some commonly used information schema views and the typical purpose of each.

It is important to note that the information schema views are security dependent. That is, users will only be able to see information about objects to which they have been granted the appropriate permissions.

Locking and Concurrency

To ensure that resources are available to multiple users at a time, individual sessions must lock data before they attempt to modify it. While certain information is locked, no other users can modify the same information. A major performance enhancement in SQL Server 2000 is the ability to perform row-level locking. This allows users to lock only a specific row within a table—instead of the table itself—while making changes. Row-level locking therefore allows multiple users to modify the same table at the same time. SQL Server also supports row locks (partial or complete) when accessing indexes, tables, and databases. The result is that locking will have less of an impact on overall concurrency. Covering all of the issues related to locking can be quite complex and is covered in detail in Chapter 5.

Network Communications

The real purpose of your database is to communicate with clients, whether they are end users who query your application directly, client/server applications, or other database servers. In order for clients and the database server to communicate, a common method of data transfer must be determined. The default selections for network libraries (shown in Figure 1-12) will be appropriate for most TCP/IP-based environments. SQL Server can use any number of network libraries to communicate, but each must be enabled separately on both the client and the server.

Table 1-7 lists the available protocol types and the typical users of each.

If you're having trouble connecting to a SQL Server installation, the protocols likely are configured incorrectly. It has become increasingly common to connect to database servers over the Internet. Although this is supported using the TCP/IP protocol, you must also make sure that there are no firewalls that block the appropriate communications ports. These options can be modified after SQL Server installation by using the Client Network Utility and Server Network Utility programs in the Microsoft SQL Server 2000 program group.

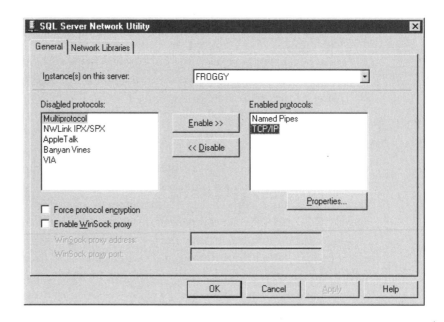

FIGURE 1-12

Selecting SQL
Server 2000
Server network
library options

Note that the use of encryption can be a very useful option for increasing the security of connections to SQL Server that occur over the Internet.

TABLE 1-7

SQL Server 2000
Network
Libraries

Protocol	Suggested Type of Client	Notes
AppleTalk	Macintosh clients	Uses local AppleTalk zone for communications
Banyan VINES	VINES clients	Supports SPP communications; only available on Intel platform
Multiprotocol	All	Uses any protocol type; data and authentication encryption are possible
Named pipes	Windows 95/98/ME and Windows NT/2000 only	Works on TCP/IP, NetBEUI, or IPX/SPX networks
NWLink IPX/SPX	Novell NetWare clients and servers	Can connect to NetWare Bindery
TCP/IP	All (requires TCP/IP connectivity)	Uses TCP port 1433 by default and can work over the Internet; also supports MS Proxy Server

Working with SQL Server 2000

So far, we have been talking about SQL Server architecture. This topic is somewhat theoretical, but it is extremely helpful in understanding how SQL Server works "under the hood." Now, it's time to look at what you—the database administrator or implementer—work with daily. One of the most welcome enhancements to SQL Server 2000 is easier administration. Database servers used to be the domain of specialized administrators who understood the architecture of the product and used archaic commands to interact with the machine. Realizing that not all systems administrators are also DBAs, Microsoft has greatly simplified the processes involved with designing, implementing, and managing a database solution. We have already talked about such features as dynamic file management, but that's just scratching the surface. SQL Server 2000 includes many enhancements that improve manageability and decrease time spent in administration. Those who have worked with other RDBMSs will find the tools in SQL Server 2000 to be intuitive and easier to use. Let's start with the heart of the administrative interface.

Enterprise Manager

The central portion of the SQL Server interface is Enterprise Manager. Microsoft has standardized on moving its various heterogeneous tools to a single, extensible interface called Microsoft Management Console (MMC). Enterprise Manager is a plug-in that works within MMC to provide a uniform look and feel between different types of administration tools. It uses HTML capabilities to provide clear information about the status of databases and the various options available. Figure 1-13 shows the sort of information you might see in Enterprise Manager.

Almost all of the functions you will regularly have to perform on an installation of SQL Server can be performed from within this interface. Enterprise Manager supports accessing remote servers from within a single interface. A list of all the tasks available would be impossible, but Microsoft has taken the time to make some of the most complex operations accessible using wizards. A good example is the Database Maintenance Plan Wizard, which can automatically create and schedule jobs for performing database backup operations.

FIGURE 1-13

Viewing server
information in
SQL Server
Enterprise
Manager

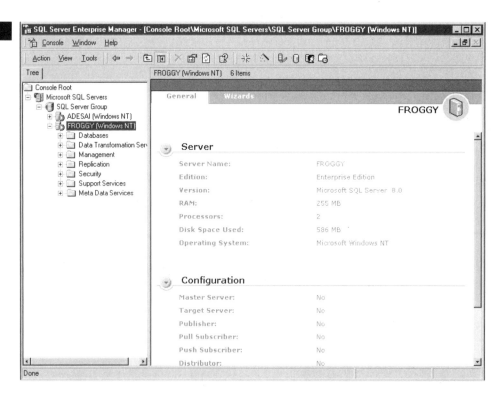

It's very important for technical professionals to choose the best tool for the job. Working with SQL Server 2000 is no exception. Fortunately, you have many different tools at your disposal. The one that many database developers and administrators become familiar with is Enterprise Manager. The graphical interface of Enterprise Manager is certainly user friendly, but it's not always the best way to perform specific tasks. For example, if you need to run a query or make a change to many databases on your server, it might be much more efficient to perform the actions via Query Analyzer (which we'll cover later in this section). Through a well-designed script, you might also have a set of code that you can reuse in the future. Many experienced database administrators and developers collect libraries of scripts that they can use, should the need arise. In such an instance, you'll be using SQL Server 2000's tools to build some of your own! Always remember that choosing the right tool is an important first step to any solution.

Database Schemas

A *database schema*, defined simply, is a statement of the relationships between database objects. Specifically, this means the relationships between tables using primary keys and foreign keys. A great deal of time can (and should!) be spent in designing a database schema that meets business requirements. Usually, a database schema is represented in an Entity Relationship Diagram (ERD). These diagrams should display information about the tables in a specific database schema and document their interactions. Developers and database administrators can use ERDs when programming or managing database objects.

To make the task easier, SQL Server Enterprise Manager includes a tool that can be used to simplify many of the tasks involved. By using this tool, you can quickly and easily create, manage, and maintain database tables and definitions. Figure 1-14 shows a database schema for the *Pubs* sample database (which is installed with SQL Server). The diagram tool can be accessed via Enterprise Manager by clicking the Diagrams object within the contents of a database.

FIGURE 1-14

Viewing database schema information in Enterprise Manager

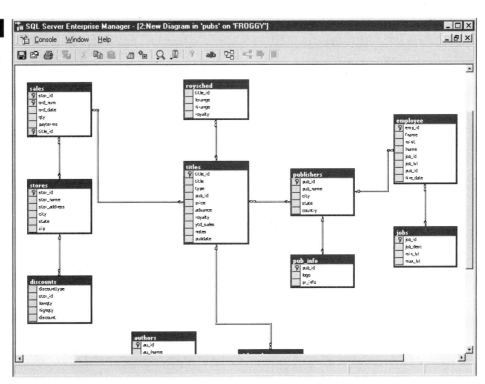

Be sure that you are very comfortable with the tools in Enterprise Manager that can be used for creating and managing relationships between tables. Expect to see database structures presented in this format on the exam.

Data Transformation Services

On many different data platforms and RDBMSs, transferring data between systems can be quite a headache. Different database servers store information using various data types and in proprietary structures. Often, transferring information requires exporting information to a standard comma-separated values (CSV) file and then manually importing the information. Microsoft has made the entire process much easier by providing Data Transformation Services (DTS) with SQL Server 2000. This architecture allows database designers and administrators to easily transfer information between supported information types. Through various interfaces, DTS supports moving information to and from other relational and nonrelational structures, such as Microsoft Excel and Access files, or from other database servers, such as Oracle. The easiest way to transfer information is to use the DTS Import/Export Wizard (see Figure 1-15), which is included with SQL Server. The wizard walks you through the creation of basic packages that transfer data.

FIGURE 1-15

Using the DTS
Wizard

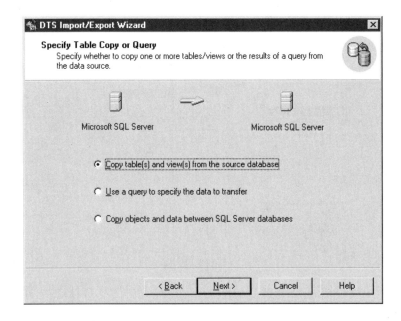

In addition to performing the important tasks of transferring information between heterogeneous sources, DTS goes one step further in letting you modify data as it is transferred. This is extremely important, because various systems might use different formats for the same information. For example, one database might store the information about a customer's status as Active or Inactive, whereas another might have a true/false setting for a column entitled Active. This can be used for data warehousing or for moving heterogeneous data into a single, uniform repository. Figure 1-16 shows a sample DTS package that copies data from several sources into a single database server.

In some cases, you might want to run an operation just once (to copy a database, for example). In others, however, you might want to periodically coalesce data from multiple sources or perform exports to another server. To support this, DTS operations can be saved as "packages," which can be stored on SQL Server for later use. The packages can also be modified as business requirements change. Finally, you can easily schedule a package to be executed at any time. For database developers, DTS also supports the export of packages to Microsoft Visual Basic files. This code can

FIGURE 1-16

A sample DTS package

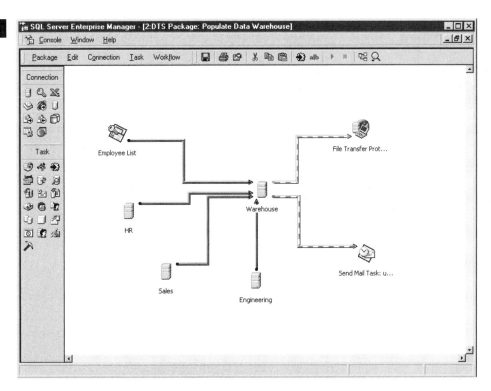

then be used as a reference for creating custom applications based on DTS functionality. The end result is a lowered learning curve and a great savings in time and effort to move data between applications, databases, and servers. We'll cover DTS in much more detail in Chapter 7.

SQL Query Analyzer

Although many of the operations you'll regularly perform on a SQL Server installation can be performed through Enterprise Manager, certain operations are easier to perform from a command-based environment. SQL Query Analyzer is an excellent tool for performing ad hoc queries against a database and for performing administrative functions using Transact-SQL. If you're a database developer that's new to SQL Server 2000, it's likely that Query Analyzer will soon become your best friend. By using SQL Query Analyzer for executing database commands, you'll be able to see the output of your query in either standard text form or within a grid. Figure 1-17 shows the results of a query in text mode.

FIGURE 1-17

Viewing query results in text mode

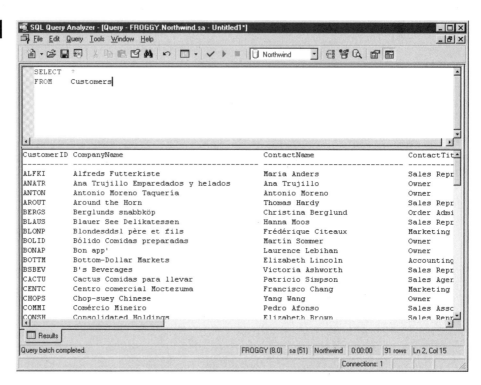

Developers can create some large and complicated queries, so the color-coding features of the SQL code can make managing long statements much easier. SQL Query Analyzer's usefulness doesn't stop there, however. In addition to being able to execute ad hoc queries, you can choose to view graphical statistics on the operations of a query (see Figure 1-18). Later in this chapter, we'll see how this function can be useful for finding performance problems.

One of the most difficult parts of using Transact-SQL is in remembering command syntax. This is especially true if you're not used to development. With SQL Server 2000, Microsoft updated Query Analyzer to include several extremely useful features. First is the option to view lists of database objects within the Query Analyzer Objects window (as shown in Figure 1-19).

By simply right-clicking a database object, you can quickly and easily generate scripts related to working with the object (see Figure 1-20). Additionally, these scripts might include replaceable parameters that allow you to replace options through the use of a dialog box.

FIGURE 1-18

Viewing information related to query statistics

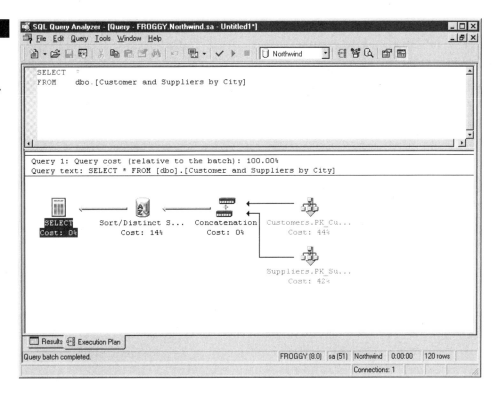

FIGURE 1-19

Viewing
information about
database objects
in Query
Analyzer

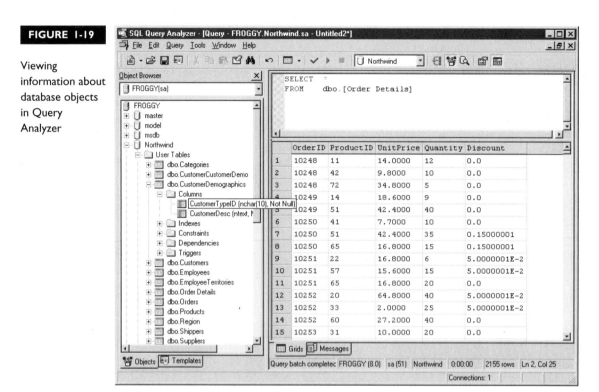

In the list of database objects section, you'll also be able to view lists of functions and other information that you can commonly use when working with Transact-SQL. Overall, Query Analyzer is a flexible and powerful tool for Transact-SQL development, and you'll spend a lot of time with it as you prepare for the exam.

Developing SQL Server Applications

The database server by itself can be useful, but before your end users will be able to take advantage of the information stored in it, you'll need to develop appropriate applications. We've already discussed some of the various roles that database servers might assume within your environment. Here, we'll look at just a few of the programming concepts related to working with SQL Server 2000. Unfortunately, we don't have the space to cover all the details. Since it is an important real-world topic, however, let's start by looking at typical application architecture and then look at data access methods.

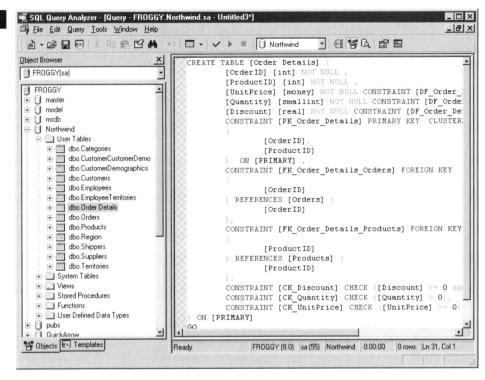

FIGURE 1-20

Creating scripts
for database
objects

n-Tier Client/Server Architecture

In many database applications, client software connects directly with a database server to obtain data for processing. For example, an order entry terminal at a store might use TCP/IP to communicate with a central inventory database server located in the "back office." This is the simplest client/server format, and it works well in some situations. The main benefit is that these types of applications are easy to develop initially. However, there are several drawbacks. First of all, much of the business logic needed to process data is stored on the client. Whenever this information changes or business rules are updated, client software must be upgraded. In most cases, this involves visiting each of the client machines and installing updates. Another potential drawback is in the area of scalability: if the database server or the client is overloaded with work, the user will experience slow response times and throughput. Overall system performance is based on that of the clients and servers.

Database servers are commonly used as part of a multitier, client/server architecture. Such architectures are often called "n-tier," signifying that the application consists of more than one tier. Here, a front-end client program (either a Visual Basic application or an Active Server Page (ASP)–based Web application) connects to a middle-tier server that contains the business rules. These data objects are then responsible for obtaining and processing the information requested from the clients. How is it more efficient to have multiple machines perform the work of just one? There are two main benefits.

First, the middle-tier server can be optimized for performing business rules operations only. It can pool together multiple requests for information and share these connections to the database server. The benefit for the database server is that it has to communicate directly with only one machine—the middle-tier server. Because database connections can use many resources to establish and destroy connections, this can represent a significant performance increase. An effective network design will optimize the bandwidth between these two machines, further increasing overall information throughput.

I promised two benefits of multitier solutions. We've already covered performance. The second is scalability. If, for example, it is found that the performance of middle-tier components is inadequate, an additional middle-tier server might be implemented to share the workload. Similarly, multiple database servers could provide the data required for the middle-tier components to continue to work at peak performance. Using this modular approach, code and hardware resources can be optimized independently at multiple levels. Additionally, it can be much easier to manage code and security settings when all the components are not located within one single piece of code.

Accessing Data from Applications

Many different methods can be used to access data from a SQL Server installation. Many are supported for backward compatibility, while others optimize performance and ease of use. The three main methods for accessing data from applications include Open Database Connectivity (ODBC), ActiveX Data Objects (ADO), and OLEDB. Which option you choose will be based on the requirements of your application and the development environment in which you work. For example, for Web-based applications, the ease of use of ADO makes it a good choice. ADO is also well supported in such development tools as Microsoft Visual Basic and Microsoft Visual Interdev.

For further information on data access methods, see SQL Server Books Online and the Microsoft Developer Network (MSDN) Online Web site at http://msdn.microsoft.com.

Programming Options

Microsoft has allowed external developers to access various portions of the SQL Server 2000 API. Table 1-8 lists the various APIs available. Although most users will not need to use these features in order to use the product, some businesses will want to create custom tools for their own use or to market commercially. Again, for more information, see SQL Server Books Online or http://msdn.microsoft.com.

SQL Server 2000 Analysis Services

In addition to the ability of SQL Server to serve as a powerful and flexible "back-end" RDBMS, SQL Server offers many useful features for storing and managing large amounts of data. Additionally, it includes new features for analyzing your data. In this section, we'll look at how decision-support services are supported in SQL Server 2000.

In SQL Server 2000, Microsoft has renamed and enhanced SQL Server 2000's Online Analytical Processing (OLAP) functionality. There are now two main components in what is called SQL Server 2000 Analysis Services. First, there is an

TABLE 1-8 Various APIs Supported by SQL Server 2000	**API**	**Application**	**Notes**
	Data Transformation Services API	Providing highly customized DTS tasks	Can be used for creating customized packages that modify, import, and export data
	Open Data Services API	Creating SQL Server extended stored procedures	Adds the benefits of working with languages such as Visual C++
	Replication Component Programming API	Setting up and managing SQL Server replication	Provides greater control over the replication process for use in custom applications
	SQL Control Manager (SCM)	Controlling SQL Server services	Can be used to start, stop, and pause SQL Server services
	SQL Data Manipulation Objects (SQL-DMO)	Managing and modifying SQL Server configuration and settings	Useful for creating custom SQL Server administration and management tools

improved and enhanced OLAP Services engine. Internally, this is referred to as OLAP 8.0. Second, there is a new data-mining engine. Let's look at these features in greater detail.

Data Warehousing

Data warehousing is the act of taking information from various heterogeneous sources and storing it in a common location for data analysis. There are several challenges that systems and database administrators might face when creating a data warehouse. These are as follows:

- **Design of the data warehouse schema**   The creation of denormalized database schema that facilitates the types of reporting that will be common for users in the organization. It is absolutely critical that this phase include input from business leaders from throughout an organization. Often, multiple schemas will need to be created to accommodate various requirements. The design of the schema itself will play a large part in the overall success and usefulness of the data warehouse.

- **Population of the data warehouse**   Information from several heterogeneous sources will need to be copied to the data warehouse. Data may come from a variety of platforms (such as relational and nonrelational databases), and may require "scrubbing" to iron out differences in data structure. In many cases, automated processes will be required to routinely refresh the information stored in the data warehouse.

- **Management of the data warehouse**   By their very nature, data warehouses tend to be large databases. Systems and database administrators must find ways to address performance and data storage concerns for the database.

- **Analysis**   The end goal of most data warehouse projects is the extraction of useful information. Reporting is extremely important for business decision makers and other "data consumers."

Since analysis is a big part of this type of information, "decision support" is the term often used to describe the purpose of data warehouses. Various tools in SQL Server 2000 can be used to help in this goal. Earlier, we discussed how the Data Transformation Services (DTS) can be used to merge data from many different sources into a single repository. Also, we covered the storage architecture of SQL

Server. SQL Server 2000 can support databases that are multiple *terabytes* in size. These features and capabilities make SQL Server 2000 a good choice for developing a data warehouse. Of course, the data warehouse itself is not very useful if you don't analyze the information in meaningful ways.

Analysis Services and Online Analytical Processing (OLAP)

Many organizations go to great lengths to collect information, but fall short of the goal when it comes to analyzing the information to obtain useful results. For example, designing a system that collects all the information reported by store cash registers at the point of sale is much easier than combining this information with data from other stores and then forming reports that provide meaningful strategies. It is well beyond the scope of this book to explain the intricacies of developing a well-designed OLAP solution. Suffice it to say that it takes a lot of careful planning and solid understanding of the information that you plan to analyze. Figure 1-21 shows the SQL Server 2000 OLAP Manager interface. Using this application, you can easily design and customize data cubes for later analysis.

FIGURE 1-21

Using the SQL Server 2000 Analysis Manager

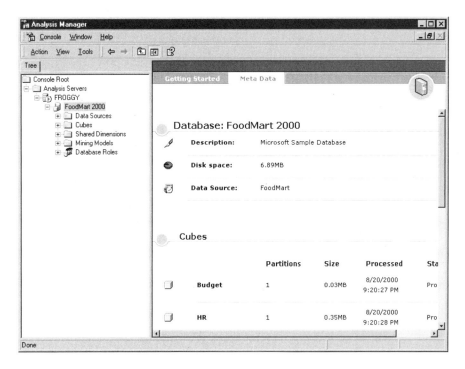

FIGURE 1-22

Using Pivot
Tables to view
and analyze
OLAP-based data

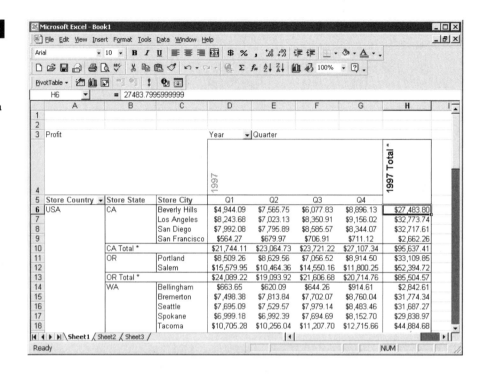

On the client side, you'll need to have a tool that is easy enough for end users to access. Microsoft Excel 2000 provides many features for accessing OLAP information. The most obvious is the use of the PivotTables feature, shown in Figure 1-22. PivotTables provide interactive data analysis, based on a graphical system. Instead of rephrasing SQL query syntax, the user only needs to drag and drop various columns into place to change views. When connected to an OLAP server, however, the PivotTables feature is greatly enhanced. The user can now form complex data relationships on two or more axes of the "cube." Furthermore, Microsoft has provided for storing *offline cubes*—data structures that store the information that is likely to be used in your OLAP analysis, except that it is stored on your local machine until needed. With this feature, queries can be run much more quickly (since they minimize data transfers on the network) and can even be run when not connected to a network at all.

Data Mining

New in SQL Server 2000 is a data-mining engine. The concept behind data mining is to allow users to find patterns of information in their data. The results from performing well-designed data-mining approaches can be very helpful in making business decisions. For example, suppose your database tracks sales that occurs at stores throughout the country. In addition to tracking the sales of specific items, you also track information about the buyers (such as their location, income, and gender). You can use data-mining techniques to find repeating patterns in the data. You might find, for example, that customers with high incomes located in the Northeast United States are much more likely to buy more of product A, while the product is not very well-received in other markets.

Figure 1-23 provides an example of the SQL Server 2000 data-mining engine.

English Query

If you're a DBA who does little database development, you've probably wondered why SQL syntax is so cryptic. Actually, compared to other "programming languages," the syntax and rules of SQL are quite simple. However, for most people, it's still easier to use a database application designed to develop a "quick report" than it is to design and generate the report manually. Realizing this, Microsoft has included the

FIGURE 1-23

Viewing data-mining information in SQL Server 2000 Analysis Manager

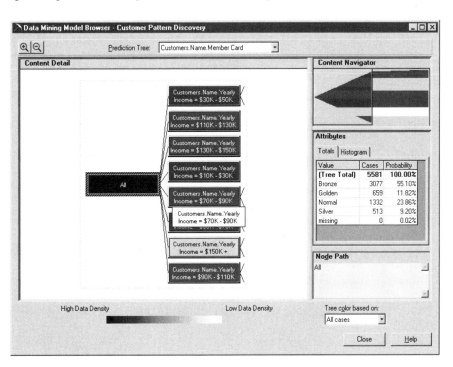

English Query application, which allows database administrators to create relationships between various types of database information. For example, suppose you program relationships such as "Customers have addresses" or "Orders are shipped to customers." Based on these relationships, English Query can create SQL statements out of phrases such as "How many parts did Store #112 sell in the first quarter of 1999?" If you've ever been on the receiving end of a call from a manager who wants you to design reports, you can see how this feature might be very helpful!

In SQL Server 2000, Microsoft has greatly enhanced the tools used to create English Query information (see Figure 1-24). This allows database developers to more easily bring plain-language querying functionality into their applications.

CERTIFICATION SUMMARY

That was a *lot* of information to cover in so few pages! As mentioned at the beginning of this chapter, the goal here was to provide an introduction to the architecture of SQL Server 2000. This chapter should have given you an overview of the types of problems that SQL Server is designed to solve, and how you can use it to solve those problems. We chose to focus on the architecture of SQL Server—how the product

FIGURE 1-24

Viewing information in the English Query Project Wizard

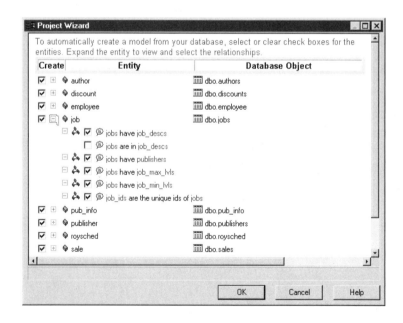

works "under the hood." We'll see many more examples (in greater detail) in upcoming chapters.

With this solid understanding of the inner workings of SQL Server 2000, we can move onward to diving into the details of database design and implementation with SQL Server 2000. In Chapter 2 we'll begin by covering the important topics that are related to database design.

SELF TEST

The following questions will help you measure your understanding of the material presented in this chapter.

1. Which of the following editions of SQL Server 2000 supports advanced features such as indexed views, log-shipping via the GUI in Enterprise Manager, and support for advanced hardware platforms? (Choose all that apply.)

   A. Developer Edition

   B. Standard Edition

   C. Windows CE Edition

   D. Enterprise Edition

   E. All of the above

2. You are a database developer for a small organization that uses SQL Server 2000. You want to be able to quickly and easily create database tables and you want to graphically depict the relationships between these tables. Which of the following SQL Server tools can be used to perform this task?

   A. Enterprise Manager

   B. Profiler

   C. Analysis Services

   D. Query Analyzer

   E. None of the above

3. You are troubleshooting a problem in which certain users are unable to connect to your SQL Server installation from remote machines. You suspect that the problem is related to connectivity for specific clients, since most users can access the server normally. Which of the following tools would be most helpful in diagnosing and fixing the problem? (Choose all that apply.)

   A. Profiler

   B. Query Analyzer

   C. Enterprise Manager

   D. Server Network Utility

   E. Client Network Utility

4. Which of the following features of relational database systems is used to improve the performance of querying tables by storing subsets and pointers to data pages?

   A. Indexes

   B. Functions

   C. Views

   D. Triggers

   E. None of the above

5. Which of the following features of SQL Server 2000 allows users to enter a query such as the following: "Which stores in the Northeast region have had sales of greater than $20,000?"

   A. Natural Language Querying

   B. English Query

   C. Transact-SQL

   D. Analysis Services

   E. None of the above

6. Which of the following types of files would be most useful for transferring hierarchical data structures between many different business applications?

   A. SQL files

   B. RPT files

   C. CSV files

   D. XML files

SELF TEST ANSWERS

1. ☑ **A and D.** Both the Developer and Enterprise Editions of SQL Server 2000 are designed to support advanced features of SQL Server 2000. The main difference is that the Developer Edition of SQL Server 2000 is licensed only for nonproduction use.
☒ The other editions of SQL Server 2000 are designed for different purposes, but none include the advanced features implemented in the Enterprise and Developer Editions.

2. ☑ **A.** The schema editing tools within Enterprise Manager can be used to easily design and view tables and the relationships between them.
☒ The other options are all useful SQL Server 2000 tools, but they are not designed specifically for the creation of tables and table relationships.

3. ☑ **D and E.** Both the Client and Server Network Utilities can be used to determine and configure the network protocols that SQL Server clients and servers can use to communicate.
☒ The other choices are useful only when you have established communications between your clients and servers.

4. ☑ **A.** Indexes are data structures that can store information about the location of specific data. Since the query optimizer may be able to search the index instead of an entire table, this can dramatically improve the performance of data retrieval.
☒ The other options can be used to improve the performance of queries, but they do not store pointers or actual data.

5. ☑ **B.** The English Query feature of SQL Server 2000 (which must be installed separately from the main product) allows users to generate ad hoc queries in plain language.

6. ☑ **D.** Extended Markup Language (XML) files can be used to transfer hierarchical data structures between systems. Many business application vendors either already support XML or are in the process of providing support for it in the future.

MICROSOFT CERTIFIED DATABASE ADMINISTRATOR

2

Developing a Logical Database Design

I n SQL Server 2000, as with all RDBMS, relational databases begin life as a logical data model. At its simplest, a logical data model is a person's or group's view of *something*. The *something* can be virtually anything: from a basic object, like the desk I work on, to an inventory and order taking system for a billion-dollar cooperation. A logical data model is a structuring of data that is *platform independent*. This means that it is developed completely on its own, without any concern for the RDBMS that it will reside on. Once a complete and correct logical data model is developed, it can then be implemented on any number of relational database products rather easily. The more correctly work is done on the logical data model, the less maintenance and overall headaches the physical database will have.

The eventual goal of a correct and robust physical database involves three main phases. The process of defining the logical data model, or data modeling, begins with the *analysis* phase. Data analysts conduct interviews with the appropriate personnel involved to gain an accurate view of the data in question. Through analysis, data can be grouped into entities and attributes, and relationships between entities are revealed. This analysis will lead to the actual *design* phase of the logical data model. In the design phase, entities, attributes, and relationships are diagrammed, creating a conceptual view of the information being modeled. After the design phase is complete, the *implementation* phase can begin. The implementation phase involves translating the logical data model into an actual physical database. Much like the construction of a house based on detailed plans, it is the creation of the database tables, columns, and relationships that have been defined in the logical data model.

The analysis and design phases of data modeling are very interrelated and occur many times: analysis is performed that reveals information and business rules that are translated into a design. The design is then verified through additional analysis, which leads to more design. This process continues over and over until a very thorough and complete data model is developed. However, the implementation phase occurs only once. Thus it is crucial that a logical data model be verified and tested through as much analysis as possible. It is much easier to change a logical data model than it is to change the physical database structure, especially once the database is functional and servicing users.

CERTIFICATION OBJECTIVE 2.01

Defining Entities and Attributes

At the core of any logical data model are *entities* and *attributes*. An entity is basically a *thing* in the real world that will be part of the logical data model. An entity can be almost anything: a car, an order form, the person writing this chapter, etc. Entities have facts about them, known as attributes of the entity. For instance, if we were to model this book, yours truly is an instance of the Author entity. I have attributes such as a name (Jeff), height (6'2"), and weight (no comment). Likewise, the color of a car would be an attribute of the Car entity, and the order number on an order form is an attribute of the Order Form entity.

Just as things interact with each other in the real world, entities in a logical data model interact with each other to form *relationships*. For example, a Product entity is purchased using an Order Form entity, creating a relationship between the two entities.

The key terms relating to data modeling are shown in Table 2-1.

TABLE 2-1   Definition of Common Terms Relating to Data Modeling

Term	Definition
Entity or relation	A logical unit of data in the data model. This will typically translate to a database table in the physical database.
Attribute	A characteristic of an entity. This will typically translate to a table column in the physical database.
Tuple	A specific instance of an entity. This will translate to a row or record in a database table.
Entity key	An attribute or group of attributes that uniquely identifies an instance of an entity. These attributes will typically translate into PRIMARY KEY constraints in the physical database.
Relationship	The means by which entities relate to one another in the logical data model. These will typically translate to FOREIGN KEY constraints in the physical database.

Let's look at a sample logical data model to demonstrate the terms in Table 2-1.

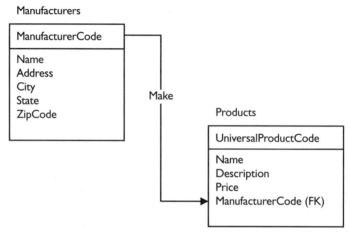

This logical data model contains two entities—products and manufacturers—represented by the large rectangles. The name of the entity is on the top of each rectangle. The entity Products has five attributes, including things like the product's name and its price, represented as text within the rectangles. The Universal Product Code attribute is the *key* attribute of products, because this value will be unique for each instance of the Product entity. Likewise, the Manufacturer Code is the key attribute for the Manufacturers entity. The Manufacturers entity also contains other attributes such as address and ZIP code. The key attributes are in the top portion of each rectangle, separated from the other nonkey attributes by a solid line. A nonkey attribute is any attribute that does not contribute to the key of an entity. There is also a relationship called "make" that exists between the two entities. This relationship can be read as a sentence in a logical data model—that is, "manufacturers make products." Notice that the Manufacturer Code attribute has been carried over or *migrated* from the Manufacturers entity to the Products entity because of that relationship, creating a *foreign key*. A foreign key is an attribute of an entity that references an attribute of another entity. In this case, each product references a manufacturer that makes each product. Finally, an instance of a product or manufacturer is a tuple, such as "Joe's Big House of Manufacturing."

Modeling Data

In any logical data model, in order to correctly define entities and attributes, careful attention is paid during the analysis phase to note keywords and phrases. When someone is describing something that is to be modeled, the nouns are typical candidates for entities and attributes. The verbs in the describing statements are typical candidates for relationships. Let's return to my desk as an example, and create a logical data model. A data analyst is given the task of defining my office in a logical data model. In describing my desk, I may make the following statements:

- My desk is brown in color.
- It's five feet long, two feet wide, and three feet high.
- It has two drawers and a cabinet underneath for storage.
- I keep my CPU in the cabinet and my monitor sits on the desk surface, as well as my keyboard and mouse.
- I keep floppy disks and CDs in the small drawer and documents in the large drawer.

Several entities and attributes become apparent in the above description. The desk itself is an entity, with the attributes of Color, Length, Width, and Height. The desk also has storage areas, such as the surface, a cabinet, a small drawer, and a large drawer. The storage areas contain various objects that I use in my day-to-day activities, such as a monitor, keyboard, and floppy disks. So, from the description, three entities have emerged: Desk, Storage Areas, and Objects. Viewed on a logical data model, we have the following:

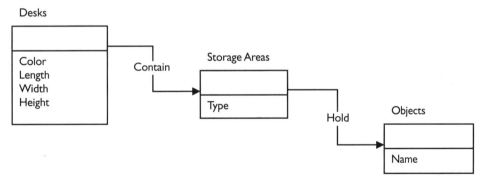

In looking at the preceding model, many questions may be popping into your head, such as why is Objects an entity? Is not an object an attribute of a storage area? And why is a storage area an entity? Shouldn't we have separate entities for each drawer, cabinet, and the desk surface? All excellent questions, I assure you, and those concerns will be addressed in upcoming sections on *normalization* using the previous example. So if you find yourself asking similar questions, congratulations! You have just the analytical mind needed for effective data modeling. For now, let's complete the process of defining the entities and attributes. You may have noticed from our current data model that none of the entities have key attributes.

Defining Entity Keys

In a logical data model, each entity must possess an attribute or group of attributes that can uniquely identify each instance of the entity. For the Desk entity, we really have no combination of attributes that will uniquely identify a desk from the attributes present. Should we even care? I have only one desk, so why do we need to uniquely identify it? At this point you'll learn a very important point about data modeling: all the necessary information is rarely, if ever, gathered on the initial analysis. Upon further questioning, we discover that my desk has an asset tag sticker on it. This can uniquely identify the desk. Also, through analysis, we discover that although only one desk is currently in my office, the possibility certainly exists that another one could fit in here should the need arise. The asset tag number becomes what's known as a *candidate key* for the Desks entity.

Key attributes in an entity can be of several types. A candidate key is an attribute or group of attributes that can uniquely identify an instance of an entity. If more than one candidate key exists, one must be chosen as the *primary key* and the remaining candidate keys become *alternate keys*. Let's use an example to illustrate: Say we are developing a data model used for tracking company assets and equipment, and we have an entity called Computers. In the Computers entity, we wish to track several attributes of each employee's computer: the processor speed, the amount of memory, the company asset tag, and the manufacturer's serial number, as shown here:

Computers

AssetTag SerialNumber Processor Memory

In this entity, both the asset tag and the serial number of the computer are unique within our organization, so we have two candidate keys for the Computers entity. The asset tag makes the most sense as primary key since we will be using this number for many operations, such as inventory, employee moves, etc. The serial number will not be used very often, probably only when dealing with the manufacturer for support issues. From the two candidate keys, the Asset Tag attribute becomes the primary key, and the Serial Number attribute becomes an alternate key.

Computers

AssetTag
SerialNumber (AK) Processor Memory

Back in our office data model, the Storage Areas entity also needs a key attribute. We have only one attribute at this point, that of Type. A type in our case would be small drawer, large drawer, surface, or cabinet. For the one desk that currently occupies the office, this may seem like a way to uniquely identify each storage area; but what if we do find ourselves in a situation where another desk occupies my office? Desks within our organization come in all shapes and sizes—some have one drawer, some have five drawers of all different sizes, some have two or three cabinets, etc. Clearly, the attribute of Type cannot uniquely identify a storage area since different desks can have common and uncommon types storage areas. The Storage Areas entity will use what's called a *concatenated primary key* in this situation. A concatenated or *compound* primary key is a primary key made up of more than one attribute; and in this case, part of the concatenated primary key is also a foreign key, migrated from the parent entity of Desks.

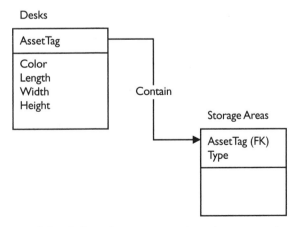

The combination of the desk and storage type has given us a primary key in the Storage Areas entity that will now uniquely identify any storage areas, irrespective of whether they put one desk or six hundred desks in my office (that would cause some space issues).

The remaining Objects entity will introduce a new type of key attribute known as a *surrogate key*. Let's say I determine there are about 50 objects stored in and on my desk. Several, such as the computer and monitor, have asset tags; but most, like my floppy disks and the photograph of my wife, don't. And this particular data model is a view of my office, not a company inventory tracking system. So the asset tag will not provide an acceptable key attribute, even if we decide later it's an attribute of the Objects entity that we'd like to store in our database. In the Objects entity, our only real choice for a primary key is the object name. But if we do choose this as our primary key, we'd have to ensure we name all objects uniquely, like "Blank Floppy Disk 1," "Blank Floppy Disk 2," etc. While this may serve our purpose, a primary key such as "The framed picture of my wife" is hardly an efficient primary key, so we'll introduce a surrogate key as the primary key of the Objects entity.

A surrogate key is a key attribute of an entity that is manufactured or created for the sole purpose of serving as the key value of an entity. A surrogate key has no business meaning, as opposed to an *intelligent key*. The key attribute AssetTag in the Desks entity is an example of an intelligent key. It has meaning in the real world. A surrogate key is typically an integer or number that can be manually entered and incremented or automatically incremented using the *identity* property of SQL Server 2000. You will learn more about the identity property in Chapter 3. Now that we've added a surrogate primary key for the Objects entity, Figure 2-1 shows the office data model with all primary keys defined.

Here are some scenarios and solutions for effectively choosing the primary key of an entity.

SCENARIO & SOLUTION

The only unique attribute in the entity is 50 characters long.	Use a surrogate key. As primary and foreign keys are often the condition on which tables are joined, 50 characters is not efficient.
You would need to use more that one attribute to guarantee uniqueness.	Use a compound primary key.
No combination of attributes can guarantee uniqueness in the entity.	That would be rare, but use a surrogate key.
There are many attributes in the entity that are unique.	Choose the one that makes the most sense as primary key.

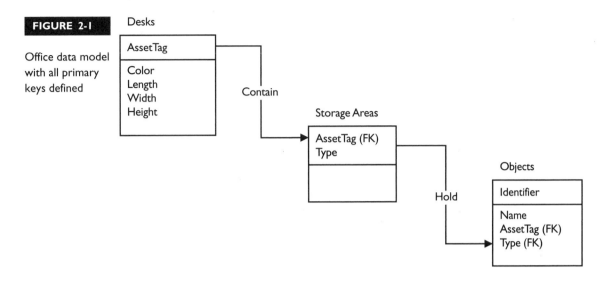

FIGURE 2-1

Office data model with all primary keys defined

Foreign Keys

The primary keys for the model have now been established. You'll notice that because of the "storage areas hold objects" relationship, the primary key of the Storage Areas entity has been migrated to the Objects entity as a foreign key. In this case, it is a compound foreign key. The foreign-key value will be an exact duplicate of the key it references back to. For example, if the Desks entity had an instance of a desk with the asset tag of 800401, the foreign key in the Storage Areas entity will also contain the value 800401. While duplicate data is something that is to be avoided in any good database design, foreign-key data is not considered redundant in the same sense. It is necessary for a foreign key to duplicate the value of the key it references in order to maintain a relationship between two entities. You will typically have a foreign key for each relationship in a data model. In our case, there are two relationships and two foreign keys defining those relationships.

Nonkey Attributes

Now that the key attributes are defined, the remaining task is to add any remaining nonkey attributes that we may wish to track in this data model. Upon further analysis, I make the following statements:

■ I'd like to keep track of the monetary value of the objects that are on and in my desk, and also be able to differentiate what belongs to me and what belongs to the company.

- Knowing the last time I cleaned my desk would also help.

- The dimensions of the cabinets and drawers would also be good to know, just in case I ever want to move things around.

Armed with this latest analysis, it's simply a matter of filling in the remaining attributes in the appropriate entities, as shown in Figure 2-2.

At this point, let's examine a question raised earlier: "Shouldn't there be a separate entity for each drawer, cabinet, and surface?" It's crucial to good data modeling and database design to ensure that entities are not duplicated. In the initial analysis, everything to be modeled is typically treated as a separate thing, and that is fine for the initial analysis. However, as the process progresses, similarities need to be noted to ensure uniqueness of the entities themselves. Let's imagine that we had created a separate entity for each type of storage area. While this might work with a small number of storage areas, what if another desk is brought into the office with five or ten drawers. We would now need to alter our data model to include five or ten more entities, one for each new drawer. And, again, the model would need to be altered should a desk be removed. Looking at the similarities of these entities, we can see that all the drawers, cabinets, and compartments share common traits such as dimensions and the ability to store objects. Our generic Storage Areas entity defines these best. Even if a scenario arises that involves multiple desks with hundreds of drawers, all of different sizes, the data model requires no modification. New additions to the

FIGURE 2-2

Office data model with nonkey attributes added

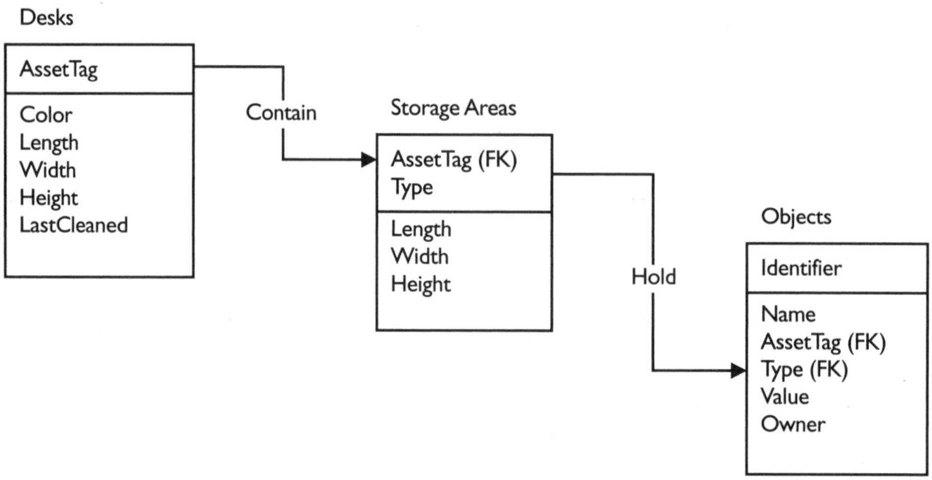

Storage Areas entity will have the key attribute of the parent desk's asset tag and the appropriate type attribute—that is Drawer 1, Drawer 2, Small Cabinet, and so on, according to whatever naming convention we adopt as a standard.

EXERCISE 2-1

Define Entities, Attributes, and Entity Keys

1. Consider the following analysis: "I'd like to create a database to store data about Little League players and the teams they play on. Currently, there are 12 teams. The team names are unique. Each team also has a unique sponsor that I'd like to track. Players may play on only one team, but each team uses the numbers 1 through 12 on the players' jerseys. I think we'll need to track the players first names, last names, jersey number, and phone numbers in case we need to contact their parents."

2. On a sheet of paper, create the entities. From the analysis, there are two entities defined: one for teams and one for players.

3. Determine key attributes for the two entities: The Teams entity will have the key attributes of TeamName and Sponsor. Both are unique, but the name of the team makes the most sense for a primary key. The Players entity has no candidate keys based on the following facts: Siblings can have the same phone number, jersey numbers are not unique, and first and last names can be shared. While the combination of first and last name might make sense, it is possible that two boys named John Smith or two girls named Mary Jones could play in the same league. The combination of FirstName, LastName, and JerseyNumber also does not work, as two girls named Mary Jones could play for different teams with the same number on their jersey. Let's take this to the extreme and say that the combination of FirstName, LastName, JerseyNumber, and PhoneNumber would be unique within the entity. However, two brothers named John Smith sharing the same phone number could play for different teams with the same number on their jersey. A surrogate key makes the most sense for the Players entity.

4. Add the remaining nonkey attributes to the entities. The Teams entity has only primary and alternate key attributes. The Players entity will have the nonkey attributes of FirstName, LastName, JerseyNumber, and PhoneNumber.

5. Add a foreign key to the Players entity referencing the primary key TeamName in the Teams entity to establish the relationship "teams are made up of players."

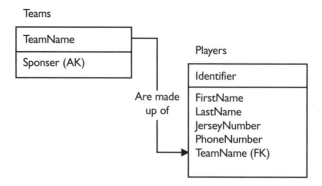

Entity Composition and Normalization

Logical database design, as with most things in life, is governed by a set of rules. These are collectively known as *normal forms*. The first three, first normal form through third normal form, were developed by Dr. E. F. Codd in 1970 based on some fairly complex mathematics. There are additional normal forms, but the first through the third are the ones you need to concern yourself with and are paramount to good database design. The other normal forms are beyond the scope of this book and cover relatively obscure conditions.

Understanding the Goals of Normalization

Applying the normal forms to database design, or *normalization*, has several benefits, including ensuring *entity integrity* and reducing redundant data to a minimum. Entity integrity states that each instance of an entity is not duplicated. Ideally, data is stored in one and only one place. When it needs to be modified, it is modified in one and only one place. Imagine a phone number that is stored in multiple entities redundantly. If the phone number were to change, and only one occurrence were updated, anomalous data would now exist in the database. Keeping your database design in compliance with the normal forms ensures that the chance of such a thing happening is minimized. However, keep in mind as you read the following sections that excessive normalization can cause performance penalties in the physical database. It is advisable, though, that all logical data models comply with third normal form, and *denormalization* be addressed after third normal is achieved. Denormalization is the process of intentionally violating the normal forms for performance increases.

The First Normal Form

The first normal form, at its most basic, states that each tuple or occurrence of an entity is exactly the same as every other occurrence of the entity. That means that each record must utilize exactly the same attributes, and that those attributes are atomic or indivisible. Each attribute must contain one and only one value and repeating groups are not allowed. Let's return to the data model of my office to demonstrate. Assume we had modeled the Storage Areas entity, as shown here:

Storage Areas

| AssetTag |
| Type |
| Length |
| Width |
| Height |
| Contents |

In this scenario, the Objects entity has been removed and the contents of a storage area have been modeled as an attribute instead of a separate entity. By virtue of the fact that a storage area can certainly hold more than one object, the Contents attribute would be multivalued. For example, in the small drawer, I may have a blank floppy disk, a SQL Server 2000 CD, and a pen. Therefore, that record of the Contents attribute would look like this: Blank Floppy Disk, SQL Server 2000 CD, Pen. Any attribute with that characteristic, usually a delimited list of items, is in violation of the first normal form. All attributes must be indivisible. We could, however, modify the Storage Areas entity to split up the list of contents as such.

Storage Areas

AssetTag
Type

Length
Width
Height
Contents1
Contents2
Contents3

In this scenario, each object will be represented as a separate attribute in the Storage Areas entity. The Contents1 attribute would contain the value Blank Floppy Disk; Contents2, the SQL Server 2000 CD; and Contents3, the Pen. However, this also is in violation of the first normal form: all records in the Storage Areas entity must be exactly the same—that is, use the same set of attributes—as every other record in the entity. Using the above model, this is not the case. There is no guarantee that each storage area will contain three and only three objects; therefore, each record in the entity will not utilize the same set of attributes. And what if a storage area is empty, or what if it contains ten items? This attribute's structure is what's known as a *repeating group*. The very nature of a repeating group requires that enough Contents attributes be provided to account for the maximum amount of objects that could possibly be placed in a storage area. This presents a challenge.

What is the maximum amount of objects that could be placed within a storage area? 100? 1,000? Do you really want a database table with 1,000 columns? The first normal form addresses this quandary by prohibiting repeating groups. If a case exists where more than one of the same attribute will be a child of an entity, this attribute is split into a separate entity, as has been done here:

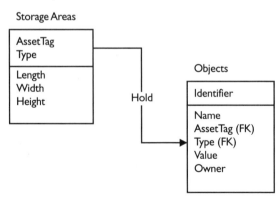

Storage Areas

AssetTag
Type

Length
Width
Height

Hold

Objects

Identifier

Name
AssetTag (FK)
Type (FK)
Value
Owner

The Second Normal Form

The second normal form builds on the first normal form by requiring that all nonkey attributes of an entity depend on the entire primary key of that entity, and that the entity be in the first normal form. A common saying is that all nonkey attributes must depend on "the key, the whole key, and nothing but the key." The following will further clarify the second normal form:

$$AB \leftarrow C \text{ and } A \leftarrow D$$

Attributes A and B represent the compound primary key of an entity. C and D represent nonkey attributes. Attribute C is fully dependent on the entire primary-key attribute of AB and complies with second normal form. However, attribute D is only dependent on part of the primary key, the key attribute A. The goal of second normal form is that the nonkey attributes of C and D both depend on the whole primary key of AB:

$$AB \leftarrow C \text{ and } AB \leftarrow D$$

Let's return to our office data model to see an example of an entity that violates the second normal form. Second normal form violations deal with partial key dependencies, so we'll use the Storage Areas entity as an example, since it uses a compound primary key. In this scenario, we've decided the unladen weight of a desk would be beneficial to track in case we ever want to move it. A Weight attribute is added to the Storage Areas entity.

Storage Areas

| AssetTag |
Type
Length
Width
Height
UnladenWeight

The Storage Areas entity is now in violation of the second normal form. While we could certainly store the UnladenWeight attribute in the Storage Areas entity, it is not dependent on the whole primary key. The weight of the desk only depends on the partial key attribute of AssetTag, not the entire key of the entity. This is a fairly intuitive violation of the second normal form; it's logical that the weight of the desk should be stored in the Desks entity. Let's explore another violation of the second normal form that is not so obvious. Consider the following model. It has two entities, one for employees and another for the skills the employee possesses.

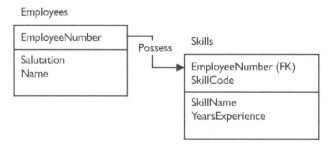

In this scenario, the Skills entity tracks the skill any employee may have, as well as the years of experience he or she has acquired in that particular skill. The combination of an EmployeeNumber and a SkillCode make up the compound primary key of the entity. In looking at the Skills entity, do all nonkey attributes (SkillName and YearsExperience) depend on the entire primary key of the entity? While the YearsExperience attribute is dependent on both an employee and a skill, the SkillName attribute depends on only part of the primary key, the key attribute of SkillCode. In order to bring this model into compliance with the second normal form, the Skills entity is split so that all nonkey attributes depend entirely on the primary key of their respective entities.

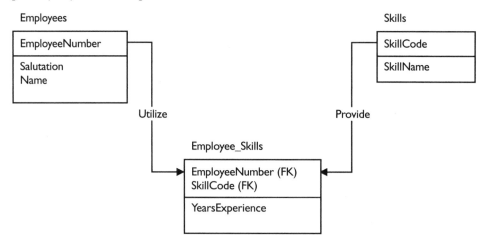

You can see that the revised Skills entity now only contains attributes relevant to skills. A new entity, Employee_Skills, is created to associate employees to their skills with a compound primary key referencing both entities. Now the nonkey attribute SkillName depends on the entire primary key of the Skills entity. Remember, to comply with second normal form, all nonkey attributes must depend on "the key, the whole key." To complete the saying with "nothing but the key," we move on to the third normal form.

The Third Normal Form

The third normal form continues to build on the second normal form by requiring that entities comply with the first and second normal forms. In addition, the third normal form requires not only that all nonkey attributes depend on the whole primary key, but also that all nonkey attributes depend on nothing but the primary key. The third normal form provides the effect of minimizing redundant data in the database by eliminating *transitive dependencies*. To illustrate the concept of transitive dependencies, consider the following:

$$A \leftarrow B \leftarrow C$$

The attribute A represents the primary key of an entity. B and C represent nonkey attributes. The attribute B is fully dependant on the primary key A. This is in compliance with the third normal form. However, attribute C does not depend on the primary key A, but instead depends on the nonkey attribute of B. This is a transitive dependency, because C does not depend directly on A. C depends transitively on A, needing B to get there. The goal of third normal form is illustrated here:

$$A \leftarrow B \text{ and } A \leftarrow C$$

Let's return to the office data model to demonstrate this further. In this scenario, we'd also like to track who is currently sitting at a desk, including their employee number, name, and salutation. We add the following attributes to the Desks entity:

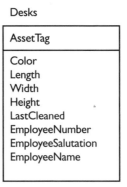

In looking at the attributes in the revised Desks entity, we can see that some transitive dependencies have been introduced. The attributes of color and the dimension attributes do indeed depend on the primary key of Desks. But consider the attributes of EmployeeSalutation and EmployeeName. Do these attributes depend on the primary key of AssetTag? What does an employee's salutation have to do with a desk? Clearly, these attributes depend on the attribute of EmployeeNumber. These dependencies must be resolved to bring our new entity into compliance with the third normal form. In order to resolve a violation of the third normal form, all nonkey attributes that depend on attributes other than the primary key are split into a new entity.

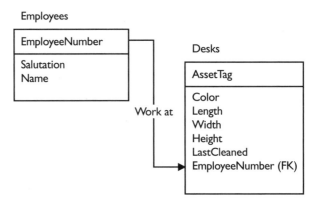

In this illustration, all transitive dependencies have been eliminated. All nonkey attributes in the newly created Employees entity fully depend on the entire primary key of the entity. Likewise, all nonkey entities in the Desks entity also depend fully on the entire primary key of that entity.

Entity Normalization

1. The following entity tracks facts about automobiles on a used car lot:

Automobiles

VinNumber
Model TireSizeFront TireSizeRear TireSizeSpare EngineSize NumberOfCylinders Horsepower Color

Assume that cars can only be one color for this exercise. Let's identify and resolve two normal form violations in the Automobiles entity.

2. There is a repeating group in this entity—that of tire size. This is a violation of the first normal form. Split the Automobiles entity to represent the relationship "automobiles ride on tires."

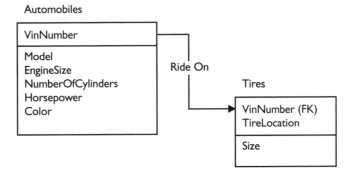

3. There are transitive dependencies in the Automobiles entity. This is in violation of the third normal form. Split the Automobiles entity to create a new entity to store all engine-related attributes. Use the engine serial number as the primary-key attribute of the Engines entity. Also include a foreign key to represent the relationship "engines power automobiles," as shown in Figure 2-3.

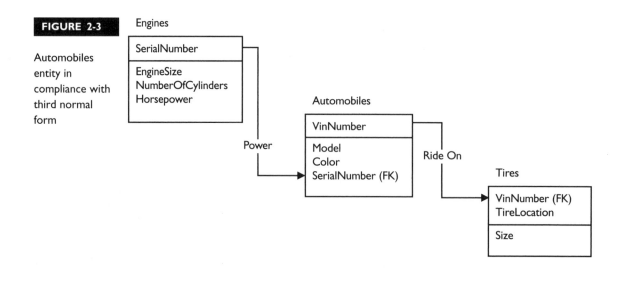

FIGURE 2-3

Automobiles
entity in
compliance with
third normal
form

Normalization Concerns and Potential Drawbacks

Third normal form, while sound in theory and certainly the ideal starting point, can lead to an inordinate amount of table joins when manipulating data. After a logical data model has achieved third normal form, it's a good idea to look at areas where excessive normalization could hinder the performance of your physical database. There is a trade-off of sorts between flexibility and performance when deciding on what degree of normalization to apply to your logical data model. Consider the data model in Figure 2-4.

This data model stores employee information such as residence and phone information. It is highly normalized, which makes it *very* flexible. It takes into account many possibilities, such as the fact that employees can share phone numbers and addresses, in the case of employees who are married or employees that are family members. Employees can also have an unlimited number of phone types, such as a home phone, work phone, pager, cell number, etc. Also, employees may have an unlimited number of addresses, such as a home address, shipping address, and billing address. In looking at the attributes of the PhoneNumbers and Addresses entities, you can see that they are also very decomposed; the phone number is made up of

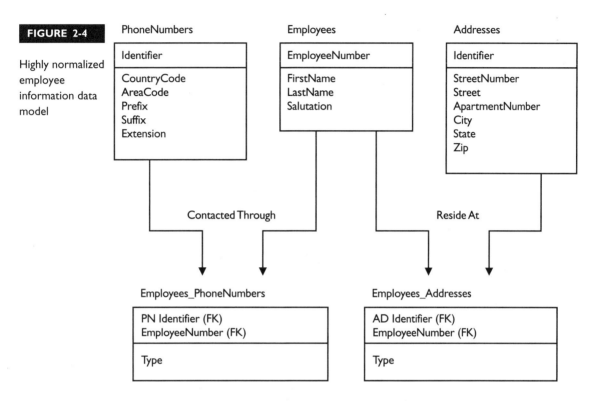

FIGURE 2-4

Highly normalized
employee
information data
model

four separate attributes; and attributes such as StreetNumber and Street, typically combined into an address attribute, have also been split.

The high degree of normalization represented in this data model will present some performance issues. Consider a seemingly simple query to retrieve an employee's name, phone number, and address information. Using the above model, this data retrieval operation will require a five-table JOIN in the physical database to return all the information required. This type of query would also be a fairly common request of the database, so the performance issue needs to be addressed by weighing the trade-off between flexibility and performance I mentioned earlier.

Denormalization

While data integrity is always of paramount importance, this would be a situation where some normal form violation needs to be explored. Thus would begin another round of analysis.

You should always try to normalize your design to third normal form in the logical data model to expose the most flexibility in the way data is stored, and then tune for performance from that point.

Having established a flexibility baseline in third normal form, the next round of analysis needs to identify what specific flexibilities are appropriate to sacrifice in the name of performance. In other words, "What can we live without to make this database run faster?" Consider the highly normalized PhoneNumbers entity for a moment. The attribute of AreaCode may indeed be appropriate for a very large corporation with offices nationwide. Regional information would need to be obtained on employees that have certain area codes. Queries such as "Show me all employees that live in the 813 or 727 area code" might be fairly common. But in the case of a small company, this would not be the case. More likely, almost all employees in a small company would have one of maybe two or three area codes. Thus, what was a common query in the large corporation might never even be issued when dealing with a small company. In this case, a single phone number attribute would serve our purpose adequately. This is an example of some flexibility that can be sacrificed.

Other solutions can be explored regarding the combining of entities to minimize table joins in the physical database. We might consider losing the flexibility of being able to store an unlimited number of phone numbers for employees as well. For example, in our small company, it's determined that we only need to track employees' home phone and work phone numbers. The data model is altered, as Figure 2-5 shows.

In the denormalized logical data model, any request for employee and phone information can now be handled with a single table operation in the physical database, which will speed performance. However, two problems have arisen because of this. First, should we ever decide that we need to track other employee numbers—such as cell phone or pager—the database will have to be modified to add another column to the Employees table. Second, we are possibly introducing redundant data into the database with this data model. If two employees share the same phone number, that number will be stored twice in the physical database. If a phone number were to change, we would now have to ensure that it is changed for both employees. These types of problems are typical when introducing a repeating group into an entity.

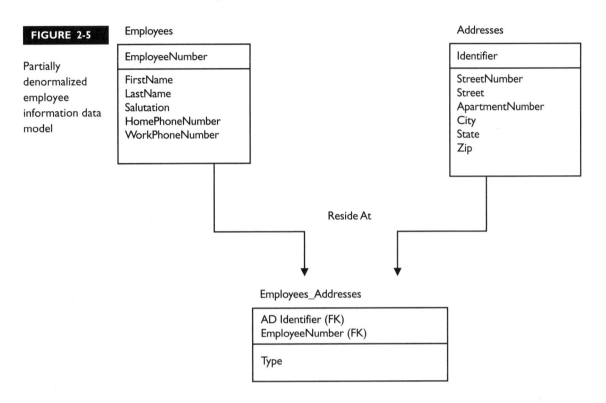

FIGURE 2-5

Partially
denormalized
employee
information data
model

The Address entity could be addressed similarly. It is decided that we only want to track the home address of each employee. The data model is modified to combine the Employees and Addresses entities, as shown here:

In the modified model, address information has now become attributes of the Employees entity. Again, we face the same problems of redundant data, as well as having to modify the physical database should we ever decide to track more than one employee address. However, any queries that request employee information now require a single table SELECT operation, as opposed to a five table JOIN in the original data model. The trade-off has been illustrated well here: Compromising flexibility and the possibility of redundant data will yield a performance gain in the physical database.

You might be wondering what the big deal is with the entity and attribute consolidation that has been performed on this data model. So what if I have to add another column to the database if we decide to track employees' cell phone numbers? Well, imagine that the data model has been engineered into a physical database. The database now contains thousands of rows, and an application has been built around it that services hundreds of users. What was simply adding an attribute at the logical level can be a major problem at the physical level. Changing the structure of tables and columns will not only require database changes, but application changes as well. This will require developer resources and expense. Structural changes also mean system downtime to the application users while the changes are implemented. What if the system is expected to be available 24 hours a day, 7 days a week? To the bottom line, it means time, money, and resources are lost.

on the
❶ o b

It is often a temptation to consolidate entities in this way to minimize the number of table joins. While it is always worth exploring, careful analysis must be performed to ensure that in the long run, the amount of denormalization you introduce will help and not hurt you.

Controlled Redundancy

Another type of denormalization involves intentionally introducing redundant data into the logical data model for the sake of performance. Consider the data model in Figure 2-6.

The data model in Figure 2-6 tracks information for a large corporation, such as employees and the departments they work for, and the locations of those departments. In this example, suppose a very common query is to obtain employee information, as well as the name of the location they work at. Satisfying this request will require a three-table join, taking information from both the Employees entity and the Locations entity. To lessen the performance impact of queries like this one,

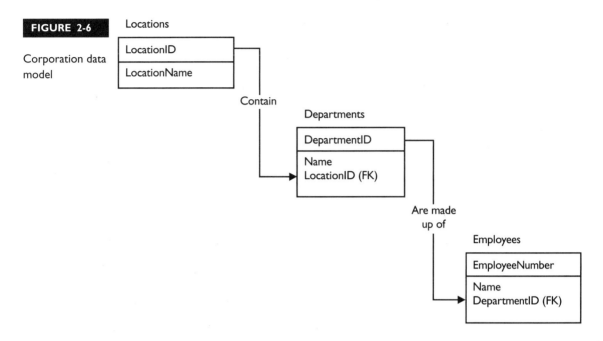

FIGURE 2-6

Corporation data model

controlled data redundancy can be introduced. This involves duplicating an attribute that is several entities away in the entity that is commonly queried. Consider this modification to the Employees entity:

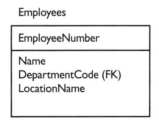

An attribute of LocationName has been added to the Employees entity, which is a duplicate of the LocationName attribute in the Locations entity. Now, retrieving employee information, as well as the name of the location in which they work, only requires querying one table in the database. However, with this type of attribute duplication, some major concerns arise.

Adding a redundant attribute as we have done requires that we ensure that the value of LocationName in the Employees entity will always be consistent with the corresponding value of LocationName in the Locations entity. This consistency is accomplished through the use of *triggers*. A trigger is a T-SQL command that the database engine will execute in the event a data modification is attempted on a column on which a trigger has been defined. (You'll learn much more about triggers in Chapter 4.) In our case, a trigger would have to be defined on the LocationName attribute in the Locations entity. This trigger will need to propagate any changes made to a LocationName value from the Locations entity to the Employees entity. It will take the changed LocationName value in the Locations entity, join the three tables, and change all the affected LocationName values in the Employees entity. This in itself will create a performance issue, if changes to the LocationName attribute are common. That is a major point of controlled redundancy; it is intended to increase performance on data retrieval operations. However, controlled redundancy creates a performance *penalty* for data modification operations. To clarify, if the LocationName attribute in the Locations entity is rarely updated, the performance gain by duplicating this value in the Employees entity would be justified. However, if the LocationName attribute were commonly modified, the trigger would need to update the Employees entity for *each* modification, basically canceling out the original performance gain. Therefore, denormalizing by introducing redundant attributes must be carefully considered through analysis. On heavily updated attributes, the problems of consistency and the performance overhead of introducing database triggers needs to be weighed to ensure that this type of duplication will actually result in a performance increase in the physical database.

Entity Lineage

There is another group of terms associated with logical data models that you should be fluent in. The terms *parent*, *child*, *grandchild*, and *grandfather* will inevitably surface in any description of a data model (and on certification exams!). These terms have to do with how entities relate to one another with regard to foreign-key relationships. For instance, consider the data model in Figure 2-7, which deals with databases, servers, and their locations.

In this data model, databases reside on servers, and servers exist at locations. The foreign-key relationships in the entities also form a sort of lineage that uses the same naming convention as a family. The Databases entity has the foreign-key attribute of ServerName that references the primary-key attribute of the Servers entity. Because of this, the Databases entity is said to be a *child* of the Servers entity. In the same way,

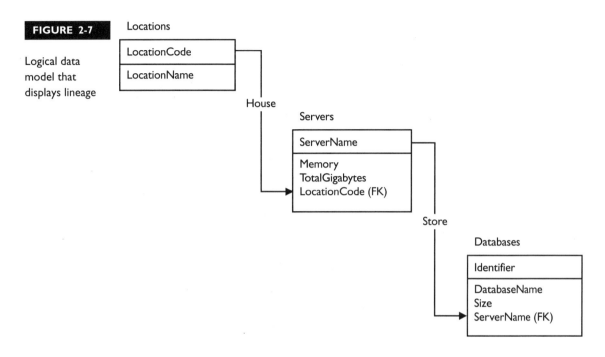

FIGURE 2-7

Logical data model that displays lineage

the Servers entity is a child of the Locations entity. It is also said that the Databases entity is a *grandchild* of the Locations entity, being a child of a child of that entity. Going in reverse, the Servers entity is a parent of the Databases entity, and the Locations entity is a grandparent of the Databases entity. Simply put, any entity that has a foreign key is considered a child, and the entity that contains the primary key referenced is considered a parent.

This is a good time to talk a little bit about convention in data modeling. It's a good idea to structure your logical data models so that the parent entities are on top, and the children and grandchildren flow down in a natural manner. While this isn't always possible for every entity, especially as models get more complex, it does make for a much more readable model.

exam
⚠atch

All of the diagrams in this chapter have been drawn with parent entities at the top and child entities underneath as much as possible, for clarity. This will not always be the case in diagrams on the exam. Remember that in an enterprise manager diagram, the parent tables will have a key icon at the parent end of relationship lines.

Another convention to address is that of naming standards for entities and attributes. While some personal preference is allowed, it is common to use plural names for entities and singular names for attributes, because an entity holds groups of records of a certain type. Some subscribe to the reverse, stating that entities should use singular naming to signify an instance of that entity. It is also advisable to use abbreviations as little as possible in data models to ensure maximum readability. Abbreviations can be considered in the physical implementation. Whatever convention you choose, the important thing is to stick with it. This ensures consistency in your model as well as your database.

on the **Job**

Keeping track of similar attributes named with different conventions on a database-wide scale can get rather annoying, so be sure to choose one convention and use it throughout the data model.

CERTIFICATION OBJECTIVE 2.03

Designing for Referential Integrity

We've had much discussion about primary keys and foreign keys, and the relationships they establish, but let's look a bit deeper into why all this matters. While PRIMARY KEY constraints enforce entity integrity, FOREIGN KEY constraints ensure that referential integrity is maintained.

PRIMARY and FOREIGN KEY Constraints

When you create a primary key in SQL Server, duplicate values are prohibited from being inserted into the database by means of a unique index created on the table (you'll learn more about indexes in Chapter 6). This enforces entity integrity and is one of the foundations of relational databases—that each entity must have a primary key, allowing each record to be uniquely identified. Imagine an entity called People with only one attribute, Name.

People

Name

Now imagine this entity has twenty records with various names of people, five of which have the value "John." While John is one of five distinct people named John out of the twenty, the database engine has absolutely no way to distinguish one from the other. There is no way to distinguish John Smith from John Stevens because there is no primary-key attribute. You could envision this on a larger scale: imagine a credit card company trying to keep track of its customers if card numbers could be duplicated! The same point applies to relational databases. Without the ability to distinguish one record from another, a sort of relational chaos ensues.

Foreign-key attributes enforce what is known as *referential integrity*. Provided an attribute is unique, a foreign key from another entity can reference it. The attribute referenced can either be the primary key of the parent entity or an alternate key from the parent entity. Alternate keys are declared in the physical database using a UNIQUE constraint or by creating a unique index on an attribute (you will read more about constraints in Chapter 3). Referential integrity prevents *data modification anomalies* in a database.

exam
Ⓦatch

Remember that PRIMARY KEY constraints are defined in all tables and that FOREIGN KEY constraints are defined in the child table only.

Data Modification Anomalies

Several problems in a database would run rampant without PRIMARY and FOREIGN KEY constraints. These are as follows:

Insert Anomalies   A record inserted into a child entity with a foreign-key attribute that does not reference a valid record in the parent table is what's known as an *orphaned record*. Consider an example: an entity called Orders has a CustomerNumber foreign-key attribute that must reference the primary key of a Customers entity, as shown here:

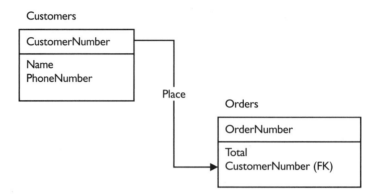

Without the referential integrity ensuring this is the case, records might be mistakenly inserted into the Orders entity that do not reference a valid customer number. In such a case, what customer should be billed for the order? Such a record is considered an orphaned record, for it has no corresponding parent record to reference.

Update Anomalies   A similar problem would exist in the absence of referential integrity concerning updates to a parent entity with a child entity referencing it. Consider the Customers entity again, and imagine that a customer number is changed. Now whatever records in the Orders entity that reference that customer number are orphaned, as they no longer reference a valid record in the Customers entity.

Delete Anomalies   Deleting a parent record from an entity that has a child entity referencing it also creates orphaned records. Imagine a record is deleted from the Customers entity that has several records in the Orders entity referencing it. The orphaned records in the Orders entity no longer point to a valid record in the Customers entity, so the problem of who should be billed for the order is once again encountered.

Referential Actions

In a logical data model, there are several means to dictate the behavior that should be taken regarding foreign-key attributes. These are collectively known as referential actions. We will concern ourselves with the two most common. These are RESTRICT and CASCADE. These actions determine what should be done in the case of a foreign-key violation—that is, an attempt is made to delete a parent record that has child records referencing it. The referential integrity that prevents the anomalies mentioned in the prior examples assumes that the *referential actions* specified for the Customers entity in the logical data model have been defined as RESTRICT. Table 2-2 describes the actions.

Let's use the Orders and Customers data model to demonstrate referential actions, as shown here:

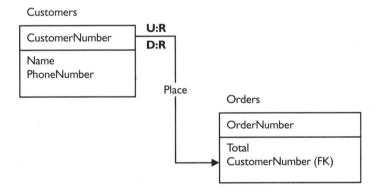

Notice that the place relationship between the Customers and Orders entities now has referential actions defined. They use the following format:

OPERATION : ACTION

The operations and actions are all abbreviated. In this case, **U:R** translates to UPDATE:RESTRICT and **D:R** translates to DELETE:RESTRICT. With the referential actions set as such, updates to the CustomerNumber key attribute in the Customers entity that have records in the Orders entity referencing it are prohibited;

TABLE 2-2   Referential Actions and Their Effects on FOREIGN KEY Constraints

Action Specified	Update to Parent Record	Deletion of Parent Record
RESTRICT	An update to the key attribute of a parent record that has child records referencing it is prohibited.	Deletion of a parent record that has child records referencing it is prohibited.
CASCADE	An update to the key attribute of a parent record also causes the foreign-key attribute of referencing child records to be updated.	Deletion of a parent record also causes any child records that reference it to be deleted.

and deletes to records in the Customers entity that have records in the Orders entity referencing it are also prohibited. Were we to change the referential actions to UPDATE:CASCADE (**U:C**) and DELETE:CASCADE (**D:C**), the situation changes. Now, any update to the CustomerNumber attribute that has referencing records in the Orders entity is cascaded, and the foreign-key attribute would also be updated. Deletes are also cascaded: For any record in the Customers entity that has referencing records in the Orders entity, upon deleting the parent records, the child records are also deleted. Take note that if a parent record that has a thousand child records referencing it is mistakenly deleted, those one thousand child records are also lost; so exercise caution when using the DELETE:CASCADE referential action.

SQL Server 2000 currently supports the CASCADE and RESTRICT (RESTRICT is called NO ACTION in SQL 2000) referential actions directly though referential integrity when defining a foreign key. The referential actions are usually declared in the CREATE TABLE statement, which will be covered in Chapter 3.

There exist other referential actions such as SET NULL. SET NULL will set the foreign-key values of a child entity to NULL if the referenced parent row is deleted. (SET NULL is not directly supported in SQL 2000, but can be implemented via database triggers.) SET NULL is not a preferred way of handling referential actions. Imagine a customer is deleted from the Customers entity that has child Orders entity records. The result of SET NULL is that all the child Orders records that referenced the parent record will have their foreign-key attribute of CustomerNumber set the value of NULL. Consequently, when looking at past orders, we will have no way of knowing who the customer was who placed the order. But if your business rules dictate that you need to use SET NULL as a referential action, it can be implemented—just not directly through referential integrity constraints.

EXERCISE 2-3

Specify Relational Actions

1. Consider the following logical data model:

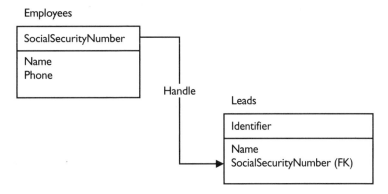

The following analysis is obtained regarding this data model: "Our Employees have self-generated leads that they try to sell products to. Each lead can only be handled by one employee. It's very important that no one accidentally change the social security number of an employee; otherwise, we'll have no way to know which lead belongs to which employee. But if an employee quits or is fired, they take their leads with them, so there is no need to track information about their leads anymore."

2. Using this analysis, establish referential actions for the "employees handle leads" relationship.

3. It's apparent from the analysis that the relationship will need to have a referential action of UPDATE:RESTRICT placed on it.

4. The fact that employees take their leads with them when they leave the company means we can cascade deletes. Declare these referential actions, as shown here:

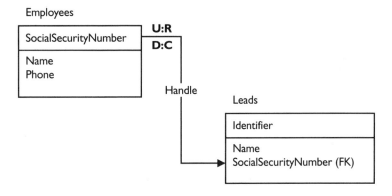

Managing Entity Relationships

We've discussed the relationship that is created between two entities when a foreign key references the primary key of a parent entity. In the preceding examples, this created what is known at a *one-to-many relationship*. There are several different kinds of possible relationships between entities or database tables, and it is crucial that you have an understanding of the common types. Microsoft likes to put lots of database diagrams on the SQL Design Exam, so it is important that you are comfortable with the various database relationships. At this point, the diagrams in this chapter will be presented using the diagramming tool of SQL Server 2000, as opposed to the simple rectangles of the preceding sections. We'll translate the entities and attributes of a logical data model into the tables and columns of a database *schema*. A database schema is just that—a schematic of a physical database. Enterprise Manager diagrams are the format used on the SQL Server 2000 exam; let's take a quick look at the format.

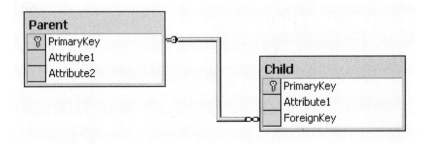

<table>
<tr><td>**Parent**</td></tr>
<tr><td>🔑 PrimaryKey</td></tr>
<tr><td>Attribute1</td></tr>
<tr><td>Attribute2</td></tr>
</table>

<table>
<tr><td>**Child**</td></tr>
<tr><td>🔑 PrimaryKey</td></tr>
<tr><td>Attribute1</td></tr>
<tr><td>ForeignKey</td></tr>
</table>

exam
⚙️atch

Be very comfortable with Enterprise Manager diagrams. They are the sole format of all the database schemas you will see on the SQL 2000 Design Exam.

In the diagramming tool, entities—now database tables—are represented by the large rectangles. The entity attributes—now table columns—are represented by text blocks within the rectangles. There is no separation of primary-key and nonkey columns within the rectangle, but the primary key of a table is now marked with the little key icon to the left of the column name. The relationship created by the foreign-key column in the child table has a line with a key at the end of it pointing to the parent table. You can access the diagramming tool of SQL Server 2000 through Enterprise Manager. Start Enterprise Manager and expand your SQL Server. Expand a Database and Diagrams is the first node. Right-click it and select New Database Diagram to create a new diagram, as shown in Figure 2-8.

Cardinality

When a relationship is defined between two tables, it has a characteristic known as *cardinality*. At its simplest, the cardinality of a relationship defines how many records of one entity relate to how many records of another entity. Cardinality is discovered during analysis as relationships are being defined. To demonstrate cardinality, imagine two entities in a data model, Cars and Tires. Assuming we are dealing with only passenger cars, each car would always have four tires. (For the purpose of the exercise, there are no spare tires.) Thus, the cardinality of the relationship of cars to tires is said to be one to four.

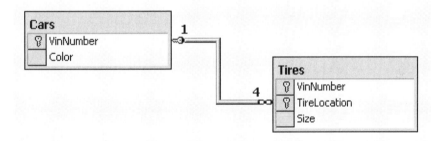

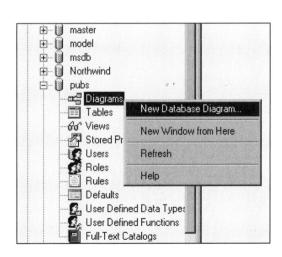

FIGURE 2-8

Accessing the diagramming tool of Enterprise Manager

You can see numbers at the endpoints of the relationship line represent the cardinality of this relationship. Each of the relationships discussed will use this style. (Relationship cardinality numbers do not appear on the exam diagrams—they are for illustration purposes only.)

Cardinality helps to more effectively define entities, as well as its main purpose— that of defining relationships. Cardinality is typically expressed from parent entity to child entity—that is, *one* record in the parent table is referenced by *many* rows in the child table.

Understanding the Different Types of Entity Relationships

Relationships can be rather simple as in the case of cars to tires; but in very complex databases, they can get a bit confusing. Let's review the most common types of relationships you may come across in a database (and on the exam). Some are fairly common and others are somewhat rare, but a clear understanding of these relationships that can exist in a database is a most important requirement for effective database design and development.

One to Many

The most common type of relationship, and the one that almost every database you will ever encounter will use, is the one-to-many relationship. As previously stated, one-to-many relationships are relationships in which one record or row in a parent table is referenced by many rows in a child table. Let's use an example database schema that represents data about the rooms in a house.

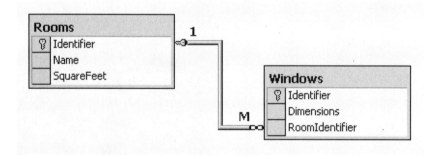

In this schema, one room may have many windows. Both the Rooms and Windows database tables have a surrogate primary key. The foreign key RoomIdentifier in the

Windows table references the primary key of the Rooms table. In a database schema, the cardinality of a one-to-many relationship is represented by a 1 at the parent end of the relationship line, and the letter *M* for "many," at the child end of the relationship line. The number of windows a room may have is irrelevant in the schema—it can be none, two, or two thousand (in the case of a glass house?)—and that is the beauty of a one-to-many relationship. It completely eliminates the need for repeating groups in a database table. A one-to-many relationship is *directly supported* by SQL Server 2000 and most RDBMS. This means that the base tables involved in the relationship require no modification, other than the addition of a foreign-key column, to establish a one-to-many relationship. It is simply a matter of defining a foreign-key relationship on the child attribute. Some relationships, such as *many to many*, are not directly supported by most relational database engines, as you will see in the next section.

Many to Many

A many-to-many relationship does not involve parent or child entities at the logical data model level. It is a relationship where many records in one entity can reference many records in another entity. Consider the many-to-many relationship of recipes to ingredients shown here.

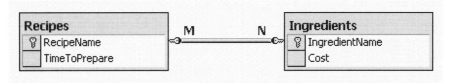

In the schema, recipes can have many ingredients. In the same way, any ingredient can be a component in many recipes, thus a true many-to-many relationship. (The relationship line for a many-to-many relationship is denoted by the letters *M* for "many" to *N*, also for "many." Using *M* twice on a relationship line is not permitted.) However, in the physical database, there is no way SQL Server 2000 (or any relational database engine for that matter) can keep track of such a relationship using the two original entities. Consider the relationship of cars to tires used a while ago. Any row in the Tires table keeps track of which car it belongs to by a foreign-key column, that of VinNumber. This works fine for a one-to-many relationship; but were we to add a foreign-key column to the Ingredients table, called RecipeName, we would have many duplicate rows in the Ingredients table: the ingredient "eggs" would be a component of several recipes, such as a cake, an omelet, muffins, cookies, etc. Thus, a duplicate row for the ingredient "eggs" would appear in the ingredients table for each recipe it was a member of.

IngredientName	Cost	RecipeName
Eggs	2.00	Cake
Eggs	2.00	Omelette
Eggs	2.00	Muffins
Eggs	2.00	Cookies

You might also notice another fact about this Ingredients table: the primary key is no longer valid, as the IngredientName of "eggs" now appears several times. The resulting duplicate data and invalid primary key are the inherent problems with trying to resolve a many-to-many relationship in a relational database: it can't be done using only the two original tables. The way a many-to-many relationship is resolved in a database is by the addition of an *association table.* An association table is a table that is created for the sole purpose of resolving a many-to-many relationship between the tables originally involved in the many-to-many relationship. Consequently, our original Recipes and Ingredients tables are resolved to a proper many-to-many relationship, like this:

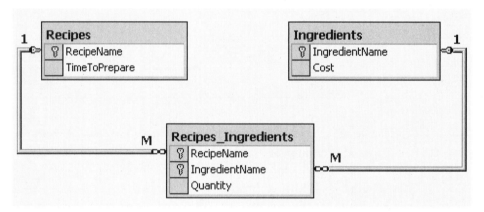

A new association table called Recipes_Ingredients had been created that references the two original entities involved in the many-to-many relationship, in essence creating two separate one-to-many relationships that the database supports. In this way, the primary keys of both tables are preserved, and no duplicate data is introduced into the database (remember, foreign-key columns are never considered duplicate data). You should notice another property of the newly created association table: It tracks any new information regarding the many-to-many relationship. When an ingredient is associated with a recipe, a new piece of information becomes necessary to track, that of quantity—that is, how many eggs are in a particular recipe? An association table provides the means of recording any additional information relevant to a many-to-many relationship.

FROM THE CLASSROOM

One to Many vs. Many to Many

It can sometimes be difficult during the analysis phase to identify which relationships are one to many and which relationships are many to many. Broad statements are typically made, such as "A recipe has several ingredients," which might tend to lead to the conclusion that "recipe to ingredients" is actually a one-to-many relationship, which it isn't. The key to correctly identifying the true nature of a relationship is to think in specific instances of entities, as opposed to the general statements about groups of data in an entity that can lead to faulty analysis. For instance, the following statement might be made: "Many football players play on many teams." While the preceding statement is indeed true, it masks the true nature of the relationship. When we begin to think in instances, the relationship exposes itself.

To qualify as a true many-to-many relationship, two statements must be true of the relationship between teams and players.

First, one specific team will have multiple players that make up the team at any given time. The first statement is true. Second, one specific player may play for more than one team at any given time. The second statement is false; a player may play for only one team at a time. Thus, the relationship of teams to players is indeed one to many. Similarly, the same two statements need to be true of the relationship of recipes to ingredients: a specific recipe is made up of many different ingredients. This statement is true. Also, any given ingredient may be a component of more than one recipe. This statement is also true, as we saw with very basic ingredients such as eggs or flour. As both of the preceding statements are true, recipes to ingredients is a true many-to-many relationship. Remember; take general statements gathered during analysis and think of them in terms of specific instances of entities to reveal the true nature of relationships.

— *Jeffrey Bane, MCSE, MCDBA*

One to One

A possible relationship of *one to one* also exists regarding the relationships of database tables to one another. A one-to-one relationship is when one record of an entity relates back to exactly one record in another entity. Direct one-to-one relationships are somewhat rare in the database world. More common is the one-to-one relationship of subtype/supertype that will be discussed in the next section. However, generic one-to-one relationships between tables are usually implemented on the physical database for space management reasons. To demonstrate, consider the following entity:

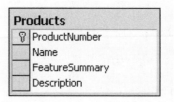

The Products table stores product information for an online store. A user is given a page of links that are made up of product names. When the user clicks on a product name, the feature summary and description are displayed. In our example, feature summaries and descriptions can get rather lengthy.

In order to understand why you would split the preceding entity into two tables and create a one-to-one relationship, it is necessary to first understand a little about how SQL Server 2000 stores data. The basic unit of storage in a SQL Server datafile is known as a *page*. A page in SQL Server 2000 is limited to 8K, or about 8,000 characters. This would create a problem for the preceding Products table, if, say, the FeatureSummary column was 2,000 characters long, and the Description column needed to be 7,000 characters long to accommodate the description with the longest length. (These may seem like excessive lengths for a single column of data, but it can and does happen.) Consequently, our row size for the Products table is now over 9K and a single row would not fit on an 8K page. The solution is to split the Products table in two, creating a one-to-one relationship.

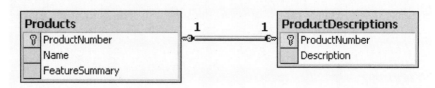

As you can see, the two new tables share the same primary key, and have a one-to-one relationship. Now the size of a row in either table is under the 8K limit and can fit on a page. However, splitting the Products table is not the only way to handle very long columns of text. The preceding diagram assumes that the FeatureSummary and Description columns were created with *Character* datatypes. (We'll discuss datatypes in an upcoming section.) If a column is declared with one of the *Text* or *Image* datatypes in SQL Server, the long text itself would be stored in a separate data page, with only a pointer to the long text field stored in the original page. Using Text or Image datatypes has the benefit of automatically taking care of splitting the table, so the split is unnecessary. However, there are other concerns with using text datatypes, which you will read about in Chapter 3.

Exceeding the 8K page-size limit is not the only reason you might consider splitting a table. As data is requested, pages are moved in and out of memory to satisfy whatever queries the database engine is servicing. That process creates overhead. To lessen the swapping of data pages in and out of memory, try to keep your rows as compact as possible. The more rows of a table that can fit on a single page of data, the better, and one way to keep your row sizes compact is to take the large and less frequently used columns in a table, split them into another table, and create a one-to-one relationship.

Subtype/Supertype

A much more common form of a one-to-one relationship is that of subtype/supertype. In a subtype/supertype relationship, one entity is a subtype or subclassification of another entity. (A subtype/supertype relationship is also referred to as a subclass/ superclass relationship.) This relationship arises when there are entities in a database that share some common traits, but not all of those traits are shared. Let's look at an example. Imagine we are tracking information about animals in a zoo. For all animals, we want to track their weight and date of birth. If an animal eats other animals, we'd like to also store how fast it can run. If an animal only eats plants, we'd like to store its favorite plant to dine on. This creates the subtype/supertype relationship shown in Figure 2-9.

As you can see, the Carnivores and Herbivores tables are actually a *type* of the Animals table. The parent table in a subtype/supertype relationship stores information common to all types. In this case, information common to both types of animals is stored in the Animals table. The Animals table has a surrogate primary key that all children tables share, and there is a one-to-one relationship between the parent table and all children tables.

FIGURE 2-9

A subtype/
supertype
relationship

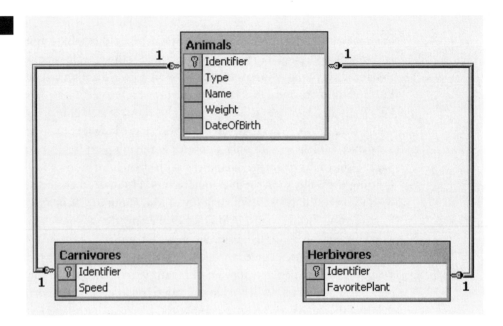

A somewhat common denormalization practice is to combine subtypes and supertypes into one table, as has been done here:

While this may save a table join between the parent and child tables, the denormalized Animals table has some relational problems. Consider the column FavoritePlant. What possible meaning will that column have to an animal that only eats meat? The preceding entity is a denormalized subtype, and as it stands now, it is storing information about two separate kinds of entities. By denormalizing this way, we have now introduced a fair amount NULLs into the database—that is, the column FavoritePlant will have no meaning for carnivores, so it will have to have a NULL value for each instance of a carnivore. While this may not be a huge problem in this example, imagine a situation with tens of subtypes and hundreds of columns that are not shared among them. The problem of the NULL values would be on quite a large scale.

Still, we have saved a table join by denormalizing in this way, which will speed data retrieval. Whether or not to combine subtypes is a question that only solid analysis of a given database can answer. Will the inordinate amount of NULL values, the increased row size, and the reduced number of rows that will fit on a data page offset the performance gain from eliminating the table join? On a large scale, this question becomes increasingly important.

Self-Referencing

Another type of foreign-key relationship is that of the self-referencing relationship. This is a case in which a foreign key in a table references the primary key of the *same* table. This type of relationship is used when dealing with hierarchical data. You will typically use a self-referencing relationship when parent and children rows have no predefined depth. For example, consider the following tables, which track products and the categories they are members of:

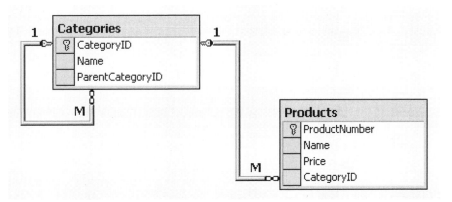

You'll notice the Categories table has a surrogate primary key that the Products table references in a traditional one-to-many relationship. Each product will be a member of one category—for instance, a product Blender will exist in the category Appliances. In the Categories table itself, you can see that the column named

ParentCategoryID has a foreign-key relationship back to the primary key of CategoryID. This self-referencing relationship allows us to keep track of category lineage. The lineages of the categories have no defined depth, meaning a category can be nested within any number of other categories. Consider the following sample rows from the Categories table:

CategoryID	Name	ParentCategoryID
1	Housewares	<NULL>
2	Kitchen	1
3	Bedroom	1
4	Appliances	2

The category Housewares has a value of NULL for its ParentCategoryID—thus, it is the top-level category, which all other categories are a member of. It has two subcategories, Kitchen and Bedroom. Both the subcategories have a ParentCategoryID value of 1. The category Appliances has a ParentCategoryID value of 2, making it a subcategory of the Kitchen entry. We can now trace the lineage of any category back to the top-level category using the ParentCategoryID column.

This manner of storing hierarchical data is what's known as an *adjacency list*. It is not the only way to store hierarchical data, but it is the most common way in use today, and more than likely the type of table structure you will come across when dealing with categories. The Categories table is also quite flexible, in that the level of nesting of categories can be of any depth, there are no restrictions on the amount of subcategories that a category can have, and so on. Self-referencing relationships are also common in organizational charts, where employee lineage is recorded. The Employees table in the sample Northwind database has such a self-referencing relationship, tracking employees and their bosses, bosses' bosses, etc.

In summary, there is a commonality to all entity relationships. Any relationship, no matter how simple or complex, is resolved to either a one-to-one or one-to-many relationship in the database schema, as these are the relationships that a RDBMS supports. In the case of many to many, an association table is added to create two one-to-many relationships. All complex relationships are resolved by manipulating database tables to create simple relationships.

EXERCISE 2-4

CertCam 2-4

Managing Entity Relationships

1. Consider the following entities:

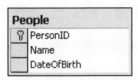

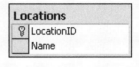

These entities will store the information necessary to build a family tree. Establish the necessary relationships to track family lines, and also to record the various locations each person in the family has lived during different stages of their lives. Add any new attributes that are necessary to establish the relationships.

2. In order to track family lines, create a self-referencing relationship in the People entity, so that the lineage of family members can be tracked. A new attribute called ParentID will be required in the People entity.

3. In order to track the locations that the people live in at various stages of their lives, create an association entity to account for the many-to-many relationship "people live at locations."

4. Add a new attribute EndDate to track the last date a person lived at a particular location. The resulting schema, with the new relationships created, looks like this:

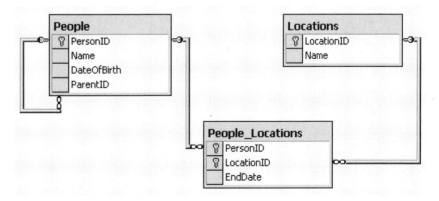

CERTIFICATION OBJECTIVE 2.05

Attribute and Domain Integrity

From the topic of referential integrity we move on to *attribute integrity*. Attribute integrity deals with the columns of database tables and ensuring the validity of the data stored within those columns. Much of attribute integrity has to do with the *domain* of an attribute. An attribute's domain defines the range and type of values that a column may store.

Designing Attribute and Domain Integrity

The domains of the attributes in a database schema are discovered during the analysis phase, after entities have been defined and relationships have been established. Each attribute that will eventually become a column in a database table must have a domain defined for it. This domain will consist of information regarding what type of data will be stored in the column, the size of the data, and the allowable values of the data. Here are some statements that begin to define an attribute's domain: "a number between one and ten," "a block of text that can be as long as two hundred characters," "a phone number that must be ten digits and ten digits only," and "a status flag that will have a value of either YES or NO." Let's take a look at a sample table and begin to define the attribute domains.

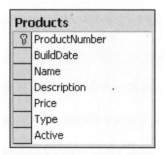

In our example, the Products table tracks various products that a computer company sells. The first step in defining the domain of an attribute is to determine what type of data it will actually store. Beginning with ProductNumber, it has been discovered through analysis that the product number is an arbitrary code assigned to each product by the company. The term "ProductNumber" can be misleading. It is important to determine the true nature of an attribute and not just assume from the name of the attribute. For example, to hear the term "serial number," we might assume that the domain of that attribute is a number. However, many serial numbers contain letters as well as numbers. Back in our example, we discover that although it has been referred to as a product number within the company for years, a product number actually consists of numbers and letters. Therefore, the ProductNumber column will be storing *character* data.

The next column we encounter is that of BuildDate. Confirmed through analysis, this column stores the month, day, and year that the product came to be. Therefore, BuildDate will be storing *date* data. The Name and Description columns of the Products table both store character data. The Price field stores the retail price of a product, making its type that of *money*. The Type column is an indicator of what type of product each row represents. In our example, the computer company sells both hardware and software. The Type column will track this piece of information. (If you're thinking that the Products table is a good candidate for a subtype/supertype relationship, you are correct. Most likely, it would have two child tables called Hardware and Software that stored type-specific attributes.) So, the Type column will also be storing character data. The Active column is used to indicate whether or not the product is still being manufactured and can be actively sold. This is a kind of attribute that is fairly common in a wide variety of tables. It allows for the storage of historical data. For example, imagine a table of employee information. If an employee were to leave, that row is deleted from the table. The alternative is to use an Active column to indicate whether or not a company actively employs the employee. In this way, when an employee leaves, the Active column is turned off, and records for all employees that have ever worked for the company are retained. The Active column is what's known as a *flag*. The flag will be switched on if the product is active or switched off if it is not active, so the Active column will store *flag* information.

Now that we have the type of data each column is going to store, we can map these types to the actual datatypes that will be used in SQL Server 2000.

Mapping Logical Attributes to SQL Server Datatypes

When any table is created in SQL Server 2000, each column must have a declared datatype. A datatype is just that—it tells the database engine what kind of data will be stored in a column. Table 2-3 lists some of the more common SQL Server 2000 system-supplied datatypes.

The range of datatypes is quite broad, able to account for any type of data that needs to be stored. When mapping types of data from analysis or a data model to the SQL Server 2000 datatypes, some guidelines should be followed. First, make sure the system datatype actually represents the type of data you are storing. An example would be storing a date in a character field. While you could do this, the column in the database would lack the integrity it would have were it declared as one of the date datatypes, say Datetime. It is not permitted to enter an invalid date into a Datetime column. For example, trying to enter 02/30/2001, an invalid date, into a Datetime column is rejected by the database engine, thereby preserving domain integrity. A character column would allow this error.

TABLE 2-3   Common SQL Server 2000 Datatypes

SQL Server Datatype	Description
Int	Whole numbers (integers) that range from approximately –2 billion to +2 billion
Smallint	Whole numbers that range from approximately –32,000 to +32,000
Tinyint	Whole numbers that range from 0 to 255
Bigint	Whole numbers that range from approximately –9 quintillion to +9 quintillion
Bit	Integer with the value of either 1 or 0
Decimal (also called numeric)	Numeric data, typically with a decimal point, with 38 total digits allowed
Money	Monetary data ranging from approximately –900 trillion to +900 trillion
Smallmoney	Monetary data ranging from approximately –214,000 to +214,000
Datetime	Stores both date and time data from the year 1753 to the year 9999
Smalldatetime	Stores both date and time data from the year 1900 to the year 2079
Char and Nchar	Character data of a fixed length
Varchar and Nvarchar	Character data of a variable length
Text and Ntext	Stores large blocks of character data
Image	Stores large blocks of binary data

Another point to keep in mind is to choose the smallest datatype possible for the data in question. You'll note from Table 2-3 that there are several datatypes for storing integer data, ranging from Tinyint to Bigint. The different various integer datatypes exist so that storage in the database can be most effectively utilized. Tinyint takes much less space to store than does Bigint, but Tinyint can only store numbers between 0 and 255. If we needed to store numbers between 5 and 50, Tinyint would be the most efficient choice.

You'll also notice that the character types of data appear twice, for example, Varchar and Nvarchar. The *N* preceding a character datatype indicates that the data in the column will be stored as *Unicode* data. Unicode data allows for larger character sets. In a regular Char or Varchar datatype, any given character can be one of only about 256 different characters. The Unicode specification allows for any given character to be one of roughly 65,000 different characters. Unicode data is useful for alphabets that require more than 256 different letters, numbers, etc.

Now that we've reviewed some of the SQL Server datatypes, let's return to the Products table and map the types of data discovered during analysis to the system datatypes. So far in our logical model, we have the following types of data to store from the Products table:

Column	Datatype
ProductNumber	Character
BuildDate	Date
Name	Character
Description	Character
Price	Money
Type	Character
Active	Flag

Beginning with ProductNumber, we've discovered that any given product number will always be 10 characters long. This is a fixed-length field, so the Char datatype is a good candidate for ProductNumber. BuildDate is a date field, so one of the date datatypes will be declared. As we are forward thinking and expect to be in business after the year 2079, Datetime is the datatype used. Name and Description are both variable-length character fields, never guaranteed to be any particular length, so

Varchar will be the datatype used. Price is a monetary value, so Smallmoney will be the datatype used. (The most expensive item we sell is under $2,000 dollars, so the Money datatype would be a waste of storage space.)

On to the Type column. This column will contain either the word "Hardware" or the word "Software" to indicate the type of product. Since both words are the same length, the fixed-length Char datatype will be used on the Type column. The Active column is a flag, basically a switch that is turned on or off to indicate if a product can be sold or not. The Bit datatype is an excellent candidate for flag data, as it only stores either 0 or 1. Having mapped all columns to system datatypes, our table now looks this:

Products

	Column Name	Data Type	
🔑	ProductNumber	char	
	BuildDate	datetime	
	Name	varchar	
	Description	varchar	
	Price	smallmoney	
	Type	char	
	Active	bit	

exam
ⓌatcH

You will sometimes have to infer the purpose of a column from its datatype. For example, if you see a bit column in a diagram, you will know some type of flag is being stored in that column. Be familiar with the common datatypes.

Certain datatypes in SQL Server 2000 require that you specify a length of the data that will be stored in the column. The next step to designing domain integrity is to determine those lengths.

Attribute Length, Scale, and Precision

The majority of SQL Server datatypes are of a fixed length. Types like Integer data, money, and date/time will always take up the same amount of space in the database. However, certain types of data, mainly the character datatypes and the decimal datatype, require that you specify a length to SQL Server in order to maximize the storage efficiency of the database engine. Character data, in particular, would waste quite a bit of storage space if there were not a means to indicate how long it will be—that is, storing a piece of data that would always be five characters long in a column that reserves a thousand characters in length.

The same logic that applies to choosing the correct datatype also applies when assigning the length to a datatype: use as small a length as possible. Back in the products example, we have four fields that will require a length to be assigned to them: the fixed-length Char columns, and the variable-length Varchar columns. Beginning with the ProductNumber column, we know from the previous analysis that this field is always ten characters long, so a length of ten is assigned to this column. Likewise, the Type column will store either the word "Hardware" or "Software," both of which are eight characters long. However, the Name and Description columns will require a bit more analysis.

In digging a bit deeper, we discover that the names of products average around 30 characters. There are some exceptions as always, with the smallest product name being 15 characters and the longest being 45. Just to be safe, we reach the consensus that no product name should ever exceed 50 characters. Is it possible we could sell a product with a longer name? Certainly, but much past 50 characters, we might consider storing the name using some abbreviations. The Description column will store some lengthy character fields that vary greatly in length. Again, through analysis, a maximum length of 500 characters is deemed reasonable. Having assigned lengths to the appropriate datatypes, the Products table now looks like this:

Products

	Column Name	Condensed Type
🔑	ProductNumber	char(10)
	BuildDate	datetime
	Name	varchar(50)
	Description	varchar(500)
	Price	smallmoney
	Type	char(8)
	Active	bit

Char vs. Varchar

There is some additional overhead that is incurred in the physical database when using variable-length datatypes. For example, in a column defined as Varchar(500), consider a value that currently is 200 characters long. If that value is updated, and now is 300 characters long, the database engine requires additional resources to expand the length of the column to 300 characters. In fixed-length fields, no such expansion or shrinking takes place. However, variable-length fields utilize storage much more efficiently. It's another trade-off to consider when choosing datatypes. As a rule of thumb, use variable-length datatypes only when the length of a column will vary by a significant amount. For example, if the value of a column will be either six or seven characters long, a fixed-length datatype of Char(7) is more efficient than a Varchar(7). The storage loss of always having to store seven characters even with a value that is six characters long is not significant. But if a value can be anywhere from 30 to 100 characters long, a Varchar(100) field is much more appropriate due to the storage space that will be saved.

Scale and Precision

In the same way that character datatypes need to have a defined length, the decimal or numeric datatype also needs its length parameters declared. The two length attributes of the Decimal datatype are known as *scale* and *precision*. A Decimal datatype allows 38 total digits to be stored. Those 38 total digits include numbers on both the left and right side of the decimal point. Let's look at an example.

Consider a decimal number such as 389.0012. The total length of this number is what's known as its precision. The amount of digits to the right of the decimal point is called its scale. So, the number 389.0012 has a precision of 7 and a scale of 4. Scale can also have a value of 0. The number 389 has a precision of 3 and a scale of 0. Decimal is the only datatype in SQL Server that requires two length parameters. If no scale or precision is specified, default lengths of precision 18 and scale 0 are used.

Nullablility

The next step in designing domain integrity is determining the *nullability* of each attribute. Nullability determines, for each row in the table, whether a column is required to have a value or the column may have a NULL value. A value of NULL indicates that the value for a column is *unknown*. The word NULL originates from set theory—a NULL set is a set that has no members, or an empty set. The concept of NULL is a bit tricky to comprehend at first. Here are some points to keep in mind about a NULL value:

- It is not the same as zero.
- It is not an empty string.
- It doesn't indicate FALSE or TRUE.

All of these are valid column values in a relational database. The NULL value differs, in that the value of the column is truly not known at the time the row is inserted into the table.

NULL values can produce unexpected results in the physical database. Therefore, it's always the best practice to keep columns that allow NULL values to an absolute minimum in database design. Let's look at an example of how NULL values can cause problems. Consider the Price column in the Products table. Assume that we've decided it would be acceptable to enter new products into the table before their price has been set. In order to do so, the Price column is defined as Nullable. Products are entered, some with a monetary value in the Price column and some with a NULL price. A situation then arises where we would like to produce a report of the ten most expensive products we sell. The report is run, and it lists the ten rows in the Products table with the highest value in the Price column. Unfortunately, the report is flawed because it cannot take into account the rows in the Products table that have NULL values in the Price column. Some of the products with a NULL in the Price column could very well be among the most expensive products sold, but we have no way of knowing it. The fact that NULLs have been introduced into the column means that we can never know with certainty the most expensive products we sell. Therefore, defining the Price column as Nullable is not good design practice.

NULL values also behave unexpectedly when performing mathematical operations. Consider the following:

1 + NULL = ?

You might think that adding NULL to 1 would translate to 1 + **nothing** and equal 1. However, by default, this is not the case. Anything plus NULL equals NULL. This makes sense when you keep in mind that NULL does not mean an empty value—it means an unknown value. Therefore, 1 + NULL = NULL translates into

1 + ? = ?

Or, 1 plus an unknown value equals an unknown value. The same behavior applies to other mathematical operations: **1 − NULL = NULL, 1 * NULL = NULL**, etc. NULL values have a similar result when applied to certain *string operations*. Consider the following:

```
'Hard' + 'Drive'
```

This is what's known as *concatenating* a string. The string 'Hard' is concatenated with the string 'Drive'. In T-SQL, this concatenation would result in the following sting:

```
'HardDrive'
```

A string containing the word "Hard Drive" with a space separating the first and last string would be accomplished like this:

```
'Hard' + ' ' + 'Drive'
```

By default, just as a numeric value added to a NULL equals NULL, a string value concatenated with NULL will yield NULL:

```
'Hard' + NULL = NULL
```

This translates into the following: the string 'Hard' concatenated with some unknown string will end up looking like an unknown string. Again, this statement makes sense when you keep in mind that a NULL is unknown, not a blank value or zero.

exam

ⓦatch

Sometimes they are unavoidable, but NULL values can be problematic in a database table. Carefully consider any exam answers that suggest incorporating NULL values into a database structure.

Now that we've covered some reasons why you want to avoid NULL values, let's return to the Products table to determine the nullability of the columns. Beginning with ProductNumber, being the primary key of the Products table, this column cannot be nullable. Remember that a primary key is used by the database engine to uniquely identify the rows of a table. This would be impossible if NULL values were allowed to be inserted into the ProductNumber column. Therefore, *nullable primary keys are prohibited.* This is enforced automatically in SQL Server 2000. In order for a column to be defined as a primary key, it is not allowed to be nullable.

The BuildDate column will always be known, for the product couldn't exist without one. Likewise, a product with a NULL value in the Name column would make very little sense. However, the Description column is a possible candidate for a Nullable column. For example, assume that we have a technical writer on staff that reviews new products and writes a thorough and detailed description. This review may take a few days, and during that time the description is not known. While we would like to avoid NULLs all together, the Description column might better serve our purpose if it were nullable. An alternative solution would be to require that a very generic description be entered while the detailed description was developed. But for our purpose, we'll allow the Description column to be nullable.

We've discussed some reasons why the Price column should not be nullable. Likewise, allowing the Type column to be nullable also makes no sense. If someday we begin selling products of a different type, we could simply create a new subclass of product and store it in the Type column. The Active column also should not be Nullable. Any column that stores flag information should always contain a value. That is the purpose of the flag—on or off. In our case, this column will contain 1 if the product is available for sale, or 0 if it is not. A value of NULL would indicate that we have no idea if the product is available or not, a statement we would not enjoy making to a potential customer. The following shows the Products table with nullablility defined, having either assigned NULL or NOT NULL for each column:

Products

	Column Name	Condensed Type	Nullable	
🔑	ProductNumber	char(10)	NOT NULL	▲
	BuildDate	datetime	NOT NULL	
	Name	varchar(50)	NOT NULL	
	Description	varchar(500)	NULL	
	Price	smallmoney	NOT NULL	
	Type	char(8)	NOT NULL	
	Active	bit	NOT NULL	▼

EXERCISE 2-5

Define Domain Integrity

1. Consider the following table:

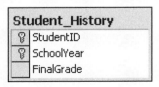

Student_History

🔑	StudentID
🔑	SchoolYear
	FinalGrade

This table tracks historical information about a student's final grades for each year in attendance at a school. Based on the following analysis, begin to define domain integrity on the three table columns: "A student ID number is always five characters long and is made up of letters and numbers. The combination of a student ID number and the year for which the grade is being tracked will uniquely identify a record. We'd like to track the final grade numerically, to the second decimal point." Perform these specific steps: assign a datatype for each column, assign a length to each column, and determine nullablility for each column.

2. Define the StudentID column with a datatype of Char. Its length will always be 5. As it is part of the primary key of the table, nullability is not permitted.

3. Define the SchoolYear column with a datatype of Datetime. It is not necessary to declare a length for the Datetime datatype. SchoolYear is also part of the primary key of the table, so nullability is not permitted.

4. Define the FinalGrade column with a datatype of Decimal. The maximum grade that can be given is 100 and grades are required to be recorded to the second decimal point. Therefore, assign a precision of 5 and a scale of 2 to the FinalGrade column. This column should also be defined as not nullable, as it is the main piece of information being tracked in the table. The completed Student_History table should look like this:

Student_History

	Column Name	Condensed Type	Nullable	
🔑	StudentID	char(5)	NOT NULL	▲
🔑	SchoolYear	datetime	NOT NULL	
	FinalGrade	decimal(5, 2)	NOT NULL	▼

Allowable Values and CHECK Constraints

The final step in designing domain integrity is to determine the *allowable values* that each column may hold. Up to this point, defining the allowable values for the columns in the Products table has partially been done: First, the datatype of a column dictates what type of data a column may hold. Next, the nullability of a column determines whether the column is required to hold a value in every row. Finally, the range of actual values, or allowable values, that a column may contain needs to be defined. This includes any *default* values that a column may have. A default value is a value that will be entered into a column if no value is provided. Allowable values no longer deal with the type of data a column will hold, but the actual data itself.

Table 2-4 offers examples of allowable values.

Defining the values allowed in each column further enhances domain integrity by preventing faulty data from being entered into a table. For instance, consider a table that stores information about the roads in Florida. A column exists in this table to record the speed limit of each road. To my knowledge, the lowest posted speed limit I've ever seen is 5 and the maximum speed limit is 70 on the interstates. A datatype of Tinyint is assigned to the SpeedLimit column, and NULLs are prohibited. However, there exists no check that would prevent a user from entering a value of 200 in the SpeedLimit column. As very few cars can even attain such a speed, this is faulty data. The user's true intention may have been to enter 20 miles per hour, but the database has no way of knowing that 200 is not a valid entry without having first defined the allowable values for the column. When we define the allowable values of 5 through 70 for the SpeedLimit column, such an error would have been prevented. (True, a user could still enter 45 when they meant to enter 5, but at that point we'd be asking the database engine to read a user's mind, which it cannot do.)

Once allowable values are defined for each column, they are implemented in the physical database by means of what's known as a *CHECK constraint*. A CHECK constraint is a clause of T-SQL that is applied to any data modification or insert. It ensures that the data being entered adheres to the limits set in the T-SQL within the constraint. CHECK constraints can be defined at the column level as we are doing, or at the table level. Table-level CHECK constraints allow a column's allowable values to be based on some other column in the table—for instance, ensuring that a ship date is greater than an order date. CHECK constraints will be covered in more detail in Chapter 3.

TABLE 2-4	Data Stored in Column	Allowable Values
Examples of Allowable Values	A social security number	000-00-0000 through 999-99-9999
	A phone number (where *N* is a number)	(*NNN*)*NNN-NNNN*
	Test grades	'A', 'B', 'C', 'D', or 'F'
	A state abbreviation (where *L* is a letter)	*LL*

Let's return to the Products table in the preceding section to define the allowable values for each column. Beginning with product number, through further analysis we discover that each product number will always start with a letter, and the last five characters will always be numbers. Therefore, the allowable values for the ProductNumber column will look like this: *LxxxxNNNNN*, where *L* is a letter, *x* is any character, and *N* is a number. The BuildDate column already has a lot of integrity built into it. Having been defined with a Datetime datatype, an illegal date cannot be entered into it. Just to be safe, we might require that a build date being entered is not some future date, but equal to today's date or sometime in the past.

The allowable values for Name and Description can be any characters within the defined length of the column, so no CHECK constraints will be necessary. The Price column brings up an interesting challenge to defining allowable values. Having been defined with the Smallmoney datatype, 'Price' is currently limited to a maximum value of about $214,000. Currently, the most expensive item sold is less than $2,000. One option is to define the allowable values as "any monetary value between $1 and $2,000." This would prevent an accidental entry of $19,000, when the intended entry was $1,900. But then the problem arises of what if we ever do sell a product that costs more than $2,000. For this reason, we'll define the allowable values of the Price column as "any monetary value, currently below $2,000, but possibly more in the future." The allowable value for the Type column is either the string 'Hardware' or 'Software'. Finally, the Active column is defined with a Bit datatype and does not allow NULLs. This means that its allowable values of 1 or 0 are already assured, so no CHECK constraint will be necessary.

With all of the allowable values defined, the CHECK constraints in Table 2-5 will be implemented in the physical database.

TABLE 2-5	**Column**	**CHECK Constraint**
CHECK Constraints for the Products Table	ProductNumber	Any value entered must have the format *LxxxxNNNNN*, where *L* is a letter, *x* is any character, and *N* is a number.
	BuildDate	Any date entered must be equal to or less than today's date.
	Type	Any value entered must be either the string 'Hardware' or the string 'Software'.

Default Values

In defining allowable values, it is also necessary to identify any *default values* the columns may have. A default value is simply a value that will be entered into a column if no value is provided at the time the row is entered. Consider a table that stores address information. In this table is a column called Country with a default value of 'USA'. Any address entered into this table with no value for the 'Country' column will automatically have the value 'USA' assigned to it by the database engine. Default values are useful when a column will contain the same value the vast majority of the time. Returning to the Products table, the columns BuildDate and Active are good candidates for default values. The majority of products are entered into the Products table on the build date of the product, so a default value of today's date makes sense in the BuildDate column. Also, most products entered into the table are also available for sale, so we'll assign the default value of 1 to the Active column.

The completed Products table, with all domain integrity defined, is shown here (GetDate() is a T-SQL function that returns the current date):

Products

	Column Name	Condensed Type	Nullable	Default Value
🔑	ProductNumber	char(10)	NOT NULL	
	BuildDate	datetime	NOT NULL	(getdate())
	Name	varchar(50)	NOT NULL	
	Description	varchar(500)	NULL	
	Price	smallmoney	NOT NULL	
	Type	char(8)	NOT NULL	
	Active	bit	NOT NULL	(1)

CERTIFICATION SUMMARY

In this chapter, we discussed the building blocks of any physical database: the logical data model. When a building is to be constructed, workers don't just jump right in and start pouring concrete. They work from design specifications described in a blueprint. In the same way, a physical database needs it's own blueprint: the data model.

A logical data model consists of entities and attributes. Every entity requires a key attribute to uniquely identify rows. Foreign-key attributes reference key attributes in other entities, creating relationships. Entities should also be normalized, as this has the effect of keeping redundant data in a database to a minimum. Once the entities are in compliance with third normal form, denormalization can be explored to increase performance in the physical database.

Referential integrity prevents orphaned rows in a database table. Referential actions, such as CASCADE and RESTRICT, allow for better control of how referential integrity behaves for a given relationship. Many types of possible relationships can exist in a logical data model, but all are resolved to simple relationships in the physical database.

Domain integrity governs the type of data that each column in a table is permitted to store. It is defined in several ways: The datatype of a column ensures that it will only contain one type of information. Nullability determines whether or not the column is required to contain a value. Finally, allowable values determine the range of acceptable values that the column may contain, as well as any default value should none be provided.

TWO-MINUTE DRILL

Defining Entities and Attributes

❑ Entities and attributes are the foundation of a logical data model. An entity defines a group of data of the same type. Attributes are characteristics of entities.

❑ Primary-key attributes are attributes that uniquely identify records within an entity. Each entity must have a primary-key attribute. A compound primary key is made up of more than one attribute.

❑ Primary-key attributes can be of several types: intelligent (an attribute with business meaning, like a social security number) or surrogate (an attribute created solely for the purpose of serving as the primary key of an entity).

❑ Foreign keys are attributes in an entity that reference a key attribute in a parent entity, creating a relationship. Foreign keys may reference primary-key attributes, or alternate key attributes.

Entity Composition and Normalization

❑ Normalization is the process of organizing entities and attributes so that they comply with what are called *normal forms.*

❑ The first normal form states that all attributes must not be decomposable (represent a single thing) and not repeat (as in repeating groups).

❑ The second normal form requires that in addition to complying with the first normal form, all attributes within an entity be dependent on the entire primary key of that entity. Second normal form violations frequently occur in tables with compound primary keys.

❑ The third normal form requires that in addition to complying with the first and second normal forms, all attributes must depend on nothing but the primary key of an entity and not on other attributes. The third normal form eliminates transitive dependencies from an entity.

Designing for Referential Integrity

❑ Entity integrity is established through primary-key constraints. Referential integrity is established through foreign-key constraints.

❑ The purpose of referential integrity is to eliminate the possibility of orphaned records in an entity. Orphaned records are records whose foreign key does not reference a valid parent record.

❑ SQL Server 2000 provides the ability to control the behavior of referential integrity. Updates and deletes to parent entities can be CASCADED or RESTRICTED. Restricted is called NO ACTION in SQL Server 2000.

Managing Entity Relationships

❑ Relationships have a property known as *cardinality*, which determines the number of instances of each entity that will be involved in the relationship.

❑ In a logical database model, many types of database relationships exist; but no matter how complex, all relationships in a physical database are resolved to either a one-to-one or a one-to-many simple relationship.

Attribute and Domain Integrity

❑ Attribute and domain integrity involves defining the characteristics of the data that will be stored in a database column.

❑ All logical datatypes in a data model must be mapped to SQL Server datatypes, and in some cases a length must be declared. This process involves choosing the most compact datatype and length for each attribute.

❑ Other characteristics that must be declared include nullablility, allowable values, and default values.

SELF TEST

The following questions will help you measure your understanding of the material presented in this chapter. Read all the choices carefully because there might be more than one correct answer. Choose all correct answers for each question. Just like on the real exam, you may need to use some scratch paper to draw out the scenarios, in order to gain a better conceptual view of the problem being presented.

Defining Entities and Attributes

1. Identify the best candidates for entities. Use this initial analysis from a dog breeder: "I have about 30 dogs currently, of various breeds. I need to track each dog's breed, as well as their date of birth. It's important for me to know which ones are pregnant, as they require a special dog food and need to be kept in a separate kennel." (Choose all that apply.)

   A. Dogs

   B. Breeds

   C. Pregnant

   D. Kennel

2. Which type of attribute establishes a relationship to another entity?

   A. Primary key

   B. Surrogate key

   C. Foreign key

   D. Alternate key

3. A logical data model has two entities: Products and Manufacturers. Each product is built by one manufacturer. Which of the following should you perform on the entities? (Choose all that apply.)

   A. Create a primary key in the Manufactures entity.

   B. Create a foreign key in the Manufacturers entity.

   C. Create a primary key in the Products entity.

   D. Create a foreign key in the Products entity.

4. Consider the following entity. This entity will store information about stock prices. At the end of each trading day, the stock symbol, the date, and the average price for that date will be stored. What is the best primary key for this entity?

Averages

StockSymbol Date AverageCost

A. The StockSymbol attribute.

B. The AverageCost attribute.

C. A compound primary key made up of the stock symbol and date attributes.

D. There are no good candidate keys in this entity. Create a surrogate primary key.

Entity Composition and Normalization

5. A logical data model exists with an entity that has been modeled with a repeating group. Which normal form does this violate? (Choose the best answer.)

A. The first normal form

B. The second normal form

C. The third normal form.

D. All of the above.

6. Which of the following statements are true of denormalization?(Choose all that apply.)

A. It gives greater flexibility in the way that data is stored.

B. It can increase performance of the physical database by reducing the amount of table joins.

C. It helps minimize duplicate data.

D. It requires no additional analysis.

7. A logical data model has several entities. What is meant by the following statement: "Entity A is a grandchild of entity B."

   A. Entity A has a foreign key that references entity B.

   B. Entity A has multiple foreign keys that reference entity B.

   C. Entity A has foreign keys that reference entity B and also other entities.

   D. Entity A does not reference entity B, but references a different entity that references entity A.

Designing for Referential Integrity

8. What type of integrity does a primary key enforce?

   A. Referential integrity

   B. Entity integrity

   C. Attribute integrity

   D. Domain integrity

9. An entity called Child has a FOREIGN KEY constraint the references an entity called Parent. The referential actions for this relationship have been defined in SQL Server 2000 as ON DELETE NO ACTION. A row is accidentally deleted from the parent table that has child rows referencing it. What is the result in the database?

   A. The child rows that referenced the deleted parent row are deleted as well.

   B. The child rows that referenced the deleted parent row are retained, but the foreign-key attribute is set to NULL.

   C. The row in the parent table cannot be deleted because it has child rows referencing it.

   D. The child rows that referenced the deleted parent row are retained, and the foreign key is not altered.

Managing Entity Relationships

10. How should you resolve a many-to-many relationship between two entities so that the relationship will be supported by a RDBMS?

    A. Create a new association entity. Create a surrogate primary key in the new entity. Create foreign-key attributes to the primary keys of the original entities. Add any additional attributes that track information relating to the many-to-many relationship.

    B. Create a new association entity. Create a compound primary key in the new entity consisting of foreign-key attributes referencing the primary keys of the original entities. Add any additional attributes that track information relating to the many-to-many relationship.

    C. Pick one entity as the child entity. Create a foreign-key attribute in the child entity that references the primary key of the parent entity.

    D. Create two new association entities, one for each original entity. Create a foreign-key attribute in each new entity that references a primary key in one of the original entities. Add any additional attributes that track information relating to the many-to-many relationship.

11. Consider the following analysis: "We have many docks here at the marina. Each dock can hold up to eight boats. Boats can park at whichever dock has free space. We're only interested in where a boat is currently docked." What kind of relationship would you create between the Docks and Boats entities?

    A. One to many

    B. Many to many

    C. One to one

    D. Self referencing

12. Which of the following are reasons to create a true one-to-one relationship by splitting an entity into two? (Choose all that apply.)

    A. The length of a row in a table will exceed 8,000 characters.

    B. There are infrequently requested columns in a table that are significant in length.

    C. There is a column in a table that stores flag information.

    D. The table has a foreign key that references its own primary key.

Attribute and Domain Integrity

13. You are analyzing a column of a table that will store numeric information. The column will store numbers between 0 and 200 most of the time. On occasion, the column may be required to store a number as high as 300. How would you ensure attribute integrity on this column?

A. Define the column with a datatype of Tinyint.

B. Define the column with a datatype of Smallint. Use a CHECK constraint to ensure that no values greater than 300 can be stored in the column.

C. Define the column with a datatype of Int. Use a CHECK constraint to ensure that no values greater than 300 can be stored in the column.

D. Define the column with a datatype of Char. Use a CHECK constraint to ensure that only numeric values less than 301 are stored in the column.

14. Which statements are true of a NULL value?

A. It is a blank value like an empty string.

B. It equates to zero.

C. It is an unknown value.

D. It equates to a value of false in mathematical operations.

15. Two entities exist in a logical data model: entity 1 and entity 2. You want to ensure that values entered into a certain column in entity 1 are within the range of values stored in a similar column in entity 2. The column values in entity 2 are unique. How would you establish the domain integrity for the column in entity 1?

A. Use a CHECK constraint.

B. Use a trigger.

C. Define the column as Nullable.

D. Use a FOREIGN KEY constraint.

16. How does a default value enhance the domain integrity of a column?

A. It ensures that if no value is provided, a NULL value will be entered into the column.

B. It automatically enters a zero into numeric columns when no value is provided.

C. It ensures that if no value is provided, the value defined as the default will be entered into the column.

D. It automatically enters an empty string into character columns when no value is provided.

17. What would be the best way to define a column that will store information about the state of a piece of equipment regarding whether or not it is currently running?

   A. Use a Char(7) datatype and a CHECK constraint to ensure that only the values of Running and Stopped can be entered into the column.

   B. Use a Char(1) datatype and a CHECK constraint to ensure that only the values of R and S can be entered into the column.

   C. Use a Bit datatype and define the column as not nullable.

   D. Use a Bit datatype and a CHECK constraint to ensure that only the values of 0 and 1 can be entered into the column.

LAB QUESTION

You have just been employed by Acme Builders as a database developer. Your first task is to improve upon Acme's current database design. The Enterprise Manager diagram of the current database schema is shown here.

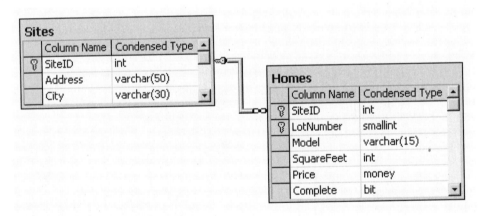

The Sites table contains information about the blocks of property Acme has purchased and can build on. The Homes table contains a row for each lot at a particular site, including the model of the home built or currently being built, the square footage and price of the home, and a flag attribute to determine whether the home construction is completed or not.

Acme has been having trouble maintaining the amount of duplicate data stored in the database. In the Homes table, a particular model's price and square footage are repeated each time that model is built on a lot. Another problem is that home prices increase each year, and Acme would like to know what the price of a home was at the time of building.

The database is used only during business hours, and the development staff has offered its full support to perform any application modifications necessary. You are given the following requirements regarding the database redesign:

1. Reduce the amount of redundant data stored in the database.

2. Comply with third normal form.

3. Add a means by which to record the price of a home when it was built, in addition to the current price.

How would you modify the current schema to complete the three requirements?

SELF TEST ANSWERS

Defining Entities and Attributes

1.   ☑   **A** and **D**. From the breeder's statements, we can conclude that dogs are housed in kennels. Both dogs and kennels are good candidates for entities based on this initial analysis.

      ☒   **B** and **C**. Neither breed nor pregnant are good candidates for entities. Breed is an attribute of a dog. Pregnant is also an attribute of a dog, a flag indicating whether or not a dog is pregnant.

2.   ☑   **C**. A foreign-key attribute references a key attribute in another entity, thus establishing a relationship.

      ☒   **A**, **B**, and **D** are incorrect because they do not establish a relationship. A primary key allows rows to be uniquely identified within an entity. An alternate key also uniquely identifies instances of an entity, but does not serve as the primary-key attribute. A surrogate key is a key created for the sole purpose of being the primary key of an entity when no other attributes or combination of attributes make good candidates.

3.   ☑   **A**, **C**, and **D**. A and C are correct because every entity must have a primary key defined. D is also correct, as each product will reference its manufacturer.

      ☒   **B** is incorrect. There is no need to create a foreign key in the Manufacturers table, as it is the parent entity. Remember, foreign keys are always created in the child entity or table.

4.   ☑   **C** is the best choice for the primary key of this entity. Since each stock symbol will have one entry per day, the combination of the StockSymbol and Date attributes will uniquely identify an instance of the entity.

      ☒   **A** cannot be the primary key, because the same stock symbol will be entered into this entity each day. **B** is also not a good choice for primary key, because the possibility exists that different stocks will have the same average price. **D** is also not a good choice. While you could create a surrogate primary key for this entity, it is always best to use an intelligent primary key, one that has actual business meaning.

Entity Composition and Normalization

5.   ☑   **D** is the correct answer. While this is a first normal form violation, remember that normal forms are cumulative. To be in second normal form, an entity must also be in first normal form. To be in third normal form, an entity must also be in first and second normal forms.

      ☒   **A**, **B**, and **C** by themselves are incorrect, as all three normal forms are violated by a repeating group.

6. ☑ **B** is the only statement that is true of denormalization. It often results in the combining of entities, which reduces the amount of table joins in the physical database.

   ☒ **A** is incorrect. Denormalization actually reduces the amount of flexibility in the way that data is stored. **C** is also incorrect as denormalization can introduce redundant data into a database. **D** is completely false, as appropriate denormalization requires careful analysis to perform correctly.

7. ☑ **D** is the correct answer. A grandchild is an entity that is a child of a child of the parent entity. Entity lineage uses the same terms as a family.

   ☒ **A**, **B**, and **C** are all incorrect. The statements in those answers would make entity A a child of entity B.

Designing for Referential Integrity

8. ☑ **B.** PRIMARY KEY constraints enforce what is known as entity integrity. This means that each instance of an entity is uniquely identifiable.

   ☒ **A**, **C**, and **D** are all incorrect. Referential integrity is enforced through FOREIGN KEY constraints. Attribute and domain integrity are enforced through datatypes, allowable values, and nullablility.

9. ☑ **C** is the correct answer. The key to this question is "in SQL Server 2000." Remember, the referential action of RESTRICT is called NO ACTION in SQL Server 2000. Therefore, if a DELETE statement affects a row in the parent table that has child rows referencing it, an error will be generated and the DELETE operation will not occur.

   ☒ **A** is incorrect because that result would require a setting of CASCADE. **B** is also incorrect because that would require a referential action of SET NULL. **D** is also incorrect, as this result would not occur no matter which referential action was specified.

Managing Entity Relationships

10. ☑ **B** is the correct way to resolve a many-to-many relationship. A new association entity is created. The primary key of this new entity consists of the migrated primary keys from the original entities involved. Any information having to do with the many-to-many relationship is also tracked in the new entity.

    ☒ **A** is incorrect. While you could resolve the relationship in this way, there is no need to create a surrogate key in the new association entity. **C** is incorrect, as a many-to-many relationship cannot be resolved in the physical database using only the original entities. **D** is also incorrect because only one association entity is necessary to resolve a many-to-many relationship.

11. ☑ **A** is the correct answer. From the analysis, it is apparent that "docks store boats." One dock can store many boats, but a boat may be parked at only one dock at a time.

    ☒ **B** is incorrect. In order for this to be a many-to-many relationship, a boat would need to be able to park at multiple docks at one time. Since no mention was made of retaining historical information, we are only concerned with where a boat is currently docked. Therefore, the Boats entity would have a foreign-key attribute indicating what dock it's currently parked at. **C** is incorrect, as a dock can hold up to eight boats. **D** is incorrect because a self-referencing relationship has to do with hierarchical data.

12. ☑ **A** and **B** are correct. The maximum size of a table row in SQL Server 2000 is about 8,000 characters. Both of these are reasons to split a table into two tables and create a one-to-one relationship.

    ☒ **C** is incorrect because storing flag information in a table takes up very little space. **D** is also incorrect, as this statement would warrant a self-referencing relationship—not a one-to-one relationship.

Attribute and Domain Integrity

13. ☑ **B** is the correct answer. The Smallint datatype uses the least amount of space in the physical database for the requirement of storing numbers up to 300. A CHECK constraint will ensure that no values greater than 300 can be entered into the column.

    ☒ **A** is incorrect because the Tinyint datatype can only store numbers up to 255. **C** is incorrect because the Int datatype can store numeric information in the neighborhood of billions, and would waste space in the physical database. **D** is incorrect because we are attempting to store numeric information, not text.

14. ☑ **C** is the only statement that is true of a NULL value. It literally translates into "unknown."

    ☒ **A** is incorrect because an empty string is a valid piece of data in a character column. Likewise, **B** is incorrect because zero is a valid value in numeric columns. **D** is incorrect, asperforming mathematical operations on a NULL value will, by default, equate to NULL, not false.

15. ☑ **D** is the correct answer. Since the column values in entity two are unique, establishing a FOREIGN KEY constraint on the column in entity 1 will ensure that the values entered are within the range of values that exist in the column in entity 2.

    ☒ **A** is incorrect because a CHECK constraint cannot reference columns in other tables. **B** is also incorrect. Although you could use a trigger to ensure this integrity, FOREIGN KEY constraints are the recommended way to handle such a requirement. Triggers always add performance overhead to the database. **D** is incorrect because defining the column as nullable will not accomplish the requirement—it will only ensure that NULL values cannot be entered into the column.

16. ☑ **C.** A default value enhances domain integrity by automatically entering a specified value into a column if no value is provided.
☒ **A, B,** and **D** are all incorrect, although you can define a default value as any value that the requirements dictate.

17. ☑ **C.** The Bit datatype is the best choice for the requirements. A Bit datatype defined as NOT NULL takes up very little space and can only store the values 0 or 1.
☒ **A** and **B** are incorrect, although they do accomplish the requirement. Using the Char datatype for this type of column will require a CHECK constraint that the bit column does not. **D** is also incorrect as a bit column can only store 0 or 1 by design, so no CHECK constraint is necessary.

LAB ANSWER

This problem of redundant data is fairly common in tables with compound primary keys. In looking at the Homes table, it becomes apparent that there is a transitive dependency. The square footage and current price are dependent on the model of home being built, not the primary key of the Homes table. This is the source of the redundant data, and it will need to be resolved by modifying the Homes table to store only the attributes specific to a model of home, including the current price and the square footage. A new association table called Sites_Homes will also need to be created, to store the information specific to a lot.

The requirement to add a means by which to record the price of a home when it was built will also be addressed in the new association entity. Attributes in the new association entity will be recorded at the actual time a home is built (the coming together of a site and a home), so it can also store historical information. The revised database schema also complies with third normal form; so all three of the requirements have been met, as shown in Figure 2-10.

FIGURE 2-10

Lab answer

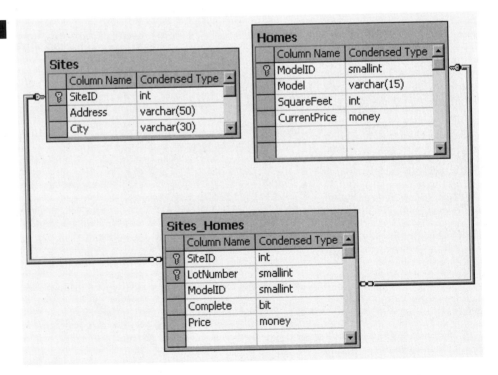

MICROSOFT CERTIFIED DATABASE ADMINISTRATOR

3

Implementing a Database

I n Chapter 2, the topic of logical database design was covered in depth. The next step in developing a database is to implement that logical design. The topics discussed in Chapter 3 are the first steps involved with the implementation phase of the database. Throughout this chapter, there will be examples derived from a small data model (see Figure 3-1) that show some of the tables available in the Northwind database, a database that is installed as part of SQL Server 2000. The chapter concludes with some exercises to review the topics covered on the test in this chapter.

CERTIFICATION OBJECTIVE 3.01

Planning for Storage Management

In previous releases of SQL Server, planning for storage management was considerably more complicated than with the SQL Server 7.0 and the 2000 release. Gone are the days of allocating drive space through devices and manually separating the transaction logs from the datafiles.

Determining Space Requirements

Based on the logical design, it is the database administrator's job to determine the space requirements for the database. The reasons for estimating this information at the beginning of the process are that this will drive hardware purchases, hardware configuration, and performance of the database, and help set other long-range decisions associated with supporting the database.

To estimate the size of the database, take into account the physical objects in the database—including tables and indexes. While views are an abstraction of data that is stored in the tables referenced by the view, indexes produced on any views should be included. See Chapter 4 for more information on views. For tables, estimations are based on the datatypes being used and approximations made on row numbers and row growth. SQL Server Books Online provides more detail for estimating size based on specific database implementations.

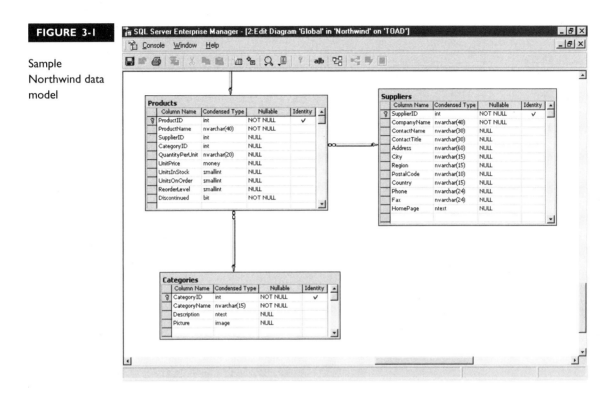

FIGURE 3-1

Sample
Northwind data
model

Understanding Files and Filegroups

There are three types of files in SQL Server:

- **Primary** The primary file is a required file that the database uses to store all the information for starting the database. This file can also be used to store table data.

- **Secondary** These are any files that are created in addition to the primary file that is used to store user-defined data. Any tables created have access to these files.

- **Transaction log** These files, sometimes referred to as log files, store all the log data for a database. Transaction logs are detailed in the next section.

There can be only one primary file in a database. The secondary files are optional and are meant to allow for more flexible architectures. If the database grows to be too large to be contained in a single file, either due to operating system limitations or drive limitations, the secondary files can be used. Multiple files can also allow data and tables to be spread across multiple physical drives. This can have some performance advantages. The support for multiple files lends itself to the next topic, which is filegroups.

on the
Job

An important note about using multiple files for performance reasons is that they must be on separate physical drives. Splitting a file across logical drives is often counterproductive because it causes disk head contention when trying to access and write to two files on the same physical drive.

As the number of files increases, it becomes more of a concern to easily administer the database. To help with these problems, SQL Server allows a group of files to be treated like a single file. These groups of files are referred to as filegroups. A filegroup can be referenced during table and index creation, as well as during backup strategies. There are some rules for filegroups:

■ While a filegroup can have one or more files, a file can only be associated to one filegroup.

■ Transaction log files are never a part of a filegroup.

■ Filegroups and the files in them cannot be shared across databases.

Every database creates a primary filegroup and assigns the primary file to that group. Secondary files are allowed to belong to the primary filegroup as well. When a table or index is created, the default filegroup is primary unless specified in the CREATE TABLE statement or a new default is set in the database.

Any type of file in a database contains default properties that govern its growth. Figure 3-2 shows the settings for a datafile in Enterprise Manager. A user can set whether a file automatically grows and how quickly it grows, and defines an upper limit for how big the file can grow.

When choosing to allow SQL Server to automatically grow the file, additional settings are required. SQL Server can grow the file as a percentage of the current size of the file, or it can allocate a specific amount. This growth can be limited by a second setting of maximum file size. A specific maximum size can be set, or the growth can be left unlimited. If the growth is unlimited, only operating system constraints and disk drive capacity limit the growth.

When a file in the database is full, the database returns errors to users when they try to insert, update, or delete. This behavior will occur whenever the file is full and

FIGURE 3-2

Setting file
properties in
Enterprise
Manager

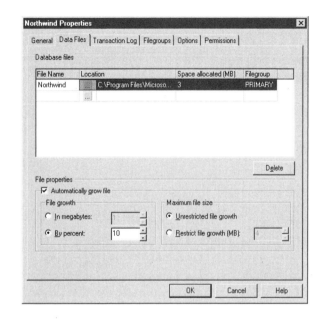

cannot allocate more space. Whether the settings do not allow the file to grow or whether the disk drive is full, the database behaves the same way.

on the
job

In a production environment, it is important to keep track of all these settings. Typically, allowing files, especially transaction logs, to grow to an unlimited size is dangerous because a runaway query that deletes, updates, or inserts data can force the transaction log to continue to grow and fill your disk, which would cause problems for this database and any others that happen to reside on the same disk.

Understanding the Transaction Log

Through the logging mechanisms in SQL Server, the transaction log stores a history of all database changes. The transaction log records all data changes, as well as the transaction information that caused the change. The transaction log records enough information so that any transaction can be reversed if needed. This is used during transaction processing (covered in Chapter 4), as well as for recovering from a failure of the database. While all the information to perform these actions is stored in the transaction log, the logs and the backing up of those logs can be maintained in ways to suit individual environments that may have different requirements.

For this reason, the management of the database transaction log is very important when determining a backup and recovery strategy. How the transaction log is maintained is set by the recovery model. The recovery model can be simple, full, or bulk-logged.

When a transaction has been completed in the simple recovery model, the information stored in the transaction log associated to that transaction is reclaimed. This limits the size and growth of the transaction logs while allowing for disaster recovery to restore the previous values of any inserts, updates, or deletes that had not been completed. This may provide easy administrative overhead, but it exposes the database to the potential loss of great deals of data. In fact, the simple recovery model exposes all transactions that have been completed since the last database backup has been done. Many times this will be used in development environments where performance is critical and there is no need to recover test data.

The second recovery model is the bulk-logged model. This model provides more recoverability than the simple recovery model, but it does not provide point-in-time recovery. During bulk-logged recovery, the transaction log tracks the individual transactions normally acting upon the database. Bulk-loading operations, such as the bcp utility, select into commands, creating indexes, and operations involving text and image data, are logged before and after the bulk load ends. This allows for limited logging during bulk processing and assists with performance. The downside is the loss of work should a failure occur during the bulk load.

The final recovery model is the full recovery model. This model stores all the transaction information both before and after a transaction completes. This model allows for a point-in-time recovery since the transaction information is available for all transactions. Because the database tracks all this data, the disk is constantly being written to while the database is active. This data continues to be written to the transaction log until a backup is done, which truncates the log. If backups of the transaction log or the database are not performed, the transaction log file continues to grow and consumes more and more drive space until some event truncates the log or the drive can no longer allocate more space. For this reason, transaction logs can be backed up and moved to another directory, left where they are, or moved to a tape backup, depending on the available resources. These transaction log backups are critical to restoring the database to a point in time since they are applied to the database after any full or differential backups have been applied. Transaction log backups are also utilized in the bulk-logged recovery model.

These recovery models offer a range of flexibility for different environments. If the environment needs change, the recovery model can also change. These decisions and the implementation of these decisions can be altered and improved during the lifetime of a system.

Implementing the Physical Database

SQL Server 2000 allows the user to create a database and tables from Enterprise Manager and from Query Analyzer. Query Analyzer requires Transact-SQL statements to create, alter, and drop objects. Enterprise Manager provides a user interface that gives the user this functionality without knowing the specific syntax

FROM THE CLASSROOM

Backup and Recovery Strategies

While Exam 70-229 requires only a beginning understanding of the subject of backup and recovery, it is probably the most important job of a DBA. For those that doubt this, imagine if something happened to your production servers and there was no way to recover the data. Not only would the company be out of potentially weeks, months, and maybe years of data entry and processing, your job would probably be on the line.

The first step in a good backup and recovery strategy is to do a thorough job of interviewing customers. The customer is the one that gives you the best idea of usage patterns because they are the people that use the system. These people are the ones that can tell you whether the system has to be 24/7 or just running every Wednesday from noon to 6. These answers are the tools needed to define your backup and recovery strategy. The technical portions can be sorted out fairly easily after you know what needs to be done.

More information on this topic can be found in the SQL Server Books Online and books devoted to this topic such as *SQL Server 2000 Backup and Recovery* from Osborne/ McGraw-Hill.

—Craig Robinson

for each object. While learning Transact-SQL and developing upgrade scripts, Enterprise Manager provides a method to see the Transact-SQL required in Query Analyzer. Using the Save Change Script button, Enterprise Manager displays the commands needed for the desired change.

exam

🖤**atch**

Enterprise Manager is a useful tool during development, but the exam requires that you understand the syntax involved in creating and altering these objects. For this reason, the examples and exercises stay focused on the command syntax rather than the use of Enterprise Manager.

Creating the Database

Now that there is an understanding of files and filegroups, as well as a logical design, the next step is to begin implementation. Before the database is created, it is important to point out that all new databases that are created use the model database as the template. The model database is a database that is created by default when SQL Server is installed and acts as a template for all subsequent databases. If there are tables, procedures, users, views or any other object in the model database, those objects are created in the new database. New databases also assume the database properties that the model database has unless they are expressly overridden in the CREATE DATABASE command. Now that this is covered, the database can be created.

To start, a simple example of creating a database uses the following code, which creates the Test database:

```
CREATE DATABASE Test
```

As with most CREATE commands in SQL Server 2000, the CREATE DATABASE command can be brief. The reason for this is that SQL Server takes all the default values, including file size, from the model database. The only issue in question is the location of new data and transaction log files. A default is defined during installing of the server, but to change these values, right-click the Server node in Enterprise Manager. The default location for both the datafile and the transaction log can be set on the Database Settings tab. In Figure 3-3, the default data directory is being set to C:\Database\Datafile and the default log directory is set to C:\Database\LogFile.

With these as the defaults, the primary datafile is created as C:\Database\Datafile\ Test_Data.mdf and the transaction log file is created as C:\Database\Datafile\ Test_Log.ldf. The .mdf and .ldf file extensions are the defaults for the primary and log files, respectively. Secondary files have a default extension of .ndf. These file extensions

FIGURE 3-3

SQL Server
Properties dialog
box used to alter
the default file
locations

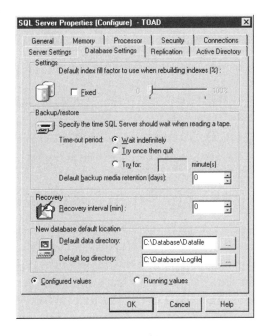

are not enforced by the database. They are the default naming convention. The CREATE DATABASE command does not require the use of the model database properties, though. These can be specified during the database creation. The following is a framework for the CREATE DATABASE command:

```
CREATE DATABASE <databasename>
 ON <filegroup_definition>(
<file_definition>
)
LOG ON (
<file_definition>
)
```

Taking the elements from this framework, the first term, filegroup definition, allows the user to specify the name of the filegroup. If the datafiles are to reside in the primary filegroup, the filegroup definition is left off. When a filegroup name other than primary needs to be used, the syntax is FILEGROUP filegroupname. After the filegroup definition, one or more file definitions can be listed. The file definitions belong inside their own set of parentheses and are separated from each other with commas. For example, if the Test database had one file in the primary filegroup and two files in the Test1 filegroup, the syntax would look like the following:

```
CREATE DATABASE Test
ON ( <file_definition>),
FILEGROUP Test1 (<file_definition>),(<file_definition>),
LOG ON (<file_definition>)
```

In the example, the ON keyword is not repeated for each filegroup. It serves to separate CREATE DATABASE from the remaining portion of the statement. It should also be noted that since the filegroup is not specified for the first file definition, it is kept in the primary filegroup. In the primary filegroup, the primary file resides. To specify which file is the primary file, precede the file definition with the keyword PRIMARY. If PRIMARY is not specified, the first file definition in the primary filegroup is set as the primary file.

The file definition has a few more options than the filegroup definition. The following parameters can be specified, in this order, in the file definition of any of the three file types:

Option Name	Description	Usage
Name	Logical name for the file.	This is required except during a reattach method of CREATE DATABASE.
Filename	Name and location of the file.	If the file definition is specified, this is a required value.
Size	The initial size of the file.	Whole number values that can use the KB (kilobyte), MB (megabyte), GB (gigabyte), and TB (terabyte) suffixes. Default is MB. For primary datafile, uses the size of the primary file in the model database. Secondary and transaction log defaults to 1 MB.
Maxsize	Maximum size of the file. This value accepts the UNLIMITED keyword as a value.	Whole number values that can use the KB (kilobyte), MB (megabyte), GB (gigabyte), and TB (terabyte) prefixes. Default is MB. If the Maxsize parameter is not specified, UNLIMITED is default.

Option Name	Description	Usage
Filegrowth	Specifies the growth method, percentage or absolute, and rate of growth.	Whole number values that can use KB, MB, GB, TB, or %. Default is MB. A % denotes a percentage increase. When percentage increase is chosen, growth is rounded to the nearest 64KB. Value of 0 denotes no growth.

Using these parameters, the Test database can be further defined:

```
CREATE DATABASE Test
ON PRIMARY (Name = 'Test_Data', Filename = 'C:\Database\Datafile\test_data.mdf',
 Size = 4 MB,
 MaxSize = 16 MB,
 FileGrowth = 2MB),
FILEGROUP Test1 (Name = 'Test1_data1',
 Filename = 'C:\Database\Datafile\test1_data.ndf',
 Size = 2 MB,
 MaxSize = 8 MB,
 FileGrowth = 500KB),
(Name = 'Test1_data2',
 Filename = 'C:\Database\Datafile\test2_data.ndf',
 FileGrowth = 10%)
LOG ON (Name = 'Test1_log',
 Filename = 'C:\Database\Logfile\test_log.ldf',
 Size = 4 MB,
 MaxSize = 16 MB)
```

Even though there are parameters missing in some of the file definitions, the default values are taken and the database is created. There are two more parameters that can be specified for CREATE DATABASE: the collation specification and the FOR ATTACH parameter.

The collation definition allows a DBA to set a database to support a different method of sorting the data in the database. There are many different collations that can be reviewed in SQL Server Books Online.

Another parameter in the creation of a database is the FOR ATTACH parameter. SQL Server allows for a database to be detached from a SQL Server instance and reattached. Detaching and reattaching databases can be used to move databases between machines; or if someone needs to reinstall SQL Server, they can detach the old database and reattach after the reinstall. The act of detaching a database removes references to the physical files and filegroups from the SQL Server instance.

The primary file stores all the references to supplemental files and transaction log files. This allows for all the files to be moved to a new location and reattached. When reattaching, SQL Server is given the location of the primary datafile and the other files are assumed to be in the same physical location. If this is not the case, the file locations are required in the CREATE DATABASE command.

To detach a database using Enterprise Manager, follow these steps:

1. Select the database to be detached.

2. Right-click the database and a menu will come up.

3. Choose the ALL TASKS menu item and a submenu will appear.

4. From this submenu, select the Detach Database...task.

5. The window displayed in Figure 3-4 appears.

6. After all the active connections are disconnected, selecting OK will detach the database.

To detach a database using T-SQL in Query Analyzer, the user can use the sp_detach_db command. Since the Query Analyzer session would be considered an active connection, the user cannot be connected to the database that is being detached. The following code detaches the Test database:

```
Exec sp_detach_db 'Test','true'
```

In this procedure, the first parameter is the database name that should be detached. The second parameter defines whether or not the database updates statistics before the database is detached.

Detaching a SQL
Server database

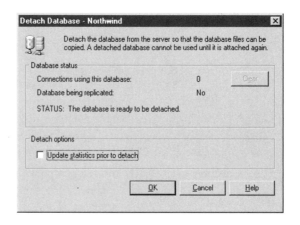

Now that the database is detached, the data and log files can be moved to another server or can be reattached to the same database. The first step is to find all the data and log files that need to be reattached. Once the files are in their new locations, there are a few ways to reattach the database.

To attach a database using Enterprise Manager, follow these steps:

1. Right-click the database folder in the SQL Server instance.

2. Choose the ALL TASKS menu item and a submenu will appear.

3. From this submenu, select the Attach Database...task.

4. The window displayed in Figure 3-5 appears.

5. Find the primary file for the database that needs to be reattached.

6. The remaining files are listed in the file list below the primary file. This will include log files as well.

7. The Attach As field defaults to the database name when it was detached. This can be edited.

Using the CREATE DATABASE command, the sp_attach_db procedure, or the sp_attach_single_file_db procedure, the database can also be attached. The CREATE DATABASE command is shown here:

```
CREATE DATABASE Test
    ON PRIMARY (Filename = 'C:\Database\Datafile\Test_Data.mdf')
    FOR ATTACH
```

FIGURE 3-5

Attaching a SQL
Server database

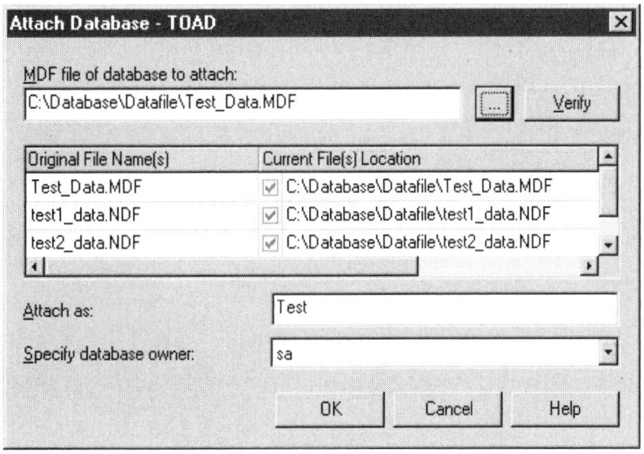

This syntax can be extended to list all the files. If all the datafiles are not listed in the CREATE DATABASE statement, they must be in the same directory as they were when detached. If they have been detached when in the C:\Database directory on the first machine, they would need to be in C:\Database directory on the next machine when attached. If the log file is not found in the same place as when detached, a new log file will be created in the same directory as the primary datafile. This is the only file that can be re-created during the attach procedure.

The sp_attach_db and sp_attach_single_file_db procedures work in a similar manner to the CREATE DATABASE command. If the log files or the supplemental datafiles are not in the same directory as when they were detached, the sp_attach_db procedure is the procedure to use. The reason for this is because the sp_attach_db procedure takes arguments for each of the files needed to attach the database. The sp_attach_single_file_db procedure only accepts the name of the primary file. Typically, the use of this procedure is limited to where the only file for the database is the primary file or where the file locations have remained the same as when detached. If any of the secondary files have been moved since the database was detached, the procedure fails, and the sp_attach_db procedure must be used. If the transaction log files are not available, a warning message is sent to the user, and the files are re-created. When moving databases between servers or to another drive on the same machine, the sp_attach_single_file_db procedure cannot be used. The syntax for sp_attach_single_file_db is listed here:

```
Exec sp_attach_single_file_db 'Test',
'C:\Database\datafile\Test_Data.mdf'
```

As with the sp_detach_db procedure, the first parameter is the database name. In this case, the second parameter is the file location for the primary file. With the sp_attach_db procedure, additional parameters are added for each file that needs to be attached.

After a database is created, it may be necessary to create new secondary files to expand the database. To create a new secondary file or to alter an existing file, the ALTER DATABASE command should be used, as shown here:

```
ALTER DATABASE Test
    ADD FILE 'C:\Database\Datafile\Test1_DATA3.ndf' TO FILEGROUP Test1
```

This statement adds a new datafile to the Test database. The new file is being added to the Test1 filegroup. The default filegroup is the primary filegroup unless specified otherwise. Some of the more common ALTER DATABASE commands are outlined in the following table:

Option Name	Description
REMOVE FILE <logical filename>	Removes references to the file and deletes the physical file associated with the logical file. The file must be empty to remove. The primary file cannot be removed.
ADD FILEGROUP <filegroup name>	Adds a filegroup with the name supplied in the filegroup name.
REMOVE FILEGROUP <filegroup name>	Removes the filegroup by name. Like REMOVE FILE, this can only be done if the filegroup is empty. The primary filegroup cannot be removed
MODIFY FILE <file definition>	Modifies an existing file. Can be used to alter the size of the file and the growth specifications. The file cannot be shrunk with this parameter.

Creating Tables

Now that the database is created, the first object that will be covered is the table object. There are two distinct types of tables. There are permanent tables, which represent the physical tables that are persistent within the database; and there are temporary tables, which are tables that reside in memory. Permanent tables are the standard tables that are documented in the logical design. These tables store data that needs to be retained for long-term storage. Temporary tables are generally used in programming and act as temporary containers for data processing. Among temporary tables, there are two separate flavors. The first are GLOBAL temporary tables. These tables reside in memory and can be shared across sessions in the database. This means that UserX can log in to the database and create a GLOBAL temporary table and UserY can later log in and access data in this temporary table as long as UserX has not terminated their connection or explicitly dropped the table. When UserX disconnects from the database, the GLOBAL temporary table is dropped only if it has been explicitly dropped with the DROP TABLE command or if no users have active connections that reference the table. This means that if another user has accessed the table, the table will not be dropped until that user has disconnected as well. The second type of temporary table is a LOCAL temporary table. These temporary tables can only be seen during the current, active connection. They are not shared across sessions and are dropped when the connection is dropped or the table is explicitly dropped. To define either a GLOBAL or LOCAL temporary table, the table name is prefixed with a single pound sign (#) for LOCAL temporary tables and double pound signs (##) for GLOBAL temporary tables. Permanent tables cannot include the pound sign in the name. All tables have the same rules as far as syntax. They can have up to 1,024 columns, follow the naming rules for identifiers, and the naming of columns in the tables must be unique. The only restriction on LOCAL temporary tables is that their names are limited to 116 characters. This is because the database appends a unique identifier on LOCAL temporary tables as an internal reference to limit the scope to the single connection.

When dealing with tables and objects associated with them, the syntax to use is the CREATE TABLE and ALTER TABLE commands. Anything that can be accomplished in an ALTER TABLE statement can also be implemented in the CREATE TABLE command. The difference is that the CREATE TABLE command creates a new table while the ALTER TABLE statement requires that the table already exist.

The first step is to look at the CREATE TABLE command for the Products table in Figure 3-1. This statement only includes required parameters to create this table. Later in this section, some of the optional parameters, including constraints, are explained.

```
CREATE TABLE Products (
    ProductID           int             NOT NULL IDENTITY (1,1),
    ProductName         nvarchar(40)    NOT NULL,
    SupplierID          int             NULL,
    CategoryID          int             NULL,
    QuantityPerUnit     nvarchar(20)    NULL,
    UnitPrice           money           NULL,
    UnitsInStock        smallint        NULL,
    UnitsOnOrder        smallint        NULL,
    ReorderLevel        smallint        NULL,
    Discontinued        bit             NOT NULL
    )
```

This syntax should look familiar to most individuals with a beginning level of database development, so let's begin by understanding what each line means. Of course, the initial line issues the command and identifies the table by name. In the example, the name is simply Products. If necessary, the user can include the fully qualified name, which includes the database name and owner or just the owner. In

SCENARIO & SOLUTION

You need to create a report that stores a list of product names, processes those rows, and later reports on the results.	Create a LOCAL temporary table to store the data, process the data as appropriate, and return the results. By placing this in a temporary table, the base data in the database is not altered.
A batch process needs to build a list of all products and calculate regional sales results. The batch process creates a separate process for each region to process rows for its region. In the end, all the regional results need to be sorted together and returned to the client.	Create a GLOBAL temporary table at the beginning of the batch process and have each of the regional processes place its data in the same table. In the end, the batch process can select all the rows and return the results.

the preceding example, the name would look something like this with the database name and owner:

```
CREATE TABLE Northwind.dbo.Products (...
```

By default, this information is the current database and the current database user for the active login, and is not required when creating the table.

exam
Ⓦatch

Many questions throughout the exam show a table or view including the fully qualified path. This is important for distributed queries and understanding this allows a user to select, insert, update, and delete from tables on remote servers and other databases on the same server.

The next lines are the column list for the table. This is a comma-separated list that stores a column definition for each column. A column definition contains the column name, datatype, and whether the column is NULL or NOT NULL. For the first column, the column name is ProductID, datatype is integer, and it acts as an IDENTITY column. The second column is ProductName with a datatype of nvarchar(40) and is NOT NULL. The columns continue until the end of the table.

The NULL/NOT NULL condition states whether the column is required or not. This should be determined in logical design. Columns that are NOT NULL never allow NULL values, while NULL columns allow NULL values. If this statement is left off, the default is to allow the column to be NULL. There is one notable exception.

The exception is when creating an IDENTITY column. Making a column an IDENTITY column carries the following restrictions and rules:

- The column is NOT NULL. The NOT NULL attribute is not required when specifying the column as IDENTITY, but it can exist.

- The column cannot have a default value applied to it; default values are covered more in depth in the next certification objective.

- An IDENTITY column allows datatypes that conform to the integer format. This includes the various sizes of integers (tinyint, smallint, int, and bigint), as well as other numeric values that conform to the integer format, such as numeric(p,0) and decimal(p,0); and the scale is zero so there are no numbers behind the decimal. This restricts the value to integers only. For more information on datatypes, as well as precision and scale, refer to Chapter 2.

- There can only be a single IDENTITY column per table.

There are also a number of properties and functions associated with the IDENTITY column that can be returned to the calling user. For a detailed list of these items, refer to Microsoft SQL Server Books Online.

Usage of the IDENTITY column requires the keyword IDENTITY along with two parameters. Using the preceding example, IDENTITY (1,1), the first parameter denotes the seed value, the value assigned to the column during the first insert, and the second is the increment amount, the amount that the seed is increased at each subsequent insert. The parameters are optional. If no parameters are provided, the defaults are (1,1). When using the parameters, both seed and increment values are required. Only providing one results in an error. For the example, the ProductID column could have been as in the following:

```
CREATE TABLE Products (
    ProductID   int   IDENTITY,
    ProductName ...
```

on the Job

IDENTITY columns are commonly used as surrogate primary keys to allow for easier implementation of foreign keys.

To assign a table to a specific filegroup in the database, the CREATE TABLE command is followed by the ON filegroup parameter. If the Products table needed to be created in the Test1 filegroup, the previous command would look something like this:

```
CREATE TABLE Products (
    ProductID int IDENTITY,
    ProductName ...
)
ON Test1
```

If this parameter is left off, the default is the database default filegroup. Each database can have a different default filegroup. In a new database, this is set to the primary filegroup, since this is the only filegroup that is assured of being present. To change the default filegroup, the following command can be executed in Query Analyzer:

```
ALTER DATABASE <database name>
MODIFY FILEGROUP <filegroup name> DEFAULT
```

This sets the default filegroup for the database to the new filegroup. From then on, any objects created without explicitly being created in another filegroup are created in this filegroup.

While the CREATE TABLE statement generates a table, any subsequent changes can be performed with the ALTER TABLE command. After time goes by, a column may need to be added, the datatype may need to be changed, or the column may need to be changed from NULL to NOT NULL, or vice versa. For example, say the preceding application required a new column to store a discount rate that is a whole number between 0 and 100. The following statement adds this column:

```
ALTER TABLE Products
    ADD DiscountRate int NULL
```

This example adds a nullable column named DiscountRate allowing values −2,147,483,648 through 2,147,483,647. A first step would be to limit the column to a Tinyint instead of an Int. The syntax to alter an existing column follows:

```
ALTER TABLE Products
    ALTER COLUMN DiscountRate tinyint NULL
```

This ALTER COLUMN statement can only be executed if the data satisfies the rules for implicit data conversion. So, if the column were altered from NULL to NOT NULL, all rows would be required to have a value for this column. If the column were converted from Int to Tinyint, as in the previous example, all the values in the column must be inclusive of 0 and 255. If the column were changed from Int to a different datatype such as Nvarchar or Nchar, it would need to be a type-safe conversion. Otherwise, the ALTER TABLE statement generates an error to indicate why the data cannot be converted. In the following certification objective, Ensuring Data Integrity, the column is further limited to values between 0 and 100.

SQL Server 2000 also allows a column to be dropped. To drop a column, the column must not be referenced in foreign keys or have other constraints applied to it. The ALTER TABLE command to drop a column is outlined here:

```
ALTER TABLE Products (
    DROP COLUMN DiscountRate
```

The datatype specification and NULL/NOT NULL constraint do not need to be specified. In fact, specifying these values results in a syntax error.

on the job

Since Enterprise Manager generates a script to apply changes made in the GUI, many developers use these scripts to apply the changes to other machines. These scripts rarely use an ALTER COLUMN or DROP COLUMN statement. They typically generate a temp table and move all the data to the table and move it back or rename the table. There are performance reasons not to move your data from table to table and back. There are three things to consider when deciding which way to go: how much time is available in the production environment for an upgrade, comfort in changing the script generated by Enterprise Manager, and personal preference of the developer.

CertCam 3-1

EXERCISE 3-1

Creating a Database and Implementing Tables

Create a database named **ExamNotes** with tables to store a list of students, tests they have taken, and whether they have passed.

   1. Open Query Analyzer and connect to the master database with a sysadmin account.

2. Execute a CREATE DATABASE command to define a database named **ExamNotes**. Create a supplemental file in a filegroup named **Success**.

3. From the database drop-down in Query Analyzer, change the database for the current connection to the newly created **ExamNotes** database.

4. Create a table named **Student** with columns of **StudentID** INT IDENTITY and **Name** Nvarchar(200) NOT NULL.

5. Create a table named **Exam** with columns of **ExamID** INT IDENTITY, **Name** Nchar(6), **Title** Nvarchar(50) NOT NULL, and **Description** Nvarchar(2000).

6. Since a student can take multiple tests, create a table **StudentExam** with columns **StudentID** and **ExamID** both as Int and NOT NULL. Additional columns should be **Passed** bit NOT NULL, and **DateTaken** Datetime NULL.

CERTIFICATION OBJECTIVE 3.03

Ensuring Data Integrity

During database development, there are many different methods for data to get into the database. With the growth of business-to-business support and the portability of data in XML files and other forms of data exports, a DBA is required to put certain restrictions on the data that is allowed to be inserted into the database. These restrictions ensure data integrity across the database so that when reports or other applications retrieve data from the database, everything is consistent. In the end, a database is a repository for data that needs to be organized and follow some rules.

Data integrity comes in multiple forms. There is entity integrity, domain integrity, referential integrity, and user-defined integrity. These can be implemented with constraints as well as triggers.

Implementing Constraints

A table is comprised of various columns, and those columns can have certain attributes that must be enforced when inserting, updating, and deleting data in order to ensure data integrity. These attributes or rules are enforced through an object called a *constraint.* These constraints are stored in the database and associated with the table and column that the constraint affects. The five types of constraints are UNIQUE KEY, PRIMARY KEY, FOREIGN KEY, NOT NULL, and CHECK constraints. Each type of constraint follows the basic framework outlined as follows:

```
ALTER TABLE <Table Name>
ADD CONSTRAINT <Constraint Name>
<Constraint Type> <Constraint Definition>
```

UNIQUE KEY Constraint

When a table has a column or columns that identify each row uniquely, those columns can be implemented as a UNIQUE KEY constraint. If a key has multiple columns, it is referred to as a compound key. A UNIQUE KEY constraint allows for one or more of the columns in the key to be NULL. The rule here is that NULL is treated like any other value and must be unique unless it is part of a key with multiple columns, and then the combination would need to be unique. A table can have multiple unique keys. Using the model in Figure 3-1, the following would be an implementation of a unique key on the SupplierID/ProductName column combination:

```
ALTER TABLE Products
   ADD CONSTRAINT UK_Products
       UNIQUE (SupplierID, ProductName)
```

This constraint enforces that any supplier cannot have duplicate product names in the Product table. Some important notes from the preceding statement are that the constraint type designation cannot include the KEY keyword, and the constraint definition is a comma-separated list of the columns involved in the constraint. A unique key implicitly creates an index with the same name as the constraint to assist with performance. The maximum number of UNIQUE constraints is set by the limit of indexes allowed on the table, which is 249 nonclustered indexes and 1 clustered index. The difference between nonclustered and clustered indexes is discussed in Chapter 6. A UNIQUE constraint cannot be created without producing the index.

PRIMARY KEY Constraint

An extended version of the UNIQUE KEY constraint is the PRIMARY KEY constraint. The difference between a unique key and a primary key is that the primary key consists of NOT NULL columns and there is only a single primary key allowed on a table. A primary key also implicitly creates an index. To implement this type of constraint, follow this simple example that implements the PRIMARY KEY constraint for the Products table found in Figure 3-1.

```
ALTER TABLE Products
    ADD CONSTRAINT PK_Products
        PRIMARY KEY (ProductID)
```

The constraint type for a primary key is PRIMARY KEY. PRIMARY alone gives a syntax error. A primary key can also be a compound key.

FOREIGN KEY Constraint

A third type of constraint is the FOREIGN KEY constraint. This constraint enforces relationships in the database. A foreign key is a column that refers to a unique or primary key in another table. Using the Products table from Figure 3-1, the foreign key from Suppliers to Products, represented by the SupplierID column, can be implemented with the following command:

```
ALTER TABLE Products
ADD CONSTRAINT FK_Products_Suppliers
FOREIGN KEY (Suppliers) REFERENCES Suppliers (ID)
```

The constraint definition in this case is a little more involved than just listing the column. First, the column list in the child table is included in parentheses. If this is a compound key, both columns are included in the list. The keyword, REFERENCES, is used to separate the child column list from the parent table. Following the parent table, in parentheses, the parent table column list is included. The order of the columns in the column list for the parent table must match the order of the column list in the child table.

While foreign keys do not implicitly create indexes, they are often the first candidates for an index. The biggest reason for this is that foreign keys are used in the JOIN condition of SELECT statements. By indexing these columns, the JOIN conditions have an index to reference when processing the statement, rather than full table scans. For more information regarding indexes and their performance benefits, see Chapter 6.

One of the benefits of SQL Server 2000 is the ability to CASCADE DELETE. In most cases, the foreign key acts as protection against deleting a parent row if it is being referenced by a child row. There are occasions, however, when the child rows are there for the sole purpose of further defining the parent entity, and serve no additional purpose. These dependent rows should be removed when the parent is deleted, but the application does not really need to know that these rows exist. In these cases, the user wants to issue one DELETE statement and wants all the rows to be deleted. This is the reason that databases commonly have a CASCADE or RESTRICT clause, which defines whether the DELETE of the parent should automatically CASCADE down to the child rows of the foreign key and delete them along with the parent row or whether the deletion of a parent row should be prevented if it is referenced by the foreign key. The implementation of a CASCADE or RESTRICT is done as an optional parameter in the constraint syntax. The default in SQL Server 2000 is to RESTRICT on delete. Figure 3-6 shows a pair of tables that have a dependent relationship. The DepartmentHoliday table exists only to store information for the Department table. There is no reason to prevent the deletion of a department because there are holidays associated with it. In this case, it would be better to remove these rows automatically.

The following statement implements the relationship between the Department and DepartmentHoliday tables as a CASCADE DELETE:

```
ALTER TABLE DepartmentHoliday
   ADD CONSTRAINT FK_DepartmentHoliday_Department
   FOREIGN KEY (DepartmentID) REFERENCES Department (ID) ON
DELETE CASCADE
```

With this attribute turned on, the application can delete the Department and the DepartmentHoliday rows with a single statement.

The DELETE action is not the only occasion when the foreign keys will automatically affect child rows. SQL Server 2000 allows for the update of the parent row to cascade down to the child rows. The syntax is similar to the DELETE CASCADE statement with the replacing of DELETE with the UPDATE keyword. So, if the primary key is updated in the parent row, the child rows that reference the primary key are also updated. This does not carry over to other columns. It is only the key column in the parent table that triggers the update.

FIGURE 3-6

Tables for
CASCADE
DELETE example

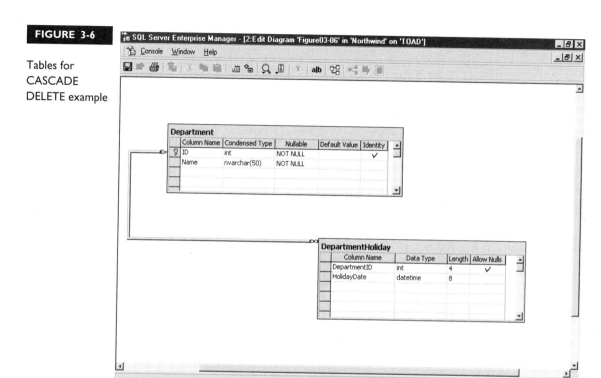

CHECK Constraint

The fourth type of column constraint is the CHECK constraint. These constraints are very useful when enforcing business rules on the data being placed in the tables. These constraints restrict the data allowed in the columns. An example from Figure 3-1 would be on the UnitsInStock column. In order to ensure that negative values never get into this column, a CHECK constraint can be implemented.

```
ALTER TABLE Products
   ADD CONSTRAINT DF_Products_UnitsInStock
      CHECK (UnitsInStock >= 0 or UnitsInStock IS NULL)
```

This constraint definition is merely the column and what values are allowed. While this constraint is on a numeric column, any logical operation that evaluates to a True or False value can be implemented in a CHECK constraint.

NOT NULL Constraint

The fifth type of constraint that can be placed on a table or column is the NOT NULL constraint. This constraint is perhaps the most straightforward of all the constraints, in that its sole purpose is to determine whether a column can contain NULL values. In a way, it is a simple form of the CHECK constraint. These constraints are not named or created in the same way as the other constraints. They are more closely referred to as an attribute of a column. In fact, this constraint does not use the ADD CONSTRAINT syntax that has been used for the other constraints. This constraint is implemented when the table or column is created. If the user decides that the column should be NOT NULL after the column has been created, the ALTER COLUMN parameter is used to add this. The following example adds the NOT NULL constraint to the Discontinued column of the Products table in Figure 3-1:

```
ALTER TABLE Products
     ALTER COLUMN Discontinued bit NOT NULL
```

Default Constraint

Default constraints insert a specified value if a value is not provided. If the INSERT statement explicitly states that a NULL is being inserted, a NULL will be inserted and override the default. Given the table in Figure 3-7, if the following INSERT statement is executed, col1 has a value of 1 and col2 has a value of NULL:

```
Insert into Test1 (col1, col2) values (1,NULL)
```

The row for the next INSERT statement has values of 1 for both columns:

```
Insert into Test1 (col1) values (1)
```

As stated here, the reason for this is that the NULL is expressly defined in the value list. For more information, see Chapter 5 where the INSERT statement is outlined. The syntax for a default constraint is in the following ALTER TABLE command:

```
ALTER TABLE Products
   ADD CONSTRAINT DF_Products_UnitPrice
   DEFAULT 0 for UnitPrice
```

This statement adds a default constraint on the UnitPrice column of $0 when a UnitPrice is not given. The constraint definition gives the value to be used, followed by the FOR keyword, and then the column to which the default applies. A default constraint can be applied to any type of datatype column except for IDENTITY and

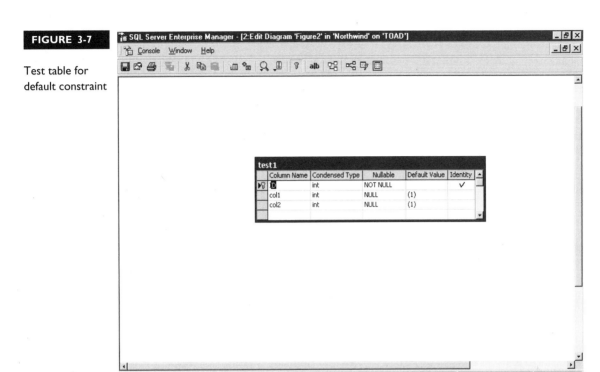

FIGURE 3-7

Test table for default constraint

timestamp columns. The reason for this is that the values for these columns are already being generated by the database and the default cannot override that action.

on the **Job**

While it is more convenient to include foreign keys and other constraints in the CREATE TABLE statement, converting customer data presents a significant obstacle to this implementation. Often it becomes necessary to drop or disable the foreign keys at the beginning of the script and then create or reenable the foreign keys at the end of the script. This implementation allows the data to be converted without running into constraint errors that stop the script.

All of these constraints can be added through the ALTER TABLE commands given in the previous examples, or they can be included in the original CREATE

TABLE command. The following statement is the CREATE TABLE command from the beginning of the objective with the constraints added:

```
CREATE TABLE Products (
    ProductID         int             IDENTITY (1,1)
        CONSTRAINT PK_Products PRIMARY KEY,
    ProductName       nvarchar(40) NOT NULL
        CONSTRAINT UK_Products UNIQUE ,
    SupplierID        int             NULL
        CONSTRAINT FK_Products_Suppliers
            FOREIGN KEY REFERENCES Suppliers(ID),
    CategoryID        int             NULL
        CONSTRAINT FK_Products_Categories
            FOREIGN KEY REFERENCES Categories(ID),
    QuantityPerUnit   nvarchar(20) NULL
        CONSTRAINT CK_Products_QuantityPerUnit
            CHECK (QuantityPerUnit >= 0 OR QuantityPerUnit IS NULL),
    UnitPrice         money           NULL
        CONSTRAINT DF_Products_UnitPrice DEFAULT 0,
    UnitsInStock      smallint        NULL,
    UnitsOnOrder      smallint        NULL,
    ReorderLevel      smallint        NULL,
    Discontinued      bit             NOT NULL
)
```

Some important differences in the syntax for these constraints are that the column name is not repeated in the constraint definition, the constraint and constraint name are optional, and the NOT NULL constraint is implicitly created as part of the attributes for the Discontinued column. If the constraint name is not provided, SQL Server provides a name.

on the Job

Many development shops have naming standards for the database, but they stop at the table or column level. Naming standards that extend to the database objects, such as constraints, are crucial when dealing with production environments. Since every machine may provide a different name for a constraint, it becomes difficult to remove or alter a column if the constraint name is not known. This was even more important in older versions of SQL Server.

Another method of enforcing data integrity is through the use of triggers. Using triggers, the DBA can enforce business rules that cannot be defined by the constraints. For more information about triggers, including when and how they work, refer to Chapter 4.

CertCam 3-2

EXERCISE 3-2

Adding Data Integrity to the ExamNotes Database

1. Open Query Analyzer and connect to the ExamNotes database that was created in Exercise 3-1.

2. Create a primary key on the Student table using the StudentID column.

3. Create a foreign key between the Student table and the StudentExam table using the StudentID column between the tables.

4. Create a primary key on the Exam table using the ExamID column.

5. Create a foreign key between the Exam table and the StudentExam table using the ExamID column between the tables.

6. Create a default constraint on the StudentExam.Passed column to make the default 1 (True).

7. Modify the DateTaken column so that it no longer accepts NULL values. Assume that there are no rows in the table with NULL values.

CERTIFICATION SUMMARY

This chapter took a look at transforming the logical design into a physical database. The database itself must be created and files must be created to store the information. After creating the database, the tables can be created. This chapter explains the use of the CREATE TABLE command. For subsequent changes to the table, the ALTER TABLE command allows a DBA to do anything that could have been done on the initial CREATE TABLE command.

While the table is the repository for the data, the constraints and triggers are what make sure the data makes sense. By looking at the various constraints found in SQL Server, the methods of enforcing data integrity are reviewed. Whether it is enforcing a NOT NULL constraint on a required column or performing a CASCADE DELETE on a foreign key, this chapter shows what these constraints mean and when they should be used.

TWO-MINUTE DRILL

Planning for Storage Management

❑ There must be one and only one primary datafile.

❑ Data and transaction logs are never in the same files.

❑ A filegroup cannot be shared between two databases.

❑ Tables and indexes should be used when estimating the size of the database.

❑ Unlimited file growth is only limited by the operating system and the physical disk capacity.

Implementing the Physical Database

❑ The model database acts as a template database. When creating a database, the model database provides the default settings and creates the same objects as found in the model database.

❑ GLOBAL temporary tables can be shared between sessions while LOCAL temporary tables cannot.

❑ If a log file is not found when attaching a database, a new log file is automatically created.

❑ A table can be stored in a specific filegroup if the ON filegroup parameter is specified.

❑ Fully qualified object names include the database name, object owner, and the object name.

Ensuring Data Integrity

❑ Foreign keys must be associated to a unique or primary key in the parent table.

❑ Default constraints only work when the column is not referenced in the insert. If a NULL is explicitly inserted, the default is not used.

❑ When using a CASCADE DELETE, the deletion of the parent rows automatically deletes the child rows.

❑ Constraints can be embedded in the CREATE TABLE command. As long as the parent table exists, a FOREIGN KEY constraint can even be created.

❑ Primary and unique keys generate an index automatically.

SELF TEST

The following questions will help you measure your understanding of the material presented in this chapter. Read all the choices carefully because there might be more than one correct answer. Choose all correct answers for each question.

Planning for Storage Management

1. What should be taken into account when estimating database growth?

   A. Tables

   B. Indexes

   C. Number of views that are implemented

   D. Estimated increase in the number of rows

2. A database on the server is returning errors stating that the filegroup is full. The files in that filegroup are set to grow automatically by the default of 10 percent. How would this be corrected?

   A. Clear the stored procedure cache and reboot the server.

   B. Restart the SQL Server services and turn single-user mode off for those databases.

   C. Remove unneeded files from server, install a new disk drive, move files to a new physical disk, or shrink database files to allow for more space to be allocated.

   D. Disconnect active connections and restore database to last backup.

3. What database term signifies multiple files being logically defined as a single unit?

   A. RAID array

   B. Filegroup

   C. File directory

   D. Active Directory

4. How many log files can be contained in a single filegroup?

   A. 1,024

   B. 512

   C. 256

   D. 0

5. Which is/are valid recovery model(s) for a database?

   A. Complex

   B. Simple

   C. Bulk-insert

   D. Full

Implementing the Physical Database

6. What is the name of the file that is created by default as part of a database?

   A. Default

   B. First

   C. Alpha

   D. Primary

7. What syntax is used to create a new database?

   A. COPY DATABASE

   B. exec sp_attach_db

   C. CREATE DATABASE

   D. MODIFY DATABASE

8. What is the maximum number of columns that can be on a single table?

   A. 512

   B. 1,024

   C. 256

   D. 255

9. Which of the following would be the fully qualified name for the Product table that is being stored in the Test database and a database owner of dbo?

   A. Test.dbo.Product

   B. dbo.Product

   C. dbo.Test.Product

   D. dbo.Product.Test

10. How is a database detached?

    A. sp_detach_single_file

    B. sp_detach_db

    C. sp_move_database

    D. Choose the Detach Database option from All Tasks.

11. When attaching a database, what happens if there is no log file in the directory that the log file was detached from?

    A. A message is returned to the user stating that the file cannot be found and the attach fails.

    B. While attaching, a search is done on the directory recursively, and, if not found, an error is sent and the attach action terminates.

    C. A new transaction log will be created in the same directory that the original transaction log was located before the database was detached.

    D. A new transaction log is created in the same directory as the primary file.

12. Which is a type of temporary table?

    A. Session

    B. LOCAL

    C. Database

    D. GLOBAL

Ensuring Data Integrity

13. The Product table has a relationship to the Manufacturer table on the ManufacturerID column. How can this foreign key be implemented?

    A.
```
CREATE TABLE Product (
ProductID int NOT NULL,
ProductName varchar(50) NOT NULL,
ManufacturerID int NULL CONSTRAINT FK_Product_Manufacturer REFERENCES
Manufacturer (ID)
)
```

    B.
```
ALTER TABLE Product ADD CONSTRAINT FK_Product_Manufacturer FOREIGN KEY
(ManufacturerID) REFERENCES Manufacturer (ID)
```

C. `ALTER TABLE Product ADD CONSTRAINT FK_Product_Manufacturer REFERENCES Manufacturer`

D. `ALTER TABLE Product ADD FK_Product_Manufacturer REFERENCES Manufacturer (ID)`

14. Which type of data integrity cannot be implemented with an ALTER TABLE command?

A. NOT NULL constraint

B. CHECK constraint

C. Table trigger

D. FOREIGN KEY constraint

15. A table in the database has been in production for a few months. A new column needs to be added. The column cannot allow NULL values and has a default of 0. How can this be done?

A. Add the column along with a default constraint of 0.

B. Add the column to the table, update the values to 0, add a default constraint of 0, and then alter the column so that it is NOT NULL.

C. Add the column and add a CHECK constraint to ensure that it only allows 0.

D. In a single statement, add the column along with a default constraint of 0 with the WITH VALUES parameter to populate the existing rows.

16. When a foreign key is implemented, what must be present in the Parent table to enforce the key?

A. Unique key

B. All the columns must be NOT NULL

C. Primary key

D. Default constraint

17. If there is a relationship between the Product and Supplier tables that requires that products that belong to a specific supplier be deleted if the supplier is deleted, how could this be implemented?

A. `ALTER TABLE Supplier`
   `ADD CONSTRAINT FK_Product_Supplier ProductID REFERENCES Product (ID)`

B. `ALTER TABLE Product`
   `ADD CONSTRAINT FK_Product_Supplier SupplierID REFERENCES Supplier (ID)`

C. `ALTER TABLE Product`
`ADD CONSTRAINT FK_Product_Supplier SupplierID REFERENCES Supplier (ID)`
`ON DELETE CASCADE`

D. `ALTER TABLE Supplier`
`ADD CONSTRAINT FK_Product_Supplier ProductID REFERENCES Product (ID) ON`
`DELETE CASCADE`

LAB QUESTION

Company X has decided to upgrade all their database server hardware. They want to bring in new hardware and move all the databases to the new servers. Currently, all databases consist of a single datafile and one log file. The new machines have multiple physical disk drives that need to be utilized. Define a thorough project plan to handle the migration of the databases and the new implementation.

SELF TEST ANSWERS

Planning for Storage Management

1. ☑ **A, B,** and **D.** These items take up physical space on disk.
   ☒ **C.** Views look at data that is in the tables. They do not actually store any information on disk. Some views do allow indexes to be implemented on them, but it is still the index that stores the data, not the view.

2. ☑ **C.** When individual databases no longer accept connections, the most likely reason is that the drive is full. While the file is set to automatically grow, the growth cannot take place because of lack of disk space.
   ☒ **A.** This solution may work temporarily, but it does not really solve the problem. **B** is incorrect because once connections start again, the first action that requires an insert or update and the file to grow will trigger the same problem. **D** would be totally unnecessary and would only delay the problem until the datafile needed to grow again.

3. ☑ **B.** Filegroup is the term used for a group of files being administered together.
   ☒ **A** is incorrect. RAID array refers to hard drive configurations. **C** is incorrect. A file directory is the hierarchy of the file system. **D** is incorrect. Active Directory is a directory service in Windows 2000.

4. ☑ **D.** Transaction log files cannot be members of filegroups.
   ☒ **A, B,** and **C** are incorrect because they are greater than 0 and a transaction log cannot be a member of filegroup.

5. ☑ **B** and **D.** The third recovery mode is bulk-logged.
   ☒ **A** and **C.** Bulk-insert is not the name of the third recovery mode. It is actually bulk-logged.

Implementing the Physical Database

6. ☑ **D.** A database always creates a primary file. The primary file always exists in a primary filegroup.
   ☒ **A** is incorrect because there is a default filegroup, but it is not named default. **B** and **C** are incorrect because the file that is created is the primary file.

7. ☑ **B** and **C.** If the datafile is still available from a database, a new database can be created by attaching those files (sp_attach_db).

☒   **A** is incorrect. There is no such Transact-SQL command. **D** is incorrect. There is no such Transact-SQL command. To modify the database, the ALTER DATABASE command is used. Also, the database must already exist to issue this command.

8. ☑   **B.** The maximum number of columns is 1,024.

      ☒   **A, C,** and **D** are incorrect because the maximum number of columns for a table is 1,024.

9. ☑   **A.** The proper order for declaring the fully qualified name of a table is the DatabaseName.OwnerName.TableName. Queries across machines can also put the machine name in front. It always goes from broad to specific in object naming.

      ☒   **B, C,** and **D** are incorrect. These are all either out of order or incomplete.

10. ☑   **B** and **D.** These two options will detach the data and log files from the database and will remove references to the database in Enterprise Manager.

      ☒   **A.** There is no such command. There is the sp_attach_single_file command, though. This allows for individuals to place their files in the same relative position on the disk drive and the attach will find them. **C** is incorrect because it is not a Transact-SQL command.

11. ☑   **D.** If there is no log file specified or found in the default location of where the file used to be, a new file is created in the directory where the primary file is. This even overrides the default log file parameter set for the database.

      ☒   **C** is incorrect, because if the file is in the original directory and not referenced in the ATTACH command, the file will be reused. If it needs to create a new one, it will be in the same directory as the primary file. **A** and **B** are incorrect because the file is created and used with no further action from the user or database.

12. ☑   **B** and **D.** Local temporary tables provide temporary storage of data in a table structure without actually storing the information long term on disk. GLOBAL temporary tables do the same thing, but allow other sessions to access the data in the temporary table.

      ☒   **A** is incorrect. While the LOCAL temporary table is confined to the session, the table is not referred to as a Session temp table. **C** is incorrect. While the GLOBAL temporary table is available to the database, the table is not referred to as a Database temp table.

Ensuring Data Integrity

13. ☑ **A and B.** The foreign key can be implemented either during creation or after the fact. The downside to implementing this during creation is that the Manufacturer table would have to already exist for the table to be created.

    ☒ **C** is incorrect because it is missing the parent table column list in the definition. **D** is incorrect because it is missing the CONSTRAINT keyword in the definition.

14. ☑ **C.** Triggers are objects that are created with a CREATE TRIGGER command. This is discussed in more detail in Chapter 4

    ☒ **A.** NOT NULL constraints may not be implemented as an ADD CONSTRAINT syntax, but they are implemented as part of the column definition or when altering a column. **B** and **D** are incorrect because they are implemented with the ADD CONSTRAINT syntax. They can also be implemented as part of the CREATE TABLE syntax as outlined in the chapter.

15. ☑ **B and D.** The column can be added as a single statement, as listed in option D, or can be done in steps, as in B.

    ☒ **A** would seem to work, but it would need to explicitly state that the constraint was being added WITH VALUES as in **D**. **C** is incorrect because a CHECK constraint limits the values going into the column. It does not provide default values.

16. ☑ **A and C.** A foreign key must reference a unique row in the parent table. To do this, it references against a unique or primary key.

    ☒ **B** is incorrect because in compound keys, one or more of the columns can be NULL and used in a unique key, which, in turn, would be used in the foreign key as the reference. **D** is incorrect because default constraints only populate columns when not specified in the INSERT statement. They are not used in foreign-key constraint implementation.

17. ☑ **C.** The foreign key is relating the Product.SupplierID column to the Supplier.ID column successfully. The ON DELETE CASCADE enforces that the child (Product) records are deleted when the parent (Supplier) is deleted.

    ☒ **A** and **D** are both incorrect. Since Product would be considered the child table, the foreign key would be on the Product table, not the Supplier table. **B** is incorrect because the syntax is correct for the relationship, but it will not CASCADE DELETE. The default action is NO ACTION, which prevents deletes rather than cascading.

LAB ANSWER

When beginning to put together a plan, the maintenance window is a very important. Since we want to totally move the databases, we can detach each database in the SQL Server instance on the old machine. Mirror the file system from the old machine on the new machine. This way the C:\Database\Data directory still holds all the primary files. Now that all the primary files are in place, run sp_attach_single_file to re-create the databases. Since there is only one primary file, there is no need to run the sp_attach_db. Also, be sure to do full database backups before the move so that the log files do not have to be moved as well. The sp_attach_single_file will create a new log file for each database.

Now that the databases are created on the new machine, plan on creating multiple files for each database on the separate physical disks. Then create a filegroup to group the database datafiles. Remember that datafiles and filegroups cannot be shared between databases. Set the default filegroup to the new filegroups.

4

Programming Business Logic

Implementing Advanced Database Objects

Databases can be implemented as a simple repository of information. With proper maintenance, the data should remain available and protected for years and years. While this may serve the purpose of many environments, additional functionality is required for others. This functionality may include providing reports, processing the data, and enforcing business rules on the data in the database. To accomplish these goals, SQL Server offers some objects in the database other than just tables and indexes.

These objects include views, stored procedures, triggers, rules, defaults, and—new to SQL Server 2000—user-defined functions. These objects can resolve any number of issues that come up when developing a database. This objective deals primarily with creating and using these objects. Chapter 5 covers Transact SQL, or T-SQL, more in-depth and expands upon what can be included in these objects.

Views

The first of these objects that are discussed are views. Sometimes referred to as virtual tables, views provide an interface for users to retrieve data in a format that is different than the base tables. The information is not stored a second time on disk for the view; instead, the view is executed and the data is stored in memory while being used. In many respects; a view can be treated like a table. One can reference a view in a SELECT statement, an INSERT, UPDATE, or DELETE statement can be run against it; and a view can be referenced in another view, procedure, or function. Of course, there are restrictions that also may apply to whether the view can be involved in these actions. The exceptions and rules are outlined next.

When implementing views, the syntax is as simple or complex as the SELECT statement it contains. As with most objects, a view has a declaration and a definition. The view declaration follows the normal CREATE <OBJECT TYPE> <OBJECT NAME> format. Here is an example of the declaration for the TestView view:

```
CREATE VIEW TestView AS
```

In this case, the object type is VIEW and the object name is followed by the AS keyword. Many database objects have the AS keyword to separate the declaration and the definition.

Like a table name, the view name can be fully qualified and would include dot notation for the database name and owner of the object.

In the preceding example, the view name is provided and little else. This is not always the case. A common item in a view declaration is a column list. The column list is a comma-separated list contained in parentheses directly after the view name. This list provides the name for each column in the select list. The column list provides names based on relative position in the select list and does not look for column aliases or other naming in the select list for hints. While this is optional, it is used most often for more complex view definitions that may include UNION statements, computed columns, or a column name represented more than once in the SELECT.

Another part of the view declaration is defining any view attributes. A view can have one or more of three attributes. The attribute name follows a WITH keyword and is between the AS keyword and the definition of the view. The first view attribute is ENCRYPTION. When specifying this attribute, the view definition is encrypted when selected from the system tables. This also prevents the view from being published during replication. Replication is discussed in the next certification objective. SCHEMABINDING is the next view attribute. SCHEMABINDING actually binds the view to the tables and columns that are involved in the view. The result here is that if a table is involved in a view with SCHEMABINDING, it cannot be altered or dropped without causing an error. To resolve the error, the view must remove the references to the affected columns or tables, or the view can be re-created without SCHEMABINDING. To specify SCHEMABINDING, all objects in the SELECT statement must contain the object's owner before the object name. The final type of view attribute is VIEW_METADATA. VIEW_METADATA returns information to the client that allows the client to specify what the source tables are for the view.

After these attributes have been declared for the view, the view definition is provided. In the case of a view, the definition is a SELECT statement. The SELECT statement can contain multiple tables, other views, computed columns, aggregates, and any other syntax that is normally found in a SELECT statement. The syntax for a SELECT statement is covered more in-depth in Chapter 5. A simple example of a view is shown here:

```
CREATE VIEW EmployeePhoneList
WITH ENCRYPTION, SCHEMABINDING
AS
SELECT FirstName, LastName, HomePhone, Extension
FROM dbo.Employees
```

In this example, which uses the Northwind database installed with SQL Server 2000, the EmployeePhoneList view selects four columns from the Employees table. Since the view has the SCHEMABINDING attribute set, the table must include the table owner—in this case, dbo. When a user selects from this table, they can view only the four columns defined in the SELECT. This restricts the remaining columns from viewing by the user. This restriction of viewable columns is a major benefit of views when implementing security for the database. If the Employees table stored a yearly salary, not everyone should have the ability to view that kind of sensitive information, while the phone numbers are less sensitive. Security implementations and the use of roles in that implementation are covered in more depth in Chapter 8.

The first topic that is discussed is whether the view is updatable without using an INSTEAD OF trigger. For a view to be updatable, it must follow these rules:

- Cannot contain aggregates in the select list.

- Statement cannot include operators such as DISTINCT, GROUP BY, TOP, and UNION. These operators have the effect of limiting or combining rows that would otherwise be a part of the SELECT statement.

- Statement must contain at least one table and must contain a column selected from that table.

- No column in the select list can be a concatenation or other derivation of other columns.

After the SELECT statement has been included, the view can contain one more item. The WITH CHECK OPTION option can be added to the end of the view. This restricts the user from updating the view in such a way that it would remove the row from the view. So, if the WHERE clause in the SELECT statement had a restriction to only include WHERE name = 'X', the name column could not be updated to a value other than 'X'.

FROM THE CLASSROOM

Coding Practices in the Database

The following topics cover coding in and for the database. In the day-to-day duties of a database administrator, this form of coding may come up only rarely. Despite the rather infrequent use, learning how to write efficient and correct procedures and functions is extremely important. If one of these objects is not coded and tested well, the code can continue to run—causing runaway processes and potentially altering data that cannot be corrected or restored.

For those of you with a programming background, the following topics should serve as a refresher. The basic principles are all there from procedural development. The code is executed one line at a time, and conditional statements define the path the procedure takes. Unlike Java and C++, T-SQL does not support object-oriented principles such as inheritance, overloading, and type casting.

—Craig Robinson

Stored Procedures

Stored procedures, or procedures, are blocks of T-SQL code stored in the database that can be called and executed from an external source, and can accept zero or more parameters. These parameters can be INPUT or OUTPUT parameters. A stored procedure can also return a single integer value that can be used to indicate the state of the procedure. The source can be an ODBC client, a procedure, a trigger, or any other calling client that has execute permissions on the procedure. To have a returned value other than an integer, user-defined functions should be used.

exam
ⓦatch

While stored procedures are not designed to have return values besides integers, there are ways to return a result set to a client. If a SELECT statement is issued in the body of the procedure, the calling client can process those rows. Methods for accessing these results are outside of the scope of test 70-229. They are related to client-side programming tools such as ADO in Visual Basic.

Stored procedures can accept zero or more parameters. The maximum number of parameters is 2,100. There are two types of parameters that can be used in a stored procedure. They are INPUT and OUTPUT parameters. INPUT parameters allow the calling agent to pass in a value for the stored procedure to use when executing the procedure. An OUTPUT parameter is a value that is set inside the stored procedure and the calling agent can access the value after the stored procedure has completed. To specify a parameter, a name, datatype, and parameter type must be set. INPUT parameters do not require any keyword, since all parameters are assumed to be INPUT. The keyword for OUTPUT parameters is OUTPUT. The OUTPUT keyword follows the name and datatype of the parameter. In certain situations, a parameter may not be defined by the calling application. In these cases, a default can be assigned to INPUT parameters. The default follows the datatype and is an equal sign followed by the value. This value can be anything that would be consistent with the datatype declared for the parameter.

Now that parameters have been discussed, the CREATE PROCEDURE syntax can be covered. The following example declares a procedure with three parameters. The first is an INPUT parameter with no default value. The second is another INPUT parameter that contains a default value. The third value is an OUTPUT variable:

```
CREATE PROCEDURE HelloWorld
@name varchar(80),
@location varchar(80) = NULL,
@date_executed datetime OUTPUT
AS
```

Naming of parameters follows the standards of naming variables. In the statement above, the parameters are separated by a comma; and when all the parameters are listed, they are followed by the AS keyword. Unlike the column list in the view declaration, the parameters are not enclosed in parentheses. When calling this procedure, the parameters can be referenced by relative position or by name. The following code calls the HelloWorld procedure. The first example calls the procedure using named parameters while the second is using the relative position:

```
EXECUTE HelloWorld @location = 'Minnesota', @name = 'Charlie
Brown',
    @date_executed = @return_value OUTPUT

EXECUTE HelloWorld 'Charlie Brown', 'Minnesota', @return_value
OUTPUT
```

In the two examples, the second parameter, @location, could have been left out. The procedure would still work because a default value was specified in the procedure declaration. If a default is not provided, the parameter would be required and an error would occur if the second parameter were not provided. In the first example, the @location parameter could just be left out and the default would take care of it. If the second parameter were left out of the second example, the third parameter would have to be a named parameter. The procedure call does not know that a parameter has been intentionally left out of the middle of the list. Only the final parameter can be left out without changing to named parameters. This is another advantage of using named parameters. If new parameters with defaults are added, the calls to the procedure do not require an update. The output parameter is explained later in this section.

The definition of a stored procedure can be any block of Transact-SQL code that needs to be executed. Typically, the variables needed for the stored procedure are kept at the beginning of the procedure. This is not required, though. Using the DECLARE statement, a variable can be placed anywhere in the procedure, as long as it is declared before the variable is referenced by the executing code. For the HelloWorld example earlier, the procedure body might look something like this:

```
CREATE PROCEDURE HelloWorld
@name varchar(80),
@location varchar(80) = NULL,
@date_executed datetime OUTPUT
AS
DECLARE @print_string varchar(200)
DECLARE @Return int

SET @date_executed = GetDate()

IF @location is NULL
   SET @print_string = 'Hello '+@name
   SET @Return = 1
ELSE
   SET @print_string = 'Hello '+@name+', welcome to '+@location
   SET @Return = 0

PRINT @print_string
RETURN @Return
```

Using the DECLARE statement, the variable is named and the datatype, including length, is specified. As with all local variables in SQL Server, the variable name must be preceded by a single @ symbol. The SET command assigns a value to a variable. The @date_executed variable is assigned a value using the SET command. The next step is to check whether the @location variable is NULL or not. If it is NULL, the procedure takes one path. The ELSE statement covers all conditions not contained in the initial IF statement. The PRINT statement at the end prints the string placed in the @print_string variable that was set in the IF...ELSE block. The PRINT statement does not return values to the calling procedure. It prints out to the Query Analyzer results pane. Print is used primarily for debugging, since it does not output to the client except in Query Analyzer.

on the
Job
SQL Server 2000 has implemented a debugger in Query Analyzer that can be very helpful in development of stored procedures and user-defined functions. SQL Server Books Online has more information about configuring and using the debugger for testing code.

The procedure also declares a variable to pass back as a return value. In the example, the variable is set depending on the execution path. If the @location variable is NULL, the @return variable is set to 1. Otherwise, @location is set to 0. The final line in the procedure returns this variable back to the procedure.

One of the statements in the preceding example is setting the @date_executed variable. This is the OUTPUT parameter. An OUTPUT parameter can be used in stored procedures to allow a procedure to pass back a value to the calling client. Continuing the HelloWorld example, the following code uses this OUTPUT parameter:

```
Declare @output_value datetime
Declare @return_value int
execute @return_value = HelloWorld 'Charlie  Brown','Minnesota',@output_value OUTPUT
print @output_value
print @return_value
```

If this code is executed in Query Analyzer, the result is the current date and time being printed, and the return value, @return_value, of the procedure being printed follows. The first line declares the variable that the OUTPUT parameter is being assigned to in the block. The next line declares the variable that is returned from the procedure. The third line executes the stored procedure and puts in the variable that was defined in the third parameter. Just like during the procedure declaration, the OUTPUT keyword must follow the parameter, including in the call. The result is that the @outputvalue is set in the procedure by the SET @date_executed = GetDate() line in the procedure. The @outputvalue variable can be referenced in subsequent commands and operations.

A return value can be set as an integer. When the value needs to be returned, the RETURN keyword is followed by the integer to pass back. User-defined functions allow more flexibility for return values. The different types of returned values for functions are covered in the next section, "User-Defined Functions."

Like views, stored procedures can have options. These are placed in the same relative position between the procedure declaration and the AS keyword before the definition. The options for a procedure are ENCRYPTION and RECOMPILE. ENCRYPTION is the same as with views. It will encrypt the procedure definition in the system tables. The RECOMPILE option sets the procedure so that it recompiles before every execution instead of caching and reusing that execution plan. The downside of using the WITH RECOMPILE option is that SQL Server cannot reuse the execution plan. This causes the procedure to run slowly, since it has to re-create the execution plan each time the procedure is called. For this reason, the WITH RECOMPILE option should be used infrequently and only where the parameters that are passed in would necessitate a different execution plan used.

User-Defined Functions

User-defined functions, or functions, are new to SQL Server 2000. They are similar to procedures with one notable exception. A function provides a defined return value. The returned value can be of any valid datatype and is explicitly returned in the function definition. Based on the return type, there are three types of user-defined functions. The differences are based on the type of return value that each has.

The first type is a scalar function. The scalar function returns a scalar value. This would be any single value of a standard datatype. The remaining two types both involve the Table datatype. There is an inline table–valued function and a multistatement table-valued function. The inline table–valued function does not have a function body. It is just a SELECT statement in the declaration. A multistatement table–valued function also returns a table, but the rows in that table are defined in the function body. Examples for both of these types of functions are given after the Table datatype has been discussed.

The Table datatype is a new feature in SQL Server 2000. It is used to define a structure by which data can be returned between blocks of code. Like a physical table, the Table datatype consists of columns with datatypes. A variable would be declared as the Table datatype, and subsequent inserts and updates can access this variable as if it were any other table. This is similar to temporary tables, in that it is not physically stored on disk. One of the differences is that the Table datatype can be passed as a variable instead of referencing a temporary table that may be out of scope. The following example creates a variable of Table datatype:

```
Declare @TestTable table (ID int, Name varchar(50), Description
varchar(200))
```

Like any other variable declaration, the datatype follows the name of the variable. In this case, the type is Table. Of course, any table needs to have a list of columns. To define the columns for the Table datatype, a column list is enclosed in parentheses. Constraints and other attributes normally associated with a table apply to the Table datatype as well. This means that CHECK constraints, default constraint, IDENTITY attribute, and everything else can be placed in a table variable. This structure allows a result set to be returned. This is especially helpful in functions.

When a function returns a table variable, it is treated as a result set and can be included in the FROM clause of a SELECT statement. This flexibility allows functions to be placed inline with SQL statements in the SELECT, FROM, and WHERE clause. This has been true for just system functions in the past.

To construct any user-defined function, the syntax would be CREATE FUNCTION. The declaration looks like this example:

```
CREATE FUNCTION <FUNCTION NAME> (<PARAMETERS>)
RETURNS <RETURN VALUE>
WITH <FUNCTION OPTION>
AS
BEGIN
<FUNCTION BODY>
END
```

Parameters are defined in much the same way as procedures. Some of the differences are outlined here:

Parameter Usage	Procedure	User-Defined Function
Number of parameters allowed	2,100	1,024
Output parameters allowed	Yes	No, functions do not allow output parameters, since they can return a value.
Input parameters allowed	Yes	Yes
DEFAULT keyword required for default parameters	No (Default parameters can be omitted.)	Yes; @parameter = DEFAULT is required to set the default value. Omitting a parameter causes an error.
Parameters enclosed in parentheses after object name	No	Yes

As has been discussed, the <RETURN VALUE> in the earlier example can be one of three things. The first, for scalar functions, is the datatype that is to be returned. There is no need to specify a variable name as with output parameters in procedures. For inline table–valued functions, the TABLE keyword is placed here. The multistatement table–valued function also has the TABLE keyword. In this case, a variable is declared with the datatype of Table and the column list, including constraints and attributes, for the table. The variable declared for the return value can be referenced in the function body.

The <FUNCTION OPTION> settings are similar to view options without the VIEW_METADATA option. Functions can have ENCRYPTION and SCHEMABINDING only. ENCRYPTION, like for a view, specifies that the function is encrypted when stored in the database so that it cannot be retrieved from the system tables. SCHEMABINDING has the same effect as with views in that it binds itself to the tables that it references. When this is turned on, it prevents schema modifications that would affect the objects in the function.

After this is set, the function body can be written. This is whatever block of code is appropriate for the function. One thing that needs to be done at this point is to return the result for the function. For scalar functions, the keyword RETURN should be followed by the scalar value that needs to be returned. This can be a variable that has been defined in the function body or a constant, if that is appropriate. For inline table–valued functions, the function body is left out and only the RETURN keyword exists. After the RETURN keyword, a SELECT statement is placed inside parentheses that define the result set that should be returned.

The select list sets the column list of the table that is returned. The BEGIN and END keywords are not used in this type of function. The next example is an inline table–valued function that returns all the employees from a department that has been passed into the function:

```
CREATE FUNCTION EmployeeByDepartment (@DepartmentID INT)
RETURNS TABLE
AS
RETURN (SELECT * FROM Employee WHERE DepartmentID =
@DepartmentID)
```

The multistatement table–valued function follows the function body with the RETURN keyword followed by the variable on the returned table, as defined in the function declaration. In this example, the EmployeeByDepartment() function above is changed to a multistatement table–valued function:

```
CREATE FUNCTION EmployeeByDepartment (@DepartmentID INT)
RETURNS @EmployeeList TABLE (ID int, LastName varchar(25),
EmployeeNumber smallint, HireDate datetime)
AS
BEGIN

INSERT INTO @EmployeeList VALUES SELECT ID, LastName,
EmployeeNumber, HireDate Employee WHERE DepartmentID =
@DepartmentID

RETURN @EmployeeList
END
```

on the **job** *Looking at the examples above, the question can be raised of why this would not be included in a view instead. For performance reasons, these functions are considerably faster because they provide a parameterized view. The database does not have to return all employees if the client really only wants the subset. This can be a significant performance gain, depending on the views in the database.*

To drop a function, the syntax is DROP FUNCTION <FUNCTION NAME>. To update a function, replace the CREATE FUNCTION keywords with ALTER FUNCTION. This updates an existing function to the new definition.

Triggers

Triggers provide an automatic action to take place when a specific triggering action takes place on a table or view. There are two types of triggers available in SQL Server 2000. They are the INSTEAD OF and AFTER triggers. Each of these types can apply to three separate actions that are performed on the table or view. An INSERT, UPDATE, OR DELETE statement, can cause the trigger to execute. A single trigger can be written that fires for one or more of these events. By specifying each action in a list, the trigger can fire for each of these actions. All triggers in SQL Server are statement level. For example, if an UPDATE statement affects 2,000 rows in a table, the AFTER trigger fires once after all the rows have been updated.

There is one notable command that circumvents triggers. The TRUNCATE TABLE command deletes all the rows in a table, but it does not trigger a DELETE trigger if one exists on the table. The reason for this is that TRUNCATE TABLE does not go through the normal process of deleting rows. Since TRUNCATE TABLE bypasses the transaction log, it does not fire triggers on a table. TRUNCATE TABLE also is not allowed on tables that are involved in a FOREIGN KEY constraint.

First, the basic trigger syntax should be covered. The first step is the trigger declaration. A trigger is different from the previous objects in that it is related to a specific table or view. For this reason, the declaration requires more information— namely, what table the trigger acts on, what type of trigger it is, and when the trigger should fire. The following example shows the template for a trigger declaration:

```
CREATE TRIGGER <Trigger Name> ON <Target Table>
<Trigger Type> <Triggering Action>
AS
```

In the template above, the <Target Table> is the table or view that the trigger references. The <Trigger Type> specifies whether the trigger is an INSTEAD OF trigger or AFTER trigger. The <Triggering Action> specifies whether the trigger acts on an INSERT, an UPDATE, or a DELETE. When the trigger needs to be associated to more than one action, the <Triggering Action> can be a comma-separated list containing one or more of the actions.

An INSTEAD OF trigger is frequently used to update a view that is usually not updateable. This is because an INSTEAD OF trigger replaces the triggering action with whatever is defined by the trigger. So, if an INSERT statement is being issued against a table with an INSTEAD OF trigger on the insert action, the trigger will fire, but the initial insert does not occur. This is why they are named INSTEAD OF triggers. Instead of the action taking place, the action defined in the trigger takes place. Of course, the trigger can issue an INSERT statement in the trigger, and those rows are inserted without interference from the INSTEAD OF trigger. The INSTEAD OF trigger occurs before any of the table constraints are processed since it replaces the insert. An important restriction of the INSTEAD OF trigger is that it cannot conflict with a cascading referential constraint. This means that an INSTEAD OF DELETE trigger cannot be placed on a table that participates in a relationship with a DELETE CASCADE. The same is true for INSTEAD OF UPDATE triggers which cannot be placed on a table that participates in a relationship with an UPDATE CASCADE. Another restriction of INSTEAD OF triggers is that they cannot be placed on views that have the WITH CHECK OPTION set. A final restriction allows only a single INSTEAD OF trigger per triggering action on a table or view. This means that there can be a maximum of three INSTEAD OF triggers, since there can be a separate trigger for INSERT, UPDATE, and DELETE.

AFTER triggers are ones that occur after the statement has completed. This includes the processing of any constraints. Since the data has already been affected, processing in an AFTER trigger cannot change the data as it is being modified. Subsequent updates or deletes would need to be issued to affect the rows. SQL Server also allows the FOR keyword to substitute for the AFTER keyword during trigger declaration. These two keywords have identical behavior. Multiple AFTER triggers are allowed on a single table. Each table is allowed multiple separate triggers per triggering action. When multiple AFTER triggers are specified, the user is allowed to specify which trigger is first and last. Only the first and last triggers can be specified. The triggers in the middle are not of a specific order. To specify the first and last triggers, the sp_settriggerorder system stored procedure can be used. The following example sets the trgTest_u update trigger as the first trigger:

```
Execute sp_settriggerorder 'trgTest_u', 'first', 'UPDATE'
```

This procedure has three parameters. The first parameter, @triggername, is the name of the trigger to be set as first or last. The second parameter, @order, defines whether the trigger should be first or last. The accepted values for this parameter are first, last, and none. The NONE keyword is used to reset a trigger that was set as first and last on a previous occasion. The third and final parameter, @stmttype, specifies which triggering action the trigger applies. Since a trigger is allowed to be associated to more than one triggering action, this parameter cannot be assumed from the trigger. None of these parameters are optional.

During the processing of a trigger, there are two tables that are available for processing. They are the Inserted and Deleted tables. During trigger execution, these two tables allow the user to select the values from the altered rows. Of course, during a DELETE statement, the Inserted table would have zero rows, while an INSERT statement produces zero rows in its Deleted table. It is only during UPDATE statements that both of these tables are populated. These tables can be joined in statements in the trigger body and can have cursors created to loop through them. They are treated like any other table. The only issue is that the scope of these tables is restricted to the trigger.

The trigger body can be written in much the same way as any procedural block. Local variables can be set and used in the trigger. Stored procedures and functions can be called. Views can be used. The trigger can even reference objects outside the current database using distributed queries.

on the
job

The downside for triggers is that developers of the client-side application sometimes do not realize a trigger is implemented and do not know how or why certain actions take place. Unlike a procedure or function, a client does not explicitly call triggers.

Defaults

Default constraints are something that has been covered in Chapter 3 as part of the discussion on constraints. There is a second type of default that is an object in the database that is often used when a specific value is required on a variety of columns across the database. The default constraint is more common and has the advantage of being tied directly to a table. Another advantage of a default constraint is that multiple default constraints can be assigned to a column, while only a single default object can be bound to a column or user-defined datatype. User-defined datatypes are discussed later in this chapter. As with default constraints, a default cannot be assigned to a column that is of the TIMESTAMP datatype or is an IDENTITY column.

on the
job

The default object has been maintained for backward-compatibility use. The default constraint should be used wherever a default is required.

To create a default object, use the CREATE DEFAULT statement. The following example creates a default with the value of 'Microsoft Certified':

```
CREATE DEFAULT Certification AS 'Microsoft Certified'
```

Now that the default has been created, it can be attached to a specific column. To do this, use the system procedure sp_binddefault. The sp_binddefault procedure accepts the default name as the first parameter, @defname, and the table name and column for the second parameter. The following example assigns the default to the Employee.Certification column:

```
Exec sp_binddefault Certification, 'Employee.Certification'
```

The second parameter, @objname, needs to be the column name using dot notation to specify the table. A default cannot be assigned to a column that has a default constraint already applied. Now, the column will be populated with the string 'Microsoft Certified' whenever a statement inserts a row into Employees without specifying the Certification column. Just like the default constraint, the default is not used if the Certification column is specified and a NULL value is explicitly passed. If the column name does not contain a table and column name using dot notation as shown, the bind procedure assumes that the default is being defined to a user-defined datatype.

In this case, a third parameter—@futureonly—is accepted that binds the default to all columns that are currently of that user-defined datatype, or assigns it only to future instances of the user-defined type. If left NULL, which is the default, all current instances of that user-defined type inherit this default. If the string 'futureonly' is given, only new columns using this user-defined datatype inherit the default.

To remove the default from the column or user-defined type, the sp_unbinddefault procedure should be used. This procedure accepts two parameters. The first parameter, @objname, is the name of the column that has the default bound to it. Since only a single default can be assigned, there is no need to specify the name in this procedure. The second parameter, @futureonly, applies only to user-defined datatypes. This parameter is optional and defaults to NULL. The parameter specifies whether the default is being unbound for all current columns or future columns using the user-defined datatype. Like the sp_binddefault syntax, the default of NULL removes the default for all columns that are of the user-defined type. The 'futureonly' string unbinds the default only to new columns being created using the user-defined datatype. This leaves the current columns with the default.

To drop a default from the database, the DROP DEFAULT syntax is used. The following code drops the Certification default defined in the previous example:

```
DROP DEFAULT Certification
```

If the default is still bound to a column or user-defined type, the previous statement returns an error. At this time, the default should be unbound from the column using the sp_unbinddefault syntax, and the DROP DEFAULT can be reissued.

on the
job

Stored procedures can use relative positioning or parameter names to set and pass parameters. System stored procedures, such as sp_binddefault, can be executed the same way. Naming is sometimes safer to do when creating scripts so that if the sequence of parameters changes, the script can still work.

Rules

Just as the default object is a backward-compatible version of the default constraint, the rule object acts much the same way as CHECK constraints. Much like the CHECK constraint, a rule defines a range of values or conditions that must be met for the value to be valid to populate the column. If an invalid value is provided, the rule will return an error and the insert or update is prevented. This includes default values that are being inserted either through a default or default constraint. If the rule only allows integers between 1 and 200, a default of 500 can be bound to the column; but when it is used, an error occurs.

To implement a rule, the CREATE RULE syntax is used. After the rule name, the condition is given. The condition requires that a variable be presented in the comparison. The variable name is not really important other than that it follows the rules of variable naming and that it is preceded with an @ symbol. The following code implements a rule to limit values to be between 0 and 100:

```
CREATE RULE Percentage AS @value >= 0 AND @value <= 100
```

As with the other objects, the keyword AS is used to separate the name and the definition—in this case, the condition. The variable in the condition could be named anything and not change the condition. Using the sp_bindrule system procedure, a rule can be bound to an individual column or a user-defined datatype. Similar to the sp_binddefault procedure, there are three parameters available.

The first parameter, @rulename, specifies the name of the rule to be applied. The second parameter, @objname, is the column or user-defined datatype that the rule applies.

If the object that receives the rule is a user-defined type, the third parameter, @futureonly, can be used to specify whether the rule applies to all user-defined datatypes in the database, or it will only apply to future uses of the user-defined datatype. Just like sp_binddefault, the parameter default is NULL. That means that all current and future columns of this type have the rule applied, and the 'futureonly' value for the parameter limits the rule to only new columns of this user-defined datatype.

To unbind the rule, the sp_unbindrule system procedure is used. The parameters are the same as in sp_unbinddefault. The first is the name of the object, @objname, that has the rule bound to it. If this is a user-defined datatype, the second parameter, @futureonly, can be used to specify whether the unbind applies to all instances of the user-defined datatype or unbinds future uses of the user-defined datatype.

To remove a rule from the database, the DROP RULE syntax should be used. Once again, the rule cannot be applied toward any columns or user-defined datatypes if it is to be dropped. It must first be unbound, and then dropped.

User-Defined Datatypes

In the previous objects, rules, and defaults, the user-defined datatype has been mentioned. A user-defined datatype is just what its name implies. A user is allowed to create a datatype that can then be used throughout the database. User-defined datatypes ensure that all instances of a type of object have the same datatype and length.

To create a user-defined datatype, the following three items are defined: a name, the system datatype it is based on, and nullability. The sp_addtype system procedure is used to add the type to the database. For example, a description field may need to be implemented to always be of Varchar(200) and be NOT NULL. The following code adds a user-defined datatype that could be used in subsequent tables:

```
Execute sp_addtype 'Description', 'varchar(200)', 'NOT NULL'
```

In this procedure, the first parameter, @typename, names the type that has been added. When using the type in tables, this name appears where the datatype is normally. The second parameter, @phystype, sets the user-defined type to be of this datatype and length. Any system datatype is available to create a user-defined type. The third parameter, @nulltype, specifies whether the column allows null values. The accepted values for this parameter are NULL, NOT NULL, and NONULL. NULL is the default value and does not have to be specified. NOT NULL and NONULL are synonymous and denote the column cannot contain NULL values. This parameter must be enclosed in quotation marks when given. The fourth parameter, @owner (which is not shown), is the owner of the datatype. This parameter defaults to the current logged-in user.

Once the datatype is added, it can be used as any other datatype would. Now that this new datatype is being defined for the database, rules and defaults can be assigned before using the column. This allows the user to implement business rules to all instances of the column throughout the database with a single object rather than adding a CHECK and a default constraint to every instance of the column.

To remove a user-defined datatype from the database, the sp_droptype procedure is used. The parameter for this procedure is @typename, which is the name as specified in the sp_addtype function. Since the name must be unique within the database, regardless of owner, the owner does not need to be included. The only restriction before dropping a custom datatype is that it cannot be referenced in any tables or other database objects.

CertCam 4-1

EXERCISE 4-1

Create a User-Defined Type and Utilize It in a Table

1. Open Query Analyzer and log in to the Northwind database.

2. Issue the following command to create a user-defined datatype:

   ```
   execute sp_addtype 'Percentage' ,
   'decimal(5,2)','NONULL'
   ```

3. Create a rule that restricts this value to be between 100 and 0.

   ```
   CREATE RULE PercentageRange as @value >= 0 AND @value
   <=100
   ```

4. Now, bind the rule to the user-defined datatype Percentage.

   ```
   execute sp_bindrule 'PercentageRange', 'Percentage'
   ```

5. Next, create a table using the new user-defined datatype.

```
CREATE TABLE ExerciseCompletion (Name varchar(50),
PercentComplete Percentage)
```

6. Finally, let's test the rule and the user-defined datatype.

```
insert into ExerciseCompletion (Name, PercentComplete)
values ('Exercise1', 100)
insert into ExerciseCompletion (Name, PercentComplete)
values ('Exercise2', 50.5)
insert into ExerciseCompletion (Name, PercentComplete)
values ('Exercise3', 102)
insert into ExerciseCompletion (Name, PercentComplete)
values ('Exercise4', -1)
insert into ExerciseCompletion (Name, PercentComplete)
values ('Exercise5', 'Fail')
```

7. Of the above inserts, numbers 3 and 4 fail because they break the rule applied to the Percentage user-defined type. Number 5 fails because it is not a decimal.

CERTIFICATION OBJECTIVE 4.02

Implementing Advanced Database Features

The objects in the previous certification objective are some of the advanced objects that allow for business rules and business logic to be enforced in the database. There are also some database features that extend the database functionality. Some of these features include partitioning data, replicating across databases, error handling in the object reviewed in the previous sections, and the impact of transactions when processing data. These features allow safer development and engineering by the DBA and development team.

Partitioning

Partitioning data is a process by which data can be split into separate tables based on analysis of usage patterns. The division of data between tables increases performance because larger tables require additional time to scan the table or scan the indexes, since there are so many rows. There are two main methods of partitioning data: horizontal and vertical.

Horizontal Partitioning

The first method of partitioning data is horizontally. This method divides one large table into multiple smaller tables, all with the same structure. To divide the rows, criteria need to be defined by the user so that the tables can contain constraints to enforce the criteria that have been defined. The result is that selects, inserts, deletes, and updates only access the table and indexes that hold and reference the data in the statement. This can greatly improve performance because instead of dealing with a table with ten million rows, the user is only dealing with a table of one million rows.

The most common example is archiving data by year. If transactions in a table span many years and the system does not require day-to-day use of the older data, the older data can be subdivided by year into separate tables. In the simple example that follows, the Sales_Figures table contains all the sales for the last five years including the current year:

```
CREATE TABLE Sales_Figures
(Sales_Figures_ID   INT,
 Product_ID         INT,
 Quantity_Sold      INT,
 Sales_Amount       money,
 Sales_Date         datetime)
```

To divide the data into multiple partitioned tables, the user creates five tables with the same columns with names that should identify each as part of the group. Using the example above, the table can be named Sales_Figure_*XXXX*, where *XXXX* is the year of the data in the table. A constraint can then be placed on the Sales_Date column to limit values between the data range for that year. Of course, how can this be implemented to hide the fact that there are now five tables that contain the data that was in one table? To accomplish this, SQL Server implements partitioned views.

Partitioned views join data across the tables and hide the location of the data. A partitioned view is a query that spans the tables to join all the data for the partitioned data. In the following example, the sales region data resides in separate tables and the partitioned view hides this implementation from the user:

```
CREATE VIEW Sales_Figures
AS
   SELECT * FROM Sales_Figures_1997
UNION
   SELECT * FROM Sales_Figures_1998
UNION
   SELECT * FROM Sales_Figures_1999
UNION
   SELECT * FROM Sales_Figures_2000
UNION
   SELECT * FROM Sales_Figures_2001
```

To a user, this view appears to be a table available for reporting. With INSTEAD OF triggers, the view can be implemented as an updateable view that logically separates the data out to its respective table. The end user gets all the performance gains this provides and no code needs to be rewritten after the database changes have been implemented.

Vertical Partitioning

While horizontal partitioning divides the rows of a table into separate tables, vertical partitioning actually separates columns of a table into separate tables. Vertical partitioning is often covered in proper logical design, since normalization is a form of vertical partitioning. Another method of vertical partitioning is row splitting.

Normalization should be handled during initial database logical design and has been covered in Chapter 2. Row splitting is a method of dividing certain columns into a separate table. Unlike in horizontal positioning, where the data between tables is unrelated, the vertically partitioned rows are related by some unique identifier for each row. Row 128 in the first table corresponds to row 128 in the second table. The columns that should be divided into their own tables are columns that are infrequently used. The goal, unlike in horizontal partitioning, is to limit row length rather than number of rows. This kind of partitioning needs to be implemented very carefully. If implementation requires a scan of two very large tables, performance is actually affected negatively. This also introduces another cross-join to any SELECT statements that access all the columns in the rows.

Replication

Replication is a process by which a database can publish data to an external source. Whether it is another database, an Access database, or other client, the data in a database can automatically keep other data sources synchronized. Replication, like partitioning, takes detailed planning and is highly customizable. The flexibility of replication allows a variety of client types to be involved. Whether a sales person is only online once a month or a remote sales office needs an up-to-date inventory, there is a replication option that satisfies the requirement. There are three separate types of replication in SQL Server and each offers its own benefits and disadvantages.

In all three of these replication types, there are basic concepts and terms that are critical in the discussion. Whenever replicating data, everything starts with a publisher server. The publisher monitors the databases and prepares data for replication. On the publisher, the publication database resides. This database stores all the data and objects that are copied to subscribers. On the publication database, publications can be set up that are logically grouped pieces of information that should be distributed together. When dealing with larger data sets, publications can help limit what data is being synchronized between the publishers and the subscribers. The subscribers are the database servers that can be updated with information from the publisher. By referencing the publications in the publication databases, the subscriber can request, or subscribe, to a publication, and the subscriber is updated with this information during replication. A subscriber does not have access to individual pieces of the publication database or even part of a publication. The subscriber must accept the entire publication.

During replication, the publisher and subscriber act on each other through actions of pushing and pulling information between them. If a publisher has an update to a publication that is subscribed to, replication settings act to push the data from the publisher to the subscriber. In other cases, where the subscriber is offline for prolonged periods of time and cannot have information pushed to it, the subscriber can pull a publication. These actions are determined when setting up the replication model for the individual environment being set up.

The publisher and subscriber store all the databases in a format that can be accessed by the end user. To facilitate the replication process, a distributor server is also required. The distributor server contains distribution databases that store all the replication history, metadata, and transactions based on the type of replication being used. This distributor can be on the same physical machine as the publisher or can be moved to a remote machine. By offloading the distributor to another machine, the resources needed to support replication are moved to that machine. A single distributor can support multiple distribution databases. This allows the machine to be tuned to support the kind of disk storage and network resources needed for the distribution.

Understanding Merge, Transactional, and Snapshot Replication

When deciding to implement replication, the user has three different types to choose. Based on the descriptions, it is relatively easy to determine which method is best for each environment. Some replication methods give almost real-time updating of servers, while others update at set intervals that may be days or weeks apart. Still others wait for the publishers and subscribers to both be online.

The first type of replication is merge replication. Merge replication allows both the publisher and subscribers to be offline and make updates to their respective sets of data. Typically, merge replication is used when the data sets in each of the subscribers are somewhat autonomous, and there are minimal conflicts when the databases are eventually synchronized. In this type of replication, the distributor has very little overhead. The distributor is only responsible for storing the metadata and the synchronization history.

Transactional replication is a bit more reliant on the publisher being the primary source of data. Transactional replication offers the subscribers an initial snapshot of the data. That snapshot is subsequently updated with transactions as they are applied to the publisher database. Using the transaction log of the publishing database, subscribers are sent or pushed out subscriptions of data that they require. In situations in which subscribers do not have a reliable or consistent connection, the subscriber can pull the data when their connection is active. Transactional replication maintains the lowest latency for updates, since transactions can be applied at any time. The distributor plays a larger role in transactional replication because it stores all the intermediate transactions between replication. When the database is in continual use, the replication transactions are stored on the distributor until the subscribers are available for the publication. The distributor is still responsible for the metadata and synchronization log.

Snapshot replication is the least demanding of the replication options. With snapshot replication, the subscribers are sent a new point-in-time edition of the data. Individual updates are not recorded while snapshot replication is enabled. This is best when the data is mostly static and the database can be fully restored at any time.

The distributor in snapshot replication must store the snapshots and the synchronization log. Due to the size of the snapshots, this can be resource intensive.

Updateable Subscriptions

When using snapshot and transactional replication, the data in the subscriber databases is typically read-only. This way, the subscribers can report on the data in that database. SQL Server does allow the subscribers to update the data, given some additional configuration. If the databases are always connected (common in transactional replication), the immediate updating can be set. This sends updates from the subscriber to the publisher, as well as the normal publisher to the subscriber. When the databases are offline, queued updating can be utilized. If the databases are connected the majority of the time, but may occasionally be disconnected, immediate updating with queued updating as a failover can be set. This maintains immediate updating while online and then switches to queued updating when they disconnect.

Queued Updating During transactional and snapshot replication, the publisher is updated with the subscriber data when the sources are online if using immediate updating. When a subscriber is offline, these transactions reside on the client for a time until a connection to the publisher is restored. When that connection is restored, the transactions must be moved into the publishing database. If queued updating is enabled as a failover for immediate updating or is the initial setting, the publisher and subscribers must both be updated.

Queued updating solves this problem by asynchronously re-creating every INSERT, UPDATE, and DELETE that has occurred while offline. This queued updating works to push subscriber data back to the publisher. If the data has been manipulated while the subscriber was offline, or if other subscribers have also updated the data, a conflict arises. All conflicts for queued updating occur on the transaction level and not the row level. To resolve these conflicts, a few rules are defined during publication creation.

Snapshot replication has two forms of conflict resolution. The first is to reinitialize the subscriber. In this situation, if a conflict occurs between the publisher and subscriber, the transactions that are queued for update are marked as "in conflict" and the queue stops. When the next snapshot is available from the distributor, the subscriber is updated with the snapshot and the transactions that were in conflict are lost. The alternative method of resolving conflicts in snapshot replication is to use publisher wins. In these cases, the transaction is maintained for the publisher. If the subscriber conflicts with a transaction in the publisher, the transaction on the subscriber is rolled back and the publisher's transaction is used going forward. Since the transaction has actually been committed at the subscriber before the conflict is recognized, the distributor generates offsetting transactions that reverse the transaction back to the state of the transaction at the publisher.

Transactional replication also has two methods of resolving conflicts. The first is publisher wins. As in snapshot replication, the transactions on the publisher take precedence and roll back any conflicts on the subscriber by sending reversing transactions back to the subscriber through the distributor. Transactional replication can also use subscriber wins conflict resolution. This states that the final subscriber update sets the state at the publisher and those updates are then replicated to the other subscribers. This is best suited to environments in which different subscribers are not updating the same sets of data or publications.

After all the conflicts are resolved, the list of conflicts is available to view on the publisher. This list can also be sent down to the subscribers. The Conflict Viewer can scroll through all the conflicts, but there is no automated way to update the rows if they were incorrectly resolved.

Understanding Transactions

Transactions offer users a method of grouping discrete actions and processing them at a single time. This group of actions is sometimes called a logical unit of work. Microsoft defines a logical unit of work to have the four properties. They refer to these properties as the ACID test. The four properties are atomicity, consistency, isolation, and durability. The first property, atomicity, means that the whole unit of work occurs or the whole unit of works fails. If there is an UPDATE statement, an INSERT statement, and a DELETE statement, if the DELETE statement fails, the whole transaction fails. The second property, consistency, states that everything that happened in the transaction is consistent when the transaction completes. All constraints pass, all indexes are updated, and all data is in the same state. The third property, isolation, means that the unit of work preserves the state of data during the transaction. If a table is in a certain state at the beginning of the transaction, another transaction cannot change the state of that data. The fourth and final property, durability, states that the transaction is final. Once the transaction is complete, the modifications are permanent and cannot be restored to the previous state without another transaction to explicitly reverse the original.

Transactions are critical to development so that data can be transitioned from one state to another. Without transactions in the database, SELECT statements could never know what data to retrieve, indexes would never be updated, and there would be no way to undo actions dependent upon the success of another action. Transactions and their isolation level determine locks in the database. The locking mechanism in SQL Server preserves the ACID properties of transactions. If transactions are not implemented properly, a database system can be locked and prevent anybody from even reading data from the system. Limiting the size of a transaction is the best way to limit the locks being held on the tables and resources involved, as well as freeing those locks as soon as possible.

When and How to Use Transactions

There are three modes of transactions when dealing with the database. The default mode is AUTOCOMMIT. When AUTOCOMMIT is set, each Transact-SQL statement is its own transaction. If the transaction succeeds, the transaction commits. If it fails, the transaction performs a rollback. This limits the duration of locks being held, but it is not always the best way to perform transactions.

Often, a transaction needs to involve more than just one statement. The remaining two modes offer the ability to group more than one transaction. The first of these is EXPLICIT transaction mode. In EXPLICIT transaction mode, the beginning and end of a transaction must be explicitly defined. To begin a transaction, the keywords to use are BEGIN TRANSACTION. By beginning the transaction this way, SQL Server is preparing to hold all locks until one of two things occur. The transaction would need to be committed or rolled back. To commit a transaction, the COMMIT TRANSACTION statement is used. By committing the transaction, the statements in the transactions are saved to the database and the locks on those resources are released. This allows other users in the database to have access to the new data, as well as the data that was previously locked. To roll back the transaction, the ROLLBACK TRANSACTION statements are used. This command reverses all Transact-SQL statements that were issued during the transaction. If an error occurs during the transaction, the transaction is automatically rolled back. To conform to a transaction's ACID properties, commits and rollbacks are all-or-nothing commands. If there is a need to only commit one or two of the statements in the transaction while rolling back another, the transaction should most likely be divided into more discrete transactions. The BEGIN TRANSACTION keywords can be used without turning on explicit transaction mode.

When nesting transactions—or just for clarity in coding—SQL Server allows the user to name transactions. Naming transactions extends the BEGIN TRANSACTION command. A simple example is displayed here:

```
BEGIN TRANSACTION T1
INSERT INTO Test VALUES (1, 'First Transaction')
COMMIT TRANSACTION T1
```

In the previous example, the name T1 is given for the transaction. When using the ROLLBACK TRANSACTION or COMMIT TRANSACTION, the transaction name can be provided but is not used to reference the original BEGIN TRANSACTION command. It is only allowed to facilitate readability during coding. This becomes more useful when nesting transactions, as shown here:

```
BEGIN TRANSACTION T1
INSERT INTO Test VALUES (1,'First Transaction')
BEGIN TRANSACTION T2
INSERT INTO Test VALUES (2, 'Second Transaction')
BEGIN TRANSACTION T3
INSERT INTO Test VALUES (3,'Third Transaction')
COMMIT TRANSACTION T3
COMMIT TRANSACTION T2
COMMIT TRANSACTION T1
```

In the above example, there are three transactions that are opened. Each time a new transaction is created, the @@TRANCOUNT system variable is incremented. The only time a transaction can be committed is when the @@TRANCOUNT is equal to 1. So, when the COMMIT TRANSACTION T3 is issued, the transaction is not committed. Instead, the @@TRANCOUNT variable is decremented to 2. The commit of the outermost transaction, T1, commits all interior transactions since the @@TRANCOUNT is equal to 1. COMMIT WORK and ROLLBACK WORK are the functional equivalent of COMMIT TRANSACTION and ROLLBACK TRANSACTION, respectively. The difference is that COMMIT WORK and ROLLBACK WORK cannot be used in situations in which the transactions have been named. In both of the cases, the WORK keyword can be left off and the command works the same way.

The third transaction mode is an IMPLICIT transaction mode. This mode does not explicitly state the beginning of each transaction. Each new transaction begins directly after a commit or rollback statement. To set the IMPLICIT transaction mode, the SET IMPLICIT_TRANSACTIONS command is issued. The parameter for this is either ON or OFF. If the command sets the IMPLICIT_TRANS-ACTIONS OFF, it reverts back to AUTOCOMMIT mode.

Transaction Isolation Levels

Four isolation levels exist in SQL Server. These isolation levels determine how locks are placed and held during transactions. Locks are the objects that SQL Server uses to mark rows and columns as being in use. Some locks allow the data to be updated but not added to. Other locks only allow viewing and do not allow modification of any kind. The transaction isolation level defines the extent of the locking, the types of locks, and the restrictions that the locks enforce. The first is the READ UNCOM-MITED isolation level. This only ensures that normal data integrity is upheld in the database when reading. This is the only isolation level that can read uncommitted data, or dirty reads. This is typically not a safe method, since the data being read may or may not ever be committed to the database. This is the lowest transaction isolation level. The second isolation level, READ COMMITTED, is the default isolation level. This level preserves shared locks, and thus restricts against dirty reads. The data may be changed before the end of the transaction. A third isolation level is REPEATABLE READ. It takes the READ COMMITTED isolation level one step further and locks out the data that has been retrieved, so that it is not updateable until the lock—and the transaction—have completed. It does allow phantom or new rows to be inserted into the objects that are being manipulated. The final and most restrictive isolation level is SERIALIZABLE. This takes the updateable locks and adds a lock to prevent new rows being inserted into the tables involved in the transaction. This is a very dangerous isolation level and should be used with caution. It is so dangerous because every transaction must happen serially, which hurts performance and can cause serious blocking in the system.

To change the transaction isolation level of a specific connection, the following command is issued. The <ISOLATION LEVEL> setting is one of the isolation levels just described.

```
SET TRANSACTION ISOLATION LEVEL <ISOLATION LEVEL>
```

Error Handling

While coding procedures, functions, and triggers, it is sometimes necessary to handle certain errors that come up. Either the parameters passed in are not appropriate, or, for some reason, a business rule to be enforced by one of these objects has been broken. SQL Server has a mechanism to handle these errors and to communicate the problems to the client. Not all error handling involves custom user-defined errors. There are system errors that can be captured and handled inside a procedure or function. This is required to do one or more of the following: roll back a transaction and alter the flow of the program.

System Errors

After each Transact-SQL statement, an error code is generated. When everything operates correctly and without errors, the error code is 0. When an error does occur, the error message number is set. To check this value, the @@ERROR global variable is used. As with other global variables that maintain their scope outside individual transactions, the @@ERROR variable can be referenced until another Transact-SQL statement is issued, which resets this value. This poses an interesting situation, in that the @@ERROR value must be checked after each statement that may fail.

Since many errors do not stop a transaction, checking the @@ERROR variable allows the developer to check for an error, and subsequently roll back or commit the transaction. This relies on the use of transactions, as described in the previous section. Some errors may even be a trigger for populating tables that keep track of success and failure.

on the *Job*

During batch processing and importing of data, error handling is a good way to populate log tables, so that the valid rows can be inserted successfully and the failed rows can be kept in the log tables. The exercise at the end of this objective covers a scenario like this.

User-Defined Errors

To raise a user-defined error, the method to use is the RAISERROR command. This command allows the flexibility to raise errors exactly like a system error message. The RAISERROR command can raise two general types of errors. An error can be raised that is a text string or can reference a user-defined error message that is stored in the database for use throughout the database. To create a user-defined error message, the sp_addmessage procedure is used. This procedure stores a user-defined error message in the database and allows parameters to be included so that the error message can be customized further when called from any block of Transact-SQL code in the database.

The RAISERROR command acts to raise errors during execution. The syntax for RAISERROR is shown here:

```
RAISERROR ( message number or message text, severity, state,
arguments for message)
```

The first argument for RAISERROR defines what error is being raised. If the user wishes to use a predefined user-defined error message, the number of that message is placed here. User-defined messages are discussed later in this section. Language settings are not specified and are taken from the current session's language setting. If the error message is not defined in the database, the error message can have an ad hoc message. The message text is a string that allows arguments to be specified. The severity sets how the error should be handled by the application. During the discussion on user-defined messages, later in this section, the severity parameter is explained in more detail. The setting in RAISERROR overrides the setting of the error message when using a user-defined message. The argument is required and does not default to the severity of the user-defined error message. The state parameter is used primarily for errors that can occur for a variety of reasons. SQL Server generates different states for the same error to allow technical support to troubleshoot the problem in more depth. Typically in user-defined messages, the state should be 1. These parameters are followed by the arguments defined in the message. These are ordered arguments and are not named. After these arguments, options can be set.

Valid options for RAISERROR are LOG, NOWAIT, and SETERROR. The LOG option sets whether the error is going to be sent to the Microsoft application log. When the LOG option is used with the RAISERROR command, the setting defined in the user-defined message is overridden. NOWAIT sends the error to the user before continuing the transaction. The SETERROR option assigns the message ID to the @@ERROR variable. For errors greater than 10, this is not very helpful because the @@ERROR is automatically set to the message ID. However, information messages, severities 1–10, set the @@ERROR variable to 0 by default. If a message ID is not provided, the SETERROR option assigns a value of 50000 to the @@ERROR variable. During the preceding discussion on raising errors, user-defined messages have been discussed. When the error is required across the database, SQL Server allows text and other options to be saved at the database level using the sp_addmessage system procedure. The sp_addmessage procedure has three required parameters. The outline that follows displays all the parameters available for this procedure:

```
sp_addmessage @msgnum, @severity, @msgtext, @lang, @with_log,
@replace
```

The first three parameters are required. The combination of @msgnum and @lang is the unique key for error messages. @msgnum is an Int datatype that signifies the message identifier when it is called from RAISERROR. The reason for the combination of @msgnum and @lang being the unique key is that localization may require the same error message to be in the database multiple times in different languages. When the @lang parameter is omitted, the @lang is set to the language for the session. This is most commonly the same as the database language setting. For user-defined errors, @msgnum starts at 50001. SQL Server system errors reserve numbers lower than this.

The @severity parameter is a Smallint datatype that signifies how severe the error is. A 10 severity denotes an informational message only. Error information is not sent to the client. It acts much the same way as a PRINT statement. Severity levels 11–16 signify there was a problem with data entered that can be corrected. The error message is sent to the user, but the batch or transaction is not stopped. While a user can create errors with a severity level of 17–25, user-defined errors should only use these rarely. These errors denote system-level problems involving resource allocation and other system problems, possibly involving hardware. These errors should always be reported to the system administrator or DBA for resolution. Severity levels 20–25 signify a fatal server error and can be the cause for restoring the database. Since severity levels of 19 or higher are so severe, only the sysadmin is allowed to add messages in this range.

The @msgtext parameter allows the user to define the custom text to send to the client when the error is raised. This parameter is an Nvarchar(255) datatype. To allow values to be passed into the message, a character to denote the type of value being passed in should follow a variable preceded by a % sign. The following table outlines the accepted characters and the values they expect:

%s	String values
%d or %I	Signed integer
%p	Pointer
%o	Unsigned octal
%u	Unsigned integer
%x or %X	Unsigned hexadecimal

These values are also used when declaring a message inline as part of the RAISERROR procedure.

The @lang parameter states which language the message applies. Valid values are anything that can be defined for the database language setting. This parameter is optional and is set to the session language if not specified in the call.

@with_log gives the message logging capabilities. The default is False. If set to True, the message appears in the Microsoft application log found in the Event Viewer. By default, the SQL Server log also receives an entry when this setting is True. Only sysadmins can set this option on an error message. If this is not set for the message when created in the database, the log option can still be set when the error is actually raised.

@replace is the final parameter, and allows a message to be overwritten without dropping and re-creating it. The default is NULL, but setting this parameter equal to REPLACE performs a substitution for the existing message.

If an error message needs to be reset so that it has a different logging action, the sp_altermessage procedure is available. The three parameters are @message_id, @parameter, and @parameter_value. At this time, only the with_log parameter can be reset. If the @parameter equals with_log, the third parameter can be set to False or True to switch the logging mode. Of course, the @message_id parameter is the message number from the sp_addmessage procedure.

To drop a user-defined message, the sp_dropmessage procedure can be used. By executing the sp_dropmessage command and passing in the message number as the @msgnum parameter, the message is dropped. A second optional parameter, @lang, allows a user to drop messages for specific languages. The default here is the current session language setting.

Checking for Errors During Data Migration

In this exercise, error checking allows business rules to be enforced in an INSTEAD OF trigger. By raising an error in the trigger, the batch insert is allowed to continue without stopping. A CHECK constraint could be implemented to force the price to be positive, but a CHECK constraint stops the batch. An INSTEAD OF trigger is used rather than an AFTER trigger so that the data is checked before going in the table.

1. Log in to the Northwind database using Query Analyzer, or any database available to create some objects.

2. Create a table, Books, with the following command:

```
CREATE TABLE Books (ID int IDENTITY(1,1), Name varchar(50),
Price money)
```

3. Create a table, ImportBooksError, with the following command:

```
CREATE TABLE ImportBooksError (Name varchar(50), Price money,
ErrorMessage nvarchar(255))
```

4. Now, create INSERT statements for a list of books that need to be imported from an Excel spreadsheet or some other source. Following is a list of INSERTS that should be used:

```
INSERT INTO Books (Name, Price) VALUES ('Book1',10)
INSERT INTO Books (Name, Price) VALUES ('Book2 with negative
price',-10)
INSERT INTO Books (Name, Price) VALUES ('Book3',25)
INSERT INTO Books (Name, Price) VALUES ('Book4',100)
```

5. Create the following trigger on the Books table. This trigger will allow an import to complete while rejecting rows that have a negative price.

```
CREATE TRIGGER trgBooks_I ON Books
INSTEAD OF INSERT
AS
DECLARE @Name varchar(50),
    @Price money,
    @ErrorMessage nvarchar(255)
DECLARE InsertedCursor CURSOR FOR
    select name, price from inserted
```

```
BEGIN
  OPEN InsertedCursor
  FETCH NEXT FROM InsertedCursor INTO @Name, @Price
  WHILE (@@FETCH_STATUS = 0)
  BEGIN

    IF (@Price >= 0)
    BEGIN
        insert into Books (Name, Price) values (@name, @Price)
    END
    ELSE
    BEGIN
        SET @ErrorMessage = N'Price is a negative amount.'
        RAISERROR (@ErrorMessage, 16, 1)
    END
    if (@@ERROR <> 0)
    BEGIN
      insert into ImportBooksError (Name, Price, ErrorMessage)
            values (@Name, @Price, @ErrorMessage)
    END
    FETCH NEXT FROM InsertedCursor INTO @Name, @Price
  END
CLOSE InsertedCursor
DEALLOCATE InsertedCursor
END
GO
```

6. Execute all the INSERT statements.

7. Select the rows from both tables.

8. The INSTEAD OF trigger populates the Books table with the valid books records while populating the ImportBooksError table with the books with a negative price.

CERTIFICATION SUMMARY

In this chapter, two certification objectives covered objects that assist developers and DBAs to enforce business logic. The chapter covers the creation of triggers, stored procedures, user-defined functions, and views. This was just a beginning look at creating these objects, along with some rules and restrictions involved in creating and using them. Chapter 5 gives further insight into the Transact-SQL necessary to build fully functional objects.

The chapter also covered objects, rules, and defaults, which can be bound to columns to act similar to constraints. These objects are also bound to a user-defined datatype that allows developers to extend system datatypes. User-defined datatypes, rules, and defaults are all tools to implement objects database-wide for consistency.

The second certification objective covers some features that assist with performance, supporting remote clients, and maintaining data consistency. Error handling has also been covered, so that the user is allowed to create new errors in the database. With these user-defined errors, the RAISERROR procedure provides a mechanism for users to throw back errors and messages that are not normally enforced with database objects.

✓ TWO-MINUTE DRILL

Implementing Advanced Database Objects

- ❏ Views are not stored physically on disk and are sometimes referred to as virtual tables.

- ❏ A view declaration may contain a column list that acts as an alias for columns in the view.

- ❏ Views are updateable if they do not use aggregate functions or derived columns, or involve UNION statements. DISTINCT, GROUP BY, and TOP operators also prevent a view from being updateable.

- ❏ INSTEAD OF triggers can be implemented on views to allow views that are not updateable to be updated.

- ❏ Triggers have two tables, Inserted and Deleted, that reference the inserted and deleted rows of the statement, respectively. These tables reside in the scope of the trigger only.

- ❏ All SQL Server triggers are based on the entire statement. There are no row-level triggers.

- ❏ Stored procedures allow output parameters that can set variables in the calling client.

- ❏ User-defined functions provide three types of return values: scalar, inline table–valued, and multistatement table–valued values.

- ❏ The Table datatype can be used to return a result set from a function in the inline table–valued and multistatement table–valued functions.

- ❏ User-defined datatypes extend system datatypes to be used across the database.

- ❏ Rules and defaults behave similarly to CHECK and default constraints, respectively. They are best suited to user-defined datatypes because they can be bound to the user-defined datatype and the constraints do not have to be applied to each column.

- ❏ Rules and defaults can be bound or unbound to specific columns or user-defined datatypes. To drop rules and defaults, they cannot be bound to any active columns or user-defined datatypes.

Implementing Advanced Database Features

- ❏ Partitioning data spreads data across multiple servers.

- ❏ Partitioned views act to hide the implementation of partitioned data. INSTEAD OF triggers act to allow INSERT, UPDATE, and DELETE statements to be issued against the view and modify the data in the base tables.

- ❏ Replication implements Publishers to push data out to remote machines. Subscribers are allowed to pull data.

- ❏ User-defined error messages are allowed to enforce business rules and logic.

- ❏ User-defined error messages are unique based on their message number and language. This allows the same message for multiple languages to be referenced by the same message number.

SELF TEST

The following questions will help you measure your understanding of the material presented in this chapter. Read all the choices carefully, because there might be more than one correct answer. Choose all correct answers for each question.

Implementing Advanced Database Objects

1. Rules can also be implemented as which type of constraint?

   A. FOREIGN KEY constraint

   B. PRIMARY KEY constraint

   C. CHECK constraint

   D. Default constraint

2. How many parameters are allowed for a stored procedure?

   A. 1,024

   B. 2,100

   C. 512

   D. 20

3. Which view option restricts dropping or altering tables that the view references?

   A. WITH RESTRICTCHANGES

   B. WITH SCHEMABINDING

   C. sp_restrict_database_changes

   D. CREATE VIEW

4. Which option, available to views, stored procedures, and user-defined functions, is used to prevent the body of an object from being retrieved from the system tables?

   A. sp_encrypt_body

   B. WITH HIDEBODY

   C. sp_hidecode

   D. WITH ENCRYPTION

5. An updateable view selects all the employees whose manager is Jane Smith. This view allows Ms. Smith to update data concerning her employees. How can this view prevent Jane from changing the manager of these employees?

   A. Place a CHECK constraint on the view.

   B. Define a default on the Employees table.

   C. Add the WITH CHECK OPTION at the end of the view.

   D. Add an INSTEAD OF trigger that checks the manager name and makes a RAISERROR call if it is not Jane Smith.

6. The Test table has four triggers on the UPDATE action. One of the triggers, TRIGGERTEST1, must occur after the remaining three to clean up data. How could this trigger be defined as the final trigger to execute?

   A. `ALTER TRIGGER TRIGGERTEST1 AS LAST UPDATE`

   B. `sp_settriggerorder 'TRIGGERTEST1', 'final', 'UPDATE'`

   C. `sp_settriggerorder 'TRIGGERTEST1', 'last', 'UPDATE'`

   D. `ALTER TABLE Test ALTER TRIGGER TRIGGERTEST1 last`

7. What type of data can be returned from a stored procedure through the return code?

   A. Double

   B. Varchar

   C. Text

   D. Int

8. There is a view that contains a DISTINCT in the SELECT to eliminate duplicate rows. How can the view be updated?

   A. An UPDATE statement can be issued directly against the view.

   B. Apply an AFTER trigger on the view. Issue an UPDATE against the view.

   C. Apply an INSTEAD OF trigger on the view that updates the base tables used in the view. Issue an UPDATE statement against the view.

   D. Create a procedure that reads all the rows in the view and updates each row by issuing an update on the view for each row.

Implementing Advanced Database Features

9. A company has five sites across the country residing on a wide area network (WAN) to share network resources. Each site has a separate product catalog that is frequently updated and sales figures that are updated throughout the day. The main office is responsible for company-wide reporting and tracking accounts. What form of replication would be best suited to this scenario?

   A. Transactional replication

   B. Merge replication

   C. Mirror replication

   D. Snapshot replication

10. What is the default transaction isolation level for SQL Server?

   A. SERIALIZABLE

   B. READ UNCOMMITTED

   C. READ COMMITTED

   D. REPEATABLE READ

11. Which transaction isolation level allows dirty reads?

   A. READ COMMITTED

   B. REPEATABLE READ

   C. Inline table-value

   D. READ UNCOMMITTED

12. Which severity level sets the @@ERROR variable to 0?

   A. 10

   B. 11

   C. 25

   D. 1

13. Which replication method requires that the subscriber databases be reset for each update?

   A. Snapshot replication

   B. Merge replication

   C. Transactional replication

   D. Mirror replication

14. Which property of transactions signifies that all statements in the transactions are processed or none of the statements are processed?

    A. Atomicity

    B. Consistency

    C. Isolation

    D. Duration

15. When does the @@ERROR value get set in a block of code?

    A. After each INSERT statement

    B. After each UPDATE statement

    C. Right before the COMMIT TRANSACTION statement

    D. After each SET command

16. Given the statement, RAISERROR ('Please Wait for Process to Complete', 10, 1) WITH SETERROR, what is the @@ERROR global variable set to after the statement is issued?

    A. 0

    B. 50000

    C. 60000

    D. 'Please Wait for Process to Complete''17.

    During database maintenance, a script is run that manipulates data throughout the database. This script needs to have exclusive access to the objects that it is modifying when it is modifying those objects. How could this be set for the duration of the scripts connection?

    A. SET TRANSACTION ISOLATION LEVEL REPEATABLE READ

    B. SET TRANSACTION SERIALIZABLE

    C. SET TRANSACTION ISOLATION LEVEL SERIALIZABLE

    D. BEGIN TRANSACTION AS SERIALIZABLE

LAB QUESTION

MacroWare Michigan wants to expand their sales territory and become MacroWare USA. The first phase is to create satellite offices in California, Texas, Florida, and Hawaii. Each office outside the home office of Michigan is the home base for a group of sales people. Every two months,

MacroWare updates their product catalog to reflect price changes, as well as addition and removal of certain products based on sales numbers.

Each sales person is assigned a laptop and is told to keep a product catalog on their system. While on the sales call, they are allowed to check inventory on their machines and place pending orders. When the deal is finalized, they are required to dial up to their satellite office to approve the sale by verifying the available inventory. Each region has a warehouse and inventory that they keep track of daily. The home office in Michigan wants to be able to run reports and check all inventory across their satellite offices.

Formulate a database strategy that satisfies all the database requirements that are presented by this expansion.

SELF TEST ANSWERS

Implementing Advanced Database Objects

1. ☑ **C.** Rules enforce which values populate a column just like a CHECK constraint. In most situations, CHECK constraints are actually more appropriate.
   ☒ **A** is incorrect because foreign keys are only implemented as FOREIGN KEY constraints. Triggers could also enforce this behavior. **B** is incorrect because primary keys are only implemented as PRIMARY KEY constraints. Triggers could also enforce this behavior. **D** is incorrect. Default constraints can be implemented as DEFAULT objects.

2. ☑ **B** is correct. The maximum number of parameters for a stored procedure in SQL Server 2000 is 2,100.
   ☒ **A, C,** and **D** are incorrect because the maximum number of parameters for a stored procedure in SQL Server 2000 is 2,100.

3. ☑ **B** is correct. The SCHEMABINDING option binds the view to the tables that it references. When this is not set, changes to the tables that are referenced are not prevented. The view becomes invalid after the change.
   ☒ **A** and **C** are not correct and are not SQL Server commands. **D** is incorrect. While the option is set on the CREATE VIEW statement, CREATE VIEW does not have to specify this option.

4. ☑ **D** is correct. All of these objects allow the WITH ENCRYPTION option. This option encrypts the data in the system tables so that it cannot be selected from the database.
   ☒ **A, B,** and **C** are incorrect. These are not valid SQL Server procedures or options.

5. ☑ **C** is correct because the WITH CHECK OPTION restricts updates on a view to ensure that the rows would remain in the view after any updates. **D** is correct because an INSTEAD OF trigger could be placed on the view. This trigger could be written so that it disallows updates that affect the Manager column.
   ☒ **A** is incorrect. CHECK constraints cannot be assigned to views. **B** is incorrect because a default would not restrict the values in the table. It would only serve to populate the column when not included in the INSERT statement.

6. ☑ **C** is correct. The sp_settriggerorder procedure sets the first and last triggers if multiple triggers are assigned to the same table.
   ☒ **A** is incorrect. A trigger cannot be altered to set this as its order. **B** is incorrect because it uses the FINAL keyword where it should use the LAST keyword. **D** is incorrect because altering the table cannot alter a trigger.

7. ☑   **D** is correct. Stored procedures can only return an Int as a return code.
  ☒   **A** is incorrect because a Double is not a valid SQL Server datatype. **B** and **C** are incorrect because stored procedures can only return a single Int return code.

8. ☑   **C** is correct. DISTINCT causes the view to not be updatable. By applying an INSTEAD OF trigger, the update can be handled by the trigger by updating the appropriate base table.
  ☒   **A** is incorrect because the DISTINCT keyword makes the view nonupdatable. **B** is incorrect because an AFTER trigger cannot be placed on a view. **D** is incorrect because the view is not updatable for the reason in answer A. Whether the update comes in a procedure or function; the view is still not updatable.

Implementing Advanced Database Features

9. ☑   **A.** Transactional replication keeps subscribers up-to-date using the transaction log and propagating changes out for a point-in-time replication. Based on the reliable connection provided by the WAN, and the need to keep the catalog updated throughout the day, transactional replication provides the most up-to-date copies. **B** is correct because the data is divided among the sales regions. This would minimize conflicts during merge. While the WAN should ensure a constant connection, the ability to disconnect and later synchronize the data would be an advantage for downtime caused by maintenance. Updates could be scheduled to be continuous.
  ☒   **C** is incorrect because mirror replication is not a valid replication method. **D** is incorrect because snapshot replication forces the databases to be restored. This would be inefficient since each sales region subscriber would be forced to restore throughout the day.

10. ☑   **C** is correct because the default isolation is READ COMMITTED.
  ☒   **A, B,** and **D** are incorrect because the default transaction isolation level is READ COMMITTED.

11. ☑   **D** is correct because it is the only isolation level that allows these dirty reads.
  ☒   **A, B,** and **D** are incorrect because they all hold varying degrees of locks while reading, which prevents dirty reads.

12. ☑   **A** and **D** are correct because severity levels between 1 and 10 are informational messages and set the @@ERROR = 0.
  ☒   **B** is incorrect. It is the lowest level severity level that results in an error being generated. The @@ERROR would be set to the message number or 50000 if the error is generated from a RAISERROR with only a message statement. **C** is incorrect—25 is the highest severity. The @@ERROR is set to the message number or 50000, as in B.

13. ☑ **A** is correct because snapshot replication pushes snapshots of the database out to subscribers. It does not keep track of individual transactions.
    ☒ **B** and **C** are not correct. They keep synchronized by schedule or they have queued updating when synchronizing after being disconnected. **D** is incorrect because it is not a valid replication type.

14. ☑ **A** is correct because atomicity signifies that a transaction must be a logical unit of work that is either all committed or all rolled back.
    ☒ **B** is incorrect because consistency states that all data must be in a consistent state after the transaction is completed. Any action that is going to take place has taken place. **C** is incorrect because isolation means that the transaction is reading data that will not change during its transaction. **D** is incorrect because duration means that after the transaction is complete, what happened in the transaction will be permanent.

15. ☑ **A** is correct because the @@ERROR variable gets set after each statement. **B** is correct because the @@ERROR variable gets set after each statement.
    ☒ **C** is incorrect because the @@ERROR is set after a statement, and there is no indication of what occurred before the COMMIT TRANSACTION. **D** is incorrect because the SET command is a Transact-SQL command that does not produce an error.

16. ☑ **B** is correct. Even thought the severity level is in a range not normally able to trigger the setting of @@ERROR, the WITH SETERROR option is turned on. This sets the @@ERROR to the message number or 50000, depending on whether the message was added using sp_addmessage or a message text was passed into RAISERROR. Since the message text is given, it is set to the default 50000.
    ☒ **A** is incorrect. If the WITH SETERROR option were not specified, the value would be 0 since the severity level is between 1 and 10. **C** is incorrect because the @@ERROR is set to 50000 by default and not 60000. **D** is incorrect because the @@ERROR defaults to 50000 and not the message text when a message number is not provided.

17. ☑ **C** is correct. The command to set a connection to the SERIALIZABLE transaction isolation level is SET TRANSACTION ISOLATION LEVEL <ISOLATION LEVEL>.
    ☒ **A** is incorrect. While the syntax is correct, the isolation level is incorrect. REPEATABLE READ does lock all the rows that it is reading, but new rows can be inserted. SERIALIZABLE prevents even this. During a data conversion, the lock needs to prevent new data that could possibly not be converted. **B** is incorrect. The syntax to change the isolation level is not correct. **D** is incorrect. The BEGIN TRANSACTION statement starts an explicit transaction. The AS SERIALIZABLE is not a valid option.

LAB ANSWER

The first issue to deal with is the fact that each satellite office maintains its own inventory while the home office needs to know information for all regions. A possible method to do this is to connect the satellite offices together using some form of LAN so that data can be partitioned across the satellite office inventory databases. This allows the data to stay on the individual office systems while other offices can access all the data via partitioned views that retrieve the data from the various regions. The next issue to deal with would be keeping the sales people with a current product catalog. Since the product catalog is updated infrequently and the sales people never add products to the catalog, a snapshot replication could be set up to allow sales people to pull a new snapshot whenever the catalog is updated.

The final issue is for the verification of inventory before sales. Setting up an inventory system with merge replication between the sales people and their home satellite office provides a way for the sales people's inventory systems to be updated when their machine is brought online. While offline, they could enter pending orders and check for existing inventory. When online, the replication would synchronize the databases and the order could be verified.

5

Manipulating Data Using Transact-SQL

T he Structured Query Language, or SQL, is the standard means used to communicate with a relational database. The American National Standards Institute, or ANSI, publishes a formal standard regarding the syntax of compliant SQL statements. Most relational databases, to varying extents, support ANSI-92 SQL. The ANSI standard is an attempt to allow cross-platform portability between applications that access relational databases by ensuring that database manufacturers support a consistent syntax of SQL. The level of support for ANSI SQL varies from database to database, and no RDBMS fully supports ANSI-92. Most database vendors support some level of ANSI-92 SQL, and then add their own platform-specific enhancements to the language. While most extensions to the ANSI standard tend to be useful, they hinder the *portability* of an application. Portability is a measure of how easily an application running on one system may be ported to another system. Using SQL that conforms to the ANSI standard as much as possible ensures that your applications will be as portable as can be.

There exist many different flavors of SQL from a variety of vendors. For instance, PL/SQL, the language of Oracle databases, has marked differences from the SQL syntax used with DB2, IBM's database system. However, both versions have some support for the ANSI standard. Microsoft's implementation is known as T-SQL, or Transact-SQL. T-SQL offers what's known as entry-level ANSI-92 support with the addition of a useful variety of extensions specific to SQL Server 2000. While these extensions give the database developer a more powerful tool, platform-specific T-SQL extensions will only function with SQL Server 2000 and, in some cases, previous versions of SQL Server.

CERTIFICATION OBJECTIVE 5.01

Overview of Coding SQL Queries

The language of SQL can be broken down into three main categories: DDL, or data definition language, concerns itself with the creation of database objects such as tables, views, and stored procedures. Data control language, or DCL, is used to assign permissions to database objects and manage database users. DCL will be covered in detail in Chapter 8. The third category of SQL, data manipulation language or DML, is the category of SQL this chapter will focus on. DML is used for adding, modifying, or retrieving the information stored in database tables.

The true beauty of DML lies in its simplicity: four basic commands are the foundation for data manipulation in SQL. However they are very flexible in syntax, allowing for the creation of very complex operations. Table 5-1 shows these commands and their usage.

In the next four sections, we will discuss the ANSI 92 syntax for the commands in Table 5-1, and then build upon that syntax with T-SQL extensions. The examples and exercises in the following sections will use the Northwind sample database that installs with SQL Server 2000. Begin a Query Analyzer session from the SQL Server program group and enter the connection information for your SQL Server, as shown in Figure 5-1.

Note that you will be modifying data in the Northwind database in the following sections. If you wish to preserve the data as it exists at installation, make sure that you perform a backup of the database, and then restore it when you've completed this chapter.

The SELECT Statement

Easily the most common statement in the language of SQL, the SELECT statement provides the means to return the data stored in database tables or views. This data can be returned to an online application for user interaction and modification, or to a reporting tool like Excel or Crystal Reports, or simply displayed in a tool like Query Analyzer. The basic syntax of the SELECT statement is shown here:

```
SELECT columns FROM table or view WHERE condition ORDER BY columns
```

The SELECT statement, much like all SQL statements, is very readable. The syntax states "SELECT the columns I specify FROM this table WHERE this search

TABLE 5-1		
	Statement	**Usage**
The Commands of Data Manipulation Language in SQL	SELECT	Used for retrieving the values in the rows and columns of database tables or views
	INSERT	Used for adding rows to database tables
	UPDATE	Used for modifying the values in the columns of database tables
	DELETE	Used for removing rows from database tables

FIGURE 5-1

The Connection
dialog box in
Query Analyzer

condition is met. ORDER the result set BY the columns I specify." Let's look
at some examples. Execute the following SELECT statement in Query Analyzer:

```
SELECT ProductName FROM Products
```

This statement returns the values stored in the ProductName column for all rows
in the Products table. To return multiple columns in a SELECT statement, a comma
is used to separate column names. The following statement returns all product names
and their respective prices from the Products table:

```
SELECT ProductName, UnitPrice FROM Products
```

To return all of the columns in the Products table, you can either type all the
column names separated by commas, or use the asterisk as a shortcut. The following
statement will return all columns for all the rows in the Products table:

```
SELECT * FROM Products
```

Column and Table Aliases

Up to this point, only column names have been specified in the select list of the
SELECT statement. Column names may also be preceded by the originating table
name. While in a single table select this is typically not necessary, you will discover
in the upcoming section on table JOINS that this becomes a requirement. The
syntax looks like this:

```
SELECT Products.ProductName, Products.UnitPrice FROM Products
```

Each column is preceded by its table name, separated by a period. Column and table names can also be aliased to other labels in the SELECT statement. This can produce a more readable result set. In this next example, the table name of Products has been given the alias of Prod, and the column UnitPrice has been given an alias of Price. Any alias can be used, but it is common to use single letters or abbreviations when aliasing a table name.

```
SELECT Prod.ProductName, Prod.UnitPrice AS Price FROM Products
AS Prod
```

In the result set of this statement, the column header of UnitPrice has been replaced with a header titled Price. The column name has been aliased using the AS clause. The table name of Products has also been aliased using an AS clause to a new name of Prod. Also note that in the select list the columns are now preceded by the alias of Prod, instead of the original table name Products. This practice saves a lot of typing when dealing with joins of many tables.

on the
job

The naming of a column does not stop with just the table name and column name. In SQL 2000, columns can use up to a four-part naming convention. For example, a column named Price in a table named Products owned by DBO on a server named SQL1 could be referenced as SQL1.DBO.PRODUCTS.PRICE. Multipart naming becomes important when dealing with data from other databases or servers, as Chapter 7 will show.

The DISTINCT clause

One of the more useful of the SELECT statement clauses is DISTINCT. This clause has the effect of eliminating duplicates in a result set. The following SELECT statement returns all of the values in the CategoryID column of the Products table:

```
SELECT CategoryID FROM Products
```

Note that this query returns 77 rows of data, many of which are duplicates. To eliminate the duplicates and return only the unique CategoryID values, the DISTINCT clause is used.

```
SELECT DISTINCT CategoryID FROM Products
```

This SELECT statement returns only the eight distinct values in the CategoryID column, eliminating the duplicate values. The DISTINCT clause may also be used with multiple columns. Consider the following query:

```
SELECT SupplierID, CategoryID FROM Products
```

This query also returns 77 rows, including duplicates. Execute the same query using the DISTINCT clause.

```
SELECT DISTINCT SupplierID, CategoryID FROM Products
```

Notice that the result set contains some duplicates in the SupplierID column and some duplicate values in the CategoryID column. However, any duplicates involving the combination of SupplierID and CategoryID have been removed. The effect of using DISTINCT with multiple columns will remove any duplicate rows involving *all* of the columns specified in the select list.

Concatenating Fields

The values of character columns in a table can be merged in SQL, or concatenated, producing a new column that contains the values of the original columns added together. ANSI-92 SQL uses a double pipe (||) as the concatenation operator. However, T-SQL uses the plus sign to indicate string concatenation. To demonstrate, execute the following query:

```
SELECT ProductName + ' ' + QuantityPerUnit AS Products
FROM Products
```

The preceding query concatenates the values of the ProductName and QuantityPerUnit columns to form a new column aliased as Products. A space is included between the two columns for readability. The ANSI standard for concatenating strings is shown here:

```
SELECT ProductName || ' ' || QuantityPerUnit AS Products
FROM Products
```

This query returns the same data, but it generates an error in Query Analyzer because SQL Server 2000 does not support the ANSI concatenation operator.

The WHERE Clause

Most of the time, you will not require that all rows from a table be returned in a SELECT statement. Usually, subsets of rows that meet a certain criteria are required by an application. The WHERE clause of the SELECT statement allows search conditions to be applied to columns, and rows returned accordingly. For example, the following statement returns all rows from the Products table that have been discontinued:

```
SELECT * FROM Products WHERE Discontinued = 1
```

The logic applied to a search condition in a WHERE clause is what is known as a *predicate*. In the above example, the predicate used was equality. Only rows where the value of the discontinued column equals 1 were returned. Predicates are by no means limited to equality. Table 5-2 shows some of the more common predicates of the WHERE clause.

To illustrate, the following statement will return all products with a UnitPrice value greater than $50.00:

```
SELECT * FROM Products WHERE UnitPrice > 50
```

The BETWEEN predicate of the WHERE clause takes two arguments to create a range of values to search on. For example, the following statement returns all products with a UnitPrice value between $20 and $30:

```
SELECT * FROM Products WHERE UnitPrice BETWEEN 20 AND 30
```

TABLE 5-2	Predicate	Usage
Common Predicates of the WHERE Clause	=	Returns the row if the column specified equals the specified value
	>	Returns the row if the column specified is greater than the specified value
	<	Returns the row if the column specified is less than the specified value
	BETWEEN	Returns the row if the column specified is between the specified values
	IN	Returns the row if the column specified matches one of the specified values
	LIKE	Returns the row if the column specified matches a pattern specified

The IN predicate of the WHERE clause accepts a list of values, separated by commas. If the column specified matches any of those values, the row is returned. The following will return all products with a price of $10, $15, or $20:

```
SELECT * FROM Products WHERE UnitPrice IN (10, 15, 20)
```

The LIKE predicate of the WHERE clause is used to test a pattern match in a string value. Almost any pattern can be specified using LIKE and *wildcards.* Wildcards are special characters that will not be applied literally to the search condition, but instead will be used to match a pattern. The wildcards are

- ■ _ The underscore will match any single character.
- ■ % The percent sign will match one or more characters.
- ■ [ ] Will match a single character in the specified range or set of values
- ■ [^] Will match a single character not in the specified range or set of values

For example, the following returns all products whose name begins with the letter *C:*

```
SELECT * FROM Products WHERE ProductName LIKE 'C%'
```

This tests for the character *C* followed by any number of other characters. The next statement will return all rows whose name has a first letter of *C* and a third letter of *A.*

```
SELECT * FROM Products WHERE ProductName LIKE 'C_A%'
```

NOT NOT can be applied to any predicate in the WHERE clause to specify that the rows should only be returned if the search condition is False. For instance, to return all rows in the Products table whose names do not begin with the letter *C,* this statement is used:

```
SELECT * FROM Products WHERE ProductName NOT LIKE 'C%'
```

For comparison operators such as equal, greater than, and less than, an exclamation point is substituted for NOT. The following statement will return all rows from the Products table whose price is not greater than $10:

```
SELECT * FROM Products WHERE UnitPrice !> 10
```

Note that "not equals" can be expressed as != or <>.

Specifying Multiple Search Conditions   More than one predicate can be specified in the WHERE clause. This allows for multiple columns to be tested against search conditions. The predicates are separated by one of two operators: AND or OR. AND will return all rows where both conditions are True. OR will return all rows where either condition is True. For instance, the following statement returns the two rows from the Products table where both of the conditions are True:

```
SELECT * FROM Products WHERE SupplierID = 1 AND CategoryID = 1
```

However, the next statement returns 13 rows from the Products table because it will return a row if *either* condition is True:

```
SELECT * FROM Products WHERE SupplierID = 1 OR CategoryID = 1
```

ORDER BY

By design, table rows in a relational database are never guaranteed to be in any particular order. While this is not a problem for most operations, when it comes time to present data to a user, the ORDER BY clause of the SELECT statement allows for an ordering of the result set to be specified. To illustrate, issue the following statement:

```
SELECT ProductName, Discontinued FROM Products
```

This returns the name of all products in the Products table, as well as the flag value, Discontinued. Issuing the above statement may return the data needed, but the result could be much more readable. The next statement uses an ORDER BY clause:

```
SELECT ProductName, Discontinued FROM Products
ORDER BY Discontinued
```

Now, all products available for sale are shown first, followed by discontinued products. The ORDER BY clause is not limited to one column. To return the product names in alphabetical order within each category, the following statement is used:

```
SELECT ProductName, Discontinued FROM Products
ORDER BY Discontinued, ProductName
```

This produces a much more readable report. The ORDER BY clause can also order rows in descending order by specifying DESC after the column name. You may also specify ASC for ascending order; but this is the default order, so ASC is optional. The following statement will return product names in reverse alphabetical order within each category:

```
SELECT ProductName, Discontinued FROM Products
ORDER BY Discontinued ASC, ProductName DESC
```

CASE

SQL provides a means with which to alter the values returned from column values as they are queried. By using the CASE expression, column values returned from table rows can each be examined, and conditional logic can then be applied. CASE is often useful in increasing the readability of a result set. To illustrate, execute the following query:

```
SELECT ProductName, Expense = CASE
WHEN UnitPrice < 10 THEN 'Cheap'
WHEN UnitPrice < 50 THEN 'Moderate'
WHEN UnitPrice < 100 THEN 'Expensive'
ELSE 'Very Expensive'
END
FROM Products
```

In the preceding query, a new column called Expense is created. The value of Expense is based on the value of the UnitPrice column being returned by each row. Each of the three WHEN keywords indicate a condition that must be met in order for the value specified after the THEN keyword to be applied. The ELSE keyword sets the value of the Expense column if the value from UnitPrice does not meet any of the previous conditions defined by WHEN.

The WHEN keyword within a CASE statement uses a predicate like the WHERE clause of a SELECT statement. In this query, the less-than predicate has been used. Other predicates such as equal and greater than can also be used in a CASE expression.

Subqueries

A powerful feature of the SELECT statement is the ability to nest queries inside of each other. This allows for a SELECT statement to use more complex search conditions, such as comparing a column to values in another table. A subquery is enclosed in parentheses, as shown here:

```
SELECT ProductName, UnitPrice FROM Products
WHERE CategoryID =
    (SELECT CategoryID FROM Categories
     WHERE CategoryName = 'Beverages')
```

This SELECT statement uses a subquery to return products that exist in a category called Beverages. The subquery returns the CategoryID value of the category named Beverages from the Categories table, and then that value is tested against the CategoryID column in the Products table. A subquery is not limited to returning one value. A subquery can return a list of values, as shown in the next statement:

```
SELECT ProductName, UnitPrice FROM Products
WHERE CategoryID IN
    (SELECT CategoryID FROM Categories
     WHERE CategoryName = 'Beverages' OR CategoryName = 'Seafood')
```

In this statement, the subquery now returns two CategoryID values from the Categories table. Each of the two values is then tested against the CategoryID column in the Products table, using the IN predicate of the WHERE clause.

Subqueries can be nested within other subqueries as well. The following statement shows a subquery within a subquery, using three tables total. It returns all suppliers that supply products in the category of 'Beverages'.

```
SELECT CompanyName FROM Suppliers
WHERE SupplierID IN
    (SELECT SupplierID FROM Products
     WHERE CategoryID =
         (SELECT CategoryID FROM Categories
          WHERE CategoryName = 'Beverages'))
```

EXISTS and NOT EXISTS   Another way to begin a subquery is by using the EXISTS or NOT EXISTS predicate of the WHERE clause. The EXISTS predicate is a bit different from the other predicates of the WHERE clause. In the preceding examples of subqueries, the subquery itself is performed first, and the result set from the subquery is used in the *outer* query. The outer query is simply the query that calls a subquery. To illustrate, consider the following SELECT statement:

```
SELECT ProductName FROM Products
WHERE CategoryID in
    (SELECT CategoryID FROM Categories
     WHERE CategoryName = 'Beverages')
```

In this statement, steps occur in the following order: the subquery retrieves a CategoryID value of 1 from the Categories table. This resulting value is then plugged into the outer query. At this point, the outer query is executed and would look like the following:

```
SELECT ProductName FROM Products
WHERE CategoryID in (1)
```

Using the EXISTS predicate of the WHERE clause creates what is known as a *correlated subquery*. A correlated subquery is a subquery that cannot exist in and of itself: it references a column in the outer query. In a correlated subquery, the subquery is executed for each candidate row in the outer query. Let's look at an example. The following is the same SELECT statement, this time using EXISTS instead of IN:

```
SELECT ProductName FROM Products
WHERE EXISTS
    (SELECT * FROM Categories
     WHERE CategoryName = 'Beverages'
     AND Products.CategoryID = Categories.CategoryID)
```

As opposed to other subqueries, the steps in this correlated subquery occur in a different order. First, the outer query is executed to retrieve a candidate row for the subquery. The subquery is then executed using the criteria of the row returned from the outer query. You'll note that the columns in the subquery need to be prefaced with their respective table names in order to define the column on which the subquery and outer query will be joined. To clarify, let's look at the steps of the correlated subquery: the outer query retrieves a row from the Products table. This row has a value of 1 in the CategoryID column. That value is then used in the subquery, and would now look like this:

```
SELECT * FROM Categories
WHERE CategoryName = 'Beverages'
AND 1 = Categories.CategoryID
```

This query equates to True, as the CategoryID for the row with the CategoryName of 'Beverages' is indeed 1. Therefore, the original row in the outer query is included in the result set. Next the outer query retrieves a row with a value of 2 in the CategoryID column. This value is then plugged into the subquery and would look like this at this point:

```
SELECT * FROM Categories
WHERE CategoryName = 'Beverages'
AND 2 = Categories.CategoryID
```

This subquery equates to false, as 'Beverages' does not have a CategoryID value of 2. Therefore, this row is not included in the result set. This process continues until each row in the outer query has been tested against the subquery. To simplify, a correlated subquery works in the reverse order of a regular subquery: the subquery is executed for each row in the outer query.

NOT EXISTS can be used to test for the nonexistence of rows in the subquery. The following SELECT statement returns all products that do not exist in the category of 'Beverages':

```
SELECT ProductName FROM Products
WHERE NOT EXISTS
    (SELECT * FROM Categories
     WHERE CategoryName = 'Beverages'
     AND Products.CategoryID = Categories.CategoryID)
```

This is simply the reverse of the original SELECT statement: the CategoryID for each row in the Products table is tested against the subquery, only this time the rows that don't have a CategoryID value of 1 are returned.

on the job *The EXISTS and NOT EXISTS predicates have an advantage over their counterparts, IN and NOT IN. With EXISTS, you can specify SELECT * as opposed to SELECT ColumnName in the subquery. This allows the query optimizer to more efficiently choose indexes for the subquery. EXISTS and NOT EXISTS can sometimes yield dramatic performance results vs. IN and NOT IN.*

There are more clauses and features of the SELECT statement that will be discussed in the section on summarizing data, but you now have a solid foundation on which to build.

The INSERT Statement

We've covered how to retrieve table rows based on search criteria. Adding new rows to a table is accomplished using the INSERT statement. The basic syntax of the INSERT statement is as follows:

```
INSERT INTO TableName
(ColumnList)
VALUES
(ColumnValue1, ColumnValue2...)
```

A column list is provided directly after the table name, surrounded by parentheses. The keyword VALUES then indicates the values for the columns in the new row. Let's look at an example. In the following, we'll insert a new row into the Territories table for Sarasota, Florida:

```
INSERT INTO Territories
(TerritoryID, TerritoryDescription, RegionID)
VALUES
(34231, 'Sarasota', 4)
```

The values specified in the last line of the INSERT correspond directly to the column names in the column list. However, it is not always necessary to provide a value for each column in an INSERT statement. Columns defined as nullable, or columns with a default value, do not have to have a value declared, as shown in this example:

```
INSERT INTO Customers
(CustomerID, CompanyName)
VALUES
('ACMMA', 'Acme Manufacturing')
```

The Customers table in the Northwind database has 11 columns. However, the above INSERT succeeds because the other nine columns allow NULL values. In the case of the preceding INSERT, a new row is inserted into the Customers table, but all columns except CustomerID and CompanyName have been inserted with a value of NULL.

If a value is being provided for every column in a table, the column list is not even necessary. In the following example, we'll insert another row into the Territories table for San Diego, California:

```
INSERT INTO Territories
VALUES
(92138, 'San Diego', 2)
```

In the preceding, the column list has been eliminated completely because we have provided a value for each column in the table in the same order as the columns appear in the Territories table. However, it is always advisable to include a column list in the event the underlying table structure changes.

Another case, specific to SQL Server, in which you would not provide a value for a column in an INSERT statement is if the column has been defined with the IDENTITY property. Columns defined with the IDENTITY property will autoincrement a numeric value each time an INSERT occurs. Attempting to specify a value for such a column will cause the INSERT to fail. This behavior can be overridden by setting IDENTITY_INSERT to ON, which will allow a value to be specified for a column defined with the IDENTITY property.

A powerful feature of the INSERT statement is that the column values for new rows needn't be explicitly defined: they can be based on values in other tables. To illustrate, create a new table in the Northwind database called NewTerritories that mirrors the layout of the Territories table.

```
CREATE TABLE NewTerritories
    (TerritoryID nvarchar(20) PRIMARY KEY,
     TerritoryDescription nchar(50),
     RegionID int)
```

The following INSERT statement will insert every row from the Territories table into the table just created:

```
INSERT INTO NewTerritories
SELECT * FROM Territories
```

Values from other tables and explicit values can also be combined in one INSERT statement, as just shown. The following example will insert a row into the Customers table using an explicitly defined CustomerID value, and a CompanyName value retrieved from the Territories table:

```
INSERT INTO Customers
(CustomerID, CompanyName)
SELECT 'SARAS', TerritoryDescription FROM Territories
WHERE TerritoryID = '34231'
```

Subqueries may also be used for the values of an INSERT statement, as shown here:

```
INSERT INTO Customers
(CustomerID, CompanyName, ContactName)
SELECT 'SANDI', (SELECT TerritoryDescription FROM Territories
WHERE TerritoryID = '92138'), 'Jeff'
```

on the job *Note that in cases where the inserted values reference other tables, the VALUES keyword is not specified. Specifying VALUES in such a situation will result in a syntax error.*

The UPDATE Statement

After inserting rows into a database table, situations arise where values in the particular columns of a row will need to be updated. Updating rows is actually one of the most common tasks an application will perform on a database: a result set is presented to a user for review using the SELECT statement, the user then modifies certain fields of the result set, and the changes are made to the table rows using the UPDATE statement.

The basic syntax of the UPDATE statement is as follows:

```
UPDATE TableName
SET Column = NewValue
```

Let's use an example to illustrate. The following UPDATE statement will set all of the products in the Northwind database to a status of Discontinued:

```
UPDATE Products
SET Discontinued = 1
```

Executing this statement sets every value in the Discontinued column to a value of 1 for each row in the Products table. While updating every row in a table can be useful, the UPDATE statement supports the use of the WHERE clause to allow specific rows to be updated. The following statement will remove the Discontinued status from all products with a price greater than $20:

```
UPDATE Products
SET Discontinued = 0
WHERE UnitPrice > 20
```

Multiple columns may be modified using a single UPDATE statement. The following statement sets the Discontinued flag to 1, and the UnitsInStock value to 0 for all the products with a price of less than $20:

```
UPDATE Products
SET Discontinued = 1, UnitsInStock = 0
WHERE UnitPrice < 20
```

Much like the INSERT statement, the new values specified in an UPDATE statement can reference values in other tables. The following statement updates the product name of the row with a value of 1 in the ProductID column with a value obtained from another table:

```
UPDATE Products
SET ProductName =
    (SELECT TerritoryDescription
     FROM Territories WHERE TerritoryID = '92138')
WHERE ProductID = 1
```

This statement uses a subquery to obtain a new ProductName value from the Territories table. The value returned by the subquery is then applied to the row in the Products table with a value of 1 in the ProductID column. T-SQL allows the UPDATE statement to reference other tables using a table JOIN as opposed to a subquery. Table joins will be discussed in an upcoming section.

The DELETE Statement

The final command in DML is the DELETE statement. DELETE allows for the removal of rows from database tables. After being deleted, the row(s) affected no longer exist in the database. The basic syntax of the DELETE statement is shown here:

```
DELETE FROM Tablename
WHERE (search condition)
```

Much like the UPDATE statement, the DELETE statement allows for the use of a WHERE clause to specify a subset of rows to delete in a table. It is very important to use a WHERE clause when deleting table rows. The following statement does not use a WHERE clause and as such will delete all rows from the CustomerDemographics table:

```
DELETE FROM CustomerDemographics
```

The following statement uses a WHERE clause to delete the row for San Diego from the Territories table:

```
DELETE FROM Territories
WHERE TerritoryID = 92138
```

Deletes, much like updates, can also reference rows in other tables. The following DELETE statement uses a subquery to delete all rows in the Territories table that are not assigned to any employee:

```
DELETE FROM Territories WHERE NOT EXISTS
    (SELECT TerritoryID FROM EmployeeTerritories
    WHERE Territories.TerritoryID =
    EmployeeTerritories.TerritoryID)
```

In T-SQL, deletes can also use table joins to reference other tables. Joins will be discussed in the next section.

Joining Tables

By design, a relational database stores data in many different tables that reference each other through relationships. Normalization can be thought of as the process that splits information into logical groupings that become database tables. To perform the reverse and recombine the data in the underlying tables back together, table joins are used with the four DML commands.

Joining database tables using SQL is a very common practice, especially in databases that have a high degree of normalization. There are several types of joins that can be used in SQL, each designed for specific conditions when recombining tables.

Equijoins and Inner Joins

The equijoin is one of the most common joins you will use in a relational database. It is a situation in which two or more tables are joined based on columns from each table *equating* to each other. (The equijoin is also known as an *inner join*.) It is very useful for reassembling data that has been logically split up into multiple tables. Let's look at a very basic equijoin:

```
SELECT P.ProductName, C.CategoryName
FROM Products AS P JOIN Categories AS C
ON P.CategoryID = C.CategoryID
```

This SELECT statement uses an equijoin to combine the names of products retrieved from the Products table with the names of categories retrieved from the Categories table. The keyword JOIN is used in the FROM clause separating the tables involved in the join. The ON clause is specified following the table names to define the columns on which the tables involved will be joined. In this case, the tables are joined on the CategoryID column. This join condition states that each product name will be displayed with its respective category name based on the CategoryID column being equal in both tables. Simply put, the join looks at the CategoryID value for each row in the Products table and fetches the CategoryName value with the same category ID in the Categories table.

The AND keyword can be used in the ON clause to specify that more than one condition is being used to join tables. The following uses the same join but limits the result set to the product named 'Tofu':

```
SELECT P.ProductName, C.CategoryName
FROM Products AS P JOIN Categories AS C
ON P.CategoryID = C.CategoryID
AND P.ProductName = 'Tofu'
```

When an inner join of this type is specified using some condition other than equality, it becomes what's known as a *conditional join*. A conditional join is a type of inner join that is based on any predicate used in a WHERE clause. An equijoin itself is actually a form of conditional join that uses equality as the join condition. When a join condition other than equality is used, the join becomes conditional. The following will illustrate a conditional join:

```
SELECT P.ProductName, C.CategoryName
FROM Products AS P JOIN Categories AS C
ON P.CategoryID <> C.CategoryID
AND P.ProductName = 'Tofu'
```

The preceding SELECT statement returns seven rows of data. It uses a conditional join to display all of the categories that the product 'Tofu' is *not* a member of. In this case, all categories except Produce are returned, because Produce is the category of the product 'Tofu'.

As previously stated, equijoins and conditional joins are all types of inner joins. Inner joins are by no means limited to two tables. Joins of four, five, or more tables are not at all uncommon in larger databases.

The following SELECT statement joins three tables to return the category name and supplier name for the product named 'Tofu':

```
SELECT P.ProductName, C.CategoryName, S.CompanyName
FROM Products AS P JOIN Categories AS C
ON P.CategoryID = C.CategoryID
AND P.ProductName = 'Tofu'
```

```
JOIN Suppliers as S
ON P.SupplierID = S.SupplierID
```

The Products table is joined to the Categories table on the condition of the CategoryID column being equal, and the product name having a value of 'Tofu'. After those conditions are specified in the ON clause, another JOIN keyword is added to join the current result set to the Suppliers table. Another ON keyword is used to specify the condition of the second join, the SupplierID columns having equal values. As the preceding syntax demonstrates, for each JOIN that occurs in a statement, the ON keyword is specified to declare the conditions of the current join.

Outer Joins

Another method of joining tables is by using what's known as an *outer join*. Outer joins are used in situations in which the rows in one table may or may not match rows in other tables. Outer joins are very common when using SQL to generate reports. Consider a list of customers that have money at a bank. Some of the customers have checking accounts, some have savings accounts, and some have both. In order to generate a report of all customers and the types of accounts they have, it will be necessary to use an outer join on the Customers and Accounts tables, because each customer row may or may not have rows in a particular Account table.

There are three types of outer joins: left outer joins, right outer joins, and full outer joins. In order to fully understand each type of join, it is necessary to cover the concepts of *left and right result sets.*

Left and Right Result Sets
In dealing with table joins, no matter how many tables are involved, the terms *left result set* and *right result set* apply to each instance of a join in any particular statement. To demonstrate these concepts, consider the following, which represents a three-table join.

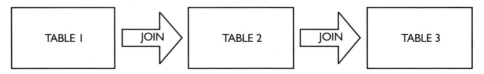

When a table join occurs, each JOIN keyword is treated separately from every other join in the statement. In this illustration, a table join will occur twice. At the point the first JOIN keyword is encountered, each table is treated as being either on the left or the right of the join. To illustrate, when the first JOIN keyword is encountered in the three-table join, conceptually it looks like this:

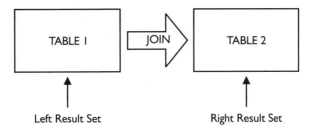

At the point before the joining of Table 1 and Table 2 occurs, the rows from Table 1 are considered the left result set, or left of the JOIN keyword, and the rows from Table 2 are considered the right result set, or right of the JOIN keyword. The rows from both Table 1 and Table 2 are then joined based on the join conditions specified creating a new result set, as shown here:

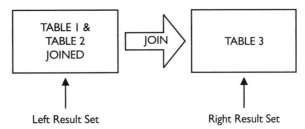

At the point of the next join, the joined rows from Table 1 and Table 2 have merged to become the left result set. The next table to be joined, Table 3, has become the right result set. This process continues on until all tables involved in the statement have been joined. Irrespective of how many tables are involved in a join, each instance of the JOIN keyword deals with a left result set that consists of all joins performed up to that point, and a right result set that is the next table that the current result set will be joined with.

Left Outer Joins   Now that you have an understanding of left and right result sets, let's take a look at the first type of outer join, the left outer join. In a typical inner join, the rows in the left table that have no matching rows in the right table will be excluded from the final result set. Consider the following query that uses an inner join:

```
SELECT C.CustomerID, O.OrderID
FROM Customers AS C JOIN Orders AS O
ON C.CustomerID = O.CustomerID
ORDER BY O.OrderID
```

This SELECT statement joins every row in the Customer table with every row in the Orders table to show a list of customers and the orders that they have placed. However, this query does not include customers that have not placed any orders in the result set. In order to include all customers irrespective of whether or not they have placed an order, a left outer join is used, as shown here:

```
SELECT C.CustomerID, O.OrderID
FROM Customers AS C LEFT OUTER JOIN Orders AS O
ON C.CustomerID = O.CustomerID
ORDER BY O.OrderID
```

Now we have a full listing of customers along with all the orders that each customer has placed. A left outer join returns *all* rows in the left result set. If a customer has not placed any orders, a NULL value is displayed in the OrderID column of the final result set. Since the statement uses an ORDER BY OrderID, the customers with no orders are displayed first. Left outer joins are designed to work in that fashion: if a row from the left result set has no corresponding rows in the right result set, the columns in the right result set will display a NULL value.

Any particular statement is not limited to using the same type of join for each table to be joined. Inner and outer joins can be combined in the same statement. For instance, the following SELECT statement performs a left outer join of the Customers and Orders table, then an inner join on the Orders and Shippers tables:

```
SELECT C.CustomerID, O.OrderID, S.CompanyName
FROM Customers AS C LEFT OUTER JOIN Orders AS O
ON C.CustomerID = O.CustomerID
JOIN Shippers AS S
ON O.ShipVia = S.ShipperID
ORDER BY O.OrderID
```

This statement returns customers and the orders that each customer has placed, as well as the company that shipped each order. However, you will notice that the result set from the above query has once again eliminated the customers that have no corresponding rows in the Orders table. This is because of the second JOIN keyword, the inner join that joins the result set from the first join to the Shippers table. Any customers that have no orders will naturally have no rows in the Shippers table indicating who shipped the nonexistent orders. Remember: each join is considered completely on its own, independent of any other joins that have occurred up to that point. In order to retain the customers that have placed no orders, the preceding query needs to use two left outer joins as shown here:

```
SELECT C.CustomerID, O.OrderID, S.CompanyName
FROM Customers AS C LEFT OUTER JOIN Orders AS O
ON C.CustomerID = O.CustomerID
LEFT OUTER JOIN Shippers AS S
ON O.ShipVia = S.ShipperID
ORDER BY O.OrderID
```

In this query, any matching rows from the result set produced by joining the Customers and Orders table will be retained whether or not a corresponding row in the Shippers table exists. In this case, both the OrderID and the CompanyName columns will be displayed with a NULL value for each customer that has not placed an order.

Right Outer Joins   The right outer join is basically the opposite of the left outer join: all rows in the right result set are retained and any rows in the left result set that have no corresponding row are set to NULL. A good use for right outer joins is when many tables have been previously joined and you wish to compare a table to that result set, as shown here:

```
SELECT O.OrderID, S.CompanyName, E.LastName, C.CustomerID
FROM Orders AS O JOIN Shippers AS S
ON O.ShipVia = S.ShipperID
JOIN Employees AS E
ON O.EmployeeID = E.EmployeeID
RIGHT OUTER JOIN Customers AS C
ON O.CustomerID = C.CustomerID
ORDER BY O.OrderID
```

In this query, the Orders, Shippers, and Employees tables are joined using inner joins to create a result set. This result set is then joined to the Customers table using a right outer join, to display all customers irrespective of whether or not they have a matching row in that result set.

The previous SELECT statement could easily have been written using a series of left outer joins as well, as shown next.

```
SELECT O.OrderID, S.CompanyName, E.LastName, C.CustomerID
FROM Customers AS C LEFT OUTER JOIN Orders AS O
ON C.CustomerID = O.CustomerID
LEFT OUTER JOIN Shippers AS S
ON O.ShipVia = S.ShipperID
LEFT OUTER JOIN Employees AS E
ON O.EmployeeID = E.EmployeeID
ORDER BY O.OrderID
```

In simple queries, it is typically a matter of preference as to writing a statement using left or right outer joins. However, in highly complex queries involving large numbers of tables, sometimes combinations of left and right outer joins will be necessary to retrieve the data required.

on the
job
There is no such thing as a left inner join or a right inner join. Therefore, the OUTER keyword is optional in join syntax. An outer join may be coded by simply specifying LEFT JOIN or RIGHT JOIN.

Full Outer Joins   The full outer join is simply the left outer join and the right outer join combined. It retains rows in the left result set that have no corresponding rows in the right result set, and it also retains rows in the right result set that have no corresponding rows in the left result set. A good use for a full outer join would be querying two tables, Employees and Departments. A full outer join would retain all employees not assigned to a department and also retain all departments that have no employees assigned to them. To illustrate, first execute the following INSERT statement to add a row to the NewTerritories table:

```
INSERT INTO NewTerritories
VALUES
(44130, 'Cleveland', 1)
```

There now exists a TerritoryID value in the NewTerritories table that has no corresponding TerritoryID value in the Territories table, and vice versa. Execute the following full outer join:

```
SELECT T.TerritoryID, NT.TerritoryID FROM Territories as T
FULL OUTER JOIN NewTerritories AS NT
ON T.TerritoryID = NT.TerritoryID
ORDER BY NT.TerritoryID DESC
```

As you can see, the full outer join has retained rows in both the left and right result sets that have no corresponding rows in the opposite result set. Full outer joins are probably the most uncommon type of outer join; however, they are quite necessary when the difference between two result sets is a requirement.

exam
Ⓦatch

If you encounter an exam question having to do with generating a particular report, carefully consider the wording of the question to ascertain which type of joins you will need to use. Remember, a left or right outer join will probably meet the requirements unless you specifically need to see unmatching rows in both the left and right result set.

Unions   The final type of join that will be covered in this chapter is a special kind of join that doesn't even use the JOIN keyword. Known as a UNION, this type of join merges two like tables together, producing a single result set. The final result set will consist of the rows from both tables displayed as if they were all rows in the same table. Let's take a look at a SELECT statement that performs a UNION on two tables:

```
SELECT * FROM Territories
UNION
SELECT * FROM NewTerritories
```

The result set from the preceding statement produces a result set containing all rows from the Territories table, as well as all rows from the NewTerritories table. Note that a union requires no join condition; it simply concatenates all rows from one table to all rows from another table.

All of the joins up to this point that used the JOIN keyword have concatenated rows *horizontally,* or by adding new columns to the result set. The UNION operator concatenates rows *vertically,* with no modification to the column layout in either table. In order for two tables to be merged using UNION, both tables must have a similar structure. In other words, the tables must have the same number of columns using the same datatypes. However, the column names in each table do not have to be the same. By default, the column names from the first table specified will be used in the result set.

Also note that when using UNION, any rows that exist in both tables involved will not be duplicated. In order to preserve the duplicate rows in a union, you need to use UNION ALL. UNION ALL will display all rows from both tables including duplicates.

SCENARIO & SOLUTION

You need to join tables based on matching column values in a foreign-key relationship.	Use an INNER JOIN.
You need to join tables when there may or may not be matching column values.	Use an OUTER JOIN.
You need to join tables that are identical in structure, creating a single result set.	Use a UNION.

EXERCISE 5-1

Coding SQL Queries

The following exercise will use two ways to retrieve the information required. Consider the following request: "I'd like to see a list of all the customers that employee Andrew Fuller has completed orders for. I only need to see the customer ID for each customer, and I'd like the results in alphabetical order." In looking at the schema for the Northwind database, it becomes apparent that the SQL needed to satisfy this request will have to combine data from three tables: Customers, Orders, and Employees. We will use two methods to produce the desired report: first using subqueries, and then using joins.

1. Retrieve the requested information using subqueries, as shown in the following statement:

```
SELECT CustomerID FROM Customers
WHERE CustomerID IN
    (SELECT CustomerID FROM Orders
    WHERE EmployeeID IN
        (SELECT EmployeeID FROM Employees
        WHERE LastName = 'Fuller' AND FirstName = 'Andrew'))
ORDER BY CustomerID
```

This query satisfies the requirements by querying the Orders table to determine which employees placed which orders. This result set is then joined on the Employees table, limiting the result set to the EmployeeID row with the value of 'Andrew' in the FirstName column, and 'Fuller' in the LastName column.

2. Retrieve the requested information using joins, as shown in the following statement:

```
SELECT DISTINCT C.CustomerID FROM
Customers AS C JOIN Orders AS O
ON C.CustomerID = O.CustomerID
JOIN Employees AS E
ON O.EmployeeID = E.EmployeeID
AND E.LastName = 'Fuller' AND E.FirstName = 'Andrew'
ORDER BY C.CustomerID
```

As opposed to the statement that uses subqueries, this statement simply joins all three tables involved to retrieve the list of CustomerID values that have placed orders through employee Andrew Fuller. Inner joins are the only type of join used, because unmatching rows are not a consideration in any of the joins. Also note the use of the DISTINCT keyword, as this statement would produce duplicate CustomerID values for multiple orders placed by the same customer.

CERTIFICATION OBJECTIVE 5.02

Retrieving Data Using Transact-SQL

Now that you have a foundation in coding SQL statements, we'll build on that knowledge by using Transact SQL to retrieve data. The following sections will introduce you to the power and flexibility of T-SQL, especially when used for reporting purposes.

T-SQL Overview

In the first part of this chapter, we discussed the four basic statements of data manipulation language. Transact-SQL adds some very useful extensions to those commands, allowing much greater control in how a result set is eventually structured. It also allows for the use of joins in INSERT, UPDATE, and DELETE operations.

The examples and exercises in the following sections will use the Pubs sample database that installs with SQL Server 2000. Note that you will be modifying data in the Pubs database in the following sections. If you wish to preserve the data as it exists at installation, make sure that you perform a backup of the database, and then restore it when you've completed this chapter.

TOP *n*

The TOP *n* clause of the SELECT statement has the effect of limiting a result set to a certain number of rows. The *n* in TOP *n* is an integer value specifying how many rows to limit the result set to. TOP *n* dramatically simplifies structuring a result set. It is one of those commands that once you begin to use it, you'll wonder how you ever got by without it. To illustrate, execute the following query against the Pubs database:

```
SELECT * FROM Stores
ORDER BY State
```

This statement generates a result set consisting of the six rows in the Stores table, ordered by the State column. By applying the TOP *n* clause to this statement, we can limit the result set to how many rows we choose, as shown here:

```
SELECT TOP 1 * FROM Stores
ORDER BY State
```

In the preceding statement, we have executed the same query as before, but this time TOP 1 has been used to limit the result set to just the first row in the result set. Just what that first row will be is determined by the ORDER BY clause. ORDER BY becomes very important when using TOP *n*, as the column ordered by will be the value that TOP *n* uses as a reference. To illustrate, execute the following query that uses stor_id in the ORDER BY clause:

```
SELECT TOP 1 * FROM Stores
ORDER BY stor_id
```

In this case, the single row returned by the statement has changed. Since the order of the result set is now different, only the first row in the result set obtained by ordering by the stor_id column is returned.

TOP *n* can also use a keyword of PERCENT to limit result sets. When using PERCENT, the value of *n* now becomes an integer between 0 and 100. The following query returns the first 50 percent of the rows in the Stores table:

```
SELECT TOP 50 PERCENT * FROM Stores
ORDER BY Stor_id
```

Using PERCENT with TOP *n* is useful when a sampling of rows from a table is necessary. Note that specifying 0 with TOP *n* returns no rows from the original result set.

The final keyword that can be used in conjunction with TOP *n* has to do with duplicates in a result set. Specifying WITH TIES has the effect of including any duplicates of the column specified in the ORDER BY clause of the SELECT statement. Consider the following query:

```
SELECT TOP 1 * FROM Stores
ORDER BY State
```

TOP *n* first produces an ordered result set and then limits the number of rows returned. In the above statement, this causes the value of CA to appear as the first value in the result set. However, there are several rows in the Stores table that have a value of CA in the State column. To preserve the duplicate values, WITH TIES is used, as shown here:

```
SELECT TOP 1 WITH TIES * FROM Stores
ORDER BY State
```

Now the two other rows with the same value in the column specified in the ORDER BY clause as the TOP 1 row in the result set have been included. Specifying WITH TIES basically tells SQL Server to return the top rows from the result set using the integer value specified in *n*, and if there are any duplicates in the column specified in the ORDER BY clause, to include them.

Using Joins to Modify Data

We have seen how to use subqueries within an INSERT, UPDATE, or DELETE statement in the first part of this chapter. T-SQL extends on that capability by allowing these statements to reference other tables using table joins. For example, consider the following UPDATE that uses a subquery:

```
UPDATE Employee
SET job_lvl = job_lvl + 5
WHERE job_id IN
    (SELECT job_id FROM jobs
     WHERE job_desc = 'Managing Editor')
```

This modification adds 5 to the value in each job_lvl column in the Employee table for each employee row that has a job description of 'Managing Editor' in the Jobs table. The preceding statement could also be written using a table join, as shown here:

```
UPDATE Employee
SET job_lvl = job_lvl + 5
FROM Employee AS E JOIN Jobs AS J
ON E.job_id = J.job_id
AND J.job_desc = 'Managing Editor'
```

In this statement, each row in the Employee table is joined to each row in the Jobs table to determine which employees have a job description of 'Managing Editor'. The UPDATE is then performed based on the join conditions specified. Using a table join in an UPDATE has a very similar syntax to using the JOIN keyword in a SELECT statement. The WHERE clause that would normally be used if the UPDATE were using a subquery is replaced with the FROM keyword, and the join is coded from there.

exam
ⓦatch

Pay special attention to the syntax when using table joins in a data modification statement. Note that the table name is specified twice, once directly after the UPDATE keyword to indicate the table to be updated, and then again in the JOIN where the table name can be aliased. It is not permitted to alias the table name directly after the UPDATE keyword. Thus, the following would be illegal:

```
UPDATE Employee AS E
SET E.Job_lvl = ..
```

Using table joins with the DELETE statement has a similar syntax. The WHERE clause typically used to restrict the rows being deleted is replaced with the FROM clause of the JOIN syntax used in a SELECT statement. The following statement uses a subquery to remove all rows from the Employees table that have a job description of 'Designer':

```
DELETE FROM Employee
WHERE job_id =
```

```
(SELECT job_id FROM Jobs
 WHERE job_desc = 'Designer')
```

The same modification can be accomplished using a table join, as shown here:

```
DELETE FROM Employee
FROM Employee AS E JOIN Jobs AS J
ON E.job_id = J.job_id
AND J.job_desc = 'Designer'
```

Using table joins in data modification statements can greatly simplify complex operations that query values in multiple tables. Although not every subquery can be recoded to use a table join, in some cases a table join will perform better than a subquery, especially when dealing with correlated subqueries.

Summarizing Data for Reporting Purposes

Relational databases can store vast amounts of information. Consider for a moment a database that tracks customers and orders for a large corporation. Any time a customer orders something from our company, that information is recorded in a relational database with a high level of detail. Our buyers' habits, likes, and dislikes, and when, where, and how they make purchases are all stored within a relational database. What better source for making future business decisions than studying the habits of our customers in the past?

The functions of SQL can be broken down into two main categories. First, SQL is used in online applications to gather and modify corporate data. Second, it is used to query that data for reporting purposes. This section will cover the aspects of DML used for report generation. A relational database is an invaluable resource when it comes to gathering and presenting historical data for analysis, study, and review, and T-SQL is a very powerful tool for retrieving such data.

Aggregate Functions

In T-SQL, as well as ANSI-92 SQL, there exists a set of functions known as *aggregate* functions. Aggregate functions provide a way to summarize sets or subsets of data, producing a single result. They are invaluable with regard to reporting functionality. For instance, consider a table that stores order information for a company. Every so often, the company will need to know how many orders have been placed from a certain date to a certain date. Querying this table to obtain a count of orders within a certain date range is an example of using an aggregate function.

Table 5-3 lists some of the more common aggregate functions and their usage. The following sections will explore the functionality of each aggregate function.

COUNT The COUNT aggregate function is one of the most commonly used aggregates in T-SQL. It returns a count of rows or values in a result set of data. It can be used to count the values of a particular column, or give a complete count of rows in a result set. To illustrate, consider the following query:

```
SELECT COUNT(*) AS NumberOfRows FROM Discounts
```

This query returns a numeric value for the number of rows in the result set. In this case, the result set is all rows from the Discounts table. As there are three rows of data in the Discounts table, the value 3 is returned and aliased as NumberOfRows for clarity. By default, COUNT does not take into account NULL values. To illustrate, execute the following query that returns a count of the stor_id column from the Discounts table:

```
SELECT COUNT(stor_id)AS NumberOfRows FROM Discounts
```

This SELECT statement returns a value of 1. Although there exist three rows in the Discounts table, only one row has a value in the stor_id column that is not NULL, so the returned value of 1 is accurate.

The COUNT function is the only aggregate function that can take the wildcard * as an argument. All other functions require a column name to be specified. Also, the

TABLE 5-3	Aggregate Function	Purpose
Common Aggregate Functions of T-SQL	COUNT()	Returns a count of rows involved in a set or subset of data
	MIN()	Returns the minimum value of a column involved in a set or subset of data
	MAX()	Returns the maximum value of a column involved in a set or subset of data
	AVG()	Returns the average value of a column involved in a set or subset of data
	SUM()	Returns the sum of values of a column involved in a set or subset of data

COUNT function, like all other aggregate functions, takes only one argument. Thus, the following would be illegal syntax:

```
SELECT COUNT(lowqty, highqty) FROM Discounts
```

COUNT may also be used with the DISTINCT keyword, to return a count of distinct values from a result set.

MIN   The MIN aggregate function returns the minimum value of the column specified as the argument in a result set. The following SELECT statement returns the lowest price in the Titles table:

```
SELECT MIN(price) from Titles
```

Upon executing the preceding query, you should also have received a warning that the NULL values had been eliminated from the aggregate function MIN. This warning has the effect of saying, "This is the minimum value from the Price column in the Titles table that has a known—that is, not a NULL—value."

MIN is not limited to a numeric column as an argument. It can accept columns defined with most datatypes as an argument (Bit is an example of a datatype that the MIN function cannot accept). The following query returns the minimum value in the Title column from the Titles table:

```
SELECT MIN(title) from Titles
```

This query returns the value "But Is It User Friendly?". Since the argument provided to the MIN function uses a character datatype, the letter *A* is considered lowest and the letter *Z* is considered highest. (Numbers and symbols are ordered before letters in character data as well.) Therefore, the title that begins with the letter *B* is the minimum value for the Title column.

MAX   The MAX aggregate function is the opposite of the MIN aggregate function. It returns the maximum value of the column specified. The following query returns the book with the highest value in the Price column in the Titles table:

```
SELECT MAX(price) from Titles
```

As with the MIN function, MAX cannot take into account NULL values, nor can it take a column defined with a Bit datatype as an argument. Also note that specifying the DISTINCT keyword in the SELECT statement has no effect on the MIN and MAX functions. The following two SELECT statements return the same value:

```
SELECT MAX(price) from Titles
SELECT MAX(DISTINCT price) FROM Titles
```

AVG   The AVG aggregate function returns the average value of the column specified as an argument for a given result set. Unlike MIN, MAX, and COUNT, AVG can be used only on numeric columns (Decimal, Int, Float, etc.). This makes sense, as the average value of a character column has no meaning. Consider the following example that returns the average price from the Titles table:

```
SELECT AVG(price) FROM Titles
```

The AVG function can also be used in conjunction with the DISTINCT keyword. As such, it will return the average value of only the distinct values from the column specified as the argument. The following query returns a different average price than the preceding query did, as it does not take into account duplicate prices in the Titles table:

```
SELECT AVG(DISTINCT price) FROM Titles
```

SUM   The SUM function will return the sum of all values in the column specified as the argument. As with the AVG aggregate function, SUM can only be used on numeric columns. The following returns the sum of all prices in the Titles table:

```
SELECT SUM(price) FROM Titles
```

SUM can also be used with the DISTINCT keyword to return the sum of all distinct values in a column, as shown here:

```
SELECT SUM(DISTINCT price) FROM Titles
```

This query returns the sum of all prices in the Titles table, ignoring prices that appear more than once.

GROUP BY

The GROUP BY clause of the SELECT statement is where the language of SQL really shines with respect to report generation. In all of the preceding examples, aggregate functions have been applied to an entire result set. GROUP BY allows you to create subsets of data within a result set, and use aggregate functions to return values for each subset that has been defined using the GROUP BY clause. In real-world applications, aggregate functions will typically deal with a subset of data, producing a result many times for any given result set. To clarify the concept of a subset, consider the following query:

```
SELECT pub_id
FROM Titles
ORDER BY pub_id
```

This query returns a list of all values in the pub_id column from the Titles table. Each book has a publisher; and the foreign key of pub_id has many duplicate values, as publishers can publish many books. Grouping a result set into subsets has the effect of combining all identical values into a single row in the result set, creating a group. To illustrate, execute the following query:

```
SELECT pub_id
FROM Titles
GROUP BY pub_id
```

The result set from this query consists of three rows, one for each distinct pub_id value in the Titles table. While the same result set could be generated using the DISTINCT keyword, the mechanics of what's going on in the above query are a bit different. The GROUP BY clause has combined the duplicate values from the pub_id column into groups or subsets. A group defined using the GROUP BY clause is a subset or group of rows with similar values. The individual groups can then have aggregate functions applied to them. To illustrate, the following query uses the aggregate function MAX to find the highest priced book that each publisher offers in the Titles table:

```
SELECT pub_id, MAX(price) AS HighestPrice
FROM Titles
GROUP BY pub_id
```

As you can see from the result set, all of the values in the Price column have been grouped by publisher, and the maximum value in the Price column for each group has been returned, aliased as HighestPrice. To clarify creating groups or subsets of data to be used with aggregate functions, consider the following:

```
SELECT A, MAX(B)
FROM TableName
GROUP BY A
```

In this code, the request being made is this: "Find all of the values of column A that are identical and create a group of rows for each unique value of column A. Then, retrieve the maximum value of column B in each grouping of rows that have an identical value in column A."

Grouping a result set into subsets or groups provides a very powerful means to generate detailed reports. Consider the following query that not only returns the highest price of each title that a publisher offers, but returns the highest price of each title that a publisher offers in each category of book:

```
SELECT pub_id, type, MAX(price) AS HighestPrice
FROM Titles
GROUP BY pub_id, type
ORDER BY pub_id
```

In this scenario, the query creates groups or subsets of data based on two columns in the Titles table, pub_id and Type. The query basically states, "Retrieve the maximum price for each book, this time grouped not only by publisher, but also by the type of book." The subset or group of rows for each publisher now has its own subset of rows, one subset for each type of book offered. The aggregate function of MAX is then applied to each type group of each pub_id group of the whole result set from the Titles table. One value of the MAX function is returned for each grouping of rows specified in the GROUP BY clause.

When using GROUP BY, it is necessary to include all of the nonaggregate columns specified in the select list in the GROUP BY clause. This makes sense when you consider an example. The following uses the same select list as the preceding query, but does not include all of the columns in the select list in the GROUP BY clause:

```
SELECT pub_id, type, MAX(price) AS HighestPrice
FROM Titles
GROUP BY pub_id
ORDER BY pub_id
```

Executing this query will generate an error in Query Analyzer. The problem with this query is that a grouping of the pub_id column is specified, with the aggregate function of MAX specified on the Price column. This in itself is fine, but the select list also states that we wish the value of the Type column to also be included in the result set. Since each grouping of the pub_id column contains several rows with differing values in the Type column, which value of Type should the query return? The database engine cannot answer this question without more information, so an error is generated. Either the Type column needs to be specified in the GROUP BY clause, or an aggregate function needs to be applied to the Type column itself. The following query will not generate an error, because by using an aggregate function on the Type column, it can return a single result for each grouping of publishers:

```
SELECT pub_id, MAX(type), MAX(price) AS HighestPrice
FROM Titles
GROUP BY pub_id
ORDER BY pub_id
```

In this query, we have given the database engine the means to select one and only one value of the Type column to return for each grouping of pub_id. In this case, we are requesting the value in the Type column with the maximum value for each group of publishers. Since the Type column is a character column, the query returns the type that begins with a letter closest to Z in alphabetical order.

In creating groups or subsets of rows from a result set, the fact that all nonaggregate columns specified in the select list must be included in the GROUP BY clause makes good sense: SQL Server must know which value for each column you wish returned in each grouping of data; and if a grouping of data contains multiple values in a given column, either that column must be specified to create a subset of data using the GROUP BY clause, or it must be specified in aggregate function to return a single value.

HAVING   Much in the same way that the WHERE clause restricts rows returned by a SELECT statement, the HAVING clause is specified to restrict the rows returned when using the GROUP BY clause. The HAVING clause is necessary when restricting rows from a result set that includes aggregate functions. To illustrate, consider the following query:

```
SELECT pub_id, MAX(price) AS HighestPrice
FROM Titles
WHERE MAX(price) > 20
GROUP BY pub_id
```

In this statement, we wish to return a result set consisting of each publisher and the maximum price from all books that each publisher offers. The predicate specified in the WHERE clause attempts to limit the result set to only those rows where the maximum price is greater than $20. The preceding query generates an error in Query Analyzer.

The problem with this query is that we are trying to limit the result set using the WHERE clause to affect an aggregate value. In SQL, aggregate values are computed *after* a WHERE clause has been applied to a result set. The order of events goes like this: a result set is generated using a SELECT statement, and is restricted to returning certain rows using a WHERE clause, and then all grouping and aggregating can take place. Therefore, a WHERE clause cannot possibly reference an aggregate value because it doesn't exist yet!

The HAVING clause provides the means to restrict a result set once aggregate values have been computed by SQL Server. The following query requests the same result set as the preceding query, but correctly uses the HAVING clause to restrict the result set based on an aggregate value:

```
SELECT pub_id, MAX(price) AS HighestPrice
FROM Titles
GROUP BY pub_id
HAVING MAX(price) > 20
```

This query returns the maximum price of all books offered by each publisher and restricts the result set to only those rows where the maximum price is greater than $20, using the HAVING clause to restrict rows based on an aggregate value.

The HAVING clause is not limited to restricting rows based on aggregate functions. It can also restrict the result set based on any column specified in the GROUP BY clause. Consider the following query that limits the result set to only publishers with a value in the pub_id column greater than 1,000:

```
SELECT pub_id, MAX(price) AS HighestPrice
FROM Titles
GROUP BY pub_id
HAVING pub_id > 1000
```

While the preceding query returns the data required, it does not use the HAVING clause correctly. The query could just as easily have used a WHERE clause to restrict the result set to publishers with a value in the pub_id column greater than 1,000:

```
SELECT pub_id, MAX(price) AS HighestPrice
FROM Titles
WHERE pub_id > 1000
GROUP BY pub_id
```

This query is much more efficient, in that it first restricts the result set using a WHERE clause to exclude rows that have a pub_id value of greater than 1,000. Then it groups that result set by publisher and computes the aggregate value. If we had used a HAVING clause, aggregate values would have been computed for each group of rows, and the result set would have been restricted to only the groups that had a value greater than 1,000 in the pub_id column. Using a WHERE clause has the effect of limiting the number of rows that aggregations will be computed for. Since the value of the column pub_id is not involved in any aggregations, it is completely legal to use within the WHERE clause.

SCENARIO & SOLUTION

You need to restrict a result set based on values in a table column.	Use a WHERE clause.
You need to restrict a result set based on an aggregate value.	Use a HAVING clause.
You need to order a result set based on values in a table column.	Use an ORDER BY clause.

CUBE and ROLLUP

There are additional keywords that can be specified with the GROUP BY clause for reporting purposes. This section will discuss CUBE and ROLLUP. These options provide a means by which to return *superaggregations* within a result set. A superaggregation is a result that considers combinations of the values in a particular column within a group of data, and returns a value that matches the aggregate function specified.

CUBE   To illustrate WITH CUBE, execute the following query:

```
SELECT pub_id, MAX(price) AS HighestPrice
FROM Titles
GROUP BY pub_id
WITH CUBE
```

The preceding query returns the highest price for each book that each publisher offers in the Titles table, this time using WITH CUBE. Note that in the result set, an additional row is now included that returns the maximum price from aggregate values in the result set. The additional row returns a NULL value in the pub_id column to indicate that the value of HighestPrice in that row is a superaggregation of the previous aggregations. Let's look at another example of WITH CUBE, this time grouping by two columns:

```
SELECT pub_id, type, AVG(price) AS AveragePrice
FROM Titles
GROUP BY pub_id, type
WITH CUBE
```

The preceding query returns the average price for all books, grouped by publisher, then by type. Let's take a closer look at the result set of this query, to demonstrate WITH CUBE.

As shown in Figure 5-2, the first two rows of the result set are the average prices of books that the publisher with a value in the pub_id column of 0736 offers grouped by type. WITH CUBE returns the third row of the result set, which is the average price of *all* books offered by pub_id 0736. This process continues in the next eight rows, for publishers with the pub_id values of 0877 and 1389. The 12th row, which contains a NULL value in both of the GROUP BY columns, is also returned by WITH CUBE. It is the average price of all books in the Titles table. WITH CUBE also generates the last six rows in the result set, which return the average price of all books in each type category.

As you can see from the result set, WITH CUBE returns quite a bit of summary information. It performs superaggregations on all possible combinations of the columns specified in the GROUP BY clause.

ROLLUP   Sometimes WITH CUBE will return more summary information than is necessary for a given query. Instead, you can specify WITH ROLLUP when grouping data. Whereas WITH CUBE returns superaggregations for all possible combinations of the columns specified in the GROUP BY clause, ROLLUP starts at the last column in the GROUP BY clause and works backward one column at a time. Consider the result set from the following query:

```
SELECT pub_id, type, AVG(price) AS AveragePrice
FROM Titles
GROUP BY pub_id, type
WITH ROLLUP
```

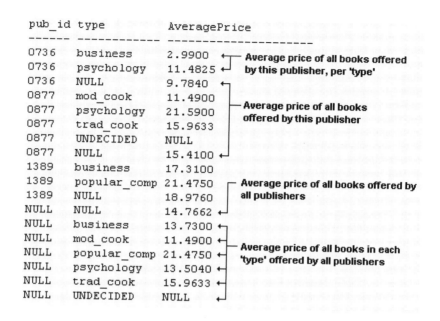

FIGURE 5-2

Query Results using WITH CUBE

```
pub_id type          AveragePrice
------ ------------  ----------------------
0736   business      2.9900      ┐ Average price of all books offered
0736   psychology    11.4825     ┘ by this publisher, per 'type'
0736   NULL          9.7840      ┐
0877   mod_cook      11.4900
0877   psychology    21.5900     ┐ Average price of all books
0877   trad_cook     15.9633     ┘ offered by this publisher
0877   UNDECIDED     NULL
0877   NULL          15.4100     ┘
1389   business      17.3100
1389   popular_comp  21.4750     ┐ Average price of all books offered by
1389   NULL          18.9760     ┘ all publishers
NULL   NULL          14.7662     ┘
NULL   business      13.7300     ┐
NULL   mod_cook      11.4900
NULL   popular_comp  21.4750     ┐ Average price of all books in each
NULL   psychology    13.5040     ┘ 'type' offered by all publishers
NULL   trad_cook     15.9633
NULL   UNDECIDED     NULL        ┘
```

This query once again returns the average price of books grouped by publisher and type. It also specifies WITH ROLLUP. The result set from the preceding query is shown in Figure 5-3.

Using WITH ROLLUP has produced a slightly different result set from using WITH CUBE. Once again, the first two rows of the result set return the average price of books in each type that the publisher with a value of 0736 in the pub_id

FIGURE 5-3

Query Results using WITH ROLLUP

```
pub_id type          AveragePrice
------ ------------  ----------------------
0736   business      2.9900      ┐ Average price of all books offered
0736   psychology    11.4825     ┘ by this publisher, per 'type'
0736   NULL          9.7840      ┐
0877   mod_cook      11.4900
0877   psychology    21.5900     ┐ Average price of all books
0877   trad_cook     15.9633     ┘ offered by this publisher
0877   UNDECIDED     NULL
0877   NULL          15.4100     ┘
1389   business      17.3100
1389   popular_comp  21.4750     ┐ Average price of all books offered by
1389   NULL          18.9760     ┘ all publishers
NULL   NULL          14.7662     ┘
```

column offers. The third row of the result set, generated by WITH ROLLUP, shows the average price of all books that the publisher offers. This process continues until the last row of the result set, where the average price of all books offered by all publishers is returned by WITH ROLLUP.

Since the columns Type and pub_id are specified in the GROUP BY clause of the query, WITH ROLLUP begins at the last column specified, Type, and works to the left. It returns aggregate information in the Type column, as you can see in rows 3, 8, and 11 in Figure 5-3. Then it moves on to the next column in the GROUP BY clause, pub_id, and returns the superaggregate value, as seen in the last row of the result set.

WITH ROLLUP has the benefit of returning a much cleaner result set than WITH CUBE; however, using WITH CUBE will return more information, accounting for all possible combinations of columns in the GROUP BY clause. In fact, as you may have noticed, using WITH CUBE includes all of the aggregate information that using WITH ROLLUP returns. Deciding which to use is simply a matter of determining how much superaggregation is appropriate in a particular result set.

COMPUTE and COMPUTE BY

COMPUTE and COMPUTE BY are leftovers from previous versions of SQL Server. They replace the GROUP BY clause in a query for the purpose of generating summary aggregate information. They are both deprecated, and most likely will not be supported in a future release of SQL Server. COMPUTE was an attempt to reproduce what is known as a *control-break* report. A control-break report generates summary information at certain controlled breakpoints in a report, hence the name. Microsoft has retained COMPUTE and COMPUTE BY for backward compatibility with earlier releases of SQL Server, but they recommend that you do not use COMPUTE. Instead, Microsoft recommends using WITH ROLLUP, or the rich set of tools provided by the Analysis Services portion of SQL Server 2000.

To demonstrate COMPUTE, execute the following query:

```
SELECT pub_id, price
FROM Titles
ORDER BY pub_id
COMPUTE MAX(price)
```

This query returns all the values from the pub_id and Price columns in the Titles table. The result set also includes an additional value after the result set that returns the maximum value of the Price column in the Titles table.

FROM THE CLASSROOM

Aggregating an Aggregate

When dealing with summary aggregate values in result sets, you will inevitably come across situations in which the requirements of a query are to perform an aggregate function on an already aggregated value. For example, the following query returns a count of how many times each job appears in the Employee table. The query basically asks how many employees hold each job.

```
SELECT COUNT(job_id)AS NumberOfRows
FROM Employee
GROUP BY job_id
```

Now that we have a count of employees for each job_id, the requirements also dictate that we return the maximum value from this result set. If aggregate functions could be performed on each other, the following query would fulfill the requirements:

```
SELECT MAX(COUNT(job_id))AS NumberOfRows
FROM Employee
GROUP BY job_id
```

However, this query is illegal. It attempts to use the aggregate function MAX on a value already aggregated by the function COUNT. Aggregates cannot take another aggregate as an argument. The solution in such a case is to use what is known as a *derived table*. A derived table is basically a subquery that is aliased, allowing it to be treated as a table with its own columns. The solution to our quandary is shown here:

```
SELECT MAX(T1.AMOUNT) AS NumberOfRows
FROM
     (SELECT COUNT(JOB_ID)AS AMOUNT
     FROM Employee GROUP BY job_id) AS T1
```

—Jeffrey Bane, MCSE, MCDBA

COMPUTE BY can also be used to create summary information. COMPUTE BY allows you to specify the breakpoints in a traditional control-break report. The column specified after the BY keyword has a similar result to specifying a column name in a GROUP BY clause. The following query is the same as the preceding query, with the addition of the BY keyword to create groups of data:

```
SELECT pub_id, price
FROM Titles
ORDER BY pub_id
COMPUTE MAX(price) BY pub_id
```

This query returns all values in the pub_id and Type columns from the Titles table. However in this query, a summary value of the maximum price is provided for each group of data, determined by the column specified after the BY keyword. A group of data or a breakpoint is created for each unique value in the pub_id column, returning three additional values containing the maximum price for each group.

Note that the additional value of summary information provided by COMPUTE and COMPUTE BY is not standard relational output. The summary information is not contained within a row, nor is it a column in the traditional sense. This is yet another reason why COMPUTE should be avoided.

on the Job

COMPUTE does have one nice feature. The output from the query looks, to some extent, like a report suitable for printing. But in the modern days of rich-looking reports created by tools such as Excel or Crystal Reports, that's not much of a benefit anymore. About the only information you need to retain about COMPUTE and COMPUTE BY is not to use them.

EXERCISE 5-2

Retrieving Data Using T-SQL

1. Consider the following request: "I'd like to know the title of the book that has had the most sales in the past, as well as how many copies have been sold." This is a seemingly simple request, but let's go over the steps to write this query. From the requirements, we can see that the information needed will come from two tables: Sales and Titles. First, we'll generate a list of all titles and the sum of sales from each order in the Sales table. The following

query returns all rows from the Sales table; groups them by title_id; and sums the column Qty, which is the quantity of a particular title sold on each order.

```
SELECT title_id, SUM(qty) AS TotalSales FROM Sales
GROUP BY title_id
ORDER BY TotalSales DESC
```

This query also orders the result set in descending order, so the maximum amount of sales will be the first row in the result set.

2. Next, we need to join this result set with the Titles table to obtain the actual title of each book, as shown here:

```
SELECT T.title, SUM(S.qty) AS TotalSales
FROM Titles AS T JOIN Sales AS S
ON T.title_id = S.title_id
GROUP BY T.title
ORDER BY TotalSales DESC
```

3. Now that we have a listing of each title and its sales, we can use the TOP *n* clause to return the row with the highest value in the TotalSales column:

```
SELECT TOP 1 T.title, SUM(S.qty) AS TotalSales
FROM Titles AS T JOIN Sales AS S
ON T.title_id = S.title_id
GROUP BY T.title
ORDER BY TotalSales DESC
```

This query has satisfied the requirements, returning the book with the title *Is Anger the Enemy?*. This book has sold 108 copies, the most of any book.

Manipulating Data with T-SQL Cursors

Relational databases and the language of SQL have their roots in mathematical set theory. As such, T-SQL returns sets of data in standard operations. However, in certain situations, the need arises for operations to be performed on a result set one row at a time. *Cursors* exist to fulfill that need. A cursor allows you to define a result set and *iterate* through the result set row by row.

For the most part, cursors are something to be avoided in relational databases. SQL Server 2000, as with most database engines, is optimized for set-based operations, not iterative operations. Using standard T-SQL commands, like the

SELECT statement, to return a result set can be orders of magnitude faster than using a cursor.

exam
Ⓦatch

If you are presented with any blocks of T-SQL code that require optimization, replacing any cursors with standard DML is a good place to start. While cursors are sometimes necessary, they are also sometimes used out of ignorance. Check to see whether the cursor can be translated into a normal SELECT, INSERT, UPDATE, or DELETE statement.

Cursors function by defining a traditional result set and acting as a pointer to individual rows of data. Operations can then be performed on a particular row of data. The pointer can then be moved from one row to another using T-SQL commands.

Using T-SQL Cursors

There are five steps having to do with creating, using, and destroying a cursor in T-SQL. Each step has a corresponding T-SQL command. Table 5-4 describes each of the commands.

To demonstrate the definitions in Table 5-4, let's look at a simple cursor defined in the Pubs database. The following cursor retrieves all rows and columns from the Publishers table:

```
DECLARE sample_cursor CURSOR
FOR SELECT * FROM Publishers
OPEN sample_cursor
FETCH NEXT FROM sample_cursor
WHILE @@FETCH_STATUS = 0
BEGIN
FETCH NEXT FROM sample_cursor
END
CLOSE sample_cursor
DEALLOCATE sample_cursor
```

Let's take a closer look at the syntax to illustrate what's going on in the cursor. First, the cursor is declared and given the name sample_cursor.

```
DECLARE sample_cursor CURSOR
```

Next the result set of the cursor is specified, and the cursor is opened, as shown here:

```
FOR SELECT * FROM Publishers
OPEN sample_cursor
```

TABLE 5-4	The Five Steps of a Cursor

Command	Usage
DECLARE	Defines the cursor. This definition includes the result set to be used in the cursor, as well as the characteristics of the cursor.
OPEN	Populates the cursor with the result set defined in the cursor declaration.
FETCH	Retrieves rows from the cursor.
CLOSE	Closes the cursor by releasing the result set. This step also releases any locks held by the cursor.
DEALLOCATE	Removes the cursor and its definition.

Opening the cursor populates it with the result set that has been specified—in this case, all the rows and columns from the Publishers table. Next, the first row from the cursor is retrieved using the FETCH command.

```
FETCH NEXT FROM sample_cursor
```

Now, a WHILE loop is created. WHILE will execute the SQL statements located between the BEGIN and END keywords for as long as the condition specified in the WHILE statement is true. In this case, a special condition has been specified using the @@FETCH_STATUS global variable. @@FETCH_STATUS will return a value of 0 for each successful fetch, and a value of −1 when the result set specified in the cursor moved past the last row. Therefore, as long as the value of @@FETCH_STATUS is equal to 0, we want to keep fetching rows from the cursor, as shown here:

```
WHILE @@FETCH_STATUS = 0
BEGIN
FETCH NEXT FROM sample_cursor
END
```

Finally, the sample_cursor cursor is closed and deallocated.

```
CLOSE sample_cursor
DEALLOCATE sample_cursor
```

As you can see from the result set, the preceding cursor really doesn't do anything extraordinary. It simply returns each row from the Publishers table, one row at a time. Notice that the output is not a single result set; each row is treated as its own result set. The real power in using a cursor lies in performing actions based on the values in certain columns from the rows in a result set.

Using T-SQL Variables with Cursors

The preceding cursor simply fetched and displayed each row from the result set defined in the DECLARE T-SQL command. Values from the columns of a row in a cursor can also be stored in T-SQL variables, allowing actions to be performed based on the values of the variables. The following cursor uses two variables to store the values of the pub_id and State columns from the Publishers table:

```
DECLARE @pub_id CHAR(4)
DECLARE @state CHAR(2)
DECLARE sample_cursor CURSOR
FOR SELECT pub_id, state FROM Publishers
OPEN sample_cursor
FETCH NEXT FROM sample_cursor INTO @pub_id, @state
WHILE @@FETCH_STATUS = 0
BEGIN
IF @state IS NOT NULL
  SELECT 'Publisher: ' + @pub_id + ' is from the great state of ' + @state
    ELSE
    SELECT 'Publisher: ' + @pub_id + ' is not from the United States'
FETCH NEXT FROM sample_cursor INTO @pub_id, @state
END
CLOSE sample_cursor
DEALLOCATE sample_cursor
```

In the preceding cursor, two variables are declared to hold the contents of the values from the pub_id and State columns from the Publishers table. Each variable is declared with the identical datatype of each column in the table:

```
DECLARE @pub_id CHAR(4)
DECLARE @state CHAR(2)
```

The cursor is then declared and opened:

```
DECLARE sample_cursor CURSOR
FOR SELECT pub_id, state FROM Publishers
OPEN sample_cursor
```

Next, the values of the columns from the first row of the result set are inserted into the two variables using the INTO keyword with the FETCH command:

```
FETCH NEXT FROM sample_cursor INTO @pub_id, @state
```

A WHILE loop is then created, based once again on the condition that the @@FETCH_STATUS global variable is equal to a value of 0:

```
WHILE @@FETCH_STATUS = 0
BEGIN
```

This time, the IF statement is used to test whether or not the value of the @state variable, fetched from the current row, contains a NULL value. If the value of the @state variable does not contain a NULL value, the current values of the two variables are concatenated into a descriptive string, as the following shows:

```
IF @state IS NOT NULL
SELECT 'Publisher: ' + @pub_id + ' is from the great state of ' + @state
```

The ELSE keyword is used to return a different string if the value of the @state variable does indeed contain a NULL value:

```
ELSE
SELECT 'Publisher: ' + @pub_id + ' is not from the United States'
```

The next row from the result set is then fetched into the two variables, completing the WHILE loop. This process will continue until all rows from the result set have been retrieved.

```
FETCH NEXT FROM sample_cursor INTO @pub_id, @state
END
```

Finally, the cursor is closed and deallocated, removing its definition:

```
CLOSE sample_cursor
DEALLOCATE sample_cursor
```

The preceding cursor illustrates how cursors use row-by-row processing to examine the results in columns, and perform actions based on the values of those columns by storing the column values in T-SQL variables.

Used in this way, cursors are a powerful tool used to create result sets that could not be accomplished with standard queries.

Modifying Table Rows Using a Cursor

Data in the underlying table rows used to build a cursor result set can also be modified based on the current position of a cursor. This is what is known as a *positioned update.* In order to perform a positioned update, the FOR UPDATE clause is added to the cursor declaration, as shown here:

```
DECLARE sample_cursor CURSOR
FOR SELECT * FROM Publishers
FOR UPDATE
```

Once the cursor is positioned on the row to be updated, the WHERE CURRENT OF clause can then be used with the DML statements DELETE or UPDATE to modify the underlying table values. To illustrate, the following statement updates the Publishers table, using the row that sample_cursor is currently positioned on:

```
UPDATE Publishers
SET City = 'Sarasota' WHERE CURRENT OF sample_cursor
```

FOR UPDATE can also be used with OF to limit the updates to only certain columns in the table. In the next example, only the columns City and State would be updatable:

```
DECLARE sample_cursor CURSOR
FOR SELECT * FROM Publishers
FOR UPDATE OF City, State
```

Positioned updates are only permitted with certain types of cursors, as you will see in the upcoming section on cursor sensitivity.

Controlling Cursor Behavior

In T-SQL, cursors have several options that can be specified in the DECLARE statement. The first option defines the *scrollability* of the cursor. The second option defines the cursor's *sensitivity*. The following sections will outline each of these options.

Scrollability   The scrollability of a cursor dictates the direction in which the rows of a cursor result set can be traversed. Scrollability can be specified with one of two values: FORWARD_ONLY or SCROLL. All of the cursors in the previous examples have been FORWARD_ONLY cursors. This means that operations on the result set of the cursor can occur only in one direction, from the first row to the last row. FORWARD_ONLY cursors support only the NEXT keyword with the FETCH command: as the cursor is only capable of going in one direction, it can only fetch the next row from the result set.

Cursors can also be defined with SCROLL. If SCROLL is specified in the cursor declaration, the rows of the cursor result set can be traversed in any direction, as well as referencing rows relative to the current row. When using SCROLL, the keywords in Table 5-5 are permissible with the FETCH command.

The effect of FETCH is that whichever row is retrieved by the FETCH command becomes the current row. For example, the current row is the first row of a cursor result set. A FETCH NEXT is specified, returning the second row of the result set. The second row of the result set is now the current row, and FETCH PRIOR will retrieve the first row of the result set, and also make the first row the current row.

Scrollability is specified in the DECLARE statement of the cursor, and FORWARD_ONLY is the default. The following T-SQL statement declares a SCROLL cursor:

```
DECLARE sample_cursor CURSOR SCROLL
FOR SELECT * FROM Publishers
```

Scollable cursors are very useful when an application accessing the database requires what's known as *next* N record browsing. Next N browsing is a case where a user is presented with only a portion of a result set. For example, a table may contain thousands of rows. However, the application only presents the user with 25 records at a time for readability. The user can then move forward or backward, traversing

TABLE 5-5 Uses of FETCH with a Scrollable Cursor

Command	Usage
FETCH NEXT	Retrieves the next row in the cursor result set.
FETCH PRIOR	Retrieves the previous row in the cursor result set.
FETCH FIRST	Retrieves the first row in the cursor result set.
FETCH LAST	Retrieves the last row in the cursor result set.
FETCH ABSOLUTE N	Retrieves the row N number of rows from the beginning of the result set if N is positive, or N number of rows from the end of the result set if N is negative.
FETCH RELATIVE N	Retrieves the row N number of rows after the current row if N is positive, or N number of rows prior to the current row if N is negative.

the record set in increments of 25 records at a time. Such a situation would not be possible with a FORWARD_ONLY cursor.

Sensitivity   Another option that can be specified when declaring a cursor is the sensitivity of the cursor. The sensitivity of a cursor dictates how the result set of the cursor behaves if changes to the underlying rows of a table involved in the cursor result set change while the cursor is open. To illustrate, consider the following scenario: a cursor creates a result set consisting of all rows from the Publishers table. While the cursor is open, another operation occurs that deletes several rows from the Publishers table. The cursor result set consisting of all rows from the Publishers table no longer reflects the actual rows in the underlying table. The cursor result set will either account for these changes or ignore them based on the sensitivity specified in the cursor declaration.

Four levels of sensitivity exist in T-SQL cursors. Table 5-6 outlines the various sensitivity options when declaring a cursor.

The level of sensitivity of a cursor is specified in the DECLARE statement. The following declares a forward-only, static cursor:

```
DECLARE sample_cursor CURSOR FORWARD_ONLY STATIC
FOR SELECT * FROM Publishers
```

Certain cursor options have incompatibilities when used together. For instance, the fetch operation FETCH_ABSOLUTE is not supported when using a dynamic

TABLE 5-6   Cursor Sensitivity Levels

Sensitivity	Effect
STATIC	The cursor creates a static result set that does not reflect any changes made to the underlying tables. Updates are not allowed in a STATIC cursor.
DYNAMIC	The cursor creates a dynamic result set that reflects changes made to the underlying tables. The order of rows in the cursor result set can change at any given fetch, based on modifications to the underlying tables.
KEYSET	The cursor creates a semidynamic result set that does not reflect INSERT operations, or updates to key columns performed on the underlying tables. The order of rows cannot change, but changes to nonkey values will be reflected.
FAST_FORWARD	This creates the fastest performing FORWARD_ONLY cursor. The cursor is also read only, and updates are not permitted.

cursor, as the result set can change while the cursor is open. Therefore, the absolute row at the beginning or end of a cursor result set is not guaranteed.

Cursors and Dynamic SQL

Dynamic SQL is a feature of SQL and T-SQL that allows the values of variables to be used in place of *object names.* You've already used many object names in the preceding examples in this chapter. An object name is the name of an object within a physical database—that is, a table name, column name, etc. Standard SQL does not allow for variables to be used as object names. To illustrate, execute the following block of T-SQL statements:

```
DECLARE @tablename VARCHAR(20)
SELECT @tablename = 'Publishers'
SELECT * FROM @tablename
```

The preceding generates an error in Query Analyzer. It attempts to use the variable @tablename as an object name in the SELECT statement, which is illegal using standard T-SQL. However, dynamic SQL allows for a string of commands and variables to be built, and then executed on the fly. The following block of T-SQL statements illustrates dynamic SQL:

```
DECLARE @tablename VARCHAR(20)
DECLARE @SqlStatement VARCHAR(50)
SELECT @tablename = 'Publishers'
SELECT @SqlStatement = 'SELECT * FROM ' + @tablename
EXEC(@SqlStatement)
```

A new string variable called @SqlStatement is declared with a character datatype. This string value of this variable is then built by concatenating the SELECT statement with the value of the variable @tablename. The string can then be dynamically executed like a normal statement using EXECUTE, or EXEC.

exam
ⓦatch

When the string value being built for dynamic SQL execution requires that a single quote be used within the string, it is necessary to escape the single quote so that SQL Server 2000 knows that you wish to insert a single quote within the string and not end the string. To illustrate, the following dynamic SQL string has embedded single quotes. The single quote is entered twice to indicate that the single quote is part of the string variable, and not terminating the string.

```
SET @SqlStatement = 'SELECT * FROM Titles
WHERE Title LIKE ''The%'' AND Royalty > 2'
```

Dynamic SQL allows for variables to be used in places where variables are normally illegal. It is also a very powerful tool when used with cursors. For example, the system view INFORMATION_SCHEMA.TABLES contains information about all tables in a database. The column table_name contains the name of each table and view. To return a list of all tables in a database, the following query is used:

```
SELECT TABLE_NAME FROM INFORMATION_SCHEMA.TABLES
WHERE TABLE_TYPE = 'BASE TABLE'
```

Armed with this information, suppose we now wish to return all rows from all tables. We can easily do this within a cursor using dynamic SQL, as shown here:

```
DECLARE @tablename VARCHAR(20)
DECLARE @SqlStatement VARCHAR(50)
DECLARE sample_cursor CURSOR
FOR SELECT TABLE_NAME FROM INFORMATION_SCHEMA.TABLES
WHERE TABLE_TYPE = 'BASE TABLE'
OPEN sample_cursor
FETCH NEXT FROM sample_cursor INTO @tablename
WHILE @@FETCH_STATUS = 0
BEGIN
SELECT @SqlStatement = 'SELECT * FROM ' + @tablename
EXEC (@SqlStatement)
FETCH NEXT FROM sample_cursor INTO @tablename
END
CLOSE sample_cursor
DEALLOCATE sample_cursor
```

When used with dynamic SQL, cursors provide a powerful way to perform operations on database objects. However, dynamic SQL is certainly not limited to allowing the values of variables to be used as object names. Dynamic SQL allows the value of a variable to be used just about anywhere in a standard SQL statement where a variable would otherwise be prohibited.

CERTIFICATION SUMMARY

Transact SQL is Microsoft's implementation of ANSI SQL. It is a powerful means by which to communicate with a relational database. This chapter discussed the subset of commands making up the data manipulation language of T-SQL. Using the four basic commands of DML, data stored in a relational database can be manipulated in most any way imaginable. Subqueries and joins allow data in multiple tables to be combined in a result set. T-SQL also provides platform-specific enhancements to the SQL standard. Extensions such as TOP *n*, and the ability to use table joins when modifying data, give database developers a very flexible implementation of SQL.

One of the main functions of T-SQL is generating reports. Aggregate functions such as MIN and MAX provide a way to summarize column values in a result set. The GROUP BY clause of the SELECT statement provides a powerful way to group data into subsets and have aggregate functions applied to them. ROLLUP and CUBE also enhance report generation by performing superaggregations on previously aggregated values.

T-SQL cursors can be used to generate a result set that can be traversed one row at a time, as opposed to the set-based operations of traditional DML. The column values from a cursor result set can be stored in T-SQL variables, allowing for conditional operations based on the values stored in the variables. Cursors can be of several types, each type producing a result set with certain characteristics. Cursors are also a very powerful tool when used with dynamic SQL, which allows for T-SQL commands to use variables in place of object names.

TWO-MINUTE DRILL

Overview of Coding SQL Queries

❑ The American National Standards Institute, or ANSI, defines the standards for the language of SQL. Microsoft's implementation of SQL, known as Transact-SQL, has entry-level compliance with the ANSI standard.

❑ T-SQL can be broken down into three categories: the data manipulation language (DML), the data definition language (DDL), and the data control language (DCL).

❑ DML consists of four basic commands: SELECT for retrieving data, INSERT for adding data, UPDATE for changing data, and DELETE for removing data.

❑ The DML commands support the use of many clauses, such as WHERE, which restricts the table rows affected by each statement.

❑ In order to reference rows in more than one table, queries can make use of subqueries or nested queries.

❑ Table joins can also be used for multitable operations. Table joins can be of two main types. Inner joins link tables based on column values that correspond to one another. Outer joins link tables based on column values that do not correspond to one another.

❑ The concept of result sets is very important when using outer joins. The result set to the left of the JOIN keyword is known as the left result set, and the result set to the right of the JOIN keyword is known as the right result set.

❑ Each occurrence of the JOIN keyword in a query is treated as a separate event; therefore, the left and right result set change each time a table join is performed.

Retrieving Data Using Transact-SQL

❑ T-SQL adds many useful extensions to ANSI SQL. TOP n is a very powerful tool that allows a result set to be restricted to a certain number of rows.

❑ Table joins in statements such as UPDATE and DELETE are also permitted in T-SQL. This allows for much more readable syntax when many tables are involved in a data modification.

❑ Aggregate functions play a big part in report generation using T-SQL. COUNT returns a count of rows in a result set. MIN and MAX return the minimum and maximum values of a column in a result set. SUM returns the sum of all values of a column, and AVG computes the average value of all values of a column in a result set.

❑ Aggregate functions are most commonly used with subsets of data. The GROUP BY clause allows for a result set to be grouped into subsets. The HAVING clause allows for the restricting of rows in a result set based on aggregate values.

❑ CUBE and ROLLUP enhance report generation by performing superaggregations. CUBE returns much more data than ROLLUP.

❑ When it is necessary to process a result one row at a time, T-SQL cursors allow for a result set to be traversed row by row. Cursors can also store column values in T-SQL variables, allowing for conditional processing.

❑ Cursors have certain characteristics that can be set in the DECLARE statement. The scrollability of a cursor determines how rows can be processed, either forward only or scroll. The sensitivity of a cursor determines how the cursor result set will reflect changes to the underlying tables.

❑ Cursors are especially useful when used with dynamic SQL. Dynamic SQL allows for SQL statements to be built from a string variable, and then executed as if the string were a traditional SQL statement.

SELF TEST

The following questions will help you measure your understanding of the material presented in this chapter. Read all the choices carefully because there might be more than one correct answer. Choose all correct answers for each question. Just like on the real exam, you may need to use some scratch paper to draw out the scenarios in order to gain a better conceptual view of the problem being presented.

Overview of Coding SQL Queries

1. Which of the following methods can be used when a query must reference rows in more than one table? (Choose all that apply.)

   A. A subquery

   B. The GROUP BY clause

   C. The CASE keyword

   D. Table joins

2. Which of the following predicates can be used with a WHERE clause? (Choose all that apply.)

   A. LIKE

   B. HAS

   C. BETWEEN

   D. WITHIN

3. When using the keyword DISTINCT in a select list consisting of three columns, how will the result set be processed?

   A. Only rows with a unique value in the first column specified will be returned.

   B. Only rows with a unique value when considering all three columns will be returned.

   C. Only rows with a unique value in the third column will be returned.

   D. An error will be generated. DISTINCT cannot be specified when the select list contains more than one column.

4. A database exists that contains two tables, Employees and Departments. Each Employee is a member of only one department. A foreign key in the Employees table references the primary key of DeptID in the Departments table. The Departments table also contains a column called

DeptName. You need to retrieve all employee information for each employee that works in marketing. How could you code the query? (Choose all that apply.)

A.
```
SELECT * FROM Employees
WHERE DeptID =
(SELECT DeptID from Departments
WHERE DeptName = 'Marketing')
```

B.
```
SELECT * FROM Employees
WHERE NOT EXISTS
(SELECT DeptID from Departments
WHERE Departments.DeptID = Employees.DeptID
and Departments.DeptName = 'Marketing')
```

C.
```
SELECT E.* FROM Employees AS E
JOIN Departments AS D
ON E.DeptID = D.DeptID
AND D.DeptName = 'Marketing'
```

D.
```
SELECT * FROM Employees
WHERE DeptID = DeptID from Departments
WHERE DeptName = 'Marketing'
```

5. You are asked to write a query that retrieves information from the Employee table in the Pubs database. The query requires each employee's first name and last name aliased as a column called FullName. However, the value of each employee's middle initial should only appear if the minit column does not contain an empty string. The middle initial should also be followed by a period, if it is present. How would code the requested query? (Choose the best answer.)

A.
```
SELECT fname + ' ' + minit + '. ' + lname
FROM Employee
```

B.
```
SELECT fname + ' ' +
IF
minit = '' THEN ''
ELSE minit IS NOT NULL THEN minit + '. '
+ lname AS FullName
FROM Employee
```

C. ```
SELECT fname + ' ' +
CASE
WHEN minit = '' THEN ''
WHEN minit <> '' THEN minit + '. '
END
+ lname AS FullName
FROM Employee
```

D. ```
SELECT fname + ' ',
CASE
WHEN minit = '' THEN ''
WHEN minit <> '' THEN minit + '. '
END,
lname AS FullName
FROM Employee
```

6. Two tables exist in a database: Orders and Products. For this example, only one product may appear on an order. You are required to produce a report that returns all orders. The report should also return all products that appear on the orders, as well as products that have not been ordered. What type of join would you use to produce the report?

   A. A left outer join

   B. A full outer join

   C. An inner join

   D. A UNION join

7. Which of the following are reasons to use the ORDER BY clause in a query? (Choose all that apply.)

   A. The query requires the result set to be ordered by a particular column.

   B. The rows in the result set need to be grouped into subsets of data.

   C. The result set requires that only rows that are in order in the table be returned.

   D. Table rows in a relational database are not guaranteed to be in any particular order.

8. Which of the following can be aliased in a query? (Choose all that apply.)

   A. Predicates

   B. Column names

   C. T-SQL variables

   D. Table names

Retrieving Data Using Transact-SQL

9. Which of the following can be used to restrict the rows returned by a result set in T-SQL? (Choose all that apply.)

   A. ORDER BY

   B. WHERE

   C. TOP *n*

   D. HAVING

10. You have been given the task of producing a report that uses the Sales table in the Pubs database. You need to determine the quantity of each title that has been sold, as well as the title that has sold the most copies. Which aggregate functions would you need to use to produce this report? (Choose all that apply.)

   A. COUNT

   B. MIN

   C. MAX

   D. AVG

11. What is meant when a result set is superaggregated?

   A. The aggregate results in a result set are restricted by a HAVING clause.

   B. The aggregate results in a result set are themselves aggregated.

   C. The subsets of data in a result set are aggregated using different aggregate functions.

   D. The subsets of data in a result set are omitted based on the aggregate values returned.

12. You are required to produce a report based on the information contained in the Sales table in the Pubs database. The report needs to produce a listing that includes stor_id value of each store, as well as each title it has sold. It also needs to include the total amount of each title that the store has sold. How would you produce the requested report?

   A. ```
SELECT stor_id, title_id, SUM(qty)
FROM Sales
GROUP BY stor_id
```

   B.  ```
SELECT stor_id, title_id, COUNT(qty)
FROM Sales
GROUP BY stor_id, title_id
```

C. SELECT *stor_id*, SUM(*title_id*)
   FROM *Sales*
   GROUP BY *stor_id*

D. SELECT *stor_id*, *title_id*, SUM(*qty*)
   FROM *Sales*
   GROUP BY *stor_id*, *title_id*

13. Which of the following T-SQL commands should be used to return superaggregate data? (Choose all that apply.)

   A. COMPUTE

   B. ROLLUP

   C. CUBE

   D. FETCH

14. You are coding the T-SQL for an application that will display a list of seats available for a play. The theater can hold 1,000 people, so you wish to present the user with only 50 available seats at a time. In the application, the user can consider those 50 seats, and then move forward or backward to consider 50 other seats. If another user reserves any seats while another user is browsing, you need that fact to be reflected to other users. What cursor options would you specify? (Choose all that apply.)

   A. FORWARD_ONLY

   B. SCROLL

   C. STATIC

   D. DYNAMIC

15. Which of the following statements are true of dynamic SQL? (Choose all that apply.)

   A. It allows a result set to be restricted without having to use a WHERE clause.

   B. It allows the values of variables to be used in place of object names in a T-SQL statement.

   C. It allows a string variable of SQL commands and variables to be built and then executed as a traditional SQL statement.

   D. It provides a means by which to perform aggregate operations on preaggregated data.

16. You have included a scrollable cursor within a certain application for your company. The cursor is declared and then opened, populating the cursor result set. A certain row is retrieved from the cursor result set and displayed to the user. The application now needs to retrieve the row

from the result set that is four rows before the current row. Which FETCH statement would you use to retrieve the requested row?

A. FETCH PRIOR

B. FETCH RELATIVE −4

C. FETCH ABSOLUTE 4

D. FETCH LAST

17. Which of the following statements is true with respect to specifying the DISTINCT keyword on a column vs. using the GROUP BY clause on a column?

A. Both DISTINCT and GROUP BY will create a subset of data based on unique values within the specified column.

B. The DISTINCT keyword returns the unique values from a column, while the GROUP BY clause will include duplicates.

C. The GROUP BY clause will create subsets of data based on unique values in the column specified, while DISTINCT will simply return the unique values from a column.

D. Both DISTINCT and GROUP BY can be used to perform aggregate functions on a subset of data, based on the column specified.

LAB QUESTION

You are employed as the database administrator for ACME Car Sales, a nationwide auto superstore. The following is a partial schema of the ACME database:

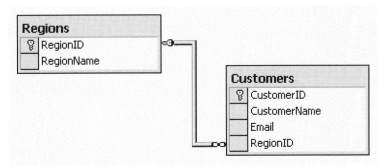

In the past, you have used the system stored procedure XP_SENDMAIL to generate and send electronic mail messages from SQL Server 2000. The partial syntax of XP_SENDMAIL is shown here.

```
EXEC MASTER.DBO.XP_SENDMAIL @recipients = 'JohnDoe@Domain.com', @message
= 'Hello John!'
```

You have been given the responsibility of sending an e-mail to every customer in the southeast region, informing him or her of ACME's big sale for the month of March. Your task is to use the XP_SENDMAIL stored procedure to send an e-mail to every customer in the southeast region, with the message "ACME is having a big March sale and invites you to attend."

You attempt to use the following subquery with XP_SENDMAIL, but find that it generates an error in Query Analyzer:

```
EXEC MASTER.DBO.XP_SENDMAIL @recipients =
(SELECT Email FROM Customers),
@message = 'ACME is having a big March sale and invites you to attend'
```

From the error, it becomes obvious to you that XP_SENDMAIL cannot accept a subquery as an argument for the @recipients variable.

What T-SQL code would you use to satisfy the requirements? You must use the following guidelines:

- You must use the XP_SENDMAIL system stored procedure.

- You must only send e-mails to customers in the southeast region.

SELF TEST ANSWERS

Overview of Coding SQL Queries

1. ☑ **A** and **D**. Both subqueries and table joins allow a query to reference rows in more than one table.

☒ **B** is incorrect because the GROUP BY clause is used to create subsets of data. **C** is also incorrect because the CASE statement is used to change column values as they are returned, usually to enhance the readability of a result set.

2. ☑ **A** and **C** are both correct. LIKE is used to match similar string values, and BETWEEN is used to match a value within a range.

☒ **B** and **D** are both wrong. HAS and WITHIN are not valid predicates of the WHERE clause.

3. ☑ **B** is the correct answer. When DISTINCT is included in a SELECT statement with multiple columns, the result will not return duplicate rows that have identical values in all the columns specified.

☒ **A** and **C** are incorrect as DISTINCT will consider all columns in the select list. **D** is also incorrect because DISTINCT can be specified irrespective of how many columns are present in the select list.

4. ☑ **A** is correct because it uses a subquery to reference the Departments table. **C** is also correct, using a table join to reference the Departments table.

☒ **B** is incorrect because EXISTS needs to be used. NOT EXISTS will not retrieve the requested information. **D** is incorrect also, as the subquery is not enclosed in parentheses.

5. ☑ **C** is the correct answer. It uses the CASE statement to test whether the minit column contains an empty string. If not, the column value plus a period is returned. All of the columns are also merged using the concatenation operator, and the new column is aliased as FullName.

☒ **A** is incorrect because it returns the value of the minit column if it is a letter or a blank string. **B** is incorrect, as the IF statement cannot be used in this way. **D** is close to being correct, but it returns three columns instead of the one concatenated column required by the query.

6. ☑ **A** is the correct answer. The wording of the question might lead you to think that a full outer join is necessary. However, a left outer join will produce a list of all orders (the left result set), as well as those products that appear on orders and those products that don't appear on orders (the right result set). Remember, a left outer join will return all rows from the left result set and rows from the right result set that match rows in the left result set, as well as those that don't match rows in the left result set.

    ☒   **B** is incorrect because a full outer join would produce redundant rows in this result set. **C** is incorrect because an inner join would only return rows from the Products table that have appeared on orders. **D** is incorrect because a UNION is used to merge two tables with an identical structure.

7. ☑ **A** is correct because the ORDER BY clause needs to be used if the result set is required to be ordered by a column value. **D** is also correct because rows in a table are never guaranteed to be in any particular order.

    ☑ **B** is incorrect because the ORDER BY clause does not produce subsets of data, the GROUP BY clause creates subsets. **C** is also incorrect, as rows in a table are not in any particular order.

8. ☑ Both **B** and **D** are correct, as column names as well as table names can be aliased in T-SQL using the AS keyword.

    ☒ **A** and **C** are incorrect. The predicate of a WHERE clause cannot be aliased, nor can a T-SQL variable be aliased.

Retrieving Data Using Transact-SQL

9. ☑ **B, C,** and **D**. WHERE, TOP *n*, and HAVING are all means by which to restrict the rows returned in a result set.

    ☒ **A** is incorrect because ORDER BY simply specifies the ordering of the rows in a result set.

10. ☑ **A** is a correct answer because the count of rows with a particular title_id value would be necessary. **C** is also correct because we would need to know the title_id that occurs the maximum number of times in the Sales tables.

    ☒ **B** is incorrect, as the minimum value of any of the columns in the Sales table would not help to produce the report. Likewise, **D** is incorrect because the report does not require any average values.

11. ☑ **B** is the correct answer. A superaggregation will apply the aggregate function specified to the already aggregated results in a result set.

    ☒ **A** is incorrect, as the HAVING clause simply limits a result set based on aggregate values. **C** is incorrect because a superaggregation applies the same aggregate function, not a different one. **D** is also incorrect because superaggregation does not omit any aggregate values.

12. ☑ **D** is the correct answer. It groups the result set into subsets based on the stor_id and title_id columns. It also includes the aggregate function SUM, which totals all the values of the column Qty for each subset of titles.

☒ **A** is incorrect. While almost correct, it does not include all of the nonaggregate columns from the select list in the GROUP BY clause. **B** is incorrect because the COUNT aggregate function simply returns a count of rows for the qty column. **C** is also incorrect, as the aggregate function SUM cannot be used with the character column title_id.

13. ☑ **B** and **C** are both correct because CUBE and ROLLUP are the recommended ways to return superaggregated data. ROLLUP tends to produce a more useful result set.
☒ **A** is incorrect because COMPUTE is only included in SQL 2000 for backward compatibility. It produces nonrelational output and should not be used. **D** is incorrect because FETCH is a command having to do with retrieving rows from a cursor result set.

14. ☑ **B** and **D** are correct. SCROLL needs to be a characteristic of the cursor, as users need to be able to browse 50 seats at a time in either direction. This would also need to be a DYNAMIC cursor, because if any other users update the base table by reserving seats, that fact needs to be reflected in the cursor result set.
☒ **A** is incorrect, as a FORWARD_ONLY cursor only allows the result set to be browsed from beginning to end. **C** is also incorrect because a STATIC cursor result set would not reflect changes to the base table made when other users reserve seats.

15. ☑ **B** is correct because dynamic SQL allows the values of variables to be used in places that they would otherwise be illegal. **C** is also correct because dynamic SQL allows for the building of a string variable that is then executed using the EXEC command.
☒ **A** and **D** are both incorrect, as dynamic SQL has nothing to do with restricting result sets, or superaggregating data.

16. ☑ **B** is the correct answer. FETCH RELATIVE −4 will retrieve the row from the cursor result set that is four rows previous to the current row.
☒ **A** is incorrect as FETCH PRIOR will return the row directly before the current row in the cursor result set. **C** is incorrect because FETCH ABSOLUTE 4 will simply return the fourth row in the result set. **D** is also incorrect. FETCH LAST will return the last row in the cursor result set.

17. ☑ **C** is the correct, because the GROUP BY clause creates actual subsets of data on which aggregate functions can be performed, while the DISTINCT clause only returns unique values from a column.
☒ **A** and **D** are incorrect because the DISTINCT clause does not create subsets of data. **B** is incorrect, as the GROUP BY clause does not filter duplicate rows, but rather creates subsets of rows based on unique values within columns.

LAB ANSWER

It is fairly clear that a table join is needed to retrieve data from both the Regions and Customers tables. The requirements dictate that the e-mail address for each customer that lives in the southeast region is returned. The first step is to code the T-SQL to accomplish that.

```
SELECT C.Email FROM Customers AS C
JOIN Regions AS R
ON C.RegionID = R.RegionID
AND R.RegionName = 'SouthEast'
```

Next, we need to plug each column value from the preceding result set into the @recipients variable in the system stored procedure XP_SENDMAIL. Since the stored procedure cannot accept a subquery as an argument, some dynamic SQL will be needed. A cursor will also be used to apply the XP_SENDMAIL stored procedure to each value in the Email column. The following block of T-SQL satisfies the requirements of the question:

```
DECLARE @Email VARCHAR(50)
DECLARE @SqlStatement VARCHAR(200)
DECLARE sample_cursor CURSOR
FOR
SELECT C.Email FROM Customers AS C
JOIN Regions AS R
ON C.RegionID = R.RegionID
AND R.RegionName = 'SouthEast'
OPEN sample_cursor
FETCH NEXT FROM sample_cursor INTO @email
WHILE @@FETCH_STATUS = 0
BEGIN
SET @SqlStatement = 'EXEC MASTER.DBO.XP_SENDMAIL @recipients = ''' + @email
+ ''', @message = ''ACME is having a big March sale and invites you to attend.'''
EXEC(@SqlStatement)
FETCH NEXT FROM sample_cursor INTO @email
END
CLOSE sample_cursor
DEALLOCATE sample_cursor
```

MICROSOFT CERTIFIED DATABASE ADMINISTRATOR

6

Tuning and Optimizing Database Performance

CERTIFICATION OBJECTIVES

Perhaps one of the most important goals of database design and implementation is performance. Users will often measure the success of an application based on how quickly it can return the data they request. If your database implementation results in a sluggish application or one that requires many minutes for simple queries to complete, the application will likely be viewed as a failure (or, at best, one that needs serious improvement). Fortunately, there are many ways that database designers can monitor and optimize the performance of their production database servers.

Performance can be monitored and optimized at multiple levels. The goal is to provide low *response times* (how long it takes to receive the first records from a query) and high *throughput* (a measure of the total number of queries that can be handled by the server in a given time). When discussing performance monitoring as related to database applications, it's important to make a distinction between these terms. Furthermore, optimization steps can often cause the balance between throughput and response times to tip in favor of one or the other. To find the optimal settings, you must understand business requirements. For example, if a user wants to scroll through a list of items, it is a good idea to return the first few items as quickly as possible. However, if a manager is creating a report on a desktop computer, it's likely that none of the calculations will be completed until all data is retrieved.

Overall database performance is based on the relationships among many different factors. You can optimize performance at one or more of several levels:

- **Server level** Performance issues related to running multiple applications on the same machine, issues with the handling of memory usage and other bottlenecks that might occur.

- **Database level** The performance related to the overall design of the database, including issues dealing with indexing, concurrency, and locking.

- **Query level** The performance of specific queries that are run on a database server system.

Fortunately, SQL Server 2000 includes several methods for monitoring and optimizing performance in each of these important areas. In this chapter, we'll look at the tools and features available for monitoring and optimizing performance of SQL Server 2000 databases.

CERTIFICATION OBJECTIVE 6.01

Monitoring and Optimizing Server Performance

The first step in optimizing performance is to look at the overall configuration of the SQL Server. At this level, you must consider details regarding the role of your SQL Server machine and the management of important computer resources. The three most important hardware-level factors that affect a database server are the CPU, memory, and physical disk decisions. In this section we'll look at how you can monitor and optimize these and other related settings to improve the overall performance of your SQL Server installation.

Using Windows NT/2000 Performance Monitor

It's often necessary to view overall system performance in relation to server resources. Windows NT/2000 Performance Monitor is the best tool for viewing and recording all of this information in a single place. When SQL Server 2000 is installed, several performance counters are added to the list of items available through Performance Monitor. One of the main challenges with using Performance Monitor is deciding *what* to monitor. To make this easier, Microsoft has included explanations of the various SQL Server–related counters that will be of interest to SQL Server DBAs (see Figure 6-1).

Although all of the counters can be useful at one time or another, you'll probably want to focus on specific counters. For example, if you're also running Internet Information Server (IIS) on the same machine, you might want to compare the number of Web users to the number of database users currently on the system.

exam
ⓦatch

In many cases, the exact counters that are available for monitoring will be based on the software you have installed and various operating system settings. For example, to view certain network characteristics, you must have the appropriate services installed (for example, the Simple Network Management Protocol [SNMP]). Or, to view information about SQL Server 2000, the database server must be installed and running on the machine you're monitoring.

For more information about monitoring server performance of SQL Server and other resources, see the Windows NT/2000 online help files.

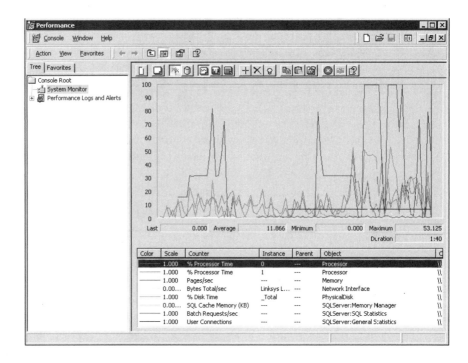

FIGURE 6-1

Managing CPU and Memory Settings

Microsoft has gone to great lengths to ensure that SQL Server 2000 is largely a
self-tuning system. That is, SQL Server 2000 monitors itself and uses monitored
statistics to adjust such parameters as caching settings and memory usage. However,
in some specific cases, you might want to manually override these parameters.

exam
ⓦatch

*In contrast to other relational database systems, Microsoft SQL Server has
been designed to be self-monitoring and self-adjusting. Since making server-
level changes will affect the performance of all databases on the server, you
should be sure you thoroughly test the effects of changes before you make
them in a production environment.*

The two most important resources that should be managed when dealing with
overall server performance are the CPU speed and memory. SQL Server is installed
with default memory and CPU usage options that are appropriate for working in most
environments. If you need to make changes, however, you have options. Exercise 6-1
walks you through the process of viewing and modifying SQL Server settings.

EXERCISE 6-1

CertCam 6-1

Setting SQL Server Memory and CPU Settings in Enterprise Manager

1. In Enterprise Manager, right-click the name of the server you want to modify and select Properties.

2. In the Memory tab, you can modify the amount of memory the SQL Server will use.

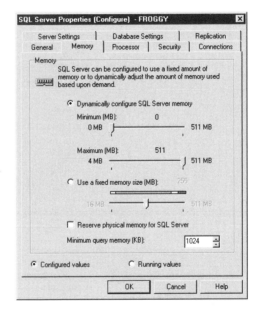

The default option—to dynamically configure memory usage—will be appropriate for most situations. If you have a large amount of RAM on the system, you might want to increase the minimum memory size. Alternatively, if your server will be running many other important applications, you might want to lower the maximum setting. If you have an accurate idea of how much memory SQL Server will typically use, you can put the value at a fixed setting. This precaution will minimize the performance overhead caused by excessive paging of information to and from the hard disk.

You can check the Reserve Physical Memory for SQL Server option if you want Windows NT/2000 to set aside physical RAM for the service. This prevents the operating system from swapping this information to disk and can increase performance. The Maximum Query Memory option specifies the limit of RAM that can be allocated to any single user transaction.

3. In the Processor tab, you can specify which CPU(s) in a multiprocessor system can be used by SQL Server. This is often useful if you want to dedicate one or more CPUs to operating system functions and other applications. The Maximum Worker Threads setting specifies how many operations SQL Server can perform simultaneously. A higher number allows more users and processes to occur, but performance might decrease as SQL Server switches between threads. If the value is exceeded, users will receive an error message when trying to execute a command.

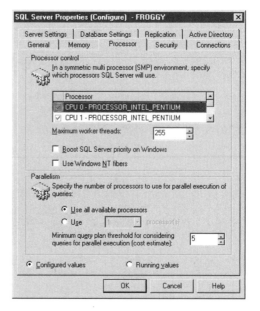

4. The Boost SQL Server Priority option is designed to give the SQL Server service more CPU time when multiple tasks are competing for resources. However, you should thoroughly test the effects of this setting, as it may provide only a marginal improvement in performance and can cause problems with other applications that are running on the same machine.

5. Finally, in the Parallelism section, you can specify whether you want SQL Server to distribute query processing among multiple processors. Multiprocessing

generally incurs overhead, and the default setting for the minimum query plan threshold will determine whether it is efficient to use multiple CPUs for this task. "Costs" are based on the time required to process a transaction. Legal values are between 0 and 32,767.

6. To accept all changes, click OK. Dynamic memory changes will take place immediately. However, note that you may be prompted to restart SQL Server before other changes take effect.

Scheduling Jobs with SQL Server Agent

In the real world, database servers experience periods of heavy load during specific times of the day. For example, users of a sales-tracking application might be much more likely to enter information during business hours. Even during business hours, servers may experience high load during the morning hours (when users are first entering the application), and during the evening (when users might be running daily reports). Load may decrease during lunch hours, weekends, or holidays.

SQL Server Agent is a component of SQL Server 2000. It runs as a service under Windows NT/2000 and can be used for creating, modifying, and executing scheduled jobs. The SQL Server Agent also runs on Windows 98, but it is limited in functionality since it runs as an application instead of as a service. Scheduling tasks to run at specific times is very helpful in optimizing performance as it can help database implementers decide when maintenance tasks should be performed. For example, it's a common practice to schedule database backups to occur during nonpeak usage hours. Similarly, if you need to run a maintenance task (such as the deletion of old records from certain temporary tables), you can create and define the job using SQL Server Agent and have it run at the times that you specify.

Before you actually create and define SQL Server Agent jobs, you must first configure the service with the settings you require.

The next exercise walks you through the various options that are available for the SQL Server Agent service.

EXERCISE 6-2

Configuring SQL Server Agent

1. In Enterprise Manager, select your server and then expand the Management folder. Right-click SQL Server Agent and select Properties. You'll see this dialog box:

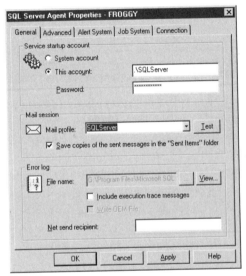

2. On the General tab, you can specify the account to be used by SQL Server Agent, the mail profile to be used for sending messages, and the name of the file to save error information to. Optionally, if you want a user to see a pop-up dialog box when errors occur, enter the name of the user who should be alerted.

3. On the Advanced tab, you can set the Idle CPU Conditions setting as desired. The Percentage Threshold setting specifies the maximum CPU usage that is allowed before the system is considered "idle," and the number of seconds specifies the minimum duration of this level of activity before tasks are run. You can also configure whether you want SQL Server Agent to restart when an unexpected stop occurs. Finally, you can choose to forward events to remote servers so that all information can be managed in a single location.

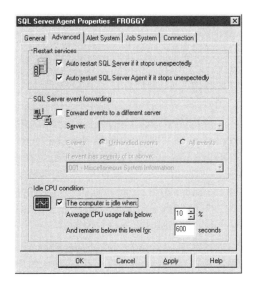

4. The Alert System tab allows you to send e-mail to a compatible pager. A failsafe operator can also be set up as an alternative recipient when an error occurs.

5. The Job System tab allows you to configure settings for the maximum log size. Here, you can also restrict access to executing operating system commands to system administrators. This option prevents users from running jobs under elevated privileges using the CmdExec procedure.

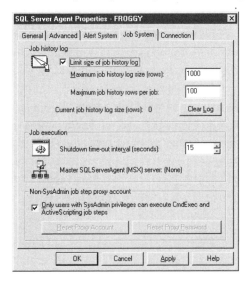

6. Finally, on the Connection tab, you can specify the account that SQL Server Agent will use to log on to SQL Server. When you're done with the configuration, click OK to accept the changes.

One way to squeeze the maximum possible performance out of your database servers is to use them when they're least busy. This is an important concept in relation to database maintenance. The properties of SQL Server Agent allow you to schedule tasks so that they occur when there is little or no activity on the database. Although it's recommended that you schedule critical jobs for times of the day or night when you know activity will be low, you can let SQL Server decide when to run jobs that can be scheduled based on load. Additionally, for simplified management (and who doesn't want that?), you can implement master and target servers. This type of setup allows you to centrally manage several servers, using one console. For details, see Books Online.

Scheduling jobs allows certain operations to occur when, for example, the staff is in a meeting or during lunchtime.

Setting Alerts

Database designers and administrators are often interested in ensuring that the databases that they manage are running within specific parameters. For example, you might want to know if the number of open transactions on a server goes above 20, as this might indicate code-related performance problems. Although you could hire someone to constantly stare at performance-related statistics and tap you on the shoulder whenever something of interest occurs, there's a much easier way to achieve the same results.

When you install SQL Server 2000, the SQL Server Agent service is also installed and configured. SQL Server Agent can be used to send alerts based on performance data. For example, if the number of user connections exceeds a certain value, a server administrator can be notified. Exercise 6-3 walks you through the process of implementing performance-based alerts using SQL Server Agent. These alerts can be used to notify you of important events on your server when they occur.

EXERCISE 6-3

CertCam 6-3

Setting Performance-Based Alerts

1. Expand the Management folder and then expand the SQL Server Agent item. Right-click Alerts and select New Alert.

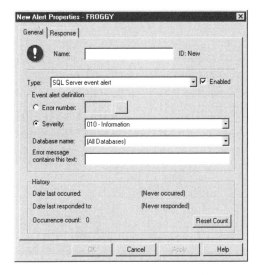

Name the alert and set the type to SQL Server Performance Condition Alert. Ensure that the Enabled box is checked.

2. To define the alert condition, choose an object and a counter. These are the same values that can be monitored by Performance Monitor (described earlier). Finally, set the alert to fire when a value is lower than, higher than, or equal to a certain number. For example, you might choose to create an alert for the following parameters:

- **Name**   High number of user connections
- **Type**   SQL Server performance condition alert
- **Object**   SQLServer:General Statistics
- **Counter**   User connections
- **Value**   Alert if counter rises above, say, 20

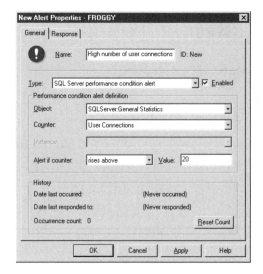

3. Optionally, you can use the settings in the Response tab to notify database administrators of problems. For example, you can execute a SQL Server job, notify operators, and/or send or log notifications in other ways.

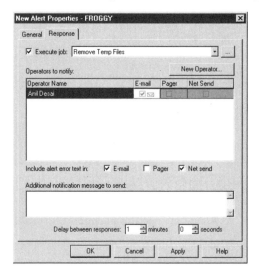

4. Click OK to accept the settings.

Alerts work by constantly monitoring Performance Monitor values on your system. When an event that meets or exceeds your characteristics occurs, the alert is fired. SQL Server Agent will then carry out any actions that you have defined, such as entering an item in the SQL Server log, executing another process or batch file, or notifying you.

on the
job
Monitoring servers is an important aspect of the job of any IT professional. When monitoring SQL Server 2000 performance statistics, be sure that you measure only what's important to you. Although it's useful to get a count of active users on a server, it can be very annoying to receive pages for every event. The end result is that you'll begin ignoring all of the erroneous or meaningless pages that you receive. For example, if you're monitoring CPU utilization, the fact that one or more CPUs reaches 100-percent utilization may not be all that important since this indicates that your machine is being used. However, if the utilization remains at 100 percent for a long period of time, this might indicate an important event. Choosing what to monitor can often be just as important as the act of monitoring itself.

As shown in Figure 6-2, SQL Server Agent includes many different types of alerts that are automatically defined upon installation of SQL Server 2000.

Monitoring Server Activity

There are several ways to monitor server activity within SQL Server. A quick and easy way to get an overview of the number of connections to your server is to use Enterprise Manager. You can simply expand the server name, click on Management and select Current Activity. Figure 6-3 shows the types of information you can expect to see in the Process Info item.

You can also obtain similar information in Transact-SQL by using the sp_who2 stored procedure.

exam
watch
Blocking is an important factor that can affect overall database performance. One of the most useful columns in the information returned by sp_who2 (and the information presented in Enterprise Manager) is the BlkBy column. This column tells you not only that a specific process is being blocked, but also provides you with details about which process is blocking it. You can use this to troubleshoot application-level problems or to correlate with end-user complaints of extremely slow transaction performance.

Viewing a list of
the default alerts
that are included
with SQL Server
2000

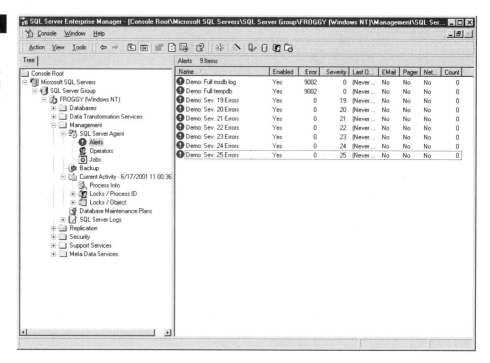

Now that we've looked at several ways to monitor and optimize overall server
performance, let's move down a level and look at how we can monitor specific types
of database activity.

CERTIFICATION OBJECTIVE 6.02

Monitoring Database Activity with SQL Profiler

Tuning performance options at the database level involves examining all the operations
that are being performed on that database over time. Normally, if you're an applications
developer, you can get a pretty good idea of how the system will perform based on this
information. One way of obtaining performance information is to add debugging
code to your application that, for example, records any queries that take longer than
a specific amount of time to run. However, this method requires application changes
and still may not provide you with all of the details that you need.

FIGURE 6-3

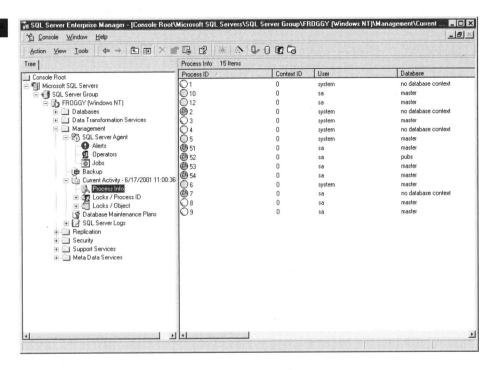

Viewing process
information in
Enterprise
Manager

Fortunately, SQL Server includes the SQL Profiler tool for measuring database server performance at several levels. In this section, we'll walk through the process of using SQL Profiler and then look at how this information can be used to optimize performance.

SQL Profiler can be used to monitor the performance of queries as they are being executed against database servers. It can display information about user logins, connections to the server, and starting and completion times for database transactions.

Creating Traces with SQL Profiler

SQL Profiler works by creating *traces*. A trace includes all of the information that you've chosen to monitor. SQL Profiler can physically store trace information in a database table or in a binary file. There are several options for the properties of a trace, including the following settings:

■ **General** Used for determining basic properties of the trace, including where the trace data will be stored.

■ **Events** A list of the types of events that are to be monitored and, optionally, recorded. The list of available events classes includes

- ■ Cursors
- ■ Database
- ■ Errors and warnings
- ■ Locks
- ■ Objects
- ■ Performance
- ■ Scans
- ■ Security audit
- ■ Server
- ■ Sessions
- ■ Stored procedures
- ■ Transactions
- ■ T-SQL
- ■ User configurable

Using the "User configurable" option, application developers can create their own event classes. These event classes can then be monitored along with the other classes. For more information, see SQL Server Books Online.

Based on this information, here are a few scenarios that you might encounter.

■ **Data columns** The specific data that is to be recorded during the trace. Many columns are available for tracing, but you may not want to select them all since this can generate a large volume of data (especially if the trace is run over an extended period of time).

■ **Filters** Rules that determine which events will be recorded. For example, you might choose to record events that originate only from a specific application, or for queries that last at least a specific amount of time.

SCENARIO & SOLUTION

You want to find queries that are performing table scan operations.	Create a SQL Profiler trace that includes information from the Scans object.
You want to monitor the performance effects of locks on your database server.	Create a SQL Profiler trace that includes information from the Locks object. This will provide you with information about which processes are holding locks, and which processes are waiting for locks to be released.
Developers in your environment want to create custom information that can be recorded using SQL Profiler.	Use the "user configurable" features of SQL Profiler to add events within the application code. Then, use SQL Profiler to monitor and record the user configurable events.

You can launch SQL Profiler directly from the SQL Server 2000 program group or from within Enterprise Manager by using the Tools menu. Exercise 6-4 walks you through the process of defining a new trace in SQL Profiler.

EXERCISE 6-4

Creating a New Trace in SQL Profiler

1. Open SQL Profiler by choosing Profiler from the Microsoft SQL Server program group.

2. Select File | New | Trace. Enter a trace name and select the server you want to monitor.

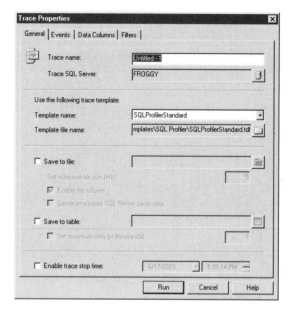

3. Choose to save the collected information to a text file or to a SQL Server database.

4. In the Events tab, add the events you want to monitor.

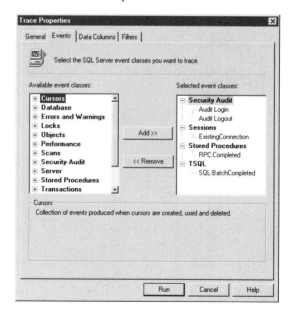

5. The lower portion of the dialog box will give you a brief description of each item.

6. In the Data Columns tab, choose the type of information you want to view for each event. Again, a brief description of each column type is provided.

7. Finally, on the Filters tab, you can select specific criteria to include and exclude in events for this trace.

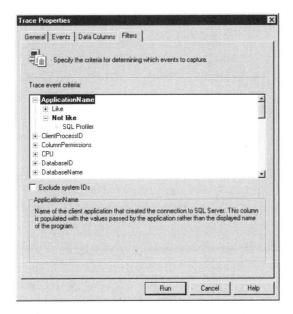

8. Click Run to execute the trace file that you have created.

Troubleshooting Performance Problems with SQL Profiler

So far, we've looked at details related to the architecture of SQL Profiler and we've walked through the process of creating a sample trace file. There are several different types of traces that you can create to solve specific types of database problems. Some examples might include

■ **Monitoring stored procedure usage**   In many applications, it's common for a few stored procedures to be called much more often than all of the rest combined. Generally, we might look for stored procedures that take a long time to execute, and then we optimize those. However, if you have a relatively quick stored procedure that executes thousands of times, it might be worthwhile to optimize that piece of code—the overall performance improvements could be dramatic.

■ **Troubleshooting locking**   Locking is an important aspect of overall system performance. When certain types of operations (such as table updates) are being performed, the process performing the change might create a lock on the object. Depending on the type of lock, this might prevent other transactions and processes from carrying out their work. The end result is generally complaints from users about slow performance. You can use SQL Profiler to monitor locking and to isolate portions of the workload that might be causing blocking issues.

■ **Monitoring application or user activity**   If your database server supports multiple applications, it's often useful to be able to isolate which of these is causing the greatest load on your server. For example, if the majority of queries are performed against database A, you might want to move this database to a different server when performance starts to become a problem.

■ **Finding the slowest queries**   Most applications have portions of code that execute less efficiently than others. Sometimes, performance issues aren't discovered until code is released in the production environment (or, slow performance only occurs when specific types of actions are performed). SQL Profiler is extremely useful for isolating queries that take a long time to complete. You can then focus on optimizing these queries to improve overall system performance.

■ **Benchmarking**   Since SQL Profiler traces can be replayed, you can create a basic reference workload that you can use to verify that changes to the application are producing actual improvements. For example, if you change a stored procedure, the overall workload should complete in less time than it took to replay the original workload. In this way, you can be sure that you're always heading in the right direction, instead of improving performance for only one area of the application while potentially reducing performance in other areas.

exam
Watch

In order to be successful in the task of optimizing databases, you must be able to sift through all of the information that you collect to find out what's really important. This generally starts by understanding the application that you're optimizing, and includes thoroughly understanding the features of the tools you plan to use. When preparing for the exam, be sure to apply SQL Profiler toward solving hypothetical performance problems, such as the ones listed in this section.

Several of the default Profiler trace templates that are included with SQL Server 2000 can be useful for monitoring these types of statistics.

Executing Traces

To execute the trace, select File | Run Traces and select either a sample trace or one that you've created. A screen will appear showing information related to monitored events, as shown in Figure 6-4. You can run multiple traces at once to record different kinds of information (for example, query performance and overall server statistics). To simulate the recorded information at a later time, you can replay a trace by using the Replay menu. Finally, to view captured information, you can select File | Open, and then select Trace File (if you've saved to a file) or Trace Table (if you've saved to a SQL Server table). Trace files can also be used with data analysis tools, such as Microsoft Access and Microsoft Excel.

If you're planning to use certain trace settings often, you can create new *trace templates.* Trace templates include all of the settings (including events, data columns, and filters) that you want to set when you start a capture. This is very useful when, for example, you might have an application that connects to many different database servers. You can simply copy the trace template to each of the machines you want to monitor, choose settings for the trace (including where the trace data should be stored), and then start the trace.

on the
Job

It's very useful to store trace information in database tables, because this provides you with a way to easily analyze large sets of results. For example, you can query against a trace table and find the worst-performing queries. Or, you can choose to delete all of the rows in the table that are not of interest to you. By using your bag of SQL tricks, trace file information stored in a table can be a very valuable asset.

FIGURE 6-4

Viewing trace file
information in
SQL Profiler

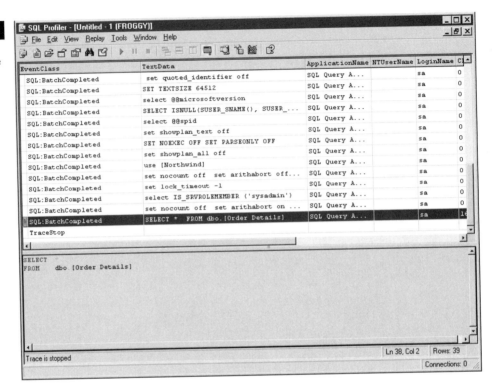

In addition to using the SQL Profiler application to manually start the monitoring of database performance characteristics, you can use built-in functions and stored procedures in SQL Server 2000 to create traces that are defined within SQL Server 2000. These traces can be configured to automatically begin whenever SQL Server 2000 is started, and they don't require that a user be logged in to the machine to run. To get started with scripting traces, you can simply choose the Script Trace option from the File menu in SQL Profiler. The resulting SQL file can be used to automatically create and define a trace in SQL Server. For more information about scripting and executing traces in this way, see SQL Server Books Online.

By now, you can probably think of a lot of different uses for SQL Profiler trace information. For example, you can create a trace that provides you with the details of which queries are being run on your production servers. Using this information, you can pinpoint queries that take a long time to run. Or, you could look for information about the most active databases on a server that hosts many different databases. And, the ability to replay trace files can be very helpful in the performance optimization process, since it allows you to record a workload, make changes (such as adding indexes or changing servers options), and then to retest using the same, original workload. In this way, you can be sure that your changes had an overall positive impact on performance.

Overall, the information provided by SQL Profiler can provide some extremely useful and relevant insight into the activity on your production servers. Later in this chapter, we'll look at how trace information can be used to optimize indexing structure. With that in mind, let's move on to the important topic of indexing.

CERTIFICATION OBJECTIVE 6.03

Designing and Implementing Indexing

Database indexes are used to speed access to information stored within SQL Server 2000 tables. We covered basic information about how indexes work in Chapter 1. Here, we'll focus on the details related to the implementation of various types of indexes, and their effects on performance.

There are several different types of indexes that are supported in SQL Server 2000. The list includes the following database objects and features:

- **Clustered index**   A clustered index contains pointers to physical data pages and determines the physical ordering of data columns within a table. You may create only one clustered index on a table. By default, when you create a table that contains a PRIMARY KEY constraint, SQL Server will automatically create a clustered index on this column. If you use a compound primary key (that is, a primary key that includes more than one column), the clustered index will be created on all of those columns. In some cases, creating a clustered index on the primary key is exactly what you want. However, based on your application design, you may want to move the clustered index to another column or columns. For example, if you have a table that contains an IDENTITY value for the ID column and stores ZIP code information, queries that look for ranges of ZIP codes will work faster if you index this column. Note that clustered indexes do not take up any additional storage space within a database, but they can reduce performance because SQL Server may have to reorganize data whenever new rows are entered into the table.

- **Nonclustered index**   Like clustered indexes, nonclustered indexes are used to speed access to specific data stored in tables within your database. The architecture of nonclustered indexes is quite different from that of clustered indexes, however. First, nonclustered indexes physically store data. Therefore, their creation requires the use of additional space within a database. Second, a table may have up to 249 nonclustered indexes. The columns that are included in the clustered index are physically stored. Query performance will improve for any operations that require information stored within an index. The indexes are also helpful in joins. A potential drawback of nonclustered indexes, however, is that they require CPU and memory resources for maintenance (that is, the indexes must be updated when changes are made to the underlying data stored in tables), and disk storage (space required for the index itself).

- **Covering index**   Deciding which columns to place indexes on is an important factor in any database design because both clustered and nonclustered indexes can lead to dramatic increases in performance. Indexes, however, impose some limitations. We already mentioned that you can only have one clustered index on a table, and that nonclustered indexes require resources for storage and maintenance. The goal for database implementers is to create covering indexes— indexes that include the columns used in a JOIN condition or in the SELECT clause of a query. Covering indexes are especially useful since they satisfy the data requirements for a query and can greatly reduce disk I/O performance impacts.

- **Indexed views**   New in SQL Server 2000 is the ability to create indexes on views. Although "traditional" views do not actually store data, the indexes can store pre-calculated aggregations of information in actual database structures. The performance impacts of creating an index on a view (especially one that requires significant resources to run) can be dramatic. However, indexed views are not without their limitations. First, there's a fairly length list of requirements for views that include indexes. For a complete list, see SQL Books Online. Next, database server resources are consumed in order to maintain indexed views. That is, whenever data changes in any of the underlying tables that are referenced by the view, the index on the view must be updated as well. Also, the indexes themselves use storage space. For certain types of views, this can require a large amount of disk space within a database. When implemented optimally, however, indexed views can be extremely useful in improving performance.

on the **Job**

Technically, indexed views are supported only on the Developer and Enterprise Editions of SQL Server 2000. In practice, however, you can actually create and manage indexed views in other editions of SQL Server 2000. The limitation is that the query optimizer will not automatically use indexed views to improve performance on these editions of SQL Server 2000. To get around this, you can use query hints to force the use of indexed views (see SQL Server Books Online for details). Overall, however, this method is difficult to implement and maintain, and is probably not a good solution in the real world.

- **Statistics**   In order to speed data retrieval and calculations, SQL Server maintains statistical information about data stored in tables. Statistics might include hints about the distribution of data in a column that stores integer values. When performing joins or searching for data in the tables, the statistics can be referenced to improve the performance of queries. As we'll see in the next section, it is highly recommended that statistics be automatically managed by SQL Server 2000.

Now that we have a solid understanding of various performance-improving database objects, let's move on to look at the details of exactly how you would implement indexes and statistics.

Creating Statistics

As we mentioned earlier in this chapter, one of Microsoft's goals with SQL Server 2000 was to greatly reduce the amount of administration required to maintain database servers by creating a largely self-tuning platform. An excellent example of this is the fact that SQL Server 2000 automatically creates, calculates, and maintains statistics for database tables. You'll probably find that the default database settings will be best for most applications.

You can, however, override the default settings for the creation and update of statistics in Enterprise Manager by viewing the properties of a database. On the Options tab (see Figure 6-5), you can specify whether you want to enable or disable the automatic creation and update of statistics. As these operations require some server resources, you might have special reasons for not performing them automatically. For the vast majority of applications, however, the automatic creation of statistics is highly recommended, as it can significantly increase performance, and it reduces administrative overhead (that is, SQL Server won't "forget" to keep statistics up-to-date).

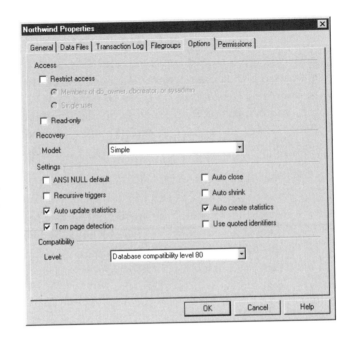

Creating Indexes

As is the case for other types of database objects, there are several different ways to create and manage indexes in SQL Server 2000. An easy way to create indexes is by using the graphical tools in Enterprise Manager. By right-clicking a table within Enterprise Manager and choosing Design Table, you'll be able to access the properties of the table. You can easily view, modify, and create indexes by selecting the Indexes/Keys tab (see Figure 6-6). Note there are options for the type of index (or key constraint), the columns to be contained in the index, and details about the index characteristics.

Although Enterprise Manager is a useful tool for creating one or a few indexes on specific tables, you will probably want to take advantage of the flexibility and maintainability of creating indexes within Transact-SQL code. The command syntax shown here can be used to create indexes in Transact-SQL:

```
CREATE [ UNIQUE ] [ CLUSTERED | NONCLUSTERED ] INDEX index_name
    ON { table | view } ( column [ ASC | DESC ] [ ,...n ] )
[ WITH < index_option > [ ,...n] ]
[ ON filegroup ]
```

```
< index_option > :: =
    { PAD_INDEX |
        FILLFACTOR = fillfactor |
        IGNORE_DUP_KEY |
        DROP_EXISTING |
    STATISTICS_NORECOMPUTE |
    SORT_IN_TEMPDB
}
```

For example, the following code will create a new index on the Authors table within the Pubs sample database (assuming that an identical index doesn't already exist):

```
CREATE INDEX [IX_AuthorInfo]
ON [dbo].[authors] ([au_id], [au_lname], [au_fname])
```

FIGURE 6-6

Viewing index information in Enterprise Manager

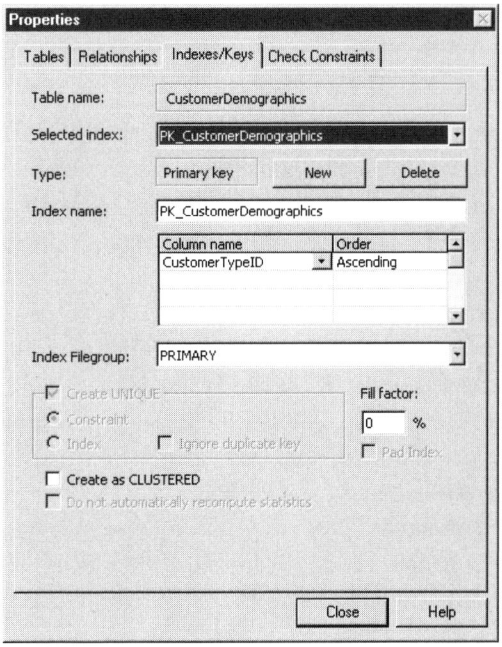

on the
()ob

When you're dealing with database objects such as indexes, it can be extremely useful to create a naming standard for indexes. One method, for example, might actually include information about the columns or usage of the index within the name of the index. Additionally, it can be useful to prefix the name of the index with some designation (such as IX_C for clustered indexes and IX_NC for nonclustered indexes). Of course, the overall value of this method depends on all database implementers and developers following the established convention. Although it might take a little bit more up-front effort, the benefits of organized naming are many and can save you a lot of time and headaches in the future!

A third method (in addition to Enterprise Manager and Transact-SQL code) is to create indexes within Query Analyzer. We'll cover this method in the upcoming section "Using Performance Features of SQL Query Analyzer."

exam
Ⓦatch

In almost all cases, there are several different ways to accomplish the same task in SQL Server 2000. A common example is an operation that can be performed in either Enterprise Manager or from within Query Analyzer (via Transact-SQL commands). If you're familiar with doing tasks one way, be sure you understand how you can use other methods before you attempt the exam.

Using the Index Tuning Wizard

Determining appropriate index placement can be a long and arduous process for any database implementer or administrator. Often, the method for determining index placement has been to examine specific commonly used queries and to identify which tables and columns are referenced. Then, educated guesses about which indexes will be most helpful are made. Next, the indexes are created and the performance effects are tested by rerunning the query. All of this can lead to a lot of work, and it might actually lead to *reduced* overall performance. This can happen, for example, if the queries examined are not often used and the indexes lead to less-than-optimal results for other queries. Although manual index optimization has made a lot of money for database administrators (and consultants), the job can seem to be a tedious and never-ending one.

Fortunately, there's an easier road to index optimizations in SQL Server 2000. Earlier in this section, we looked at how SQL Profiler can be used to capture database workload on production or test systems. Once you've captured the information you need, it's time to apply it toward the goal of choosing optimal indexing. If you're like me (averse to long, complicated, boring tasks), you'll probably want the SQL Server Index Tuning Wizard to generate index recommendations for you. The Index Tuning Wizard works by analyzing the trace information that you've captured (to either a file or to a trace table), attempting various combinations of indexes and then generating a recommendation about the types of indexes that will improve the performance of the workload.

The first step in effectively using the Index Tuning Wizard is to create an accurate trace of your workload. This can be done by using the default SQLProfilerTuning trace template. Note that in order for the Index Tuning Wizard to be able to do its job, you must trace at least the events that are included in this template (see Figure 6-7). Be sure to save your trace information to a file or to a table.

The Index Tuning Wizard can be launched from within SQL Server Enterprise Manager, SQL Profiler, or SQL Query Analyzer. The wizard walks you through the steps that are required to analyze your workload. Exercise 6-5 walks you through the steps of using the Index Tuning Wizard.

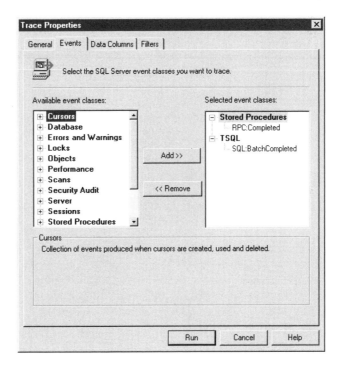

FIGURE 6-7

Viewing the default events that are recorded for SQL Profiler tuning traces

EXERCISE 6-5

CertCam 6-5

Using the Index Tuning Wizard

1. Open the Profiler program from within the Microsoft SQL Server program group.

2. Click File | New Trace. For the Template name, select SQL Profiler Tuning.

3. Click Save to File and choose a file to which the trace should be saved. Make a note of this path, as you'll need to refer to it later.

4. Leave all other options as their defaults and click Run.

5. Open Query Analyzer and run some sample queries within the Northwind database. The following queries can be used to generate some events (they all query views that are built into the Northwind database, by default):

```
SELECT * FROM [Alphabetical list of products]
GO
SELECT * FROM [Category Sales for 1997]
GO
SELECT * FROM [Current Product List]
GO
SELECT * FROM [Customer and Suppliers by City]
GO
SELECT * FROM [Invoices]
GO
SELECT * FROM [Order Details Extended]
GO
SELECT * FROM [Order Subtotals]
GO
SELECT * FROM [Orders Qry]
GO
SELECT * FROM [Product Sales for 1997]
GO
SELECT * FROM [Products Above Average Price]
GO
SELECT * FROM [Products by Category]
GO
SELECT * FROM [Quarterly Orders]
GO
SELECT * FROM [Sales by Category]
GO
```

```
SELECT * FROM [Sales Totals by Amount]
GO
SELECT * FROM [Summary of Sales by Quarter]
GO
SELECT * FROM [Summary of Sales by Year]
GO
```

Note that the queries are separated by a GO command to ensure that they show up as separate queries in SQL Profiler.

6. After you have run the queries, you should see the information recorded in the SQL Profiler display. Click the Stop button to stop recording the trace.

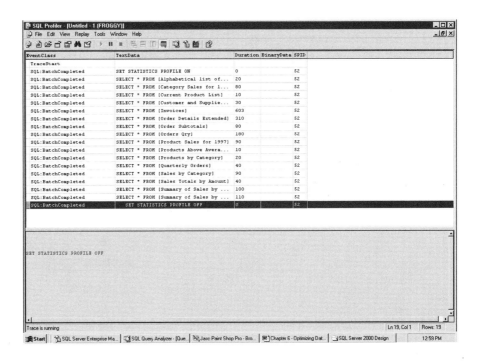

7. To start the Index Tuning Wizard, Click Tools | Index Tuning Wizard.

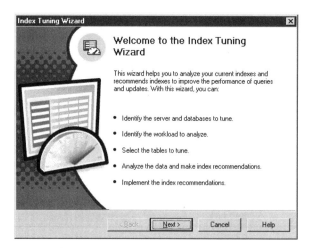

8. Click Next to begin the wizard and then log in to the server on which you created the trace.

9. In the first step of the Wizard, choose the Northwind database. Enable the Keep All Existing Indexes option and disable the Add Indexed Views option (if it is available). Leave the Tuning mode at its default of Medium. Click Next to continue.

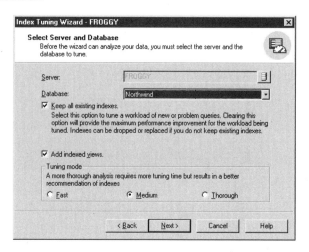

10. In the Workload option, choose My Workload File and then find the trace file that you created earlier in this exercise. Note that you can select several details in the Advanced Options dialog box. Click Next to continue.

11. Click the Select All Tables option to instruct the Index Tuning Wizard to analyze all of the tables within the Northwind database. Click Next.

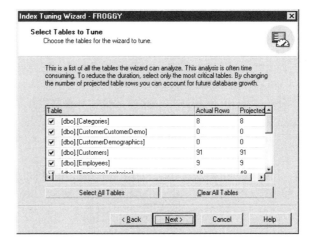

12. The Index Tuning Wizard will perform an analysis of the workload. Click Analysis to view details about the analysis. Note that you can choose from several reports listed in the drop-down box. You can also save the various reports by clicking the Save button. Click Close, and click Next to continue.

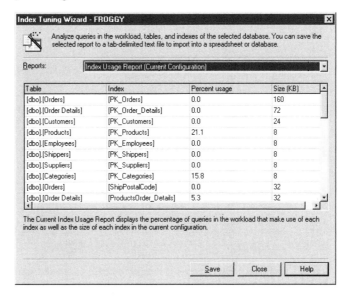

13. Since, in this case, the Index Tuning Wizard did not make any recommendations for indexing, the wizard will complete. Had recommendations been made, the wizard would offer to create scripts and/or create the indexes immediately.

Once the Index Tuning Wizard has completed, you have the option to view various reports about the workload (including table access and other related information). The wizard will then automatically create a SQL script to implement the indexes that it has recommended. You can choose to have the wizard automatically execute the recommendations or save them as a SQL script for later analysis.

If you've ever had to perform manual index analysis, you'll probably appreciate the time and effort that the Index Tuning Wizard can save you. Although the recommendations may not be perfect, they can save time and reduce errors in implementation.

CERTIFICATION OBJECTIVE 6.04

Optimizing Queries with SQL Query Analyzer

So far, we've covered methods for optimizing performance at the server level and at the database level (using features such as indexes and the Index Tuning Wizard). Now, it's time to tackle the most detailed (and in many cases, the most important) level of performance optimization: specific database queries.

At the level of the individual query, you can use features of SQL Query Analyzer to provide you with statistics and performance recommendations. These features are excellent for applications developers who want to test the effects that minor syntax changes have on performance, or optimize performance of a particularly slow-running query. In this section, we'll look at the performance-monitoring and optimization features of SQL Server 2000's Query Analyzer.

Using Performance Features of SQL Query Analyzer

SQL Query Analyzer is a powerful tool included with SQL Server 2000. On a basic level, it provides a Transact-SQL command environment for executing SQL queries.

However, it goes much further by color-coding queries and allowing users to display results in a grid format. For measuring the performance of specific queries, it can show the exact statistics for fulfilling a request. Finally, it can analyze queries and make recommendations as to which columns to place in indexes. In the next sections, we'll cover the specific types of information that can be returned by Query Analyzer.

Execution Plan

SQL Query Analyzer has the ability to return a graphical execution plan of the steps that SQL Server had to perform to obtain the results from a query (see Figure 6-8). Included are statistics related to the resource usage for the query (such as CPU time and disk I/O), along with the actual objects that were referenced and any indexes that were used. By hovering the mouse over portions of the execution plan, you will receive in-depth details about the specific operation that was performed.

If you're new to SQL Server 2000 or to relational database systems, the results from Query Analyzer might seem very complicated. However, by gaining an understanding of the types of steps that are performed (and how they can help you optimize queries),

FIGURE 6-8

Viewing a graphical execution plan in Query Analyzer

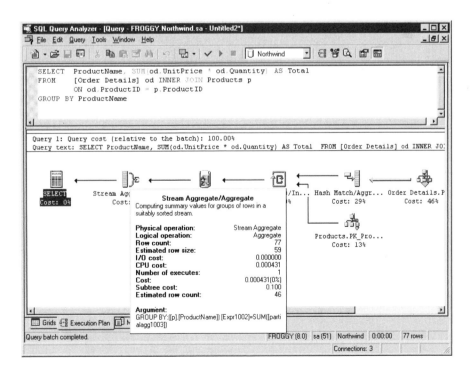

you'll be able to quickly identify inefficiencies within your queries. The following is a partial list of the types of operations that you'll find in the execution plan, along with their usefulness:

- **Table scans and clustered index scans**   In general, table and index scans are inefficient processes. When the query optimizer performs a scan, it is an indication that SQL Server had to parse through all of the rows in a given table. This is much slower than using indexes to quickly pinpoint the data that you need. If significant time is spent on these steps, you should consider adding indexes to the objects that are being scanned.

- **Table seeks and clustered index seeks**   Seek operations are more efficient than scan operations. Generally, you'll find these steps to be much quicker than similar table scans or clustered index scans. If the objects that are being referenced in the queries contain covering indexes, the query optimizer is able to utilize these indexes using a seek operation.

- **Parallelism**   If you're running your queries on a machine that has multiple CPUs, you can see how SQL Server has decided to split up the job among different processors. This might be useful, for example, if you want to estimate the performance improvements from running on production servers (vs. those in the development environment).

- **Number and size of rows processed**   A handy feature of the execution plan is that it graphically displays arrows between steps, showing the data that's passed between various operations within a query. The wider the arrow, the more rows are being processed (and, the greater the amount of memory that is used to perform the query). Very wide rows might indicate that you have forgotten a JOIN condition, resulting in a very large list of results for specific steps.

A complete list of all of the types of information returned in the execution plan is available in Books Online. Based on this information, next are a few scenarios that you might encounter.

SCENARIO & SOLUTION

You suspect that several queries are performing slowly because of missing indexes.	Use the execution plan to identify where table scans or clustered index scans are occurring.
You want to ensure that the new indexes you created are being used by specific queries.	Use the execution plan to ensure that you see table seeks and clustered index seek operations, instead of scans.
A particular query takes a long time to execute. You suspect that one or more JOIN conditions are missing.	View the number of rows processed within the execution plan to find abnormally large numbers of rows that are being passed between steps.

on the
Job *When you're optimizing performance of long-running queries, you might want to generate an "estimated" execution plan instead of running the entire query and waiting for it to finish. This will cause SQL Server to determine an execution plan for the query, but it will not actually run the query itself. The end result is that you can get the information you need quickly, without bogging down the server nearly as much as running the entire query. In order to do this, simple choose Display Estimated Execution Plan in the Query menu of Query Analyzer. You'll get an approximate result of what the execution plan might look like. Of course, the final test should always be executing the actual query.*

Server Trace

A server trace provides a basic return of the types of operations that were performed by SQL Server in order to execute a batch of SQL statements. This feature can be very helpful in determining what steps SQL Server is attempting to perform in order to complete the commands that you are sending. Figure 6-9 provides an example of the types of information that may be returned for a series of Transact-SQL batch operations.

Client Statistics

When you're dealing with database performance, the most important parameter to measure is what the end user sees. For example, it doesn't matter all that much what's going on within SQL Server if your users have to wait minutes for simple

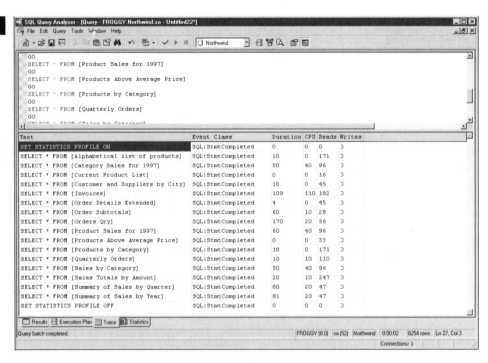

queries to execute. Query Analyzer includes the ability to view details of the query results with respect to the client. The statistics that are returned (as shown in Figure 6-10) can be useful for determining the end-user experience for certain types of workloads.

Index and Statistics Management

In addition to the performance information returned by Query Analyzer, database developers can click actual database objects and choose to correct performance problems without leaving Query Analyzer. For example, if a particular step in a query takes a long time to execute because it is performing a table scan, a developer could right-click the icon of the table that is being scanned and choose either Manage Indexes or Manage Statistics (see Figure 6-11).

From the resulting dialog box, the developer could quickly and easily create indexes or statistics. Figure 6-12 provides an example of the dialog box that is used to view and create indexes. The developer could then rerun the query to measure changes in performance and to ensure that the index is being properly used.

FIGURE 6-10

Viewing client
statistics
information in
Query Analyzer

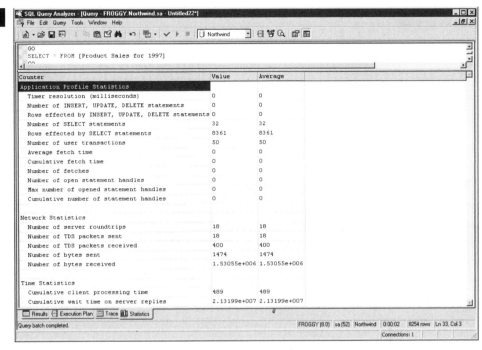

In addition to the features available via the execution plan functionality in Query Analyzer, you can choose to run the Index Tuning Wizard for a specific SQL query (or group of queries) by running the Index Tuning Wizard from within Query Analyzer. Instead of using a Profiler-generated trace file or trace table, you'll have the option of choosing SQL Query Analyzer text as the source of the workload to analyze.

Troubleshooting Query Performance

Now that we have an understanding of the types of information that Query Analyzer can return, let's look at the details of actually generating that information for some sample queries. Exercise 6-6 walks you through the creation and testing of a SQL query in Query Analyzer.

FIGURE 6-11

Choosing options
to manage
indexes and
statistics in
Query Analyzer

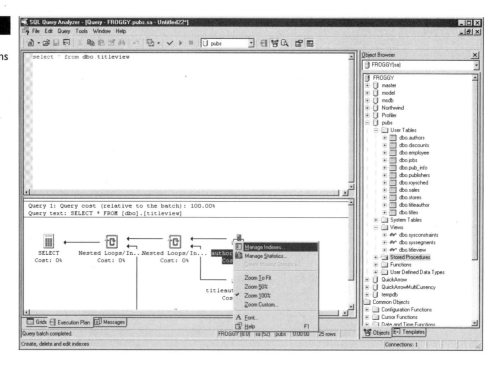

FIGURE 6-12

Viewing and
creating indexes
using Query
Analyzer

EXERCISE 6-6

Creating and Testing a SQL Query in Query Analyzer

1. Open SQL Query Analyzer either from the Microsoft SQL Server 2000 program group or by selecting Tools | Query Analyzer in Enterprise Manager.

2. If prompted, log on to a SQL Server database.

3. Type a standard SQL query in the main window. In general, the more complex the query, the more useful the information you'll receive in the next step.

4. Select Query | Display Estimated Execution Plan to execute the query and record statistics. You might have to maximize the query window to see all the information. The following query, run against the Northwind sample database, will present information similar to that shown in the next illustration.

```
SELECT productname, SUM(od.unitprice * quantity) AS total
FROM [order details] od inner join products p
ON od.productid = p.productid
GROUP BY productname
```

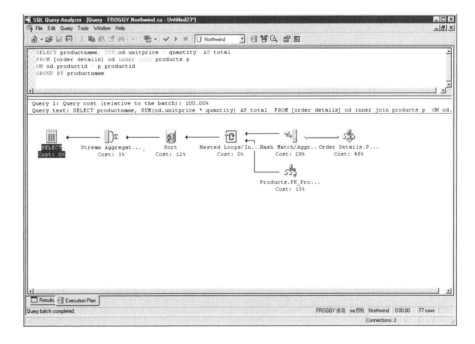

5. Hover the mouse over a specific step or arrow in the execution plan for the SQL Query. A window will pop up providing detailed information about the steps required to complete the query.

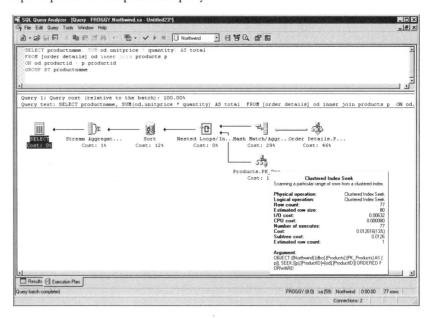

Optionally, select Query | Index Tuning Wizard to rerun the same query and to make recommendations on index implementation. This option works only for certain types of queries that can be analyzed by SQL Query Analyzer. For example, simple SELECT statements can be analyzed, whereas database management commands (such as the DBCC commands) cannot.

on the
job

A very important point to keep in mind when testing and optimizing queries is the effects of caching. A common error is to mistake the effects of caching for real performance improvements. For example, you might run a query once and measure the time it takes to complete. Then, you run the query again (unmodified), and it returns ten times faster! This is the effect of caching (of the execution plan and of data). Therefore, in order to ensure that you're getting accurate and consistent measurements each time, you can run the DBCC DropCleanBuffers and DBCC FreeProcCache between performance tests of your queries.

Using Query Governor

It is often useful to be able to limit the resources used by a single query or transaction in SQL Server. For example, executing a query that asks for the sum of all values in a 3GB table would be quite costly to perform. Other users would suffer from slow response times, and the database server itself might be significantly slowed. In many cases, such a transaction might be executed by mistake. If the transaction must be carried out, it is a good idea to schedule it to occur at a specific time when the server is expected to experience low activity levels.

SQL Server 2000 includes a server configuration parameter that can allow an administrator to limit the resources that can be used by a single operation. This option, the query governor cost limit, sets the longest time (in seconds) that a query may run. You can set this option in Enterprise Manager by right-clicking a server, selecting Properties, and then selecting the Server Settings tab. You can then enable or disable the Use query governor to prevent queries exceeding specified cost setting (see Figure 6-13).

FIGURE 6-13

Setting query governor cost settings in Enterprise Manager

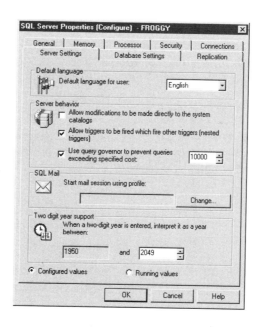

To set these options for all databases on a server, you can use the sp_configure stored procedure, as follows:

```
USE master
EXEC sp_configure 'query governor cost limit', '1'
RECONFIGURE
EXEC sp_configure
```

Before this setting will take effect, you need to stop and restart SQL Server. Finally, the query governor cost limit can be set on a per-transaction basis by using the following statement as part of a transaction:

```
SET QUERY_GOVERNOR_COST_LIMIT
```

A value of 0 will set no limit on the maximum query execution time. Any values greater than 0 will specify the number of seconds that a query may run. Note that the same query might take differing amounts of time to complete, based on server hardware configurations.

on the
Job

You should be very careful when making system-wide changes, such as setting the query governor cost option. There may be legitimate reasons for long-running queries to execute, such as month-end reports or database maintenance tasks. When the query governor cost is set, these operations may not complete, causing other application problems. Be sure to thoroughly understand your application and workload before setting this option—doing so can often avoid a lot of angry phone calls.

Using Stored Procedures

So far, we have discussed the use of stored procedures in several chapters of this book. In this section, we'll look at a quick discussion of how stored procedures can be used to optimize performance. SQL Server stored procedures use cached optimization plans to greatly speed the processing of queries. *Stored procedures* are precompiled collections of SQL statements that remain cached in memory, and they can execute up to 20 times faster than the same statement run manually. They also have the following advantages:

- **Reduced network traffic** Instead of sending large queries with hundreds of lines, a single command can be executed on the server. All the relevant processing

FROM THE CLASSROOM

Scalability and Benchmarks

People often refer to scalability when talking about the features of a database platform. However, the term itself—let alone the actual measurements—is open to interpretation. In general, we can define scalability as the ability of database server software to take advantage of upgraded hardware. The law of diminishing returns applies, though. The performance increase of adding a second CPU to a server might not be the 100 percent that one would expect, due to the overhead involved with splitting operations between processors. Many efforts have been made to ensure that the architecture of SQL Server allows for scaling to large databases and making use of advanced options, such as multiple gigabytes of physical memory and parallel processing.

When measuring performance between different systems on different platforms, it's important to have a standard test. This test should not be written to prefer any database platform over another, and should put a database through some real-world tests that can provide relevant and pertinent information. A real-world attempt at just such a test has been made by the TPM council. You can get more information at www.tpc.org. There, you'll find the actual benchmarks posted for specific database servers. One important aspect of these benchmarks is that they take the factor of cost into account. Many vendors advertise about the levels of performance that they have been able to attain using the TPM benchmarks. However, this can be largely irrelevant to most businesses, because the costs of such systems are often far out of reach for business users. What is of more interest is how much "bang for the buck" (or, more technically, "cost per transaction") one can get from a specific platform.

—Anil Desai, MCSE, MCSD, MCDBA

can be performed on the server, and only the final results are returned to the client.

■ **Modular and flexible code**   Stored procedures can call each other, and common procedures can be written only once and shared throughout a database.

■ **Streamlined security**   Stored procedures can provide embedded security permissions logic. Since a stored procedure executes with the permission of its owner, security implementation is simplified. Furthermore, the definitions of stored procedures can be stored in an encrypted form within the database, thereby protecting business logic.

Choosing the Right Tool

SQL Server 2000 provides so many different tools for monitoring and optimizing performance that the challenge sometimes becomes choosing the best tool for the job. Table 6-1 lists the tools we've discussed thus far and provides recommendations for their use.

In general, it is recommended that you use all of the various tools and features of SQL Server 2000 for improving overall system efficiency and performance. After all, highly optimized queries alone won't give you the performance you want if the server settings are not configured properly. It's a constant juggling act to optimally manage resources, but it's one that can easily pay for itself in reduced equipment costs and happier end users!

Based on this information, few scenarios that you might encounter are next.

TABLE 6-1	Tool	Best Use	Example
SQL Server Performance Monitoring Tools and Their Functions	Performance Monitor	Measuring overall system performance; measuring overall database server performance over a given period of time	Troubleshooting sluggish system performance that occurs when a server is being used for multiple purposes
	SQL Profiler	Logging performance and object access information for later analysis; monitoring multiple queries occurring on a server over a given period of time	Tracking exceptionally slow database performance that occurs when many users run a specific application
	SQL Query Analyzer	Analyzing the performance of a specific query	Determining why a specific SELECT statement seems to be running slowly
	SQL Server Alerts	Responding to a specific event of interest and notifying the appropriate personnel	Notifying a system administrator when a transaction log becomes full

SCENARIO & SOLUTION

You want to measure the overall performance of your server, including CPU and memory utilization.	Use Performance Monitor and add the appropriate objects and counters. You can also create logs of performance activity for longer-term analysis.
You want to find the worst-performing queries in your application.	Use SQL Profiler to monitor for the worst-performing queries.
You want to be notified whenever there is a large number of locks on your database server.	Use SQL Server Alerts to configure a threshold and the methods in which the SQL Server Agent should notify you should the number of locks exceed the threshold.
You want to find out why a specific query is taking a long time to execute.	Use the graphical execution plan in Query Analyzer to find out which steps are taking the most time to complete.

CERTIFICATION SUMMARY

In this chapter, we looked at the many different methods that can be used for monitoring, analyzing, and optimizing the performance of SQL Server 2000. Specifically, we examined the importance of optimizing performance at the levels of the server, of the database, and of specific queries. Through the use of tools such as SQL Profiler and the Index Tuning Wizard, you can quickly and easily identify and remove performance bottlenecks in your database implementation. The end result should be an optimally performing database server and applications.

TWO-MINUTE DRILL

Monitoring and Optimizing Server Performance

❑ The most important resources for a SQL Server machine include CPU time, disk I/O, memory utilization, and network utilization.

❑ The Windows NT/2000 Performance Monitor can be used to measure important statistics related to the overall performance of SQL Server 2000.

❑ In order to reduce the impact of certain operations, jobs can be scheduled within the SQL Server Agent to run during periods of low activity.

❑ Alerts can be created to notify database administrators of performance-related issues. Additionally, jobs can be executed to automatically take corrective action for specific alerts.

Monitoring Database Activity with SQL Profiler

❑ SQL Profiler can be used to monitor specific types of activities that are occurring on a database server.

❑ SQL Profiler traces can include various events, data columns, and filters to monitor only the information that is useful.

❑ SQL Profiler traces can be viewed on the screen, or can be stored in files or database tables.

Designing and Implementing Indexing

❑ Indexes can greatly improve the performance of database queries, but there are drawbacks to creating indexing, including overhead for index maintenance and storage space requirements.

❑ SQL Server supports the creation of many types of indexes, including clustered indexes, nonclustered indexes, and indexed views.

❑ The Index Tuning Wizard can be used to automatically generate index placement recommendations based on a representative query workload recorded by SQL Profiler.

❏ Database statistics can be used by the query optimizer to improve performance. By default, statistics are automatically created and maintained for all user databases.

Optimizing Queries with SQL Query Analyzer

❏ The SQL Query Analyzer can return many different types of performance information, including a graphical execution plan, server traces, and client statistics.

❏ From within Query Analyzer, database developers can choose to manage indexes and statistics.

❏ Stored procedures can be used to improve the performance of SQL operations, and can improve the security and manageability of database-related code.

❏ The query governor option can be used to prevent extremely long-running queries from adversely affecting overall database performance.

SELF TEST

The following questions will help you measure your understanding of the material presented in this chapter. Read all the choices carefully because there might be more than one correct answer. Choose all correct answers for each question.

Monitoring and Optimizing Server Performance

1. You are attempting to monitor SQL Server performance settings for multiple servers. You have been able to successfully add counters from three out of four servers, but you are unable to find the SQL Server object on the fourth server. Which of the following is the most likely cause of this problem?

   A. SQL Server is not installed on the fourth server.

   B. None of the servers are configured for distributed administration mode.

   C. There are built-in limitations in the version of Performance Monitor that you are using.

   D. SQL Server monitoring has not been enabled for the fourth server.

   E. None of the above.

2. You are creating a new SQL Server alert that fires whenever the number of "Lock Waits / sec" value exceeds 100. Which of the following responses can you configure for the alert? (Choose all that apply.)

   A. Execute a job that clears out temporary tables.

   B. Execute a job that runs a command line utility.

   C. Notify an operator via e-mail.

   D. Notify an operator via pager.

3. You have installed the Enterprise Edition of SQL Server 2000 on a machine that has 512MB of physical memory. What is the minimum amount of memory that you can allocate to SQL Server 2000?

   A. 0MB

   B. 16MB

   C. 64MB

   D. 256MB

   E. 512MB

4. Which of the following is a potential problem with scheduling jobs using the Start whenever the CPU(s) become idle option? (Choose all that apply.)

   A. The job will use more CPU time than it would have used had it been scheduled to run at a specific time.

   B. Based on server activity, the job may never run.

   C. Based on server activity, the job may be run too frequently.

   D. The job may execute when the load on the server is high.

Monitoring Database Activity with SQL Profiler

5. You are attempting to determine which database on a specific server is using the most resources. You configure a SQL Profiler trace using the appropriate data columns, events, and filters that you want to monitor. You want to run the trace and then store the results for later analysis. Which of the following are valid options for the output of the trace and allow for later trace file analysis? (Choose all that apply.)

   A. Output to a file

   B. Output only to the screen

   C. Output to a table

   D. Save to SQL Server Repository

6. You want to limit the capture of trace information in SQL Profiler to only queries that take longer than 5 seconds to execute. On which of the following tabs of the properties of a trace can you set this option.

   A. General

   B. Events

   C. Data Columns

   D. Filters

   E. None of the above

7. Based on a workload that you created earlier in the week, you identified several new indexes that should be created in a specific database. You have created and implemented the indexes. Which of the following features of SQL Profiler can you use to ensure that the indexes were correctly created?

   A. Filtering

   B. Trace templates

   C. Logging to database tables

   D. Replay of a previously recorded workload

8. Which of the following commands in SQL Profiler can be used to generate information for running traces without using SQL Profilers?

   A. Filtering

   B. Trace templates

   C. Script trace

   D. Replay

   E. User-configuration event classes

9. You want to create a definition of a specific set of criteria to monitor your application. You then want to use these settings on multiple SQL Server 2000 machines in your environment. Which of the following should you create?

   A. Trace file

   B. Trace table

   C. Trace definition

   D. Trace template

   E. None of the above

Designing and Implementing Indexing

10. What is the maximum number of clustered indexes that can be created on a table with a PRIMARY KEY constraint?

    A. None

    B. 1

    C. 16

    D. 256

    E. Unlimited

11. A developer runs an ad hoc query that returns only employees' first and last names from the Employee table. The query optimizer uses a single nonclustered index to obtain the information it needs. The index can be best described as which of the following?

   A. Nonclustered index with a single column

   B. An indexed view

   C. A covering index

   D. None of the above

12. Which of the following database objects is used directly by the query optimizer to determine the distribution of data within tables?

   A. Nonclustered index

   B. Clustered index

   C. Indexed views

   D. Statistics

13. Which of the following SQL Server 2000 tools can be used to created indexes?

   A. Index Tuning Wizard

   B. Profiler

   C. Enterprise Manager

   D. Server Network Utility

   E. Query Analyzer

   F. Client Network Utility

Optimizing Queries with SQL Query Analyzer

14. A database administrator wants to determine which steps of a complicated query are taking a long time to execute. Which of the following features in Query Analyzer will provide him or her with a graphical method for quickly and easily determining which steps are being performed and how long they are taking?

   A. Execution plan

   B. Client statistics

   C. Index tuning reports

   D. Server trace

   E. None of the above

15. You want to prevent several novice database administrators from running extremely long-running queries. Which of the following SQL Server 2000 options can you use most easily to do this?

    A. Give permissions to only stored procedures.

    B. Use the query cost governor.

    C. Provide the developers with a limited version of SQL Query Analyzer.

    D. Limit the amount of memory allocated to SQL Server.

    E. None of the above.

16. Which of the following options is useful for determining how much client processing time was required to process a query?

    A. Execution plan

    B. Server trace

    C. Messages

    D. Grid view

    E. Client statistics

17. Stored procedures have all of the following potential advantages over ad hoc SQL statements, except which of the following?

    A. Increase performance

    B. Easier administration

    C. Improved security

    D. Increased processing time

    E. None of the above (all are advantages of stored procedures)

LAB QUESTION

Your organization is an application service provider (ASP) that provides service to a Web-based application for several hundred customers. Each of your 20 database servers hosts several customer databases. For example, customers A, B and C may be hosted on DBServer1, and customers D, E, and F may be hosted on DBServer2. Recently, several users have complained about slow performance when performing specific operations within the application. The problems seem to have occurred recently, and no major changes (at least none that you're aware of) have been implemented on the production servers.

Several members of your organization (within and outside of the IT team) have speculated about potential causes of the problems and have recommended solutions. For example, the Executive team has recommended that additional servers be added, although this decision is based on a "hunch." Those within the IT department claim that the problem is application related (perhaps some extremely slow queries or locking problems). Database and application developers, in turn, are convinced that the problem lies in the configuration of the servers since none of these issues have been seen in the development environment. There's only one thing that everyone agrees on: the problem must be solved.

As the head of the database implementation team, it is ultimately your responsibility to ensure that the application performs adequately in production. You have performed some basic analysis of the Web/application servers and have found that they are not the bottleneck. Basic information seems to indicate that the performance issues are occurring at the level of the database server. Therefore, you need to isolate and fix the problem. How can you use the various performance-monitoring tools and features in SQL Server 2000 to determine the source of the problem?

SELF-TEST ANSWERS

Monitoring and Optimizing Server Performance

1. ☑ **A.** SQL Server must be installed on a server in order for the SQL Server object to be available.

   ☒ The other choices are either not available options or would not affect your ability to monitor performance on a remote machine.

2. ☑ **A, B, C, D.** All of the options provided are valid responses that the SQL Server Agent can perform based on the firing of an alert.

3. ☑ **B.** Regardless of the amount of physical memory that is available on a specific machine, SQL Server requires at least 16MB of physical memory to properly operate.

4. ☑ **B, C.** The option specified in the question instructs SQL Server Agent to run the job only when a specific condition is met. Since the job will only fire when the machine is considered to be idle, it is possible that a very busy server will never run the job. Conversely, it's also possible that the job will run far too often if load on the server is too low.

   ☒ **A** is incorrect because the scheduling settings should not have any direct effect on the performance of the job. **D** is incorrect since the SQL Server Agent will ensure that the job does not execute unless the server load is low (although the definition of this threshold can be changed by a database administrator).

Monitoring Database Activity with SQL Profiler

5. ☑ **A, C.** SQL Profiler has two main options for storing trace data. Both saving to a file and saving to a table can allow you to later analyze SQL Server trace data.

   ☒ **B** is incorrect since, although the information will always be displayed to screen, the data will not be saved for later analysis. **D**, the SQL Server Repository, is not an option for saving Profiler trace information.

6. ☑ **D.** The purpose of the Filters settings for a SQL Profiler trace is to limit the data collected to only the values that you're interested in monitoring. In this case, you could easily specify a filter for queries for which the duration is less than 5,000 milliseconds.

   ☒ The other options allow other settings for the properties of the trace, but they do not allow you to provide specific filtering options.

7. ☑ **D.** Once you have made changes to the database, it's always a good idea to retest performance to ensure that your changes were correct and improved performance. SQL Profiler's ability to replay a trace can be used to do this.

   ☒ The other choices are options that can be performed by SQL Profiler, but they're not directly useful in verifying the optimization of database performance.

8. ☑ **D.** Traces can be scripted from within SQL Profiler. The resulting scripts include the SQL commands that can be used to define traces that can be run using stored procedures from within SQL Server.

   ☒ The other options are features of SQL Profiler, but they are all designed to run within the SQL Profiler application.

9. ☑ **D.** The purpose of a trace template is to create a standard definition for the events, data columns and filters that you want to monitor. The trace template can then be used to create traces on multiple machines.

   ☒ The other options do not allow you to create a single trace definition, which can be applied on other machines.

Designing and Implementing Indexing

10. ☑ **B.** Any table can have only one clustered index. The fact that the table has a primary key does not affect this number, although SQL Server will automatically create a clustered index on the primary key.

    ☒ The other options are incorrect because only one clustered index can be created on a database table.

11. ☑ **C.** A covering index is one that includes all of the columns needed to complete a query.

    ☒ The other options are available as features in SQL Server 2000, but the most specific and accurate definition of the scenario described is a covering index.

12. ☑ **D.** Statistics are used by the query optimizer to determine the distribution of data in tables and to speed the retrieval of data in tables.

    ☒ The other options can be used to increase overall performance, but they are not directly used by the query optimizer to determine the best path for data access.

13. ☑ **A, C, E.** Enterprise Manager, Query Analyzer, and the Index Tuning Wizard all include features that allow the creation of indexes.

    ☒ The other tools cannot be used to create indexes within SQL Server 2000 databases.

Optimizing Queries with SQL Query Analyzer

14. ☑ **A.** The execution plan functionality in Query Analyzer returns a graphical display that details the steps that are required to complete a query.

    ☒ The other options include valuable information about the execution of queries, but their results are not graphical.

15. ☑ **B.** The query cost governor is designed to limit the resources that single queries can consume on a SQL Server machine. This will prevent the developers from accidentally running long-running queries.

    ☒ It may be possible to implement any of the other options, but this will restrict functionality and would be much more difficult to implement.

16. ☑ **E.** The client statistics option will return information about the amount of client processing time that was required to process the results of a result set.

    ☒ The other options are useful primarily for measuring server-side performance. None return information about client processing time.

17. ☑ **D.** Stored procedures usually execute much more quickly than ad hoc SQL statements; therefore, the processing time should generally decrease.

    ☒ All of the other options are potential benefits of using stored procedures.

LAB ANSWER

Isolating and troubleshooting performance problems can be difficult and time-consuming. Based on the scenario presented, the actual problem might lie in any of dozens of places. Worse yet, there could be multiple problems or circumstances that could be contributing to the overall problem. From a political angle, the finger-pointing and guesses about the problem don't help in resolving the issue.

So what's the "correct" answer to this question? The single most important aspect of troubleshooting *any* performance-related problem is to take an organized and methodical approach toward isolating the issues. Through an effective process of elimination, you should be able to pinpoint the problem (or, at the very least, determine what the problem *is not*). Based on that information, you can focus your efforts on the more likely causes.

In this specific scenario, some suspect that the problem might exist at the server level. You can prove/disprove that by using the Windows NT/2000 Performance Monitor application. By measuring statistics related to CPU, memory, and network performance, you can determine whether a hardware upgrade might help. You can also determine whether the problems are occurring on all of the machines or only a few of them. While you're working on Performance Monitor, you should be sure to measure

SQL Server statistics. Using SQL Server objects and counters, you can determine, for example, the number of queries that are running on those machines, the number of recompilations that are occurring, and how many user connections are actually created.

If, after measuring server performance, you find that you need to dive deeper into the problem, you can use SQL Profiler to measure actual query load on specific servers. For example, if you know that certain complex functionality is taking a long time, a SQL Profiler trace can help you determine whether it's a general problem, or if specific stored procedures or views are the culprit.

Finally, assuming you isolate the problem to specific queries, stored procedures, or views, you can use Query Analyzer to pinpoint the slow steps in the process. For example, you might find that a missing or out-of-date index or two are causing drastic drops in performance. Or, you might find that a few inefficient views that are called often use significant server resources.

Through this organized approach, you can take a seemingly chaotic situation and determine how to isolate and fix the issue. If all goes well, you'll quickly and easily resolve the issue. In the worst case, you can rest assured that you're taking an organized approach to eliminating potential causes of the issue.

7

Transferring Data Between Systems

CERTIFICATION OBJECTIVES

A most important part of maintaining modern databases is transferring data between systems. Data transfers will occur many times during the life cycle of a database. For example, transfers will typically take place when a database is first created. This is known as *populating* a database. When a new database is created, some or all of the data to be stored in that database will exist in other systems. Data transfers are also used to maintain the data in a database. Daily or weekly imports of data from another format are very common, and often performed to keep the data in a database up-to-date.

SQL Server 2000 provides a rich set of tools to query, change, and transfer data between SQL Server 2000 and a wide range of external sources. The data involved in these transfers can be stored in many forms: in other RDBMS products, other SQL Server databases, flat files, or XML documents, to name a few. Most of these external sources do not store data in the same way that SQL Server 2000 does. A text file for example, stores data in a different format than does an Oracle database. In turn, Oracle databases store data in a different way than SQL Server. To enable interaction with these and other systems, Microsoft uses OLE-DB technology (short for Object Linking and Embedding). SQL Server 2000 ships with many OLE-DB drivers, giving the database developer the ability to view and modify data stored in a wide variety of external formats.

SQL Server 2000 also provides an environment for the centralized administration of external databases and datasources. For example, a single SQL Server could be used to query and modify data on the local server, SQL Server databases on external servers, an Access database, and an Oracle database on another server. SQL Server also includes the DTC, or distributed transaction coordinator, which allows for remote datasources to be used within queries, stored procedures, triggers, and so on. The DTC provides a powerful way to maintain data in an enterprise environment.

CERTIFICATION OBJECTIVE 7.01

Importing and Exporting Data

Two of the most common tools you will use when transferring data in SQL Server 2000 are the *BCP* utility and *DTS*. BCP, or the bulk copy utility, is used to copy data from a database table to a data file, or vice versa. It is executed from the command line, as opposed to from within Query Analyzer. DTS, or data transformation services, is a full-blown graphical user interface that allows you to create highly complex data transfer operations in a very user-friendly way. Both are covered in detail in the upcoming sections.

BCP

The bulk copy utility has been around for a while. As such, it is one of the most fundamental ways to transfer data between systems. BCP can export the column values in a database table to a delimited or fixed-length datafile. It also has the ability to import the data stored in a datafile into a database table.

BCP is *extremely* useful in the day-to-day maintenance of a relational database. It is a quick and easy way to transfer data between like or *heterogeneous* systems. Heterogeneous data refers to data stored in many different formats, external to SQL Server. Most RDBMS products support some method of exporting the data from relational tables into a datafile. By exporting the data from a different database product into a simple text file, the data from the datafile can then easily be imported into SQL Server using BCP. The datafiles themselves only store column values; therefore, the internal workings of each database product are not relevant. BCP only deals with raw data, not how a particular implementation of a relation database product stores that data.

The examples and exercises in the following sections will use the Pubs sample database that installs with SQL Server 2000. Note that you will be modifying data in the Pubs database. If you wish to retain the data as it exists at installation, make sure you perform a backup of the Pubs database, and then restore it when you are done with this chapter. You will also need to create a new directory on your C: drive called Chapter7.

Using BCP

As stated earlier, BCP is executed via the command prompt. As such, it lacks any sort of graphical user interface. Let's take a look at the syntax of a simple BCP command:

```
BCP Pubs.dbo.Jobs OUT c:\Jobs.txt -c -Ssqlserver1 -Usa -Ppassword
```

This command exports all rows from the Jobs table in the Pubs database to a file called C:\Jobs.txt. The OUT keyword specifies the direction of the data transfer. Specifying the IN keyword would have imported the rows from the file C:\Jobs.txt *into* the Jobs table. The -c argument states that the data in the datafile will be stored in character format. The -S argument specifies the SQL Server name. The -U argument tells BCP what user ID to use as a security context to access the table, and the -P argument specifies the password.

Let's execute a simple BCP export. Start a command prompt either by selecting Command Prompt from the Accessories program group, or by selecting Run from the Start menu and typing **CMD** in the run box, as shown here.

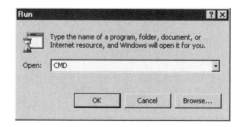

From the command prompt enter the following:

```
BCP Pubs.dbo.Jobs OUT c:\Jobs.txt -c -T
```

Upon executing this statement, a text file called Jobs.txt should now appear at the root of your C: drive. All rows from the Jobs table in the Pubs database have been exported to this datafile, which you can examine using Notepad or any text editor. In this BCP statement, the -T argument has been used to indicate that a trusted connection should be used to access the Jobs table. This replaces the -U and -P arguments, which are used to specify a SQL Server login. The -T argument specifies that whatever network login the user is currently using will be used as the Windows login to establish the security context when connecting to the SQL Server. Also, the -S argument that specifies the SQL Server involved has been omitted. BCP will default to the local SQL Server, using the default instance.

exam
ⓦatch

Be very familiar with the various arguments available to the BCP utility. Some questions on the exam may suggest using arguments of the BCP utility that don't exist.

There are a great many arguments that can be specified with the BCP utility. Tables 7-1 through 7-4 show some of the more common arguments of the BCP utility, grouped by category.

Let's illustrate some of the arguments in the tables. The following BCP command imports the first two lines of data in the Authors.txt files into the Authors table:

```
BCP Pubs.dbo.Authors IN C:\Chapter7\Authors.txt -L2 -c -T
```

TABLE 7-1	Argument	Purpose
BCP Arguments That Specify the Direction of Transfer— Only One Can Be Specified	IN	Used to transfer data from a datafile into a table
	OUT	Used to transfer data from a table into a datafile
	QUERYOUT	Uses a query instead of a table name to export a result set to a datafile

This uses the -c argument to specify that the data file is stored in character format. It also specifies the -T argument, using a trusted connection to access the Authors table in the Pubs database. The argument -L2 is also used to specify that the last line to be imported into the Authors table is the second line in the datafile.

Next, the following command exports all rows in the Employee table to a datafile called C:\Employee.txt:

```
BCP Pubs.dbo.Employee OUT c:\Employee.txt -w -oC:\output.txt -T
```

This BCP uses the -w argument to specify that the datafile will store Unicode data. It also uses the -o argument to create an output file that contains the screen output of the BCP command. The text file C:\output.txt stores the screen information from the preceding BCP command, as shown here:

```
Starting copy...
33 rows copied.
Network packet size (bytes): 4096
Clock Time (ms.): total        10
```

TABLE 7-2	Argument	Purpose
BCP Arguments That Specify the Datatypes Used in a Datafile — Only One Can Be Specified	-n	Specifies a datafile in native format. Uses the SQL Server datatype of each column in the datafile. Used when transferring data from one SQL Server to another SQL Server
	-c	Specifies a datafile in character format. Uses a Char datatype for all values in the datafile
	-w	Specifies a datafile in Unicode format. Uses an Nchar datatype for all values in the datafile

Argument	Purpose
-U and -P	Specifies the username and password for a SQL Server login to access a table
-T	Specifies that the current Windows login should be used to access a table

Output files are quite useful for capturing the screen output from a scheduled BCP command. Any errors that would normally be displayed on screen are now saved to a text file.

on the
ⓙob

The arguments of the BCP command are case sensitive. For example, the arguments -f and -F have different meanings in BCP. See SQL Server Books Online for a complete listing of all arguments of the BCP command.

Format Files   Specifying the -w, -n, or -c arguments to the BCP utility will use certain defaults when creating a datafile. First, a TAB will be used to separate column values. Second, a RETURN or newline character will separate lines of data, or rows from the database table. Consider the following lines from a datafile created using BCP in character format.

```
0736    New Moon Books           Boston    MA    USA
0877    Binnet & Hardley     Washington    DC    USA
1389    Algodata Infosystems     Berkeley    CA    USA
```

These lines are from a datafile created by exporting several rows from the Publishers table, using BCP in character format. Notice that each column value

Argument	Purpose
-F and -L	Used to specify the first and last rows from the datafile to import. Used when importing data
-S	Used to indicate the SQL Server involved in the BCP. Only necessary when the SQL Server is not the local default instance
-o<filename>	Redirects all output from the BCP command prompt to a text file. Useful when diagnosing BCP

is separated with a TAB and each row is separated by a RETURN or newline character. However, datafiles will not always use this format.

Data stored in text files will sometimes use column delimiters other than a TAB, and row delimiters other than a newline. To account for such a situation, the BCP utility allows a *format file* to be specified. A format file is a special kind of file that describes the characteristics of how the data in a datafile is stored. A format file can be specified in the BCP syntax, allowing the utility to import data stored in datafiles with custom formats.

To illustrate, consider the following sample lines from the datafile C:\Chapter7\ Stores.txt:

```
9991|Eric the Read Books|788 Catamaugus Ave.|Seattle|WA|98056
9992|Barnum's|567 Pasadena Ave.|Tustin|CA|92789
9993|News & Brews|577 First St.|Los Gatos|CA|96745
```

As you can see, the datafile Stores.txt does not use a TAB as a field terminator, but instead uses the pipe(|) character. In order to BCP the lines from this datafile into the Stores table, a format file must be used. The following command uses the BCP utility to import the data in the Stores.txt datafile into the Stores table:

```
BCP Pubs.dbo.Stores IN C:\Chapter7\Stores.txt -
fC:\Chapter7\Format.fmt -T
```

In the preceding BCP, the -f argument is specified, indicating that a format file is needed to process the Stores.txt datafile. Let's take a look at the Format.fmt format file. Use Notepad to open the file C:\Chapter7\Format.fmt, as shown here.

```
8.0
6
1  SQLCHAR  0  4   "|"    1  stor_id       SQL_Latin1_General_CP1_CI_AS
2  SQLCHAR  0  40  "|"    2  stor_name     SQL_Latin1_General_CP1_CI_AS
3  SQLCHAR  0  40  "|"    3  stor_address  SQL_Latin1_General_CP1_CI_AS
4  SQLCHAR  0  20  "|"    4  city          SQL_Latin1_General_CP1_CI_AS
5  SQLCHAR  0  2   "|"    5  state         SQL_Latin1_General_CP1_CI_AS
6  SQLCHAR  0  5   "\r\n" 6  zip           SQL_Latin1_General_CP1_CI_AS
```

The first line of the format file contains the value 8.0, indicating which version of the BCP utility is being used, in this case, 8.0, or SQL Server 2000. The next line with the value of 6 indicates that the datafile in question contains six columns. The next six lines in the format file contain information about each field in the datafile. Of particular importance to our situation is the fifth column in the format file, directly following the length of each field. This column specifies the field terminator of each column. In the case of the first five columns, the field terminator is the pipe character, enclosed in double quotes. The sixth line contains a field terminator of "\r\n". This indicates a newline in the format file, indicating that each row of data is separated by a RETURN.

Fields in a datafile can also be separated by no character, meaning that they are of a *fixed length*. Fixed-length fields always use the same amount of characters for each column value. For example, the following datafile contains data from the stores table, this time using a fixed-length format:

```
9991Eric the Read Books        788 Catamaugus Ave.SeattleWA98056
9992Barnum's                   567 Pasadena Ave.  Tustin CA92789
9993News & Brews               577 First St.Los   Gatos  CA96745
```

Notice that no field terminator is used, but each column value has the same length, irrespective of its original length. In a format file, fixed-length columns are specified using an empty string, or "".

To create a format file, simply use BCP to export table rows into a datafile without specifying any of the format arguments shown in Table 7-2. The BCP utility will prompt for each column's datatype, length, and so forth, and will allow you to save that information as a format file with whatever name you specify. The following BCP command will allow you to create a format file:

```
BCP Pubs.dbo.Sales OUT C:\Sales.txt -T
```

BULK INSERT   An alternative to using the command-line BCP utility is using the T-SQL BULK INSERT command. BULK INSERT can be used to import a datafile into a table only. You will need to use BCP to export data from a table to a datafile. BULK INSERT offers the advantage of being able to execute a BCP import from within Query Analyzer just like any other T-SQL statement. As such, it may be included within transactions, T-SQL batches, and stored procedures. The following BULK INSERT T-SQL statement loads three new rows into the Authors table in the Pubs database:

```
BULK INSERT Pubs.dbo.Authors
   FROM 'C:\Chapter7\Authors2.txt'
```

BULK INSERT has many options that can be specified. Like BCP, it can use a format file, specify the first and last rows from the datafile to be inserted, specify custom field terminators, and so forth. However, unlike BCP, you cannot specify a server name or a security context. Since BULK INSERT is executed via an existing connection to SQL Server, the server and security context have already been established.

The options in BULK INSERT are similar to the arguments in BCP; however, they are specified using a WITH clause. The following BULK INSERT imports the last two lines of data from the datafile into the Authors table:

```
BULK INSERT Pubs.dbo.Authors
    FROM 'C:\Chapter7\Authors3.txt'
WITH
(DATAFILETYPE = 'char',
 FIRSTROW = 2)
```

This BULK INSERT uses a WITH clause to specify two options: The DATAFILETYPE option specifies that the datafile uses character format. The FIRSTROW = 2 option skips the first line of data in the datafile. SQL Server Books Online has a full listing of the options for BULK INSERT.

Logged and Nonlogged BULK COPY Operations   When using BCP or BULK COPY, you can greatly speed up the process by using *nonlogged* copy operations. During a normal, or logged BCP, the transaction log records every row imported from a data file as if it were a traditional T-SQL INSERT operation, taking extra time to write to the transaction log. However, when bulk copies are performed nonlogged, the transaction log records only minimal information, just enough to roll back the copy operation should there be a catastrophic failure, thus speeding up the copy operation.

Another problem with using logged BULK COPY operations can occur when importing large amounts of data from a datafile. As each line of data imported from the datafile is logged as a traditional INSERT, the log can fill up very quickly when importing a large datafile. BCP is extremely fast and a transaction log can become full with little warning if not sized properly.

It is therefore recommended that you used nonlogged BULK COPY operations whenever possible. There is no setting to turn logging on or off when using BCP. The following criteria must be met in order for a BULK COPY operation to be nonlogged:

- The table that the datafile is being imported into cannot be involved in replication.

- The table cannot have any triggers defined on it.

- The TABLOCK hint must be specified in the BULK COPY syntax. This prevents other users from altering the table while the import is occurring. TABLOCK is an argument of the BCP utility, and an option of the BULK INSERT command.

- One of the following is true of the destination table: the table has zero rows, or the table has no indexes.

- The recovery model for the destination database is either SIMPLE or BULK-LOGGED.

If any of these criteria are not met, the BULK COPY operation will be logged. Though the criteria are stringent, nonlogged BULK COPY operations can perform orders of magnitude quicker than logged operations.

exam
ⓦatch

It is recommended that you drop all table indexes and disable all triggers on the target table when importing large amounts of data. In this way, indexes needn't be maintained and triggers will not fire as the import is occurring. Once the import is complete, the indexes can be re-created and the triggers can be reenabled.

Data Transformation Services

Included with SQL Server 2000 is an extremely powerful tool known as DTS. DTS is a full-blown application in its own right, allowing the SQL Server database developer to architect data transfers between various systems on a large scale. One of the most powerful aspects of data transformation services is the fact that the systems involved needn't necessarily be SQL Servers. Using DTS, one can transfer data between Sybase and Access tables, perform scheduled imports of text files into an Oracle database, or manipulate data stored in a FoxPro database. Whereas BCP is limited to datafiles, DTS can deal with many different systems. It is truly an enterprise data transfer management solution.

At the core of DTS is the concept of DTS *packages*. A DTS package is a data transfer operation that can be saved in a specified format for repeated use. DTS packages can be stored as files, in the MSDB database, in the Meta Data Services repository, or as Visual Basic files. To access the DTS package designer, expand the

FIGURE 7-1

Creating a new
DTS package

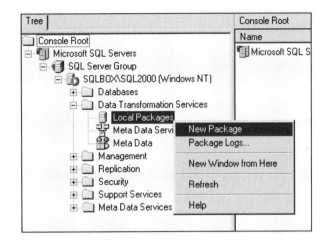

Data Transformation Services folder under your SQL Server, right-click Local
Packages, and select New Package, as shown in Figure 7-1.

The DTS Designer

The DTS designer is a user-friendly graphical interface that allows you to create
complex data transformations among many different systems. The DTS designer
interface has two main classes of objects that can be involved in a data transfer:
Connections and Tasks. These are displayed as icons in the left pane of the Designer,
as shown in Figure 7-2.

Holding the mouse pointer over each different icon in the left pane of the Designer
will display the purpose of each object. For example, the first icon in the connections
task is used to define an OLE-DB datasource, including a SQL Server. The right
pane of the DTS Designer is where the connections and tasks defined will be displayed.
Let's begin by creating a connection object to the Pubs database on your SQL Server.
Left-click the first icon in the Connection icon group, as shown here.

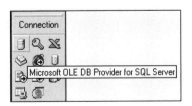

This brings up a dialog box where the properties of the OLE-DB datasource can be specified. In the first text box, type **Local SQL Server** as a name for the new connection. In the Database drop-down list, select the Pubs database. Leave all the other default options. Figure 7-3 shows the Connection Properties dialog box for the new connection.

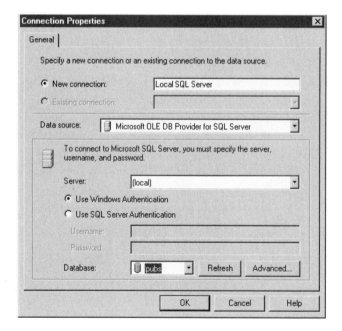

Click OK to create the new connection. In the right pane of the DTS Designer, a new icon has appeared representing the connection just created to the Pubs database. In our example, we'll be transferring rows from the Publishers table to a comma-delimited text file. To create the connection to the new text file, select the second icon in the third row from the Connection objects group of icons, as shown here.

This brings up another Connection Properties dialog box that will define the properties of the text file to be created. In the first text box, enter **PublishersFile** as the name of the new connection; and in the File Name text box, enter the path of **C:\PublishersFile.txt**. Figure 7-4 displays the Properties dialog box for the connection to the text file.

FIGURE 7-4

The Connection properties of the PublishersFile text file

Clicking OK brings up the Text File Properties dialog box. At this stage, custom row and field delimiters can be specified, as well as whether or not the text file will use delimiters, or be of a fixed length. For this example, accept all defaults by clicking Finish. This will once again bring up the Connections Properties dialog box. Click OK to create the new connection to the text file.

Now that two connections exist, a Task object needs to be created in order to transfer data between the two connections. To create a data transformation task, left-click the third icon in the first row from the Task objects group of icons, as shown here.

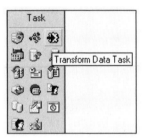

After clicking the Data Transformation Task icon, move the mouse pointer into the right pane of the DTS Designer. Once in the right pane, the mouse pointer will now include the trailing text "Select source connection." Left-click the Local SQL Server icon in the right pane to define the Pubs database as the source connection. Upon selecting the source connection, the mouse pointer will now include the trailing text "Select destination connection." Left-click the Publishers File icon in the right pane to define the text file as the destination connection. A solid black arrow now appears between the two connections to indicate a data transformation, as shown here.

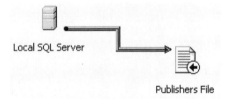

To complete the data transformation task, double-click anywhere on the solid black arrow. This brings up the Transform Data Task Properties dialog box. In the description text box, type **Publishers Data** as the name of the task. In the Table/View drop-down box, select the Publishers table, as shown in Figure 7-5.

FIGURE 7-5

The Transform
Data Task
Properties
dialog box

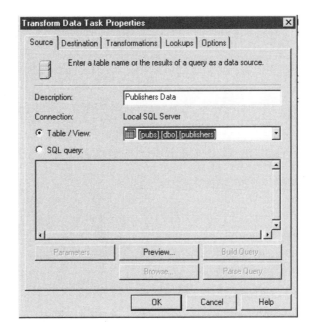

Next, click the Destination tab on the top of the dialog box. This brings up the
Define Columns dialog box where each column and its type and length can be defined.
Accept the default values by clicking Execute. Next, click the Transformations tab at
the top of the dialog box. The Transformations tab displays an arrow pointing from
each source column to each destination column, as shown here.

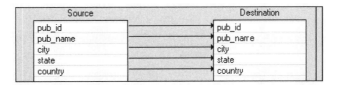

Click OK to close the Transform Data dialog box and complete the task definition.

Left-click the Package menu in the upper-left corner of the DTS Designer and select
Save to save the DTS package we just created. Enter the name **Publishers Package** in the
Package Name text box, and click OK. The package has now been saved to the MSDB
database and may be executed at any time. To execute the package, close the DTS
Designer by left-clicking the X in the upper-right corner of the package designer. The
Publishers Package now appears under the local packages node, as shown next.

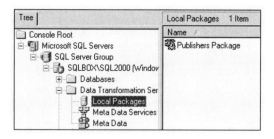

To execute the package, right-click the package name and select Execute Package. A dialog box will alert you to the successful completion of the package and a new file called PublishersFile.txt will appear at the root of your C:/ drive, containing the rows from the Publishers table in a comma-delimited text file. It is worth noting that while this same action could have been performed using BCP, DTS provides a very user-friendly way to accomplish both basic and complex BULK COPY tasks.

Transforming Data

Though every data transfer in DTS is known as a data transform task, up to this point we have transferred data from the source to the destination unmodified. DTS also has the ability to alter or reformat data as it is being transferred. This is a very powerful feature of DTS that is accessed through the Transformations tab in the Transfer Data Task Properties dialog box.

In the next example, we will use a DTS transformation to convert the data in the Pub_Name column in the Publishers table to all lowercase characters before being written to the text file. Double-click the Publishers Package previously created in the right pane of Enterprise Manager to reopen the package for editing. Open the Transform Data Task Properties dialog box by double-clicking the solid black arrow, and click the Transformations tab, as shown in Figure 7-6.

As Figure 7-6 shows, there are five black arrows pointing from each source column to each destination column. These arrows represent each column transfer involved in the task. Highlight the second arrow pointing from the Pub_Name source column to the Pub_Name destination column by left-clicking it. Note that in the second text box, the type of transformation that is taking place is Copy Column. This means that the data will be transferred from the source to the destination unaltered. To convert each pub_name value to lowercase while it is being transferred, first click Delete to remove the current transformation. The arrow for the pub_name

FIGURE 7-6

The
Transformations
tab of the
Transform Data
Task dialog box

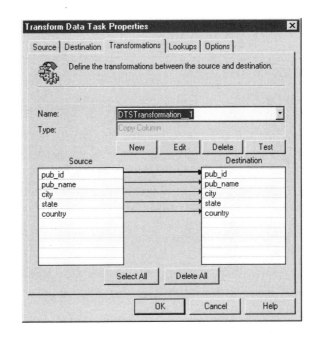

transformation now disappears. To create the new transformation, click New. This
brings up the New Transformation dialog box shown in Figure 7-7.

Highlight the fourth option, Lowercase String, and click OK. This brings up the
Transformation Options dialog box. Click OK to accept the defaults. Notice that a

FIGURE 7-7

The New
Transformation
dialog box

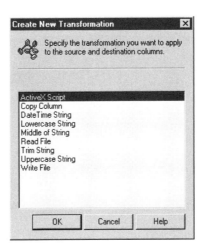

new arrow appears for the pub_name transformation that has just been created, with the type of Lower Case String. Click OK to close the Properties box, save the Publishers Package, and execute it. Upon successful execution of the package, notice that the PublisherFile.txt file has been overwritten with the same rows from the Publishers table as before, but this time the values for each Pub_Name column have been converted to a lowercase string.

Many different types of transformations are available in DTS, providing a versatile way to manipulate data while it is being transferred. Custom transformations can even be written using the Visual Basic scripting language by selecting ActiveX Script as the transformation type. This allows data to be reformatted or transformed in any number of ways and is a very powerful tool for the database developer.

exam
⚠️atch

DTS has a blatant speed advantage over BCP when dealing with multiple tables. Whereas BCP can only perform one import to or export from a table at a time, DTS can import or export data from multiple tables all at once. BCP is by nature faster than DTS, but an instance of the BCP utility can only deal with one table at a time.

The DTS package designer is a very intuitive graphical user interface for creating DTS packages. However, simple DTS packages can also be created using the DTS Wizard that is included with SQL Server 2000. The following exercise will use the DTS Wizard to perform a data transfer.

SCENARIO & SOLUTION

You need to import millions of rows from a datafile into one table as fast as possible.	Use BCP or BULK INSERT. Ensure that the target table has no indexes or triggers enabled.
You need to import a large number of rows from 50 different datafiles into 50 different tables.	Use DTS. DTS can simultaneously import data from multiple files into multiple tables.
You need to import data from an Oracle table into a SQL Server table and reformat the values of certain columns in the easiest way.	Use DTS. You could export the data from the Oracle table into a file and then use BCP to import the file into SQL Server, but DTS can reformat column values as they are transferred.

EXERCISE 7-1

Transferring Data Using the DTS Wizard

1. To initiate the DTS Wizard, expand the Pubs database in Enterprise Manager and left-click the Tables node to display all tables in the right pane. Right-click the Stores table, select All Tasks from the menu, and then select Export Data, as shown here.

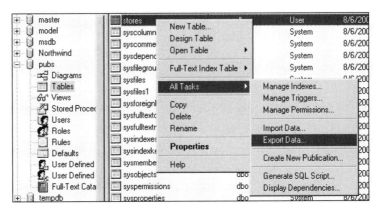

2. This will start the DTS Wizard. Click Next to bring up the Datasource Properties dialog box. Define the datasource by ensuring that your local SQL Server appears in the Server text box, and use the Database drop-down list to select the Pubs database, as shown here.

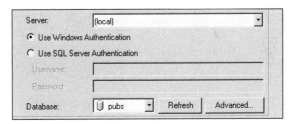

3. Click Next to open the Data Destination Properties dialog box. Once again, make sure your local SQL Server appears in the Server text box, and that the Pubs database is selected in the Database drop-down box.

4. Click Next to specify the nature of the transfer. For this exercise, select the Use a query to specify the data to transfer radio button, as shown here, and click Next.

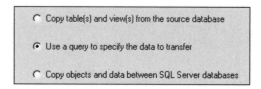

5. In the Query Statement box, type the following T-SQL command and then click Next.

```
SELECT * FROM Stores WHERE State = 'WA'
```

6. This brings up the Select Source Tables and Views dialog box. Click the word "Results" under the header Destination column and enter **WashingtonStores** as the destination table, as shown here.

7. Click Next to complete the package definition. This brings up the Save, Schedule, and Replicate Package dialog box that allows you to save, schedule, or run the package just created. Leave the default radio button, Run immediately, selected and click Next. Click Finish to execute the DTS package. Upon being notified of the successful package execution, you will find that a new table now exists in the Pubs database called WashingtonStores, which contains all rows from the Stores table with a value of WA in the State column.

CERTIFICATION OBJECTIVE 7.02

Working with External Servers

While DTS provides the tools to coordinate data transfers between many different database servers and other datasources, a rich set of T-SQL commands also exist that provide the functionality to query and modify data on servers external to the local SQL Server. SQL Server 2000 also supports the use of *linked servers*. A linked server is a virtual server that SQL Server 2000 defines by using an OLE-DB driver to establish a connection to the datasource. A linked server does not necessarily need to be a SQL Server: it can be an Oracle server, an Access database, or any datasource that can be accessed using OLE-DB.

Linked Servers and Distributed Queries

Once a linked server is defined in SQL Server 2000, it can then be accessed by traditional T-SQL commands using a four-part naming convention. This allows a linked server to be queried and modified as if it were another table in a SQL Server database. The four-part naming convention uses the following syntax:

```
ServerName.Database.Owner.[Table or View Name]
```

For example, the following T-SQL command would return all rows from a table named Employees, owned by DBO, in a database named Corporation, on a SQL Server named SQL1:

```
SELECT * FROM SQL1.Corporation.DBO.Employees
```

Linked servers are a very powerful way to manage data in an enterprise environment. Many linked servers can be defined on a SQL Server, allowing data to be maintained on a wide variety of systems from a central source. Linked servers can be defined using T-SQL commands, or through Enterprise Manager. The following syntax uses the sp_addlinkedserver system stored procedure to add a linked server called LinkedServer1, and an external SQL Server named SQL 2000.

```
EXEC sp_addlinkedserver
@server='LinkedServer1',
@srvproduct='SQLServer2K',
```

```
@provider='SQLOLEDB',
@datasrc='SQL2000'
```

This syntax specifies the name of the linked server using the @server variable. The @srvproduct variable is simply the name of the product being accessed; in this case, I used a name of 'SQLServer2K'. The @provider variable defines the type of OLE-DB driver that will be used, and the @datasrc variable specifies the name of the SQL Server. Upon executing the above statement in Query Analyzer, a new linked server will appear in the Security folder under the Linked Servers node in Enterprise Manager, as shown here:

This linked server will, of course, not function because the server does not exist, but it demonstrates the syntax of the stored procedure. Note that for SQL Servers only, if the @srvproduct variable is given the value of 'SQL Server', the remaining variables are optional. However, the value specified for the @server variable must be the actual name of the SQL Server or the server name and instance name, as shown here:

```
EXEC sp_addlinkedserver
@server='SQL2000\Instance1',
@srvproduct='SQL Server'
```

This example would add a new linked server for the named instance called Instance1 on a SQL Server called SQL2000.

Linked Server Security

When a linked server is created, it is necessary to establish the security context in which operations against the linked server will be performed. By default, the login account being used on the local SQL Server is used to test security against the linked server. However, SQL Server 2000 also supports *mapping* logins on the local server to logins on the remote server. A mapped local login will impersonate a login on the linked server to establish a security context. This enables the database administrator to more effectively control security on an enterprise-wide scale.

For example, you may only want certain users on the local SQL Server to be able to access the data on a linked server. To establish security, you would create a new login on the linked server and assign it the appropriate permissions. Then map the logins of only the users on the local server that are permitted to access the data on the linked server to the new remote login.

You can map local logins to remote logins using Enterprise Manager, or by using T-SQL. The following example maps a local login of John Smith in the Marketing domain to a remote SQL Server login called 'Remote' on a linked server named 'SQL2':

```
sp_addlinkedsrvlogin
@rmtsrvname = 'SQL2',
@useself = 'FALSE',
@locallogin = 'Marketing\Jsmith',
@rmtuser = 'Remote',
@rmtpassword = 'password'
```

In the preceding, the stored procedure sp_addlinkedserverlogin is used to map a local login to the linked server login. The variable @rmtsrvname specifies the linked server with which to establish the mapping. The @useself variable is given a value of 'False', which indicates that the local login will not use its own security context, but rather map to a remote login. The @locallogin variable provides the local login that will be mapped, and the @rmtuser variable specifies the remote login to impersonate. Finally, the @rmtpassword variable contains the password of the remote login.

The mapping of local logins to remote logins is only necessary when the concept of security is meaningful on the system being accessed. For example, establishing a linked server to a flat file would not use security of any kind. In this case, the mapping of logins is unnecessary.

EXERCISE 7-2

Creating and Querying a Linked Server

1. Ensure you are logged in to your computer as an administrator and begin a Query Analyzer session using Windows authentication.

2. Establish a linked server called AccessSample that points to the sample Access database provided with this book by executing the following stored procedure:

```
EXEC sp_addlinkedserver
@server = 'AccessSample',
```

```
@provider = 'Microsoft.Jet.OLEDB.4.0',
@srvproduct = 'OLE DB Provider for Jet',
@datasrc = 'C:\Chapter7\Sample.mdb'
```

3. Return all rows from the Employees table that exist in the new linked server using the four-part naming convention. Take note that the Jet database engine does not use the concepts of database name or object owner, which are used in SQL Server. As such, the database name and owner arguments are left blank when querying an Access database, as shown here:

```
SELECT * FROM AccessSample...Employees
```

4. Execute this SQL statement to return all rows from the Employees table in the Access database.

Using OPENQUERY

When using linked servers, the processing involved in retrieving rows from a linked datasource takes place on the local SQL Server. This can be a burden on the local processor in certain situations. Fortunately, SQL Server 2000 supports the *passing through* of queries from the local server to the linked server with the OPENQUERY command. A pass-through query is a case where the processing of the retrieval operation takes place on the remote server.

For example, consider a local SQL Server with a single 700MHz processor, that has a defined linked server that is a powerful server with eight 700MHz processors. A query needs to join five tables from the linked server and return the result set to the local SQL Server. By using OPENQUERY, the processing time involved in joining the five remote tables takes place on the remote server, and the joined result set is returned to the local SQL Server.

The syntax of OPENQUERY is similar to that of a subquery, as shown here:

```
SELECT pub_name FROM
OPENQUERY (SQL2,
'SELECT * FROM Pubs.DBO.Publishers')
```

OPENQUERY takes two arguments: The first is the linked server name, followed by the query to be executed on that linked server. The preceding statement uses OPENQUERY to return all rows from the Publishers table in the

Pubs database from a linked server called SQL2. The original SELECT statement then selects all values in the Pub_Name column from the result set returned by OPENQUERY. In the SELECT statement syntax, OPENQUERY is used in the FROM clause, much like a subquery. The result set produced by OPENQUERY can also be aliased like any other result set.

OPENQUERY is most useful when the result set that needs to be returned from the remote server requires more than a single table SELECT of all rows. In the following statement, the table join, filtering, and ordering of the result set are all performed on the linked server named SQL2:

```
SELECT * FROM
OPENQUERY (SQL2,
'SELECT DISTINCT P.pub_name FROM
Pubs.DBO.Publishers AS P
JOIN Pubs.DBO.titles AS T
ON P.pub_id = T.pub_id
AND T.price > 20
ORDER BY P.pub_name')
```

OPENQUERY is a very powerful command that can be used to place the heaviest burden of query processing on the most powerful computers in the enterprise, improving the response time of queries that involve external data.

Using OPENROWSET

OPENROWSET is another T-SQL function used for returning data from an external source accessible via OLE-DB. OPENROWSET differs from OPENQUERY in that a linked server needn't be defined for the datasource in order to retrieve data from it. OPENROWSET is useful for ad hoc queries that access a remote datasource only occasionally, thus negating the need to create and maintain a linked server entry. Like OPENQUERY, the result set returned by OPENROWSET is processed on the remote server.

Since no linked server is defined for the datasource accessed by the OPENROWSET function, the syntax contains similar information supplied to the sp_addlinkedsever stored procedure, as shown here.

```
SELECT *
FROM OPENROWSET('SQLOLEDB','SQL2';'sa';'password',
'SELECT * FROM Pubs.DBO.Titles ORDER BY title_id')
```

The preceding SELECT statement uses the OPENROWSET function to return all rows from the Titles table in the Pubs database on a remote SQL Server named SQL2, using a username of 'sa' and a password of 'password'. The first argument to the OPENROWSET function is the provider name, in this case, SQLOLEDB, which is the OLE-DB driver for SQL Server. Next SQL2 is used to indicate the name of the remote server, followed by the username and password to be used in establishing a security context. Finally, the query to be executed on the remote server is specified.

In OPENROWSET, the query itself can be substituted with an actual database object name, using the three-part naming convention of database name, owner, and object. The next example returns the same result set as the preceding example, this time using a three-part name to specify an object instead of using a query:

```
SELECT *
FROM OPENROWSET('SQLOLEDB', 'SQL2;'sa';'password',
Pubs.DBO.Titles)
ORDER BY title_id
```

on the job

When dealing with external servers that are not SQL Servers with respect to three-part naming, the concept of database name and object owner has different meanings in different systems. For example, Access has no such thing as object owners. On the other hand, Oracle uses the concept of "schema," which translates to an object owner in SQL Server. As such, the schema name is specified in place of the object owner when querying rows in an Oracle database.

The result set produced by OPENROWSET can also be aliased in the same way as the result set produced by OPENQUERY. The following joins the table Publishers on a local server with the table Titles on a remote server named SQL2, to return all unique publishers that publish books in the category of psychology:

```
SELECT DISTINCT P.pub_name
FROM Publishers as P JOIN
OPENROWSET('SQLOLEDB','SQL2';'sa';'password',
Pubs.DBO.Titles) AS T
ON P.pub_id = T.pub_id
AND T.type = 'psychology'
```

Using **OPENDATASOURCE**

OPENDATASOURCE is similar to OPENROWSET in that it is intended to be used against external datasources that are only accessed infrequently. Like OPENROWSET, connection information must be provided to OPENDATASOURCE, as no linked server is required.

OPENDATASOURCE differs from OPENROWSET in that the connection information needed to query the datasource is specified as the first part of the four-part naming convention, in place of a linked server name. The following example uses OPENDATASOURCE to retrieve all rows from the Titles table from a remote SQL Server named SQL2:

```
SELECT    *
FROM OPENDATASOURCE(
'SQLOLEDB',
'Data Source=SQL2;User ID=sa;Password=password'
).Pubs.DBO.Titles
```

Much like querying a linked server using the four-part naming convention, the OPENDATASOURCE function replaces the name of the linked server with the connection information needed to establish an OLE-DB connection to a remote datasource.

OPENDATASOURCE, much like OPENROWSET, is meant to be used against remote datasources that cannot, for whatever reason, have a linked server defined. Microsoft recommends using linked servers whenever possible when dealing with external data.

SCENARIO & SOLUTION

You need to set up a datasource that will be accessed frequently.	Use a linked server. The connection information does not need to be entered each time the datasource is queried.
You need to set up a datasource that will be accessed only once or twice a year.	Use OPENROWSET or OPENDATASOURCE.
You need to set up a datasource and security is a big concern.	Use a linked server. Linked servers allow for the mapping of logins to control security.

CERTIFICATION OBJECTIVE 7.03

XML Functionality

XML has soared in popularity since its introduction a few years back. In case you are not familiar with XML, let's have a brief overview. XML, or the Extensible Markup Language, is a standard way to structure information. It arose from the need for various entities and organizations to be able to exchange documents, usually over the Internet, in a way that all systems could understand.

Consider an example: Company A sells company B a document on a daily basis that contains information about the performance of certain stocks and mutual funds. This information is delivered in the form of a delimited text file. Company B also purchases information from other companies. Some of these documents are delivered as Excel spreadsheets, others as text files, and others as Word documents. The problem company B faces is to take all this information in different formats and store it in their database for reporting purposes. Company B would either need to employ people to enter the information manually or design custom interfaces that could read each of the documents and insert the information into their database.

The goal of XML is to end such system incompatibilities. It is a way of structuring a document that is self-defining, because the information needed to structure the document is contained within the document itself. In this scenario, if company B were to receive all information in XML format, only one interface that can parse XML would be required.

XML Document Structure

At the core of an XML document are *elements* and *attributes*. An element in XML is similar to an entity in a data model. It is a concept or thing that is being represented in the XML document. Also like entities in a logical data model, XML elements have attributes that are characteristics of the elements.

XML uses *tags* embedded within a document to specify the structure of the document. A tag in XML is similar to a tag in HTML, but XML has no predefined tags. Let's look at a sample XML document:

```
<ROOT>
 <Employee>Jones</Employee>
 <Employee>Smith</Employee>
</ROOT>
```

This XML document is a simple listing of employees. The document contains two different types of elements, ROOT, and Employee. Every well-formed XML document must contain one and only one ROOT element. ROOT is a sort of parent element that allows for a hierarchy of elements to be represented in a document.

Elements in an XML document have start tags surrounded by brackets and each element uses an end tag with a slash. The actual content of each element is entered between the start and end tags of the element. Element attributes are contained within the start tag of an element, as shown here:

```
<ROOT>
 <Employee EmployeeID = "A1">Jones</Employee>
 <Employee EmployeeID = "A2">Smith</Employee>
</ROOT>
```

In the preceding document, the attribute of EmployeeID has been added to each Employee element. End tags for each element are only necessary if an element has content, as in the case of Jones or Smith. For example, this document is a listing of only Employee ID values:

```
<ROOT>
 <Employee EmployeeID = "A1"/>
 <Employee EmployeeID = "A2"/>
</ROOT>
```

Since each Employee element contains only attributes and no content, the end tags for each element are unnecessary. Instead, a slash is entered at the end of the element tag.

The concepts of elements and attributes in an XML document work well with relational databases. An element will typically translate into a database table and an attribute will translate into a database column. As such, it is fairly simple to assemble the information in a database table into an XML document. SQL Server 2000 provides a rich set of tools for retrieving data from database tables and outputting the information in XML format.

Creating XML Output from Relational Data

To retrieve data from a database in XML format, SQL Server 2000 adds the FOR XML clause to the syntax of the SELECT statement. FOR XML produces a query result set in the form of nested XML elements, and complete well-formed XML documents can be created with a simple SELECT statement using FOR XML and Internet Explorer, as you will see in the upcoming section on IIS integration. The FOR XML clause is used with one of three keywords to specify the formatting of the XML output. These are AUTO, RAW, and EXPLICIT.

FOR XML AUTO

Using FOR XML AUTO maps each table involved in a query to an element in the XML output. Each column in the query becomes an attribute of its parent element. Let's look at an example of using FOR XML AUTO. Execute the following query using the Pubs database:

```
SELECT au_lname, au_fname
FROM Authors
WHERE State = 'UT'
FOR XML AUTO
```

This statement uses the FOR XML AUTO clause to produce a listing of first and last names of authors who live in Utah. The following is the XML output:

```
<Authors au_lname="Ringer" au_fname="Anne"/>
<Authors au_lname="Ringer" au_fname="Albert"/>
```

Each row from the Authors table has been created as an element called Authors in the XML output. The columns of Au_Lname and Au_Fname involved in the SELECT statement have been mapped to attributes of the Authors elements. Notice that using FOR XML AUTO has not produced a ROOT tag in Query Analyzer. The FOR XML AUTO clause produces what is known as a document *fragment*, or a piece of an XML document.

When the query specified in the SELECT statement retrieves data from more than one table, the XML output is nested to represent the hierarchy. The following query returns the price of each book sold for the publisher New Moon Books:

```
SELECT Publishers.pub_name, Titles.price
FROM Publishers
JOIN Titles
```

```
ON Publishers.pub_id = Titles.pub_id
AND Publishers.pub_name = 'New Moon Books'
ORDER BY Titles.price
FOR XML AUTO
```

The following is the result set:

```
<Publishers pub_name="New Moon Books">
 <Titles price="2.9900"/>
 <Titles price="7.0000"/>
 <Titles price="7.9900"/>
 <Titles price="10.9500"/>
 <Titles price="19.9900"/>
</Publishers>
```

As you can see in the result set, each table involved in the query has been mapped to an element in the XML output. The price of each book is returned as an attribute of the Titles element.

This result set, as with the previous ones, has used what is known as *attribute-centric* mapping. This simply means that all database columns are returned as attributes of their parent elements. Using FOR XML AUTO with the ELEMENTS keyword will return an *element-centric* result. This means that column values in a database table will map to subelements instead of attributes of the parent element. For example, the following query uses the ELEMENTS keyword to return the table column values as subelements:

```
SELECT Publishers.pub_name, Titles.price
FROM Publishers
JOIN Titles
ON Publishers.pub_id = Titles.pub_id
AND Publishers.pub_name = 'New Moon Books'
ORDER BY Titles.price
FOR XML AUTO, ELEMENTS
```

The ELEMENTS keyword is specified after the FOR XML AUTO clause, separated by a comma. The following is the partial result set:

```
<Publishers>
 <pub_name>New Moon Books</pub_name>
  <Titles>
   <price>2.9900</price>
  </Titles>
  <Titles>
```

```
    <price>7.0000</price>
  </Titles>
</Publishers>
```

As you can see, each column specified in the SELECT list has been returned as a subelement instead of an attribute. The ELEMENTS keyword gives greater control over how XML output will look when formatted. Both attribute-centric and element-centric result sets are valid in an XML document.

FOR XML RAW

The FOR XML RAW clause of the SELECT statement is similar to the FOR XML AUTO clause. It also uses the result set of a query to return formatted XML output; however, raw XML data has no named elements. Each element returned using FOR XML RAW will use the generic element name of "row." The following query returns several first and last names from the Authors table using FOR XML RAW:

```
SELECT lname, fname
FROM Employee
WHERE pub_id = '0877'
FOR XML RAW
```

The following is the partial result set:

```
<row lname="Accorti" fname="Paolo"/>
<row lname="Ashworth" fname="Victoria"/>
<row lname="Bennett" fname="Helen"/>
<row lname="Brown" fname="Lesley"/>
<row lname="Domingues" fname="Anabela"/>
```

As opposed to FOR XML AUTO, where each element name is mapped to the table name in the SELECT statement, FOR XML RAW has assigned the generic name "row" to each element returned in the XML result set. However, FOR XML RAW does not alter the name of the attributes in each row element. Only the element names are changed.

Uses of the FOR XML RAW clause are few. For example, an application may simply need a list of attributes from a certain element. However, most of the time, circumstances will require the named elements generated by FOR XML AUTO or FOR XML EXPLICIT.

FOR XML EXPLICIT

The FOR XML EXPLICIT clause is provided in SQL Server 2000 for cases where XML output needs to be formatted in a very specific way. It is used in situations where FOR XML AUTO cannot produce the XML format required. Generating results using FOR XML EXPLICIT is done in a very different way from using AUTO or RAW. The query used must be written in a specific way using certain aliases. The query then creates what's known as a *universal table.* A properly formed universal table is necessary when using FOR XML EXPLICIT. It is a virtual table that is processed to produce the formatted XML output.

To illustrate what a universal table looks like, first consider the following query that uses FOR XML AUTO:

```
SELECT Publishers.pub_name, Titles.title
FROM Publishers JOIN Titles
ON Publishers.pub_id = Titles.pub_id
AND Publishers.pub_id = '0736'
ORDER BY Publishers.pub_name, Titles.title
FOR XML AUTO
```

This query returns a listing of publisher elements and title elements for the publisher New Moon Books. The following is the partial result set:

```
<Publishers pub_name="New Moon Books">
 <Titles title="Emotional Security: A New Algorithm"/>
 <Titles title="Is Anger the Enemy?"/>
 <Titles title="Life Without Fear"/>
```

To produce the same XML output using FOR XML EXPLICIT, let's take a look at what the universal table would need to look like.

Tag	Parent	Publishers!1!pub_name	Titles!2!title
1	NULL	New Moon Books	NULL
2	1	New Moon Books	Emotional Securi...
2	1	New Moon Books	Is Anger the Enemy?
2	1	New Moon Books	Life Without Fear
2	1	New Moon Books	Prolonged Data D...
2	1	New Moon Books	You Can Combat C...

A universal table can seem a bit overwhelming at first, so let's break down the contents. The first column in the table, Tag, is used to signify a distinct element in the output. The next column, Parent, is used to specify which element is the parent of the current element. The columns Tag and Parent are necessary to ensure the correct nesting of the elements in the XML output. Parent has a self-referencing relationship to Tag. In our example, all rows with a Tag value of 2 have a Parent value of 1, meaning that the element with tag 1 is the parent element of tag 2.

The last two columns in the table have an apparently unusual naming convention. These columns are used to store the values of the attributes for each element. The naming convention uses the following format:

Element Name!Tag Value!Attribute Name

To illustrate, the third column in the example universal table has the name Publishers!1!pub_name. This means that the column will store the value for an attribute with the name pub_name whose element has a Tag column value of 1, and the element name is Publishers. Similarly, the fourth column in the table stores the value for the attribute named Title, for an element named Titles, with a Tag column value of 2.

Building the universal table is accomplished using the SELECT statement. As stated earlier, the query must be structured in a very specific way to produce a proper universal table. As such, a UNION will be required for each distinct element present in the query. Let's look at the first part of the query to produce the universal table:

```
SELECT 1 as Tag,
NULL as Parent,
Publishers.pub_name as [Publishers!1!pub_name],
NULL as [Titles!2!title]
FROM Publishers
WHERE Publishers.pub_id = '0736'
```

The first part of the query that builds the universal table uses aliases to create the column names in the table. The column of Tag is given a value of 1 with a Parent value of NULL to indicate that it is the topmost element in the XML output. The column Publishers!1!pub_name is given the value of the Pub_Name column from the Publishers table of the publisher New Moon Books. The column Titles!2!title is assigned a NULL value, as we are only creating the column name at this point to hold the values from the Title column in the Titles table. The result set created by this query is then joined using UNION ALL to the final part of the query, which will retrieve the values for the second element, Titles, from the Titles table.

```
SELECT 1 as Tag,
NULL as Parent,
Publishers.pub_name as [Publishers!1!pub_name],
NULL as [Titles!2!title]
FROM Publishers
WHERE Publishers.pub_id = '0736'
UNION ALL
SELECT 2,
1,
Publishers.pub_name,
Titles.title
FROM Publishers JOIN Titles
ON Publishers.pub_id = Titles.pub_id
AND Publishers.pub_id = '0736'
ORDER BY [Publishers!1!pub_name], [Titles!2!title]
FOR XML EXPLICIT
```

The remaining part of the query inserts the value of 2 into the Tag column to specify the next element. A value of 1 in the Parent column is assigned, to indicate that the new element will be a child element of the Publishers element. The remaining two columns are populated with the values of the pub_id and Titles columns, respectively. The ORDER BY clause is also used to order the results by the parent elements, followed by the child elements. Finally, the FOR XML EXPLICIT clause parses the universal table and creates the XML output shown here:

```
<Publishers pub_name="New Moon Books">
 <Titles title="Emotional Security: A New Algorithm"/>
 <Titles title="Is Anger the Enemy?"/>
 <Titles title="Life Without Fear"/>
```

exam
Ⓦatch
You need to specify an ORDER BY clause when using FOR XML EXPLICIT in order to ensure the correct nesting of elements in the XML output. It is not illegal to omit the ORDER BY clause; however, the XML output may not be formatted correctly.

FOR XML EXPLICIT Directives   After seeing the previous example using FOR XML EXPLICIT, you may be thinking that was a lot more work to produce the same result set that FOR XML AUTO can easily produce. The true power of using FOR XML EXPLICIT becomes apparent when *directives* are included in the universal table definition. A directive is a keyword that is included as part of a column name alias in a universal table that can reformat XML output. When using directives, the naming convention of the columns that hold attribute values looks like this:

Element Name!Tag Value!Attribute Name!Directive

There are many directives that can be specified when using FOR XML EXPLICIT. For example, the following query uses the "hide" directive to not display the attribute of Pub_Name in the XML output:

```
SELECT 1 as Tag,
NULL as Parent,
Publishers.pub_name as [Publishers!1!pub_name!hide],
NULL as [Titles!2!title]
FROM Publishers
WHERE Publishers.pub_id = '0736'
UNION ALL
SELECT 2,
1,
Publishers.pub_name,
Titles.title
FROM Publishers JOIN Titles
ON Publishers.pub_id = Titles.pub_id
AND Publishers.pub_id = '0736'
ORDER BY [Publishers!1!pub_name!hide], [Titles!2!title]
FOR XML EXPLICIT
```

The output from the above query does not display the pub_name attribute, but still uses the ORDER BY clause to reference it. The "hide" directive is useful for ordering output by an attribute that you do not wish to display.

The following query uses the "element" directive to create a new element called pub_name:

```
SELECT 1 as Tag,
NULL as Parent,
Publishers.pub_name as [Publishers!1!pub_name!element],
NULL as [Titles!2!title]
FROM Publishers
WHERE Publishers.pub_id = '0736'
UNION ALL
SELECT 2,
1,
Publishers.pub_name,
Titles.title
```

```
FROM Publishers JOIN Titles
ON Publishers.pub_id = Titles.pub_id
AND Publishers.pub_id = '0736'
ORDER BY [Publishers!1!pub_name!element], [Titles!2!title]
FOR XML EXPLICIT
```

The XML output from the preceding query uses the value of the attribute pub_name from the Publishers element and creates a new subelement of the same name by specifying the "element" directive. The following is the partial result set:

```
<Publishers>
<pub_name>New Moon Books</pub_name>
<Titles title="Emotional Security: A New Algorithm"/>
<Titles title="Is Anger the Enemy?"/>
<Titles title="Life Without Fear"/>
</Publishers>
```

Using directives with FOR XML EXPLICIT gives the database developer a very powerful tool to create customized XML output from relational data. However, XML EXPLICIT requires much more initial effort than AUTO or RAW. Creating an accurate universal table requires much more planning than simply adding a FOR XML clause to the SELECT statement.

on the **job**

The syntax of FOR XML EXPLICIT is very comprehensive, and can be a bit confusing. Always keep in mind that building the universal table is the hard part. Once you've pulled that off, manipulating the output using directives is fairly straightforward.

Reading XML Data with OPENXML

So far, we've learned how to retrieve relational data from a SQL Server database and format it as XML output using the FOR XML clause. SQL Server 2000 also provides the capability to do the reverse, read an XML document and format the output as a relational result set. With this capability, the information stored in an XML document can be inserted into a database table, or used to query and manipulate relational data based on the elements and attributes in the XML document. This is a very powerful feature of SQL Server 2000 that brings us closer to the original goal of XML, the sharing of documents in a platform-independent way.

Reading XML in SQL Server is accomplished using the OPENXML function. OPENXML is used along with the sp_xml_preparedocument stored procedure to create an in-memory representation of an XML document. The sp_xml_preparedocument stored procedure accepts a parameter that is known as a *handle*. The handle is a variable with an Integer datatype that will be used by OPENXML to reference the parsed document. To illustrate, the following example uses sp_xml_preparedocument to parse a simple XML document containing a list of store elements, so that it may be used by OPENXML:

```
DECLARE @handle int
DECLARE @document varchar(200)
SET @document ='
<ROOT>
 <Store stor_id="1111" stor_name = "New Book Store"/>
 <Store stor_id="1112" stor_name = "New Book Store2"/>
 <Store stor_id="1113" stor_name = "New Book Store3"/>
</ROOT>'
EXEC sp_xml_preparedocument @handle OUTPUT, @document
```

The preceding statement first declares two variables. The @handle variable will contain the handle value that will be referenced by the OPENXML function (the value is set by the sp_xml_preparedocument stored procedure). The @document variable is declared as a long character string and is then populated with an XML document using SET. The @handle variable is also declared using OUTPUT, so it may be referenced many times in a batch of T-SQL.

Once the document has been prepared, it can then be referenced by OPENXML. The OPENXML function accepts several arguments to produce the relational result set. First, the handle is provided so the function can reference the parsed XML that has been created by sp_xml_preparedocument. Next, an XPATH query is specified to determine which elements are being referenced in the XML. You will learn much more about XPATH queries in an upcoming section; but for now, know that ROOT/Store references the Store element directly beneath the ROOT element. Finally, a WITH clause is used to specify how the relational result set is to be formatted. To illustrate, the following statement uses both sp_xml_preparedocument and OPENXML to create a relational result set from the specified XML document:

```
-- Prepare the XML document
DECLARE @handle int
DECLARE @document varchar(200)
SET @document ='
<ROOT>
 <Store stor_id="1111" stor_name = "New Book Store"/>
 <Store stor_id="1112" stor_name = "New Book Store2"/>
 <Store stor_id="1113" stor_name = "New Book Store3"/>
```

```
</ROOT>'
EXEC sp_xml_preparedocument @handle OUTPUT, @document
-- Document has been prepared, use OPENXML to produce a result set.
SELECT * FROM OPENXML
 (@handle, 'ROOT/Store')
      WITH (stor_id char(4), stor_name varchar(15))
-- Remove the in memory document representation
EXEC sp_xml_removedocument @handle
```

In the preceding statement, the XML document is once again parsed using
sp_xml_preparedocument. OPENXML is then used to produce the result set: First
the @handle variable is provided to OPENXML. Next, the XPATH query is used to
specify the elements from the XML document that will be referenced. The WITH
clause then assigns datatypes to each attribute that will be returned from the XML
document. The WITH clause in OPENXML is similar to a table definition. It
specifies how to format the XML data in a relational format. Finally, the stored
procedure sp_xml_removedocument is used. This procedure simply removes the
in-memory representation of the XML document. The result set looks as follows:

```
stor_id  stor_name
----------------------
1111     New Book Store
1112     New Book Store2
1113     New Book Store3
```

The preceding examples used attribute-centric mapping to reference the values in
the XML document. Element-centric mapping can also be used in OPENXML by
including the FLAGS argument to the function. The FLAGS argument is specified
after the XPATH query, as shown here:

```
SELECT * FROM OPENXML
 (@handle, 'ROOT/Store', 2)
```

The value of 2 specifies that OPENXML should use element-centric mapping
when parsing the XML document. OPENXML defaults to attribute-centric mapping,
or it can be specified with a value of 1.

Using XML Data to Modify Relational Data

Now that we've learned how to retrieve information from XML documents and
format the information as a relational result set, let's actually do something with this

newfound power. The following example uses the same XML document to insert new rows into the Stores table in the Pubs database using OPENXML:

```
DECLARE @handle int
DECLARE @document varchar(200)
SET @document ='
<ROOT>
 <Store stor_id="1111" stor_name = "New Book Store"/>
 <Store stor_id="1112" stor_name = "New Book Store2"/>
 <Store stor_id="1113" stor_name = "New Book Store3"/>
</ROOT>'
EXEC sp_xml_preparedocument @handle OUTPUT, @document
INSERT Stores
(stor_id, stor_name)
SELECT * FROM OPENXML
  (@handle, 'ROOT/Store',1)
      WITH (stor_id char(4), stor_name varchar(15))
EXEC sp_xml_removedocument @handle
```

This time the OPENXML function is used with an INSERT statement to insert the rows of data from the parsed XML document into the Stores table, the column values having been obtained from the attributes of the XML document. Similarly, we can perform other data manipulations based on XML data values. For example, a DELETE statement can be used to remove rows from the Stores table based on values in an XML document, as shown here:

```
DELETE FROM Stores
WHERE stor_id IN
(SELECT stor_id FROM OPENXML
  (@handle, 'ROOT/Store',1)
      WITH (stor_id char(4)))
```

OPENXML gives the modern SQL Server 2000 database developer a new ability to use XML documents as a datasource for adding or modifying relational data. Along with FOR XML, SQL Server 2000 has provided the tools to effectively deal with XML data in ways never before possible. Further enhancing this tool set, is SQL Server 2000's tight Web integration, which will be discussed next.

XML Integration with IIS

The XML functionality provided with SQL Server 2000 integrates with Microsoft Internet Information Services, allowing XML output to be displayed through Internet Explorer. This allows for queries to be submitted via *HTTP*, or the Hypertext Transfer Protocol. HTTP is the language of the Internet and, once enabled, SQL Server's IIS integration allows a SQL Server database to be queried over the Internet, formatting the output as a well-formed XML document.

SQL Server's IIS functionality allows queries to be submitted using the address bar in Internet Explorer. In addition, template files that contain queries can be specified in the URL. In order to access this functionality, a virtual directory must be set up on this IIS server that will be associated with a SQL Server database.

EXERCISE 7-3

CertCam 7-3

Creating an IIS Virtual Directory for a Database

1. Ensure that Internet Information Services is installed and running properly on your computer. Create a new folder under the C:\Inetpub\wwwroot folder called Pubs. Also, create two new subfolders under the newly created Pubs folder called Template and Schema. Now, from the SQL Server program group, select Configure SQL XML Support in IIS, as shown here.

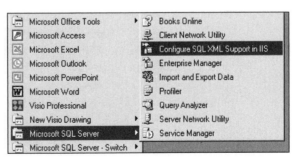

2. This brings up the IIS Virtual Directory Management MMC snap-in. Expand your server and right-click Default Web Site. Select New and then Virtual Directory, as shown next.

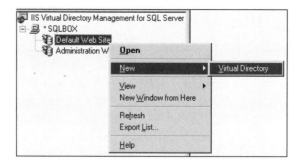

3. This brings up the New Virtual Directory Properties box. On the General tab, enter **PubsWeb** in the Virtual Directory Name text box. Also, enter the path **C:\Inetpub\wwwroot\Pubs** in the Local Path text box, as shown here.

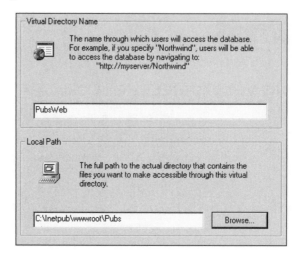

4. Click the next tab, Security. Here you can define the security context that will be used when a user attempts to query a database using a Web browser. Normally, you would want to use integrated Windows authentication, or at least basic authentication. For the purposes of this exercise, select the "Always Log on as" radio button and enter the user SA and your SA account password.

5. Click the next tab, Datasource. (You will be asked to confirm your SA password first.) Here you will define the SQL Server and database for the virtual directory. Ensure that your SQL Server is entered in the first text box, and select the Pubs database from the Database drop-down list.

6. Click the Settings tab. This tab is used to further establish security by specifying the types of queries that are allowed when using a Web browser. For this exercise, select *all* of the check boxes to allow all types of access.

7. Finally, click on the Virtual Names tab. Here you will define the three types of access that can occur through the URL. Click the New button to bring up the Virtual Name Configuration dialog box. Enter the name **Template** in the Virtual Name text box, select "template" in the Type drop-down box, and enter the path **C:\Inetpub\wwwroot\Pubs\Template** in the Path text box, as shown here.

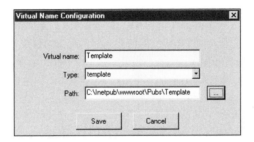

8. Click the Save button to create the new virtual name. Click New again to create the schema virtual name. Enter the name **Schema** in the Virtual Name text box, select "schema" in the Type drop-down box, and enter the path **C:\Inetpub\wwwroot\Pubs\Schema** in the Path text box. Click Save to create the schema virtual name.

9. Click New once again to create the Dbobject virtual name. Enter the name **Dbobject** in the Virtual Name text box, and select "dbobject" in the Type drop-down box. Click Save to create the Dbobject virtual name.

10. Click OK to close the Properties box, and save all changes. Test the IIS configuration by opening Internet Explorer. Enter the following as a URL, substituting the name of your IIS Server for the name "IISServer":

```
http://IISServer/PubsWeb/dbobject/stores[@stor_id='7067']/@stor_name
```

If IIS has been configured properly, you should see the text "News & Brews" appear in the Web browser.

URL-Based Querying

Once IIS has been configured for SQL XML support, a SQL Server database can be accessed via HTTP, using Internet Explorer. Whereas using the FOR XML clause in Query Analyzer produced document fragments, using FOR XML through Internet Explorer can create complete, well-formed XML documents. To illustrate, in Internet Explorer, enter the following in the URL line and press ENTER. Note that in all of the following examples, you will need to substitute the name of your IIS Server with the name "IISServer" in the URL line.

```
http://IISServer/PubsWeb?sql=SELECT stor_name FROM Stores FOR XML AUTO&root=root
```

The preceding URL query returns all stor_name values from the Stores table in the Pubs database, formatted as an XML document. The first part of the URL, before the question mark, points to the virtual directory PubsWeb, created in the previous exercise. This virtual directory can accept a query that uses FOR XML. The question mark precedes sql=, which indicates the text to follow is a query that should be issued against the database. Directly following the query text is an ampersand, followed by the ROOT keyword. The ROOT keyword is used to assign a name to the root element in the resulting XML document. The name of the root element can be anything. For instance, specifying root=top will create a root element named "top." The following is the partial result set:

```
<?xml version="1.0" encoding="utf-8" ?>
- <root>
  <Stores stor_name="Eric the Read Books" />
  <Stores stor_name="Barnum's" />
  <Stores stor_name="News & Brews" />
  <Stores stor_name="Doc-U-Mat: Quality Laundry and Books" />
  </root>
```

on the job

The ROOT keyword only needs to be included in the URL if the resulting XML document contains more than one top-level element. If the query only returns one top-level element, ROOT may be omitted.

URL-based querying is not limited to using the SELECT statement. Stored procedures can also be executed, but the stored procedure definition must use the FOR XML clause. To illustrate, create the following stored procedure in the Pubs database:

```
CREATE PROCEDURE PubsProc AS
SELECT au_lname, au_fname
```

```
FROM Authors
FOR XML AUTO
```

Once the procedure has been created, enter the following URL into Internet Explorer.

```
http://IISServer/PubsWeb?sql=EXEC PubsProc&root=root
```

The resulting XML document contains all values of the Au_Lname and Au_Fname columns from the Authors table. The following is the partial result set:

```
<?xml version="1.0" encoding="utf-8" ?>
- <root>
  <Authors au_lname="Bennet" au_fname="Abraham" />
  <Authors au_lname="Blotchet-Halls" au_fname="Reginald" />
  <Authors au_lname="DeFrance" au_fname="Michel" />
  <Authors au_lname="Yokomoto" au_fname="Akiko" />
  </root>
```

Specifying Template Files in the URL   While entering SQL queries directly into the URL line in Internet Explorer is convenient, long and complex queries can get a bit bothersome when they have to be typed over and over. Queries in the URL also are not very secure, as they expose object names in the database. Instead, SQL Server 2000 allows for *template* files to be specified in the URL. A template file is an XML document that contains a SQL or an XPATH query. Template files are stored in the directory created for the virtual name of the template type. Let's take a look at a sample template file:

```
<ROOT xmlns:sql="urn:schemas-microsoft-com:xml-sql">
  <sql:query>
    SELECT pub_name, state
    FROM Publishers
    FOR XML AUTO
  </sql:query>
</root>
```

As you can see, a template file contains an XML element called sql:query, which contains the content of the SQL query. It also contains a root element, making the template file a complete XML document. Note that the root element also has an attribute called xmlns. This attribute is what's known as an XML *namespace*. A namespace is a prefix of sorts that allows the elements in an XML document to be uniquely identified. In this case, the namespace is given the prefix sql:, which prefaces the element names in the template file. To execute the template, save the preceding template file as C:\Inetpub\wwwroot\Pubs\Template\Sample.xml. Then, enter the following into Internet Explorer:

```
http://IISServer/PubsWeb/template/sample.xml
```

A template file can also contain the header element. The header element is used to specify any parameters that are involved in the query. Header elements contain param subelements that contain the actual values. To illustrate, save the following text to new file called C:\Inetpub\wwwroot\Pubs\Template\Header.xml:

```
<ROOT xmlns:sql="urn:schemas-microsoft-com:xml-sql">
  <sql:header>
    <sql:param name='pub_id'>0736</sql:param>
  </sql:header>
  <sql:query>
    SELECT pub_name, state
    FROM Publishers
    WHERE pub_id = @pub_id
    FOR XML AUTO
  </sql:query>
</ROOT>
```

The template file uses the header and param elements to specify a value of 0736 for the variable @pub_id. Execute the template by typing the following URL into Internet Explorer:

```
http://IISServer/PubsWeb/template/header.xml
```

The template file uses the value specified in the param element to return the XML output. It will use the default value specified unless a different value is included in the URL. To illustrate, the following URL will provide a new value for the @pub_id variable, and return the row from the Publishers table with a pub_id value of 0877:

```
http://IISServer/PubsWeb/template/header.xml?pub_id=0877
```

XDR Schemas and XPATH Queries

SQL Server 2000 allows you to create *XDR schemas* of XML documents. An XDR schema, or XML-Data Reduced schema, is basically a view of an XML document that describes the structure of the elements and attributes of the document. Once an XDR schema is created to reference a document, the view can then be queried using

FROM THE CLASSROOM

What's in a Namespace?

The term "namespace" in XML tends to generate quite a bit of confusion and debate. The purpose of a namespace is to allow the unique identification of an element or an attribute in an XML document. It uses what's known as a uniform resource identifier, or URI. This is very different from universal resource locator, or URL.

URIs are used to prefix the name of an element in XML using a colon, allowing it to be universally identified. Consider database tables for a moment. A table named Employee could exist in many different databases. To allow the table to be uniquely identified on an enterprise-wide scale, it is prefixed with the database and server name using the four-part naming convention. In the same way, a URI namespace prefixes the name of an element,

allowing unique identification. Therefore, the following elements have different meanings:

\<door:knob\>

\<radio:knob\>

In the case of Microsoft template files, the URI is urn:schemas-microsoft-com:xml-sql. So what exactly does that URI point to in a Web browser? Well, nothing. As previously stated, a URI is not the same as a URL that points to a Web site. A URI used in a namespace is more of an abstract thing, not an actual resource. It exists purely for the purpose of uniquely identifying a name. However, XML is continuing to evolve as new standards are produced. In the future, URIs could point to actual resources that would contain more information about the element types, definitions, and so forth, in an XML document.

—*Jeffrey Bane, MCSE, MCDBA*

the *XPATH* language. XPATH is a very simple way to query the information in an XML document.

An XDR schema is itself an XML document containing various mappings and other information about the elements in a document. Let's take a look at a simple XDR schema:

```
<?xml version="1.0" ?>
<Schema xmlns="urn:schemas-microsoft-com:xml-data"
        xmlns:dt="urn:schemas-microsoft-com:datatypes"
        xmlns:sql="urn:schemas-microsoft-com:xml-sql">
<ElementType name="Stores" >
   <AttributeType name="stor_id" />
```

```
        <AttributeType name="stor_name" />
        <attribute type="stor_id" />
        <attribute type="stor_name" />
</ElementType>
</Schema>
```

The preceding XDR mapping schema describes an XML view of the columns in the Stores table. The root element in the XDR schema is the Schema element. Note that the Schema element contains several namespace prefixes. The ElementType element maps the Stores element to the Stores table. The AttributeType element assigns a name to each attribute, and the Attribute element maps each element to a database column. This schema uses what's known as *default* mapping. This simply means that the element named Stores maps to the database table named Stores, and the attributes map to columns in the Stores table.

To use the previous schema to create an XML view, save it to a new file called C:\Inetpub\wwwroot\Pubs\Schema\Schema1.xml. Once the schema file is saved, it can be accessed using the virtual name of the schema type created for the Pubs database. The following URL uses a simple XPATH query that returns all of the Stores elements using the mapping schema:

```
http://IISServer/PubsWeb/Schema/schema1.xml/Stores?root=root
```

In the preceding, the schema virtual name is specified after the PubsWeb virtual directory name in the URL. The schema file to be used is specified, followed by the XPATH query. In this case, the XPATH query is simply /Stores, which returns all Stores elements from the XML view created by the schema file. Also, since more than one top-level element is being returned, the ROOT keyword is included to create a legal XML document.

As previously stated, the preceding XDR schema uses default mapping. The true power of XDR schemas becomes apparent when annotations are added.

Annotated XDR Schemas   *Annotations* may be added to an XDR schema to alter the format of the XML output. Specifying an annotation in a schema file is similar to specifying a directive when using FOR XML EXPLICIT: it changes the structure of the resulting XML document. In fact, XDR schemas are a great way to restructure XML output without having to fuss with the complex syntax and universal tables involved when using FOR XML EXPLICIT.

For example, consider the following XDR schema. It uses annotations to change the names of the elements and attributes to more readable names.

```
<?xml version="1.0" ?>
<Schema xmlns="urn:schemas-microsoft-com:xml-data"
        xmlns:dt="urn:schemas-microsoft-com:datatypes"
        xmlns:sql="urn:schemas-microsoft-com:xml-sql">
<ElementType name="Shops" sql:relation="Stores" >
    <AttributeType name="StoreID" />
    <AttributeType name="StoreName" />
    <attribute type="StoreID" sql:field="stor_id" />
    <attribute type="StoreName" sql:field="stor_name" />
</ElementType>
</Schema>
```

This schema uses two annotations. The first, sql:relation, is used to map an XML item to a database table. In this case, the element is given the new name of Shops and the sql:relation annotation maps the Shops element to the Stores table in the database. The annotation sql:field is also used to rename the attributes. For example, stor_id is renamed to StoreID, and the sql:field annotation maps the attribute to the stor_id column in the Stores table.

There are many kinds of annotations that can be used in an XDR schema file. The following schema introduces the sql:relationship annotation that establishes primary and foreign keys when building an XML view from multiple tables. Save the following schema file as a new file called C:\Inetpub\wwwroot\Pubs\Schema\Schema2.xml:

```
<?xml version="1.0" ?>
<Schema xmlns="urn:schemas-microsoft-com:xml-data"
        xmlns:dt="urn:schemas-microsoft-com:datatypes"
        xmlns:sql="urn:schemas-microsoft-com:xml-sql">
<ElementType name="Orders" sql:relation="sales" >
    <AttributeType name="OrderNumber" />
    <attribute type="OrderNumber" sql:field="ord_num" />
</ElementType>
<ElementType name="Shops" sql:relation="stores" >
    <AttributeType name="StoreId" />
    <AttributeType name="StoreName" />
    <attribute type="StoreId" sql:field="stor_id" />
    <attribute type="StoreName" sql:field="stor_name" />
     <element type="Orders" >
      <sql:relationship
       key-relation="stores"
```

```
         foreign-relation="sales"
         key="stor_id"
         foreign-key="stor_id" />
      </element>
   </ElementType>
   </Schema>
```

The preceding schema uses the sql:relationship annotation. It establishes the relationship between the Stores table and the Sales table. The key-relation and foreign-relation attributes specify the primary-key table and foreign-key table, respectively. The key attribute specifies the primary key of the parent table and the foreign-key attribute specifies the foreign key of the child table, thus establishing a way to join the two tables. To retrieve the XML document, enter the following URL into Internet Explorer:

```
http://IISServer/PubsWeb/Schema/schema2.xml/Shops?root=root
```

XPATH Queries   SQL Server 2000 also supports the use of XPATH queries to retrieve information from an XML view defined by an XDR schema. XPATH is a language used to query XML documents much in the same way T-SQL queries database tables. XPATH queries can be specified in the URL and also in template files.

XPATH is a very intuitive language that allows much of the same flexibility that the SELECT statement provides when querying a database table. Let's take a look at a very simple XPATH query. Using the Schema2.xml XDR Schema from the preceding example, to retrieve a list of all Shops elements and subsequent Orders subelements, the XPATH query looks like this:

/Shops

This is what's known as a location path in XPATH. The slash in the syntax indicates the child of the current element. In this case, the current element is root, so the child of root is the first top-level element, or Shops. To return all Orders subelements, another slash is added to specify that the children of the Shops element should be returned. To illustrate, enter the following URL into Internet Explorer:

```
http://IISServer/PubsWeb/Schema/schema2.xml/Shops/Orders?root=root
```

This XPATH query returns all the Orders child elements of the parent Shops element. The partial result set is shown here:

```
<?xml version="1.0" encoding="utf-8" ?>
- <root>
  <Orders OrderNumber="6871" />
  <Orders OrderNumber="722a" />
  <Orders OrderNumber="A2976" />
  <Orders OrderNumber="QA7442.3" />
  </root>
```

At any point in the location path, *predicates* may be specified. Predicates in XPATH are similar to predicates of the WHERE clause in a SELECT statement. For example, the following URL returns the Shops element with a StoreID value of 6380:

```
http://IISServer/PubsWeb/Schema/schema2.xml/Shops[@StoreId="6380"]?root=root
```

As you can see, the predicate used is included after the location path of Shops, surrounded by brackets. This limits the resulting XML document to only the Shops elements that have a value of true for the predicate specified. Predicates in XPATH are not limited to a condition of equality. Much like the WHERE clause, conditions such as greater than, less than, and not equal may also be tested.

XPATH can also go in reverse using location paths to specify the parent of the current element. This is done by using two periods. To illustrate, enter the following URL in Internet Explorer:

```
http://IISServer/PubsWeb/Schema/schema2.xml/Shops/Orders
[../@StoreId="6380"]?root=root
```

This XPATH query returns all Orders elements where the parent Shops element has a StoreID value of 6380, by specifying two periods before the variable to be tested in the predicate.

exam
ⓦatch

Much of what has been covered about SQL Server 2000's XML functionality is case sensitive. If you are unable to get an XPATH query, template file, or XDR schema to function, case sensitivity is usually the culprit.

XPATH predicates also support the use of arithmetic operators, Boolean functions, and operators such as AND and OR. They provide a very versatile way to restrict an XML document based on search conditions.

Querying Database Objects Using XPATH   Database objects can also be queried directly in the URL, using the virtual name type of Dbobject. To illustrate, the following returns the value of the Stor_Name column from the row with a stor_id value of 6380:

```
http://IISServer/PubsWeb/dbobject/Stores[@stor_id="6380"]/@stor_name
```

Note that querying database objects using the Dbobject virtual name type can only return a single value. Multiple rows or columns in the result are not supported.

CERTIFICATION SUMMARY

Databases typically do not exist in a solitary environment. Transferring data between systems is one of the most common tasks that the SQL Server database developer must architect. SQL Server 2000 provides a comprehensive set of tools for dealing with data in the enterprise environment.

Datafiles are a common means of transferring data between systems. Both the BCP utility and T-SQL BULK INSERT command provide a fast and simple way to import from datafiles. BCP can also export data from tables into datafiles. DTS provides the ability to use datafiles as a datasource or destination, along with any number of other OLE-DB-accessible datasources, with a full-blown graphical user interface. DTS is an application in its own right, allowing complex transformations between many different systems to be defined and scheduled.

Databases hosted on many different platforms are common in the enterprise environment, and SQL Server 2000 provides many tools to effectively deal with external servers. Linked servers can be defined against any OLE-DB–accessible datasource, allowing the use of the four-part naming convention to query and modify external data. Ad hoc queries can also be specified by dynamically providing the connection information for a query using OPENROWSET and OPENDATASOURCE.

SQL Server 2000 also provides a high level of support for the Extensible Markup Language, or XML. New T-SQL commands provide the ability to read from XML documents and reformat relational data as XML output. SQL Server 2000's XML functionality can also be integrated with Microsoft's Internet Information Services, bringing XML's goal of standardized document exchange over the Internet closer to reality.

✓ TWO-MINUTE DRILL

Importing and Exporting Data

❑ SQL Server 2000 provides many tools to transfer data between systems, including BCP, BULK INSERT, and DTS.

❑ Both the BCP utility and the BULK INSERT statement can be used to import data from a datafile into a database table. However, only BCP can export data from a table into a datafile.

❑ It is important to try to use minimally logged, called *nonlogged*, bulk copies of data. This greatly speeds up the process and also lessens the possibility of the transaction log filling up during large transfers.

❑ DTS can also import data from a datafile, and it can also perform highly complex transformations between various systems.

❑ DTS uses what are known as DTS packages to define a data transformation job. DTS packages are created using the DTS Designer, or by using the DTS Wizard in Enterprise Manager.

❑ A DTS package consists of many objects known as connections and tasks. Connection objects use OLE-DB technology to define datasources and destinations. Task objects define how to transfer the data between various connection objects.

Working with External Servers

❑ Data residing on external servers can be queried and modified by establishing a linked server. A linked server is a permanent connection to an external datasource that can be accessed using the four-part naming convention.

❑ Security on linked servers is established by the process of mapping local logins to remote logins. This is done by using the sp_addlinkedserverlogin stored procedure.

❑ Linked servers can be other SQL Server databases, but they can also point to databases that run on other database systems.

❏ SQL Server 2000 also supports the use of pass-through queries, which are queries where the result set processing takes place on a remote server. OPENQUERY is a T-SQL command that specifies a pass-through query.

❏ OPENROWSET and OPENDATASOURCE are also T-SQL commands that can query and modify data on an external server. However, they are intended for infrequent use, when setting up a linked server is not practical or feasible.

❏ Since no permanent connection exists, both OPENROWSET and OPENDATASOURCE require that connection information be provided at the time the query is executed.

XML Functionality

❏ SQL Server 2000 has built-in support for XML. XML is an attempt to standardize the markup of shared documents.

❏ The T-SQL FOR XML clause allows relational data to be queried and reformatted as XML output. FOR XML AUTO and FOR XML RAW map the tables and columns in a database to the elements and attributes of an XML document.

❏ FOR XML EXPLICIT is used when XML output needs to be structured in a very specific way. It uses a fairly complex syntax that builds a universal table that is queried to produce the custom XML output.

❏ SQL Server 2000 also provides the ability to read XML data using the OPENXML system function. OPENXML is used with the sp_xml_preparedocument and sp_xml_removedocument stored procedures.

❏ SQL Server 2000's XML functionality also integrates with Internet Information Services. This allows database queries to be issued using HTTP. Complete, well-formed XML documents can be produced and displayed in Internet Explorer.

❏ Template files can also be specified in the URL that can contain a T-SQL or an XPATH query. Template files enhance the security of URL-based querying.

❏ A view of an XML document can be created by using XDR schemas. Once an XDR mapping schema is created, an XML document can then be queried using the XPATH language.

SELF TEST

The following questions will help you measure your understanding of the material presented in this chapter. Read all the choices carefully because there might be more than one correct answer. Choose all correct answers for each question. Just like on the real exam, you may need to use some scratch paper to draw out the scenarios in order to gain a better conceptual view of the problem being presented.

Importing and Exporting Data

1. Which of the following statements are true regarding the BULK INSERT command? (Choose all that apply.)

   A. BULK INSERT can be faster than using BCP to import data.

   B. BULK INSERT can be faster than using BCP to export data.

   C. You should use BULK INSERT instead of BCP whenever possible.

   D. BULK INSERT has more options than BCP does arguments for establishing the security context used to access a table.

2. You are planning to use DTS to transfer several rows of data from a SQL Server table to an Access table. You need to reformat a column containing date/time information, so it will be compatible with the Access database. Which of the following should you set up in the DTS Designer to build the package?

   A. A Connection object to establish the database connections and a Task object to transfer the data.

   B. Two Connection objects to establish the database connections and a Task object to transfer the data.

   C. Two Connection objects to establish the database connections, a Task object to transfer the data, and a Task object to reformat the data from a date/time column.

   D. Two Connection objects to establish the database connections, two Task objects to transfer the data, and two Task objects to reformat the data from a date/time column.

3. You are going to use BCP to import several rows into a SQL Server table from a datafile named D:\Imports\Newfile.txt. The datafile was originally exported from another SQL Server, so the datafile is in native format. The target table is named Sales, and it exists in the Corporation database. You need to import the data using your current Windows account information to access the table. You also need to exclude the first three lines in the datafile from the import. Which command would you use to accomplish the import?

   A. `BCP Corporation.DBO.Sales IN D:\Imports\Newfile.txt -F3 -n -T`

   B. `BCP Corporation.DBO.Sales OUT D:\Imports\Newfile.txt -F3 -n -T`

   C. `BCP Corporation.DBO.Sales IN D:\Imports\Newfile.txt -F4 -n -T`

   D. `BCP Corporation.DBO.Sales IN D:\Imports\Newfile.txt -F4 -c -T`

4. You need to import several thousand rows from a datafile into a SQL Server database. The datafile contains new information that has yet to be stored in the database, so no target table exists yet. Which of the following would you use to accomplish the import in the simplest way?

   A. BCP

   B. DTS

   C. BULK INSERT

   D. OPENQUERY

5. Which of the following are valid arguments when using the BCP utility?

   A. -t

   B. -T

   C. -2

   D. -TABLOCK

Working with External Servers

6. Two SQL Servers exist. The first is a development server called SQLDEV. All users on SQLDEV have rights to read and modify data in all the tables on SQLDEV. A linked server is established on SQLDEV, pointing to the second server, SQLHR. SQLHR contains sensitive HR information. You need to allow certain users on SQLDEV the right to select data from one of the tables on SQLHR, using the linked server. How should you accomplish this requirement?

   A. Create a new login on SQLHR and assign the appropriate permissions to the new login. Map the local logins of all appropriate users of SQLDEV to this new login.

   B. Create a new login on SQLDEV with the appropriate permissions to the table on SQLHR. Have the appropriate users on SQLDEV use the new login.

    C. Map the local logins of all appropriate users on SQLDEV to the system administrator account on SQLHR.

    D. Use DTS to import the table from SQLHR to SQLDEV. Give the appropriate users on SQLDEV the right to query the new table.

7. You have established a linked server to a SQL Server 2000 computer called SQLDEV2. You want to test the new linked server using OPENQUERY. Which of the following could you use to retrieve all values in the City column from the Publishers table on the linked server? (Choose all that apply.)

    A. `SELECT * FROM SQLDEV2`

    B. `SELECT city FROM`
       `OPENQUERY (SQLDEV2,`
       `'SELECT * FROM Pubs.DBO.Publishers')`

    C. `SELECT * FROM`
       `OPENQUERY (SQLDEV2,`
       `'SELECT city FROM Pubs.DBO.Publishers')`

    D. `SELECT city FROM`
       `(SQLDEV2,'OPENQUERY SELECT city FROM Pubs.DBO.Publishers')`

8. Which of the following can be used as a linked server datasource? (Choose all that apply.)

    A. An Oracle database

    B. A SQL Server database

    C. An Excel spreadsheet

    D. All of the above

9. Which of the following statements are true with regard to OPENQUERY and OPENROWSET?

    A. Both OPENQUERY and OPENROWSET require connection information to be provided at the time of the query.

    B. The remote data is processed locally when using OPENQUERY and processed remotely when using OPENROWSET.

    C. OPENQUERY requires that a linked server has been defined against the target datasource while OPENROWSET does not.

    D. Both OPENQUERY and OPENROWSET utilize the four-part naming convention to identify the target table.

10. You have established a linked server named ExcelLink that points to an Excel workbook that contains a worksheet named Sheet1. The Excel document is not password protected. You attempt to query the data using the following query, but it is generating an error.

    ```
    SELECT * from ExcelLink.Workbook.ADMIN.Sheet1$
    ```

    Which of the following could be causing the error? (Choose all that apply.).

    A. An Excel workbook cannot be used as a datasource for a linked server.

    B. The Excel workbook is open for use by another user.

    C. Excel does not use the concepts of database or object owner.

    D. Another user has deleted the Excel workbook.

11. Which of the following are meant for infrequent, ad hoc data retrieval from remote datasources? (Choose all that apply.)

    A. OPENQUERY

    B. Linked servers

    C. OPENROWSET

    D. OPENDATASOURCE

XML Functionality

12. You are working with a database table that contains contact information. You need to output the contents of the table as an XML document for sharing. You'd like to map each row in the table to an element in the XML document, with attributes containing the column values for each row. Which of the following would accomplish this task in the easiest way?

    A. FOR XML RAW

    B. FOR XML EXPLICIT

    C. FOR XML AUTO

    D. OPENXML

13. Which of the following are valid virtual name types in SQL Server 2000's XML integration with IIS? (Choose all that apply.)

    A. Schema

    B. Element

    C. Template

    D. Dbobject

14. You are attempting to create XML output from the rows of a database table called Products. The requirements dictate that the XML output should not contain any attributes, but instead should use element-centric mapping to the Products table. Which of the following would you use to produce the XML?

A. `SELECT * FROM Products, ELEMENTS`
`FOR XML AUTO`

B. `SELECT * FROM Products`
`FOR XML ELEMENTS`

C. `SELECT * FROM Products`
`FOR XML AUTO(ELEMENTS)`

D. `SELECT * FROM Products`
`FOR XML AUTO, ELEMENTS`

15. Which of the following statements are true regarding OPENXML? (Choose all that apply.)

A. A variable containing an XML document or document fragment needs to be provided as an argument to OPENXML.

B. OPENXML can only read XML that contains a root tag.

C. OPENXML uses a document handle to reference a representation of the XML document created by the stored procedure sp_xml_preparedocument.

D. OPENXML can use an XPATH query or T-SQL query as an argument to retrieve data from an XML document.

16. Which of the following XPATH queries would return all Employees elements that contain an attribute named LastName having a value of Jones?

A. /Employees/LastName="Jones"

B. /Employees[@LastName="Jones"]

C. /Employees/@LastName="Jones"

D. /Employees[LastName="Jones"]

17. Which of the following statements regarding XDR schemas are true? (Choose all that apply.)

A. An XDR schema creates an XML view that can be queried using XPATH.

B. XDR schemas are necessary to query a database table using FOR XML EXPLICIT.

C. Annotations can be added to an XDR schema in order to reformat the resulting XML document in custom ways.

D. XDR schemas cannot be used with template files.

LAB QUESTION

You are one of several database administrators for a very large corporation and manage several SQL Servers in the HR department. One of your servers, SQLHR1, has a linked server defined that points to another SQL Server in the payroll department named SQLPAY4. SQLPAY4 exists at a different branch of the corporation, several blocks away, and contains sensitive information. As such, even the SA account on SQLHR1 does not have rights to any of the remote tables. Your login, and several other developers' logins, have rights on the linked server through a mapped login to issue SELECT statements against a table named Rates on SQLPAY4. The Rates table contains roughly one hundred million rows.

One of your developers is writing code for a new application. The application will access the Rates table via the linked server, using the four-part naming convention and the mapped login. In order to test certain parts of the new application, the developer needs an exact copy of the Rates table, as his testing will modify data in the table and the production table cannot be altered. The test table will also need to contain the same number of rows as the production table in order to measure the speed of the new application.

Since the table is so large, it is decided to use BCP to export the rows from the remote Rates table into a datafile, and then import the datafile to a new table on a development server. However, you do not possess the password for the mapped login that the linked server uses to access the table. You try the BCP operation using a trusted connection, but your Windows account also lacks rights to access the table. To make matter worse, you discover that the DBA for the payroll server is out sick, and no one else has the rights to grant you a login to perform the BCP operation.

How can you perform the BCP operation against the linked server with only the mapped login the linked server uses? Keep in mind these requirements:

- You must use the BCP utility to export the data.

- You have no way of obtaining the password of the mapped login that the linked server uses.

SELF TEST ANSWERS

Importing and Exporting Data

1. ☑ **A** is correct. BULK INSERT runs in process of SQL Server, eliminating the need for communication between SQL Server and the BCP utility. Therefore, it can perform faster than BCP. **C** is also correct due to the speed advantage, and the fact that BULK INSERT can also be used within user defined transactions.

☒ **B** is incorrect because BULK INSERT cannot export data from a table. **D** is also incorrect because BULK INSERT uses an existing connection to SQL Server, eliminating the need to provide a security context.

2. ☑ **B** is the correct answer. Two Connection objects will be needed, one for the SQL Server database and one for the Access database. A transform data task will also be needed to transfer and reformat the data.

☒ **A** is incorrect because a separate Connection object will be needed for each database. **C** is incorrect because a separate task to reformat the data is not necessary. **D** is also incorrect because a single Task object can both transfer and transform the data.

3. ☑ **C** is the correct answer because it uses the -n argument to specify the datafile in native format. It also uses -T to establish a trusted connection that uses the current Windows login to establish security. The first three lines of the datafile are excluded by using -F4, which specifies that the fourth row of data is the start point for the import.

☒ **A** is incorrect because -F3 will begin the import on the third line of data in the datafile, only excluding the first two. **B** is also incorrect because specifying OUT in BCP will export, not import, data. **D** is incorrect, as it uses the -c argument to indicate that the datafile is stored in character, not native, format.

4. ☑ **B** is the correct answer. A DTS transform data task can be used to create a new table before an import occurs in the properties window of the transform data task. It will create table columns that mirror the columns in the datafile.

☒ **A** and **C** are incorrect because a target table needs to exist in order to use BCP or BULK INSERT. **D** is also incorrect, as OPENQUERY is not used to import data from a datafile.

5. ☑ **A** is correct because -t is used to specify a field terminator in a datafile. **B** is also correct because -T is used to indicate a trusted connection for the security context.

☒ **C** is incorrect because no such argument exists. **D** is also incorrect because the TABLOCK hint is specified using the -h argument of the BCP utility.

Working with External Servers

6. ☑ **A** is the correct answer. A new login will need to be created on SQLHR that has only the rights to query the table. The logins of the appropriate users on SQLDEV can then be mapped to the remote login using the stored procedure sp_addlinkedsrvlogin, or Enterprise Manager.

   ☒ **B** is incorrect, as the linked server on SQLDEV will need a login that is local to SQLHR, or a domain Windows account to map to. **C** is incorrect, because the sa account can also modify data in the table, and the requirements state that the users on SQLDEV should only be able to select data from the table. **D** is also incorrect because any updates to the table on SQLHR would not be reflected in the new table on SQLDEV.

7. ☑ Both **B** and **C** are correct. **B** selects the city column from a result set consisting of all rows and columns from the Publishers table. **C** selects all columns from a result set consisting of the city column values from the Publishers table.

   ☒ **A** and **D** are incorrect, as they use syntax that is illegal in OPENQUERY. OPENQUERY is specified directly after the keyword FROM in a SELECT statement.

8. ☑ **D** is the correct answer. A linked server can point to a SQL Server database, most other database products, and even an Excel spreadsheet.

   ☒ **A**, **B**, and **C** are all correct answers in and of themselves; however, **D** is the correct answer.

9. ☑ **C** is the correct answer because OPENQUERY is used with an existing linked server. OPENROWSET is used for infrequent connections and requires no defined linked server against the datasource.

   ☒ **A** is incorrect because OPENQUERY uses an existing linked server and requires no connection information in the syntax. **B** is incorrect because both OPENQUERY and OPENROWSET execute pass-through queries on the remote server. **D** is also incorrect because the server name is provided as a separate argument in the syntax of both OPENQUERY and OPENROWSET. They both use three-part naming to specify the target table.

10. ☑ **B**, **C**, and **D** are correct. **B** is correct because a linked server established to an Excel file will fail if the file is opened by another user. **C** is correct because Excel does not support the use of database or object owner in the four-part naming convention. **D** is also correct because the query would fail if the Excel file has been deleted.

    ☒ **A** is incorrect because an Excel workbook is a legal datasource for a linked server.

11. ☑ **C** and **D** are correct. Both OPENROWSET and OPENDATASOURCE are meant to be used for infrequent access to a remote datasource.

    ☒ **A** and **B** are incorrect. A linked server is a permanent connection to a remote datasource. OPENQUERY is used with a linked server to execute pass-through queries.

XML Functionality

12. ☑ **C** is the correct answer. By default, FOR XML AUTO will map each column in the underlying table to an attribute of each element in the resulting XML document.
☒ **A** is incorrect because FOR XML RAW assigns each element in the XML document a generic row identifier as the element name, thus the document would not be very readable. **B** is incorrect because FOR XML EXPLICIT is used to reformat an XML document in complex ways. **D** is also incorrect because OPENXML is used to read XML data from a document.

13. ☑ **A, C,** and **D.** Schema, template, and Dbobject are the valid virtual name types. Each is used with XML integration with IIS to access different types of objects.
☒ **B** is incorrect because element is not a valid virtual name type. An element is a part of an XML document.

14. ☑ **D** is the correct answer. ELEMENTS is an option of the FOR XML AUTO clause and is specified after the AUTO keyword, separated by a comma.
☒ **A, B,** and **C** are incorrect. Neither uses the correct syntax for specifying the ELEMENTS option.

15. ☑ **C** is the correct answer. OPENXML is used with the sp_xml_preparedocument stored procedure, which creates a handle that OPENXML can then reference.
☒ **A** is incorrect because OPENXML requires a document handle created by the sp_xml_preparedocument stored procedure as an argument, not the XML document itself as variable. **B** is incorrect because OPENXML can use any XML document fragment that has only one top-level element. **D** is also incorrect, as OPENXML uses an XPATH query to determine which elements and attributes to retrieve from the XML document.

16. ☑ **B** is the correct answer. The predicate in an XPATH query is surrounded by brackets and the attribute being tested is preceded with the @ character.
☒ **A** is incorrect because the LastName attribute is not enclosed in brackets nor is it preceded with the @ character. **C** is incorrect because the predicate is simply preceded by a forward slash. **D** is also incorrect, as the LastName attribute lacks the @ character.

17. ☑ **A** and **C** are correct. An XDR schema is an XML view that can be queried using XPATH, and annotations can be made in the XDR schema to customize the XML output.
☒ **B** is incorrect because FOR XML EXPLICIT uses a universal table, not an XDR schema to customize XML output. **D** is also incorrect because template files, as well as URL queries, can use XDR schemas.

LAB ANSWER

The simplest way to do this would be to create a new table with the identical structure of the Rates table, and use an INSERT statement to populate the new table as shown here:

```
INSERT NewTable
SELECT * FROM SQLPAY4.Database.dbo.Rates
```

However, this operation could fill up the transaction log rather quickly, and the requirements state that the BCP utility must be used. The solution is using the BCP argument QUERYOUT. In addition to OUT, which exports all the rows from the table specified into a datafile, BCP supports the use of QUERYOUT. When using QUERYOUT, a T-SQL query is specified in place of a table name, as shown here:

```
BCP "SELECT * FROM SQLPAY4.Database.dbo.Rates" QUERYOUT D:\MegaFile.txt -n -T
```

The query against the linked server is specified in place of the three-part naming convention used to identify the table to be exported. Note that this BCP operation is issued against the local server. Therefore, the mapped login that has the rights needed to perform the operation is used to issue the query, and the operation succeeds.

8

Designing and Implementing Database Security

One of the biggest concerns for IT professionals is related to implementing and maintaining adequate security policies based on business requirements. This is especially true for database implementers and database administrators, as businesses store large portions of their sensitive information within databases. It's the job of database implementers to ensure that database users can view only the information to which they should have access. This includes the design, implementation, and administration of database-level security.

In this chapter, we'll look at the steps that you can take to understand and implement security within SQL Server 2000.

CERTIFICATION OBJECTIVE 8.01

Understanding and Implementing SQL Server Security

Database server security is something that is often ignored. Perhaps one reason is that it is not clearly understood. It is imperative that you secure your operating system resources. Securing your database server platform is equally important. What is the exact relationship between operating system security and database server security? The security model of SQL Server 2000 includes many features that allow for integrating the two into a common database. Here, we'll examine the various levels of security settings, and explore how they all interact. The main levels that must be considered are as follows:

- Operating system security
- Database logins
- Database user permissions
- Object permissions

To get access to your most trusted information, users will have to be able to jump all four of these hurdles. As a DBA, your job is to ensure that the hurdles are of the proper height—that is, your security model takes into account both security and usability. Since they're so important, let's take an in-depth look at each level of permissions. In this section, let's look at the other levels and how they relate to each other.

FROM THE CLASSROOM

Addressing Overall Security

The focus of this chapter is security, an important topic for all IT professionals. However, the technical information presented here focuses on only one aspect of a much larger task. Although implementing and maintaining security for organizations' data is extremely important, this is only one part of a much bigger task. Good security practices must involve all members of an organization, and must take into account many different tools and techniques.

An often-overlooked aspect of technology-related security is that of restricting physical access to important machines. The best-designed database and operating system security measures are useless in preventing someone from simply walking into your server room and hauling off a server. Once they have physical access to the machine, they can take their time to get through any other security you have in place. Be sure that servers are kept in locked rooms and that access to these rooms is audited. It's increasingly common to implement "headless" servers—machines that have no input or output devices and are administered remotely.

Next, it's important to understand that SQL Server plays in the sandbox of many other network services. An implementation of SQL Server is only as secure as the operating system on which it runs. Without the appropriate permissions settings, for example, a user could simply copy a database backup over the network and restore it on his or her machine. Be sure that you take advantage of Windows NT and Windows 2000's security features, starting first with the domain model and Windows authentication. Administrators should be sure to regularly review security settings and

make the necessary adjustments. (There should be nothing more embarrassing than finding a Domain Administrator account for someone who left the company years ago!)

Finally, a very important area of security deals with the "people" aspect of security. This task is sometimes referred to as "social engineering." All users within the organization must learn the importance of not sharing passwords and of locking their workstations when they're away. Business should rely on security policies that are well communicated and enforced. A salesperson, for example, would never think of leaving his or her list of contacts on a competitor's desk for an extended period of time. However, he or she may think nothing of taping a password to the bottom of their keyboard.

So much depends on network-level security, and an unlocked console is a gateway to all of the permissions that a user has. This applies equally well (if not more so) to database and systems administrators. The Administrator account should rarely be used. Instead, specific accounts for each individual should be created. And, administrators should log off of workstations and servers immediately after they're finished with a task.

Overall, the job of creating and maintaining security is a huge undertaking. It's also one that's almost never done. That is, you must be constantly auditing and updating policies based on business requirements. However, like so many other IT-related tasks, the consequences of not addressing all areas of security can be disastrous. Remember: a chain is only as strong as its weakest link!

—Anil Desai, MCSE, MCSD, MCDBA

Server Logins

Microsoft has made providing for a single sign-on experience a major design goal in all of its products. Users and systems administrators alike benefit from being able to maintain and use a single account for all operations within the network. To accommodate this, the security architecture of SQL Server 2000 supports two security models:

- **Windows authentication** This mode uses built-in Windows NT/2000 user accounts that map to database server logins for permissions. In this mode, server logins are created from existing Windows NT/2000 group and user accounts. Users who have already been authenticated by an NT/2000 Server machine need not enter anymore information before connecting to SQL Server.

on the
Job

Throughout this chapter, we'll make references to Windows NT/2000 user accounts. Note, however, that the real integration between SQL Server and network directory services applies to Windows NT security (workgroup and domain mode), as well as Active Directory security. Additionally, this security model is supported on Windows XP platforms and future versions of the Windows operating system. Although the method of implementation of directory services is quite different, all of these options are compatible with Windows authentication and mixed-mode authentication.

- **Mixed-mode (SQL Server authentication and Windows authentication)** Supported mainly for backward compatibility, this security mode allows for the use of both integrated security and standard username/password combinations. Standard logins require the creation of new database server logins, including usernames and passwords within SQL Server itself. Application users can use this information to make a connection with your server. The disadvantages of this security model are the fact that you might have to support two different sets of user databases (one at the operating system level and another within SQL Server). Additionally, users will be forced to enter login information more than once to get access to the resources they require. However, non-Windows client types may not support Windows NT/2000 authentication and must use the standard username/password method.

Initially, you must set the SQL Server authentication mode during the setup of SQL Server. You'll be prompted for the security mode and (if you choose mixed mode) for a password for the built-in sa account. If SQL Server is running on a Windows 95/98/ME machine, users will not be able to use trusted connections. Therefore, Windows NT/2000–only authentication is not an available option, and all users who connect to that server will be required to provide a valid login and password.

After SQL Server is installed, you can set the SQL Server security mode within Enterprise Manager by right-clicking the name of a server, selecting Properties, and then clicking the Security tab (see Figure 8-1).

Auditing options are also available in this same dialog box. Auditing logon information is useful for holding users responsible for their actions and for managing performance. By tracking server logon information, you can increase security by finding out which users are logging in to the system, and when.

Creating SQL Server Logins

After you set the appropriate authentication mode for your installation of SQL Server, you need to create logins. A login is used to authenticate a user before he or

FIGURE 8-1

Setting the SQL Server security mode

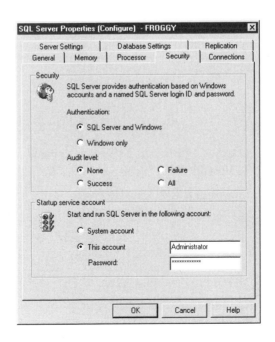

she connects to the database server. To create a SQL Server login in Enterprise Manager, use the following procedure.

EXERCISE 8-1

CertCam 8-1

Creating SQL Server Logins

1. Select the server for which you want to create a login. Expand the Security folder. Right-click Logins and select New Login. You will see this dialog box.

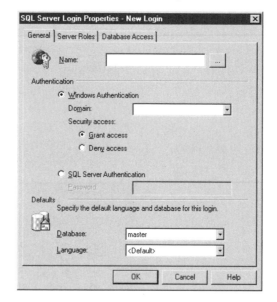

2. In the Name field, specify a unique name for the new login. This is the name a user must use to connect to the database server.

3. For Authentication, select SQL Server Authentication and enter a password to be used by a user or application to log in to the database.

4. Specify a default database to which the user will connect. Note that you may need to grant database permissions (described later) separately.

5. Click OK and then verify the password to create the new login.

You can optionally specify server roles and database roles using the other tabs in this dialog box. SQL Server login information is stored in the *Syslogins* system table (located in the master database). Password information stored in this table is encrypted. When a user attempts to authenticate, SQL Server verifies whether a login and password are present in this table, and if so, allows the login.

Mapping Windows NT/2000 Accounts

When administering user permissions in a network environment, maintaining logins at both the network operating system level and at the database level can be tedious, time-consuming, and error-prone. Windows NT/2000 accounts (groups and users) can be directly granted permissions to access a Microsoft SQL Server database if you're using Windows authentication or mixed-mode authentication. In most cases, it is preferable to grant access to Windows NT/2000 groups, to make administration easier. Consider placing all SQL Server users in one or more new Windows NT/2000 groups. If you're working in a domain-based environment, you can assign logon permissions to either global or local groups. Windows NT/2000 authentication is supported by both Windows 95/98/ME and Windows NT/2000 clients, provided that the users have accounts. Other client types (such as MS-DOS, Macintosh, and UNIX users) can only use SQL Server authentication.

on the

Job

By default, members of the Windows NT/2000 Administrators and Domain Administrators groups are granted system administrator (sa) access to the database. Although there is an option to set the password to blank, you should always set a strong password for the sa account during the installation of SQL Server 2000.

To create a SQL Server login based on a Windows NT/2000 user or group in Enterprise Manager, use the following procedure:

EXERCISE 8-2

Creating a SQL Server Login Based on Windows NT/2000 Security

1. Select the server to which you want to create a login. Expand the Security folder. Right-click Logins and select New Login. You'll see the New Login dialog box.

2. In the Name field, specify the name of a Windows NT/2000 user or group to which you want to grant login permissions. If you're working in a multidomain environment, you also need to specify the complete name, including the domain (such as Engineering).

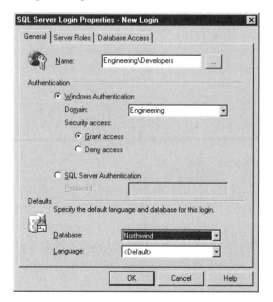

3. Leave the Authentication setting as Windows NT/2000 Authentication. Users will not need to enter a username or password to gain access. For the Security Access option, choose whether this group should be granted or denied access.

4. Specify a default database to which the user will connect. Click OK to create the new login.

You can optionally specify server roles and database roles using the other tabs in this dialog box. When a user attempts to log in to a database using Windows NT/2000 authentication, SQL Server attempts to find a matching login in the Syslogins table. If a Windows NT/2000 user attempts to log in from a nontrusted domain, he or she will be required to enter a username and password for the domain in which the SQL Server resides. The same will occur if the user is not a member of any Windows NT/2000 group or user account that has permission to log in. In either case, if a login exists, the user is allowed to connect; otherwise, an error message is returned and the user is given a chance to provide a SQL Server login (as long as SQL Server and Windows NT/2000 security is enabled). To keep track of accounts when SQL Server and Windows NT/2000 security is used, database administrators may want to avoid the creation of SQL Server login names that have the same names as Windows NT/2000 user accounts.

Database User Permissions

Although having access to a database server lets users log in, that alone does not give them the right to access information. The next step is to set permissions on logins to allow them access to one or more databases. A user must be added to a database before he or she can access any information in that database. There are two ways to add these permissions, as detailed in Exercises 8-3 and 8-4.

To add database permissions when creating a login, follow the steps in Exercise 8-3.

SCENARIO & SOLUTION	
You want only users that are members of your Windows 2000 Active Directory environment to be able to log on to SQL Server.	Configure SQL Server to use Windows authentication.
You want to allow users to log in to SQL Server using usernames and passwords that you will provide.	Configure SQL Server to use mixed-mode authentication.
You want to support the use of non-Windows client machines (for example, Macintosh or UNIX-based clients) for accessing SQL Server.	Configure SQL Server to use mixed-mode authentication and assign each user a login and a password.
You want to keep track of which users are logging in to your SQL Server, and when they log on.	Enable logon auditing by using Enterprise Manager and accessing the properties of your SQL Server.

EXERCISE 8-3

Setting Database Permissions When Creating a Login

1. When creating a new login in Enterprise Manager, click the Database Access tab in the New Login dialog box.

2. Place a check mark next to the database(s) the user should be able to access.

3. Optionally, you can assign database roles (described later) for these users.

Alternatively, you can add existing database logins to a database by following the procedure in Exercise 8-4.

EXERCISE 8-4

Setting Database Permissions When Creating a Database User

1. In Enterprise Manager, expand the object for the database in which you want to add users.

2. Right-click the Users folder and select New Database User.

3. Select a Login Name. You can use the login name as the username within the database, or you can assign a unique name.

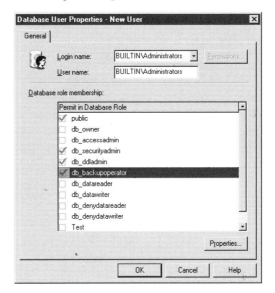

4. Add the users to any existing database roles.

So far, we've looked at the steps that are required to grant access to SQL Server databases. The next step is to look at security settings *within* a database.

CERTIFICATION OBJECTIVE 8.02

Implementing Database-Level Security

It's easier to assign permissions to groups of users who have similar functions than it is to manage individual accounts. The security architecture of SQL Server 2000 includes *roles* to make assigning permissions easier. Roles work much like groups in Windows NT/2000, but are defined based on the specific function of an individual. For example, if you have several users who should be able to view but not modify employee records, you may want to create a role called Employee Record Viewers. Another useful feature of roles is that they can contain other roles. So, for example, you might create multiple roles based on users' job functions (such as "Engineering," "Research," "Development," "Sales," and "Marketing"). Each of these roles could provide only minimal access that is required by all users that have these job functions. Then, within each of the roles, you could create roles that provide additional permissions. For example, the Engineering role may contain an "Engineering Administrators" role, which provides additional permissions.

The overall process for taking advantage of SQL Server 2000's security architecture is to define roles, assign users to roles, and then grant permissions to these roles, as shown in Figure 8-2. SQL Server logins are mapped to database user accounts. The user accounts are then added to one or more roles, and the roles themselves are granted specific object permissions.

exam
ⓦatch

Since the usage of roles is such an important practice in the real world, be sure you thoroughly understand how roles work and interact. This is especially true if you don't normally take advantage of database-level security on your SQL Server 2000 installations.

Types of Roles

SQL Server supports several different types of roles. Table 8-1 lists the different types of roles and describes the purpose of each.

With a high-level overview of the types of SQL Server roles that are available, let's drill down into the details of each of these types of roles.

FIGURE 8-2

Using roles to
manage security

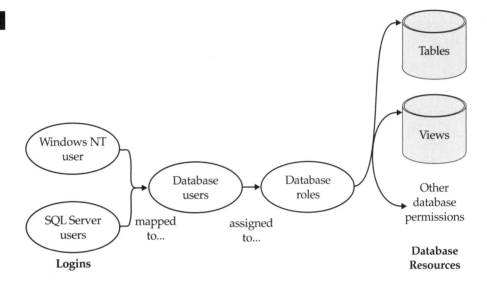

TABLE 8-1

Various Types of
SQL Server Roles

Type of Role	Function	Application
Fixed Server	Allows management of SQL Server configuration, including objects, alerts, tasks, and devices	Configuration and maintenance of the database server
Fixed Database	Allows specific database functions	Configuration and maintenance of databases
Public	Includes all users with permissions to access a database	Providing default access permissions to any user who can access the database
User-Defined Database	Provides group-based database-level permissions	Granting specific permissions to groups of users
Application	Used by a single application	Supporting applications that perform their own security control; requires a separate password

Server Roles

Database administration encompasses many different types of actions that are necessary to ensure that information is always available and that data is properly backed up. At the server level, you'll need to delegate specific tasks. Many maintenance functions are required to keep a SQL Server database operational. Managing backups, logins, and security accounts are important concerns. For small installations, it is likely that a single individual will be responsible for all of these tasks. In larger environments, however, it is more desirable to assign specific tasks to specific users. For example, one database administrator may be in charge of creating and modifying user accounts for multiple servers, while another may be responsible for managing backups on all servers.

This raises the important point about security. In the simplest implementation, you could grant all of these users full permissions on your database servers. However, this gives database administrators more permissions than they really need (generally, a bad security practice). To address this issue, SQL Server 2000 provides fixed, built-in server roles that have been created for making this process much easier. Table 8-2 lists the different server roles and their functions.

TABLE 8-2	Role	Username	Function
SQL Server 2000 Server Roles and Their Functions	Bulk Insert Administrators	Bulkadmin	Can perform BULK INSERT operations
	Database Creators	Dbcreator	Creates, alters, and resizes databases
	Disk Administrators	Diskadmin	Manages database storage files
	Process Administrators	Processadmin	Kills (stops) processes running on the server
	Security Administrators	Securityadmin	Creates and manages server logins and auditing
	Server Administrators	Serveradmin	Changes server configuration parameters and shuts down server
	Setup Administrators	Setupadmin	Manages replication, linked server configuration, some system stored procedures, and extended procedures
	System Administrators	Sysadmin	Completes control over all database functions

FIGURE 8-3

Viewing
permissions
for the Server
Administrators
server role

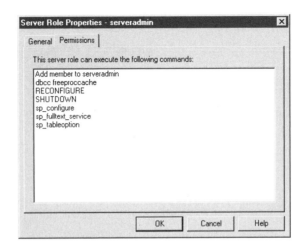

You can easily view the detailed permissions for server roles in Enterprise Manager by right-clicking the server role name, selecting Properties, and then choosing the Permissions tab (see Figure 8-3). Note that fixed server roles really are "fixed." That is, you cannot change actual permissions that are granted to members of fixed server roles, and you cannot create or delete this type of role.

Upon installation of SQL Server 2000, only the System Administrators role contains accounts. The members of this role include the Windows NT/2000 Administrators group and the SQL Server sa account. Also, note that members of each of the roles are allowed to assign the permissions of their role to another user account. For example, a user who is a member of the Setup Administrators role can add another user to this role. You can add user accounts to logins when they are created by accessing the Server Roles tab of the SQL Server Login Properties dialog box.

To add existing logins to server roles, use the following steps.

EXERCISE 8-5

CertCam 8-5

Adding Logins to Server Roles

1. In Enterprise Manager, expand the Security folder for the server you want to modify.

2. Click on Server Roles and then double-click the name of a server role in the right panel and click Add.

3. Highlight users to assign them to this role.

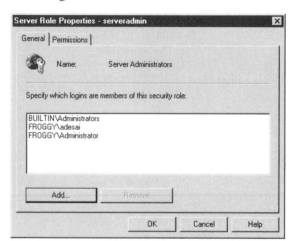

Application Roles

When it comes to designing and implementing security for real-world applications, there are several different methods that can be used. In the past, some applications might have relied only on database-level security. Every user that logged on to an application, for example, could access only the data that the database server allowed them to see. The application itself would pass the burden of managing permissions to the level of the database. From an administration standpoint, this can be very time-consuming and difficult to administer.

Large and complex database applications often enforce their own security based on business rules that are stored and enforced within the application itself. For example, an accounting package might enforce security permissions that allow a specific user to update a database only during specific hours. The application itself will use a single login and password that has access permissions to obtain and modify any data within a database. In order to secure the data, program logic within the application itself is used to determine which users can see which information.

In this type of security model, programs can use an application role to access the data it needs. Regardless of the authentication mode selected for server logins, application roles require the use of a login name, username, and password to access database information. By doing this, you can prevent DBAs from having to manage multiple accounts on the database level, and allow more complex security management within the application logic. The following exercise walks you through the process of creating a new application role.

on the Job

For highly secure applications, some implementers may want to take advantage of both application-level and database-level security. This provides the added advantage of protecting against the failure or misconfiguration of one or the other type of security. It comes at a price, however, as administrators may have to make changes in two places.

EXERCISE 8-6

Creating a New Application Role

1. In Enterprise Manager, expand the folder for the database in which you want to create a new login.

2. Right-click the Roles object and select New Role.

3. Enter a name for the application role (for example, **Accounting System**).

4. For the database role type, select Application role. Note that you will have to provide a password for this role. Enter a password that the application will use to access SQL Server and then click OK to create the application role.

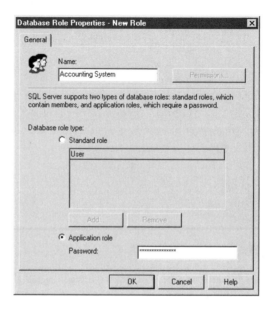

Once an application role has been created, applications can use it by first logging in to the SQL Server and then using the sp_setapprole system stored procedure (more information about security-related stored procedures is located in the section titled "Managing Security Using Transact-SQL," later in this chapter).

Database Roles

Within databases, users will be required to carry out specific functions. For small databases, a single individual might be responsible for all maintenance and administration. Large databases, on the other hand, will require that multiple users manage specific aspects of the configuration. To make managing permissions easier, SQL Server includes built-in database roles that allow administrators to easily assign only the permissions necessary for completing specific tasks. Table 8-3 lists the built-in roles generated for new databases.

Users can be assigned to any of these roles based on the requirements of their job functions. By default, whenever a user creates a database object, he or she is defined as the owner of that object. Other users with appropriate permissions may change database ownership. To remove a database owner, you must first either drop any objects owned by the user or transfer ownership to another user or role.

	Role	Permissions
TABLE 8-3 SQL Server 2000 Database Roles and Their Permissions	db_owner	Has full control of the database and its objects, as well as other maintenance and configuration activities
	db_accessadmin	Can add or remove Windows NT/2000 groups, Windows NT/2000 users, and SQL Server users in the database
	db_datareader	Can see any data from all user tables in the database
	db_datawriter	Can add, change, or delete data from all user tables in the database
	db_ddladmin	Can perform Data Definition Language (DDL) operations to add, modify, or drop objects in the database
	db_securityadmin	Can manage roles and members of SQL Server database roles, and can manage statement and object permissions in the database
	db_backupoperator	Can back up the database
	db_denydatareader	Cannot see any data in the database, but can make schema changes
	db_denydatawriter	Cannot change any data in the database
	Public	All users will automatically be members of the public role, and membership cannot be changed; default permissions on database objects are often placed on the public role

You can easily modify the membership of roles in different ways. First, in Enterprise Manager, you can access the Roles object within a database. By clicking the Add button, you can choose which users will be members of this role. Alternatively, you can view the properties of a database user and can simply check or uncheck database role membership options (see Figure 8-4).

User-Defined Database Roles

It's likely that the built-in database roles will cover many of your requirements. You can, however, create custom roles for common tasks that are performed within a database. With user-defined database roles, you can group users who have access to perform specific functions on tables, views, and other objects.

FIGURE 8-4

Modifying
database role
membership for
a user object

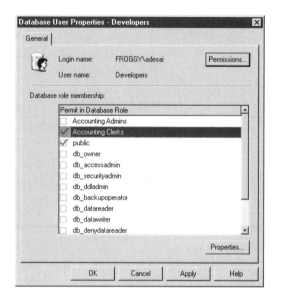

To create a new user-defined database role, follow these steps:

EXERCISE 8-7

Creating a User-Defined Database Role

1. In Enterprise Manager, expand the database in which you want to create a role.

2. Right-click Roles and select New Database Role.

3. For the Database Role Type, select Standard Role. Click Add to assign existing database users to this role. If you choose to make this an application role, it must be assigned a password.

4. Optionally, to change the permissions for the role, click the Permissions button. Using this dialog box, you'll be able to control exactly which objects are accessible to members of the role, along with the permissions they'll have.

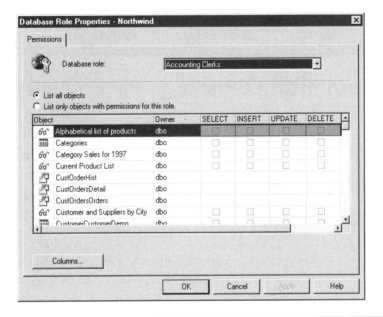

Once a role is created, you can assign users to it. A user can be assigned to multiple roles according to the needed permissions. To add users to an existing role, expand the Database Roles folder within a database. Double-click an existing role and use the Add and Remove buttons to change assigned users. All users who are members of a role will inherit any permissions assigned to the role itself. Keep in mind that permissions are cumulative, with one exception: if a user is denied permissions at the user level or in any role, he or she will not have this permission regardless of other role permissions.

SCENARIO & SOLUTION

You want all users that have access to your database to have specific permissions.	Assign permissions to the Public database role.
You want two user accounts to have full permissions for all objects within a single database on your SQL Server machine.	Assign the users to the db_owner (dbo) database role.
You want to prevent users from modifying any data or objects within a database.	Assign the users to the deny_datawriter database role.

Implementing Object-Level Security

So far, we've covered the steps that are necessary for creating server logins and databases. We also covered how you can use roles to simplify the administration of security. The final level of security—and the most granular—is at the actual level of SQL Server objects, such as tables, views, and stored procedures.

For managing security on database objects and actions, SQL Server supports three types of permissions; these are listed in Table 8-4. In this section, we'll examine these types of permissions in more detail.

exam
ⓦatch

By now, you've probably noticed that there are many different terms related to SQL Server security and that security can be assigned at multiple levels. Before you take the exam, be sure you understand the interactions of different types of permissions (for example, logins vs. database roles vs. object permissions).

Statement Permissions

Before user accounts and roles can be useful, you must assign them permissions on specific database objects. These permissions are called *statement permissions* because they control the types of commands that can be executed against database objects. The permissions possible for database objects are listed in Table 8-5

For more detailed security, you can also place SELECT and UPDATE permissions on specific columns within a database object. All database users will be members of the Public role by default, and this membership cannot be changed. This role permits them to perform functions that do not require specific permissions and to access any database via the Guest account (unless it is removed). You can define permissions by

TABLE 8-4	Type of Permission	Associated Functions
Types of Permissions in SQL Server	Statement permissions	Creating and modifying databases
	Object permissions	Executing queries that display and modify database objects
	Predefined (role-based) permissions	Tasks specific to fixed roles and object owners

TABLE 8-5	Statement	Types of Object	Function
Database Object Permissions	SELECT	Tables and views	Reads data from an existing database row
	UPDATE	Tables and views	Modifies data in an existing database row
	INSERT	Tables and views	Creates a new database row
	DELETE	Tables and views	Removes an existing row from a database
	Declarative referential integrity (DRI)	Tables	Allows users of other tables to refer to a key in the active table without having explicit permissions to view or modify that key directly
	Execute stored procedures	Stored procedures	Causes statements to execute with the permissions of the stored procedure's owner, not the executing user account

viewing either user information or database object information. To add or modify permissions for a specific database object, use the following procedure.

EXERCISE 8-8

Setting Object Permissions in Enterprise Manager

1. In Enterprise Manager, expand the database for which you want to modify permissions.

2. Expand the folder for the type of object you want to assign permissions (such as Views).

3. Right-click the name of an object, and select Properties and click Permissions. Here you can choose to list all users and roles, or just those who currently have access to the database. Note that you can further restrict permissions by clicking the Columns button. This will allow you to place permissions on specific database columns.

4. Place a check mark next to the permissions you want to grant to these database users. The meanings of the available settings are listed here.

Setting	Symbol	Meaning
Grant	Check mark	The user has permissions.
Deny	Red X	The user does not have permissions.
Revoke	Blank	Unspecified (the user can inherit permissions).

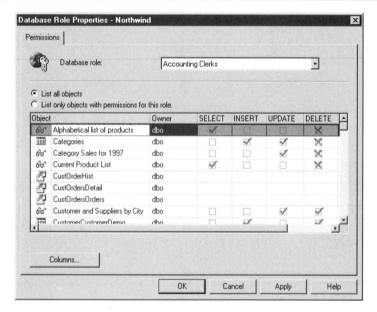

5. When finished setting permissions, click OK to make the settings take effect.

To modify permissions on a per-user basis, double-click a username in the Database Users folder within a database. Click Permissions to view the security settings for this user. In general, permissions are *additive*. That is, if a user is a member of one group that is allowed SELECT permissions on an object and another that is allowed INSERT and DELETE permissions, he or she will effectively have all three of these permissions on the object. However, if a user is a member of any group that is explicitly denied permissions to a resource, this setting overrides any other permissions. In this case, the user will not be able to perform the action until he or she is removed from the group that is denied access.

Permissions can also be set with the GRANT, REVOKE, and DENY statements using a SQL query tool. For example, the following statements grant SELECT permissions on the Employee table to the HR group and deny SELECT permissions to the Staff group:

```
GRANT SELECT ON Employee TO HR
DENY SELECT ON Employee TO Staff
```

By default, the sysadmin, db_securityadmin, and db_owner roles have permissions to perform these functions. All permissions information is stored in the Sysprotects system table. When a user executes a query or transaction, SQL Server checks for appropriate permissions in this table. Again, permissions are cumulative unless they are specifically denied. For example, if John is a member of Group 1 (which has SELECT permissions) and Group 2 (which has UPDATE permissions), he will be able to perform both functions. However, if he is also a member of Group 3 (which is denied SELECT permissions), he will be unable to query information from the object. In this case, he will receive an error message stating that he does not have sufficient permissions to execute the query or transaction.

Auditing

Though it won't necessarily prevent users from modifying information, auditing can be a very powerful security tool. SQL Server 2000 lets you automatically log actions performed by users on specific database objects. Although technically it won't prevent wrongdoing or protect data directly, auditing is a vital function of any secure database server implementation. Earlier in this chapter, we looked at how you can enable auditing of logons to SQL Server. To view auditing information, use the following procedure.

EXERCISE 8-9

Viewing Auditing Information in Enterprise Manager

1. Expand the Management folder for the server for which you want to view the audit logs.

2. In the SQL Server Logs folder, click the current log to view the most recent information, or click an archive log to view older data.

3. You can modify the view by clicking the log name and selecting View. You can also click a column heading to sort by that value.

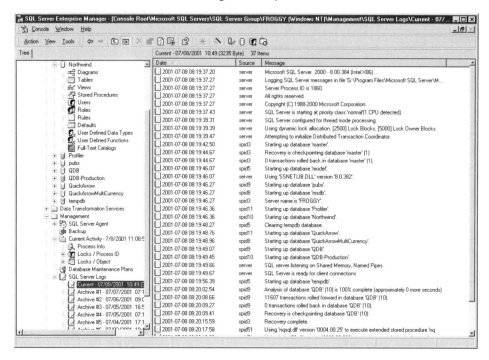

The information displayed includes the date and time of the logged item, the process ID that generated the event, and the text of the logged message. One of the most difficult parts of regularly reviewing audit logs is that there is a lot of information that is not necessarily important. To find what you're really looking for, be sure to use the filtering features in Enterprise Manager.

Specifying Auditing Settings with Alerts

In addition to the default alerts, you can track other actions of interest. You can log specific information by configuring SQL Server alerts in the SQL Server Agent alerts option. To set an alert, use the following procedure.

EXERCISE 8-10

Specifying Auditing Settings Using Alerts

1. Expand the Management folder. Expand the SQL Server Agent folder, right-click Alerts, and select New Alert. You'll see this dialog box:

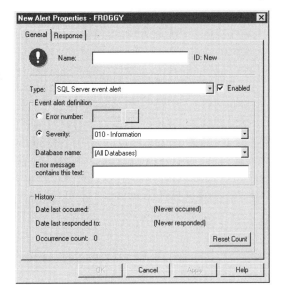

2. Name the alert and choose SQL Server Event Alert for the Type. Make sure that the Enabled check box is enabled.

3. To define the alert condition, choose to report on an error message number (which may be user defined) or on all events that have a specific severity. You can also assign the alert to only a specific database. Finally, enter the text for the error message.

4. Optionally, you can use the settings on the Response tab to notify database administrators of problems. Click OK to accept the settings.

Viewing the Activity Log

Setting auditing is important, but it is useless if the audit logs are not regularly reviewed for suspicious activity. The activity logs can contain a lot of information, making it difficult to find exactly what you're looking for. To find a specific event, you can select Tools | Manage SQL Server Messages within Enterprise Manager. You can specify text to search for, and you can restrict the search to specific error numbers or severity levels (see Figure 8-5). Once you have entered your search criteria, click Find to view the matching items.

Server messages are also written to the Windows NT/2000 application log, and can be viewed using the Event Viewer application.

Sometimes, you just want to get a quick snapshot of who's using the server and for what purpose. You can view current database activity by selecting Management | Current Activity | Process Info in Enterprise Manager. From this view, shown in Figure 8-6, you can find out which users are logged in to the database server, what operations are being performed, and which objects are currently locked. There are options to send a message to a connected user and to kill a specific process (if you have permissions).

FIGURE 8-5

Searching for activity log information in Enterprise Manager

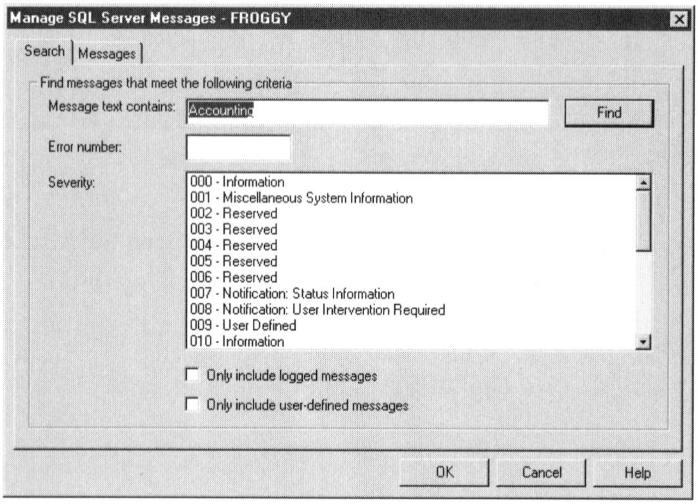

FIGURE 8-6

Viewing current database activity using Enterprise Manager

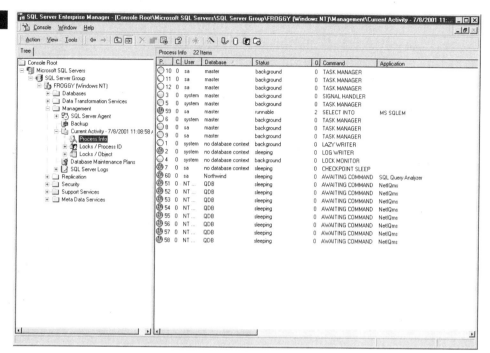

CERTIFICATION OBJECTIVE 8.04

Controlling Data Access

From a database security standpoint, working with databases that have many objects can be difficult. So far, we've discussed how you can control access to your database servers and how you can implement permissions on database objects such as tables and views. However, this is much easier said than done if your databases have hundreds of tables and have complex business rules. Clearly, it is possible to set permissions on each of these tables directly. However, there are problems with this method.

First, it's a tedious and time-consuming process to implement specific permissions for each of the roles or users to which you need to assign permissions. Second, it's an error-prone process (you're likely to overlook some portions of the database), and it's a maintenance nightmare (every time new objects are created, you must be absolutely sure that you set the appropriate permissions on them). Finally, there's still a limitation with the assignment of permissions to tables: it's difficult to restrict access to only specific columns, or to certain data values (for example, return only expenses that total less than $500). If you think that there must be a better way, there's good news in store for you!

Using Database Objects for Security

You can apply permissions on various types of database objects to better manage and enforce security. The general practice is to prevent users from accessing base tables in the database directly. Instead, they will be given permissions on other database objects that, in turn, will allow them to access the data that they need. Here are some ways in which you can use various database objects to implement security:

- **Views**   Perhaps the most commonly used method of controlling data access is views. We have discussed the many advantages of using views throughout this book, but from a security standpoint, they can be very valuable. For example, you can create a view that shows basic information about employees, but that excludes sensitive data like their salaries and Social Security numbers. Or, you could define a view that allows users to see data for only particular employees within the company (for example, only the employees that they manage). Then, you can assign object-level permissions to the view. Users of the database can then use the view to access whatever information they require. Should security changes be required (if you added a FavoriteColor column, for example), you can simply change the results of the view, and all authorized users will be able to see this value in their result set. Furthermore, views can query other views, thereby creating a chain of objects based on business rules. When portions of the logic change, only some of the views may be affected.

- **Stored procedures**   Database developers can use the power of stored procedures to perform many different types of operations using Transact-SQL. For example, stored procedures might be used for allowing certain users to update specific information within the database. Instead of giving direct access to modify data stored in base tables (which in some cases might be too liberal, or your users may not completely understand how to modify the data), you can give access to stored procedures. For example, a stored procedure called PROC_UpdateInventoryStatus might be used to allow specific users to update only inventory count information within a table.

■ **Triggers**   Instead of having end users perform certain actions performed directly by users within the database, you can create triggers to enforce the logic automatically. From a security standpoint, triggers can be used to perform the types of actions that you can't rely on users to perform. For example, suppose you want to automatically write a row to the ManagerEvent table whenever an expense of greater than $500 is input into the Expense table. One way of doing this would be to create a stored procedure that performs both updates. Another would be to create a trigger on the Expense table that automatically makes the corresponding change in the ManagerEvent table. In this way, you can secure access to the ManagerEvent table (that is, no users would be given direct access to it), while still allowing users to update expense information.

■ **User-defined functions**   Functions can operate in different ways within a database. You can create functions that return scalar data values, or you can create functions that return a table datatype. If you encapsulate some forms of business logic in functions, you can make it easy for users to access, and you can make it easier for users to get the information that they need. For example, your organization might create a function called FUNC_CalculateMarkup to determine the retail price of an object that you sell based on the cost of the object to your organization. You could then assign permissions to the function, and even users that don't have access to the base tables or business logic information will be able to calculate these values. You can also use functions similar to the way you use views for security. That is, the function can return a table datatype, and the results can be used as is or within the FROM clause of a query. Again, you can simply assign permissions to the function and prevent access to the underlying base tables.

EXERCISE 8-11

CertCam 8-11

Creating and Assigning Permissions to a View

1. In Enterprise Manager, expand the database object for the Northwind sample database. Right-click Views and select New View.

2. In the SQL Text pane, type the following SQL statement:

```
SELECT *
FROM Customers
WHERE Country = 'USA'
```

This statement will create a new view that returns a list of only the customers that are located within the United States.

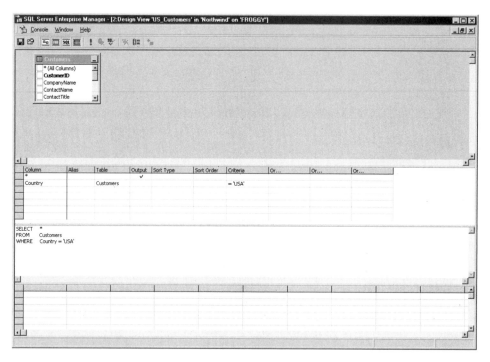

3. Click the Save icon to save the view. When prompted, name the view **US_Customers**, and click OK. Close the View Design window.

4. In Enterprise Manager, right-click the US_Customers view and select Properties. Click the Permissions button to view the permissions for the view.

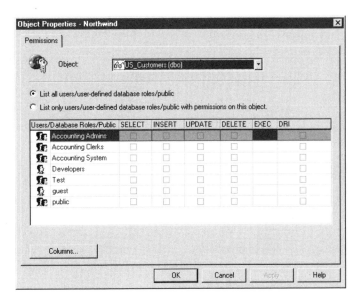

5. You will see a list of the users that have access to this view, along with their permissions on the view. Click the boxes to grant, revoke, or deny permissions for specific users. Note that you can also click the Columns button to view column-level permissions for various users.

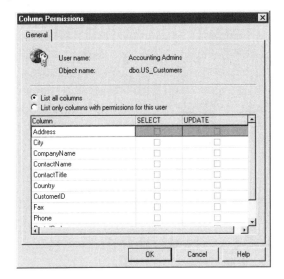

6. When you have finished setting permissions, click OK to close the Permissions dialog box.

Now that we've seen how database objects can be used to enforce security, let's look at some other important security considerations.

Applying Ownership Chains

So far, we have discussed the ideas related to how various database objects can be used to restrict access to others (mainly, to restrict direct access to database tables). One of the effects of creating objects that refer to other objects deals with the actual calculation of security permissions. The resulting set of effective permissions is referred to as an *ownership chain*. Ownership chains apply when users attempt to perform a SELECT, INSERT, UPDATE, or DELETE operation. When this occurs, SQL Server must determine whether or not the user has permissions to execute the statement.

The simplest case of an ownership chain is one in which the same user owns all referenced objects. For example, suppose a stored procedure created by User1 refers to a table, a stored procedure, and a view that is also owned by the User1. User1 then gives permissions to User2 to use the stored procedure. In this case, SQL Server must only check the permissions on the base stored procedure upon which permissions are set in order to determine whether or not User2 can perform the operation. This is sometimes referred to as an *unbroken* ownership chain (see Figure 8-7).

A more complicated situation arises when some of the objects referenced by a stored procedure or other object are owned by other users. For an example, see Figure 8-8. In this scenario, the base object, Procedure1, is owned by User1. However, the objects referenced by this procedure are owned by User2 and User3. If User1 were to give permissions to User4 on Procedure1, SQL Server would have to check the permissions on all underlying objects (as well as the base object) before it could allow User4 to perform actions on the stored procedure. User4's effective permissions on Procedure1 would be based on the combination of all permissions on the underlying objects.

Permissions Best Practices

Setting permissions on database objects can be quite complicated if you don't fully understand the implications of the settings. Major concerns should include the level

FIGURE 8-7

An unbroken
ownership chain

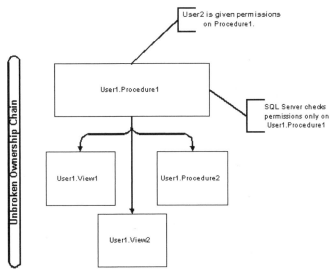

Object names are presented as ObjectOwner.ObjectName

FIGURE 8-8

A broken
ownership chain

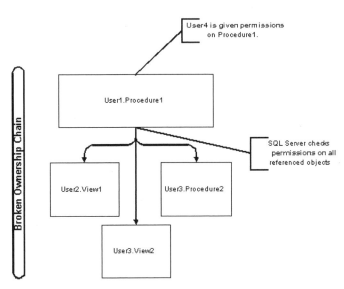

Object names are presented as ObjectOwner.ObjectName

of security provided, the ease of implementation, and the ease of administration. In general, there are several good ways to manage permissions in databases of any size:

- **Use roles to grant permissions.** Managing permissions through the use of roles is much easier than granting permissions to individual users. Roles should be designed based on specific job functions and should provide only necessary permissions.

- **Create a hierarchical role system.** Some users may require basic read access to specific tables, while others will require full access to some tables and only read access to others. Since roles can be contained in other roles, it might be worthwhile to create groups such as Employee Admins, Customer Admins, and Order Admins. Each of these roles could contain permissions specific to operations on areas of your database. Users that require access to multiple areas should be assigned to multiple roles.

- **Use stored procedures.** Apart from security management benefits, stored procedures execute much faster than the same SQL statements executed manually, and can thus cut down on network traffic. They also make interactions with database objects easier for developers and end users. By applying permissions on stored procedures (instead of the underlying objects), you can better encapsulate your business logic. This will make it easier and more secure for users to perform tasks, and it abstracts the underlying complexity of the database. For example, a stored procedure called proc_EnterNewOrder could reference several tables, views, and stored procedures to ensure that the transaction is properly completed.

- **Avoid assigning permissions directly on tables.** If your database contains an employee information table that includes basic information (such as employee names and employee numbers) and sensitive information (such as salary figures), you may choose to create a view or stored procedure that does not return sensitive data. As long as the view owner has access to the table, the user of the view will be able to access all of the data in the table. You can deny everyone access to the table except for the owner of the view or stored procedure. You can then grant users access to the view or stored procedure without worrying that they will query sensitive information.

Managing Security Using Transact-SQL

The majority of examples in this chapter have focused on the use of Enterprise Manager to create and define security permissions. As you may have guessed, the same tasks can also be performed through the use of Transact-SQL. Table 8-6 lists some of the security-related stored procedures and their functions. For a complete list of system-stored procedures and details about syntax of these commands, see the SQL Server 2000 Books Online.

These system-stored procedures offer you the ability to programmatically create and administer database-level security settings. For example, your application may want to handle the creation of new database users, or may want to change database permissions based on business rules. This can all be performed very easily through the use of stored procedures.

on the Job *The ability to script security settings can be very valuable in the real world. For example, if you need to create a large list of users, you can use Transact-SQL scripts to read the usernames (from a text file, for example), and to then create the logins using simple stored procedures. The result is much faster and more accurate than the tedious alternative—manual reentry of the appropriate accounts.*

SQL Server Security Best Practices

When dealing with database security, fitting the settings to your business requirements should be of the utmost concern. In dealing with SQL Server 2000 settings, the following measures are recommended:

- If you're using mixed-mode authentication, you should always choose to assign a strong password for the sa account during installation. Also, remember that members of the Windows NT/2000 Administrators group are automatically given the same permissions as the sa account.

- The default TCP/IP port used by SQL Server is 1433. Potential hackers will often scan for this port to find out which SQL Servers are running in your environment. Though this isn't a security breach in itself, finding the SQL Server installations in your environment may be the first step toward a hack attempt (especially on the Internet). You should use the Server Network

| TABLE 8-6 | Useful Security-Related System-Stored Procedures |

System-Stored Procedure	Purpose	Notes
sp_addapprole, sp_dropapprole	Creates or drops application roles	
sp_addlogin, sp_droplogin	Creates and deletes new logins based on SQL Server authentication	Can be used to create or delete logins if the server supports mixed-mode authentication
sp_addrolemember, sp_droprolemember	Adds or removes users from database roles	
sp_changedbowner	Changes the ownership of a database	
sp_changeobjectowner	Changes the ownership of database objects	
sp_defaultdb	Sets the default database for a user account	The default database is the one to which a user will automatically connect upon login to the server
sp_grantdbaccess, sp_revokedbaccess	Grants or revokes permissions to log in to specific databases for server logins	
sp_grantlogin, sp_revokelogin	Maps logins to Windows NT/2000 users or groups	Can be used to map Windows NT/2000 security accounts to SQL Server security if the server is running in either mixed mode or Windows authentication mode
sp_helpgroup, sp_helplogins, sp_helpntgroup, sp_helprole, sp_helprolemember, sp_helpprotect, sp_helpuser	Views security-related information for SQL Server users	
sp_password	Changes the password for a login	
sp_setapprole	Instructs the current login to assume the permissions of an application role	Useful for supported programs that take advantage of application roles within a database
sp_validatelogins	Validates mappings between Windows NT/2000 accounts and SQL Server logins	This stored procedure is useful for ensuring that the SQL Server doesn't support "orphaned" logins
sp_who, sp_who2	Displays information about the processes that are active in SQL Server	sp_who2 provides more information, including to which database each process is connected

Utility and Client Network Utility tools to change the default port to another value.

■ You should make the password for the SQL Server service accounts very difficult to guess. You'll rarely need to use this account to log in, and if you do, any administrator can always change the password. This will prevent users from accessing your networked systems using the SQL Server service accounts.

CERTIFICATION SUMMARY

In this chapter, we took an in-depth look at the security architecture of SQL Server 2000, and how you can use various SQL Server 2000 tools to implement and manage permissions based on your business requirements. We started by first examining the purpose of SQL Server logins. Then, we looked at the details of implementing database-level security, including users and roles. Finally, we covered the details of working with object-level permissions and the process of setting permissions on objects. With all of these concepts in mind, you should be able to effectively design and implement an easy-to-manage SQL Server security model.

TWO-MINUTE DRILL

Understanding and Implementing SQL Server Security

❑ Users must have a SQL Server login before they can connect to SQL Server 2000.

❑ SQL Server 2000 can be run in Windows authentication or mixed-mode authentication modes.

❑ Mixed-mode authentication allows administrators to create SQL Server–based logins that consist of a username and a password.

❑ Windows authentication requires administrators to map Windows NT/2000 security accounts to SQL Server logins.

❑ Users must be assigned permissions to access specific databases in order to connect to a database.

Implementing Database-Level Security

❑ Database users are based on SQL Server logins and are used to specify permissions settings.

❑ There are several fixed server roles that are available on all installations of SQL Server 2000. These roles provide users with specific permissions that allow server administration tasks to be performed.

❑ Application roles can be used by an application to gain full access to a SQL Server 2000 database. Regardless of the authentication model, application roles are assigned a password by the administrator.

❑ There are several fixed database roles that can be used for administering permissions within a database. In addition, user-defined roles can be created to better administer security.

❑ A recommended security practice is to assign users to roles and to then assign actual permissions to the roles.

Implementing Object-Level Security

❑ Statement-level permissions control the types of actions that database users can perform.

❑ Statement-level permissions include SELECT, UPDATE, INSERT, DELETE, DRI, and EXECUTE.

❑ Auditing can be used to record specific actions that are taken by users.

❑ Auditing information can be viewed using Enterprise Manager or by using the Event Viewer administrator tool.

❑ Object-level permissions settings include GRANT, REVOKE, and DENY.

Controlling Data Access

❑ Database objects such as views, stored procedures, user-defined functions, and triggers can be used to increase SQL Server security.

❑ A recommended security practice is to assign permissions to database objects such as views and stored procedures instead of directly to base tables, as this provides more flexibility in security administration.

❑ Ownership chains are used by SQL Server to calculate the effective permissions users should have on various database objects.

❑ Several system-stored procedures can be used to view and modify database security settings.

❑ For ease of administration, it is recommended that you create a hierarchical system of roles and then assign permissions to these roles.

SELF TEST

Understanding and Implementing SQL Server Security

1. You are configuring a new installation of SQL Server 2000 for your Accounting group. You want to support clients that are running non-Windows operating systems, and you want to take advantage of Windows authentication. Which of the following security modes will meet these requirements?

   A. Windows authentication

   B. SQL Server authentication

   C. Mixed-mode authentication

   D. None of the above

2. Which of the following icons in Enterprise Manager will allow you to view auditing information?

   A. Management | Current Activity | Process Info

   B. Management | SQL Server Logs

   C. Management | Current Activity | Locks/Objects

   D. Security | Logins

   E. Security | Server Roles

3. When using Windows authentication, based on which of the following can SQL Server logins be created? (Choose all that apply.)

   A. Usernames and passwords assigned by the administration

   B. Windows NT/2000 domain groups

   C. Local computer groups

   D. Windows NT/2000 users

   E. Active Directory users

4. You are configuring a new installation of SQL Server 2000 for your Engineering group. All supported users are using Windows-based machines and have Windows 2000 Active Directory domain accounts. You want to choose the most secure method for allowing access to your SQL Server 2000 installation. Which of the following security modes will meet these requirements?

   A. Windows authentication

   B. SQL Server authentication

C. Mixed-mode authentication

D. None of the above

Implementing Database-Level Security

5. Which of the following types of roles is designed to allow specific programs to gain full access to a SQL Server 2000 database?

A. Fixed database role

B. User-defined database role

C. Fixed server role

D. Application role

6. You want to provide Andrew with full permissions to all objects within a specific database, but you want to provide him with only the required permissions. To which of the following roles should his login be added?

A. System Administrators

B. Security Administrators

C. db_ddladmin

D. db_owner

E. None of the above

7. A database role can contain which of the following types of objects? (Choose all that apply.)

A. Database users

B. Server logins

C. Fixed server roles

D. Database roles

8. Which of the following fixed server roles has members immediately following a new installation of SQL Server 2000. (Choose all that apply.)

A. Server Administrators

B. Backup Administrators

C. Disk Administrators

D. System Administrators

Implementing Object-Level Security

9. Which of the following features of SQL Server 2000 can you use to specify which types of actions are audited?

A. Current activity

B. Performance Monitor

C. Alerts

D. sp_who

10. Which of the following permissions settings has no effect on permissions for an object?

A. GRANT

B. DENY

C. REVOKE

D. None of the above

11. You want to allow Anita, a user of the Marketing database, to add new information to the Prospects table. She should not be able to modify any existing data in the table. Which of the following permissions should she have? (Choose all that apply.)

A. SELECT

B. INSERT

C. UPDATE

D. DELETE

E. EXECUTE

12. You want to determine which users are currently connected to SQL Server 2000 and to which databases they're connected. Which of the following can you use to easily determine this information? (Choose all that apply.)

A. Current activity in Enterprise Manager

B. Event Viewer

C. Performance Monitor

D. sp_who2

Controlling Data Access

13. Paul creates a new database object that results in a broken ownership chain. At least one of the objects referenced by the database object is owned by which of the following users?

 A. Paul

 B. Another database user

 C. A member of the dbo role

 D. None of the above

14. SQL Server is attempting to calculate the effective permissions on Procedure1, an object that refers to other objects. Procedure1 refers to View1, View2, and Table1. The relationships between the objects form an unbroken ownership chain. For which of the following objects must SQL Server check security settings in order to determine the effective permissions for a user that is given access to Procedure1? (Choose all that apply.)

 A. Procedure1

 B. View1

 C. View2

 D. Table1

 E. None of the above

15. You want to create several hundred SQL Server logins based on the account information stored in a database table. Which of the following is the easiest way to perform this task?

 A. Use Enterprise Manager to create the accounts.

 B. Import the list of users using Data Transformation Services.

 C. Use Transact-SQL and system stored procedures to create the new logins.

 D. Directly modify the system tables in the master database.

16. Monica has created a script that relies on the use of the sp_addlogin stored procedure to create new user accounts. In order for this script to execute properly, the installation of SQL Server must be using which of the following security modes?

 A. Windows authentication.

 B. SQL Server authentication.

 C. Mixed-mode authentication.

 D. None of the above: sp_addlogin cannot be used from within a stored procedure.

17. SQL Server is attempting to calculate the effective permissions on Procedure1, an object that refers to other objects. Procedure1 refers to View1, View2, and Table1. The relationships between the objects form a broken ownership chain. For which of the following objects must SQL Server check security settings in order to determine the effective permissions for a user that is given access to Procedure1? (Choose all that apply.)

    A. Procedure1

    B. View1

    C. View2

    D. Table1

    E. None of the above

LAB QUESTION

You are responsible for designing the security model for your organization's payroll system. Since the data that will be stored by your application is very sensitive, security implementation and management is one of the top priorities. You have already gathered several requirements. Some of the details include the following:

- Users must be able to access data stored in the database from within a client/server application and through a Web-based application.

- There will be several different classes of users with varying levels of permissions. For example, Accounting Clerks, Accounting Administrators, and Reimbursement Staff will all require access to the information.

- Members of the Accounting department will need to have direct access to perform ad hoc queries on some database objects. This will be done primarily for the creation of custom reports at the database level.

- You will need to track when users are logging in to the database and which databases they access.

Based on these requirements, it's up to you to determine how you can best meet the security needs for your organization. The goals for the solution should include strength of security, ease of implementation, and ease of administration. Which features of SQL Server 2000 would you use to meet these requirements?

SELF TEST ANSWERS

Understanding and Implementing SQL Server Security

1. ☑ **C**. Mixed-mode authentication meets the requirements since it supports both Windows-based authentication and non-Windows clients through the use of SQL Server authentication.
   ☒ **B** is not an option for SQL Server's security mode, and **A** would not support non-Windows clients.

2. ☑ **B**. Auditing and other system-related information is stored within the SQL Server Logs. The contents of these logs can be easily viewed in Enterprise Manager.
   ☒ The other options are useful for monitoring other aspects of SQL Server's configuration, but they don't directly show auditing information.

3. ☑ **B, C, D**, and **E**. Windows authentication supports the use of all of these types of users/groups for creating SQL Server logins.
   ☒ **A** is incorrect because this type of authentication is only supported when SQL Server is running with mixed-mode authentication.

4. ☑ **A**. Since only support for Windows clients is required, Windows-based authentication is the most secure method.
   ☒ The other options do meet the requirement for the most secure solution.

Implementing Database-Level Security

5. ☑ **D**. Application roles are designed to support a single login for applications that manage their own security.
   ☒ The other types of roles are supported in SQL Server, but their primary purpose is not to support application logins.

6. ☑ **D**. A member of the db_owner role will have permissions to perform all operations within a database.
   ☒ The other choices are incorrect because they either provide too many permissions (**A** and **B**), or not enough (**C**).

7. ☑ **A** and **D**. Database roles can contain other roles or database users.
   ☒ Database roles cannot directly contain server logins, nor can they contain fixed server roles.

8. ☑ **D**. Only the System Administrators role has users automatically assigned to it after installation. The users include Domain and local Administrator accounts, as well as the sa account (if

mixed-mode authentication is selected).

☒ The other fixed server roles do not contain any members after installation.

Implementing Object-Level Security

9. ☑ C. Alerts can be used to configure which types of events cause the alert to fire, and one of the actions is for the alert to write auditing information.

☒ The other options allow you to view information about SQL Server, but they do not record or report auditing information.

10. ☑ D. All of these options have an effect on overall security permissions.

☒ All of these settings can have an effect on overall security.

11. ☑ B. With only INSERT permissions, Anita can only add new rows to the table.

☒ The other options would allow Anita to modify, delete, or query existing rows. Therefore, they do not meet the requirements.

none are specifically designed to allow the creation and modification of database objects.

12. ☑ A and D. Both the Current activity view in Enterprise Manager and the sp_who2 system stored procedure will display the desired information.

☒ The Event Viewer will not show current activity information, and the Performance Monitor only shows statistical information.

Controlling Data Access

13. ☑ B. Since the chain of ownership is broken, another user must own at least one of the referenced objects.

☒ The other options are incorrect because another user must own one of the objects.

14. ☑ A. Since the chain of ownership is unbroken, SQL Server must only verify permissions at the level of the object.

☒ SQL Server does not need to verify permissions for these lower-level objects since this is an unbroken chain of ownership.

15. ☑ C. System stored procedures and Transact-SQL code can be used to easily import the user information.

☒ The other options are not practical methods for importing the list of users.

16. ☑ C. Logins can only be created when SQL Server is running in mixed mode.
    ☒ The other options don't correctly explain the requirements,

17. ☑ **A, B, C**, and **D**. Since there is a broken chain of ownership, SQL Server must verify permissions for all of the referenced objects.
    ☒ SQL Server must check permissions on all of the referenced objects.

LAB ANSWER

The scenario that has been described might be a common one for many database implementers. As with many applications, security is a foremost concern. Fortunately, SQL Server 2000 includes many tools and functions for addressing security issues. Let's look at how you might choose to use them to solve this business challenge.

First, since the database must support a Web-based application and a client/server application, you need to determine how security will be managed. You might choose to have the client/server application manage business logic security. For this case, you would need to create only a single application role for use by the application. However, the application must also support Web-based access. You will probably need to create SQL Server 2000 roles in order to efficiently manage the types of permissions that are required.

Based on the types of users that will need access to the system, you should create roles based on job functions. For example, accounting administrators will have more authority, whereas accounting clerks might have only data entry permissions. Through the use of various objects, such as views and stored procedures, you can make sure that you can provide a very granular level of security. For example, accounting clerks may be able to see only the records that they have created themselves, whereas accounting administrators can see all records for the people that they manage.

SQL Server 2000's logon auditing is a perfect feature for supporting the requirement of recording when users access the system. You can also use the sp_who2 stored procedure or features in Enterprise Manager to view details about how your system is being accessed.

Through effective planning, you can take advantage of SQL Server 2000's security features to ensure that only authorized users can access specific data.

MICROSOFT CERTIFIED DATABASE ADMINISTRATOR

A

About the CD

This CD-ROM contains the CertTrainer software. CertTrainer comes complete with ExamSim, Skill Assessment tests, and the e-book (electronic version of the book). CertTrainer is easy to install on any Windows 98/NT/2000/XP computer and must be installed to access these features. You may, however, browse the e-book directly from the CD without installation.

Installing CertTrainer

If your computer CD-ROM drive is configured to autorun, the CD-ROM will automatically start up upon inserting the disk. From the opening screen you may either browse the e-book or install CertTrainer by pressing the Install Now button. This will begin the installation process and create a program group named "CertTrainer." To run CertTrainer use Start | Programs | CertTrainer.

System Requirements

CertTrainer requires Windows 98 or higher and Internet Explorer 4.0 or above and 600MB of hard disk space for full installation.

CertTrainer

CertTrainer provides a complete review of each exam objective, organized by chapter. You should read each objective summary and make certain that you understand it before proceeding to the SkillAssessment quiz. If you still need more practice on the concepts of any objective, use the In Depth button to link to the corresponding section from the Study Guide or review the various exercises from within the chapter.

Once you have completed the review(s) and feel comfortable with the material, launch the SkillAssessment quiz to test your grasp of each objective. Once you complete the quiz, you will be presented with your score for that chapter.

ExamSim

As its name implies, ExamSim provides you with a simulation of the actual exam. The number of questions, the type of questions, and the time allowed are intended to be an accurate representation of the exam environment. Launch ExamSim from the CertTrainer main menu after completing installation.

When you launch ExamSim, a digital clock display will appear in the upper left-hand corner of your screen. The clock will continue to count down to zero unless you choose to end the exam before the time expires.

There are two types of questions on the exam:

- **Multiple Choice**   These questions have a single correct answer that you indicate by selecting the appropriate check box.

- **Multiple-Multiple Choice**   These questions require more than one correct answer. Indicate each correct answer by selecting the appropriate check boxes.

Saving Scores as Cookies

Your ExamSim score is stored as a browser cookie. If you've configured your browser to accept cookies, your score will be stored in a file named History. If your browser is not configured to accept cookies, you cannot permanently save your scores. If you delete this History cookie, the scores will be deleted permanently.

E-Book

The entire contents of the Study Guide are provided in HTML. Although the files are optimized for Internet Explorer, they can also be viewed with other browsers, including Netscape.

CertCam

CertCam .AVI clips provide detailed examples of key certification objectives. These clips walk you step by step through various system configurations and are narrated by the authors. You can see which exercises in the book have been produced as CertCams by looking for the CertCam icon at the top of the exercise. You can also access the clips directly from the CertCam table of contents or through the CertTrainer objectives.

The CertCam .AVI clips are recorded and produced using TechSmith's Camtasia Producer. Since .AVI clips can be very large, ExamSim uses TechSmith's special AVI Codec to compress the clips. The file named tsccvid.dll is copied to your Windows\System folder when you install CertTrainer. If the .AVI clips run with audio but no video, you may need to reinstall the file from the CD-ROM. Browse to the bin folder, and run TSCC.EXE.

Help

A help file is provided through a help button on the main CertTrainer screen in the lower right-hand corner.

Upgrading

A button is provided on the main ExamSim screen for upgrades. This button will take you to www.syngress.com, where you can download any available upgrades.

MICROSOFT CERTIFIED DATABASE ADMINISTRATOR

B

About the
Web Site

A t Access.Globalknowledge, the premier online information source for IT professionals (http://access.globalknowledge.com), you'll enter a Global Knowledge information portal designed to inform, educate, and update visitors on issues regarding IT and IT education.

Get *What* You Want *When* You Want It

At the Access.Globalknowledge site, you can:

- Choose personalized technology articles related to your interests. Access a news article, a review, or a tutorial, customized to what you want to see, regularly throughout the week.

- Continue your education, in between Global courses, by taking advantage of chat sessions with other users or instructors. Get the tips, tricks, and advice that you need today!

- Make your point in the Access.Globalknowledge community by participating in threaded discussion groups related to technologies and certification.

- Get instant course information at your fingertips. Customized course calendars show you the courses you want, and when and where you want them.

- Obtain the resources you need with online tools, trivia, skills assessment, and more.

All this and more is available now on the Web at http://access.globalknowledge.com. Visit today!

MCDBA
MICROSOFT CERTIFIED DATABASE ADMINISTRATOR

Glossary

Aggregate Function   A function that is performed on column values in a set or subset of data, returning a single value. Examples include MIN, MAX, and AVG.

Alias   An alternate name assigned to a column or table name within a query or result set. Aliases are declared using the AS keyword.

Alerts   A defined response to a SQL Server event. Defined alerts are compared against events written to the Windows application log. When a match is found, the alert is executed.

ALTER (DDL)   The Data Definition Language command used to modify a database object. The database object must already exist in the system tables to be altered.

Alternate Key   An attribute that uniquely identifies rows of database table or entity, but does not serve as the primary key. When several candidate keys exist within an entity, the most logical is chosen to be the primary key. The remaining candidate keys become alternate keys.

American National Standards Institute (ANSI)   An organization that defines standards for the trade and communications industry. ANSI provides a standard for the database language of SQL, to promote compatibility and portability between database products.

Analysis Services   A set of tools provided with SQL Server 2000 that enhance online analytical processing and data warehousing. It allows multidimensional, historical data to be stored and queried

Application Programming Interface (API)   The means by which applications access SQL Server 2000. An API exposes functions and methods that a client application uses to communicate back and forth with the database engine. OLE-DB is an example of an API.

Attribute   In a logical data model, an attribute is a characteristic of an entity. Attributes in a data model are translated into table columns in the physical database. In an XML document, an attribute is a characteristic of an element.

Binary Large Object (BLOB)   Data of a very large size stored in binary format, such as graphic or audio files. BLOB datatypes in SQL Server include image, text, and ntext.

Blocking   A normal characteristic of a relational database system where one connection holds a lock on a resource and a second connection requests a lock on the resource of a conflicting type. Steps can be taken to minimize blocking, such as ensuring that transactions are kept as short as possible.

Bottleneck   The most direct source of a performance problem. Examples can include a lack of system memory, storage speed, and processor speed. Addressing a performance bottleneck will typically reveal a lesser bottleneck.

Bulk Copy Operation   The process of transferring a large amount of data into or out of a relational database table. Several methods exist to perform bulk copies, including BCP and the T-SQL BULK INSERT statement.

Bulk Copy Utility (BCP)   A command prompt utility used for importing data from datafiles into database tables, and from tables into datafiles.

Business Rule   A statement or rule about how a business is run. These rules are adhered to in the physical database using triggers, stored procedures and referential integrity, and constraints.

C2 Auditing   A government standard that dictates the level of auditing for a C2-compliant system. C2 auditing can be turned on in SQL Server 2000 to document successful and failed attempts to access database objects.

Candidate Key   An attribute or group of attributes in an entity that can uniquely identify each instance of the entity. When more than one candidate key exists, the most logical is chosen as primary key, and the remaining candidate keys become alternate keys.

Cardinality   A characteristic of a relationship that signifies how many instances of a particular entity relate to how many instances of a related entity. Examples of cardinality are one to one, one to many, and many to many.

Check Constraint A T-SQL clause that restricts the data values that may be stored in a table column. Check constraints are translated from the allowable values in a logical data model.

Checkpoint The process in which SQL Server writes modified data or log pages in the buffer cache to disk. Pages that have been modified in cache but have not yet been written to disk are known as "Dirty Pages." The checkpoint process clears all dirty pages from the buffer cache.

Clause Part of a T-SQL statement that in some way alters how the statement behaves. Examples of clauses are WHERE, HAVING, TOPn, and ON.

Index Clustering The process of using several server computers to spread processing load or for fail over capability. Windows 2000 Advanced server and Data Center server provide the ability to implement clusters.

Collation Determines how character data is sorted and compared. SQL Server 2000 supports defining collations to the column level within a single database.

Column The most atomic unit of storage within a database table. Columns are translated from attributes in the logical data model.

Commit T-SQL statement that saves all modifications made by the current transaction to the physical database. The alternative to COMMIT is ROLLBACK, which ensures that all changes made by the current transaction are not applied to the physical database.

Component Object Model (COM) An architecture specification for developing application components. COM is based on object oriented technology and is used by several APIs such as OLE-DB provided with SQL Server.

Compound Key The key of an entity that is made up of more than one attribute. A compound key can be made up of any number of entity attributes.

Computed Column   A virtual column present in a result set that is derived from other column values. An example of a computed column would be each employee's salary multiplied by 1.05 to account for a 5% raise.

Concatenation   The process of combining two character strings together to create a new string. The concatenation operator in T-SQL is the + character, therefore the T-SQL expression 'Hello' + 'world' would yield 'Hello world.'

Concurrency   The process by which SQL Server allows multiple users to access and change data at the same time within a database by using locking mechanisms.

Conditional Logic   The act of performing or not performing certain operations within a T-SQL batch based on certain conditions being true or false. Conditional logic is implemented within T-SQL by IF THEN statements, and CASE statements.

Controlled Redundancy   Introducing duplicate data within a physical database in order to realize a performance gain. Controlled redundancy is maintained through the use of database triggers.

CREATE (DDL)   The Data Definition Language command used to create a new database object.

Cursor   A special type of SQL Server object that is used to reference a result set one row at a time. A cursor can iterate through the rows of a result set, performing complex tasks on each row.

Cursor Scrollability   Determines the direction in which a cursor result set can be navigated. Examples include forward only, which means each row within a cursor result set can only be accessed sequentially; and scroll, which means rows can be fetched in either direction.

Cursor Sensitivity   Determines the way in which modifications to the base tables are reflected in a cursor result set. A static cursor will not reflect changes to the base tables in a cursor result set, whereas a dynamic cursor will reflect changes.

Data Control Language (DCL)   A group of SQL statements having to do with assigning permissions within a database. The GRANT command is an example of DCL.

Data Definition Language (DDL)   A group of statements having to do with the creation of database objects. CREATE and ALTER are examples of DDL.

Data File   With regards to BCP operations, the physical file that data is exported to or imported from. In SQL Server 2000, the actual operating system file that holds the data stored in a database.

Data Modification Language (DML)   A group of SQL statements having to do with manipulating data within a database. INSERT and UPDATE are examples of DML.

Data Transformation Services (DTS)   A companion application that ships with SQL Server used for architecting enterprise data transfers. DTS includes an intuitive graphical user interface for creating DTS packages that can be saved and scheduled for repeated execution.

Database Console Command (DBCC)   A series of T-SQL commands that check the logical and physical consistency of a database and report on other SQL Server information, such as open transactions. Some DBCC commands, such as DBCC CHECKDB, are processor intensive and should only be executed during times of low activity.

Database Options   A series of database-level settings that determine certain characteristics of the database, such as the automatic updating of statistics, compliance with ANSI standards, and the recovery model used in the database.

Database Population   The act of initially filling a new database with data existing in other systems. Tools such as BCP, BULK INSERT, and DTS are invaluable when initially populating a database.

Database User   An account that possesses rights within a database. Database users are mapped to SQL Server or Windows logins.

Datatype   The declaration of what type of data may be stored in a database column. Examples of datatypes include CHAR, VARCHAR, and INT.

Deadlock   An unresolvable case where two connections to a database each hold a lock on a particular resource and attempt to acquire a lock on the resource held by the other connection. A deadlock occurs when a connection would have to wait indefinitely for the other connection to release its lock on the resource requested.

Deadlock Victim   The connection chosen by SQL Server to be rolled back when a deadlock situation is detected. Typically, SQL Server will choose the least intensive process as the deadlock victim and raise error 1205.

Default Value   A declared value that will be inserted into a table column when no value is explicitly defined.

DELETE (DML)   The data modification language statement used to remove rows from a database table.

Delimited File   A file that contains multiple data values stored as a string. The values are separated by a certain character, or delimiter. The comma is a very typical delimiter.

Denormalization   The process by which the normal forms are intentionally violated to realize a performance gain in a database. Denormalization is fairly common when translating a logical data model into a physical database.

Derived Table   A query or subquery result set that is aliased for use within a FROM clause. The query result set is treated as a table by SQL Server, allowing it to be joined with other traditional result sets.

Distributed Query   A query that references datasources that are external to the local SQL Server.

Distributed Transaction A transaction that references datasources that are external to the local SQL Server.

Distributed Transaction Coordinator (DTC) The SQL Server service that acts as a transaction manager, which coordinates the actions of committing or rolling back transactions involving several datasources.

Distributor In replication, the server that contains the distribution database. The distribution database stores replication information including transaction and history information.

Domain In a logical data model, the characteristics of an attribute. An attribute's domain includes such factors as the type of data it will store, its nullability, and the range of values that may be stored.

DROP (DDL) The Data Definition Language statement used to remove a database object. The object must exist in the system tables in order to be affected by the DROP statement.

DTS Import Export Wizard A step-by-step wizard, included with data transformation services, that walks a user step by step through a data transformation process. Data transfer tasks created with the wizard may optionally be saved as DTS packages for scheduled execution.

DTS Package A saved object consisting of connection and task objects created using data transformation services. A DTS package is a data transformation job that can be saved in a variety of formats for scheduled execution.

Dynamic Memory Management A feature of SQL Server that allows for the database server to automatically measure performance and memory usage characteristics and to use this information to efficiently allocate memory.

Dynamic SQL A SQL statement wherein the object names being referenced are not known until runtime. Dynamic SQL allows for character strings of SQL statements to be dynamically built and executed.

Element   In XML, a thing or something that is represented in an XML document. Elements, much like entities in a logical data model, have attributes that describe them.

Encryption   The process by which SQL Server hides actual data by making it unreadable, thereby enhancing security.

Enterprise Manager   The main user interface provided with SQL Server. Enterprise manager allows for the centralized administration of multiple SQL Servers.

Entity   A logical grouping of data within a logical data model. A person, place, thing, or idea that is represented in a data model.

Error Severity Level   A numeric value that indicates the type of error that has occurred within SQL Server. These numeric values range from 0 through 25. Errors with a value of 20 or greater are considered fatal errors, and will terminate a client connection.

Escape Character   A character that indicates the character to follow is meant literally and not as an operator. An example of using an escape character is trying to include a single quote within a T-SQL string. In order to do so, the single quote must be preceded by an escape character, another single quote. Therefore to specify '*It's*' in a T-SQL string, '*It''s*' is specified so that the single quote does not end the string.

Exclusive Lock   A type of lock used to prevent other connections from acquiring a lock on a resource during an operation that modifies data. Exclusive locks are used when a connection performs an INSERT, UPDATE, or DELETE.

Execution Plan   A way to retrieve data that is stored in the procedure cache for a given query. When a query is submitted to SQL Server, it first checks the procedure cache to see if an existing execution plan for the query exists. If so, it reuses the execution plan to save the overhead of recompiling the query.

Extensible Markup Language (XML)   A standard way of structuring documents for sharing. XML uses a series of tags, similar to HTML tags, to define the structure of a document. However, there are no preset tags within XML; it is a self-defining language.

Extent   A unit of storage in SQL Server, used when allocating space to tables and indexes. A extent consists of eight pages, each 8k in size, making its size 64k. Extents can be shared by different objects or used to hold a single object.

Field Terminator   A character within a datafile that signifies the breaks between column values. The comma is a very common field terminator in datafiles.

Filegroup   A collection of storage files in SQL Server. Each database contains a default filegroup and user created filegroups can be added.

Fill Factor   Determines the amount of free space that will be left on index pages for future growth. A index's fill factor is specified as a percentage between 0 and 100. For example, an index with a fill factor of 50 will leave the leaf level index pages about half empty when the index is created.

Foreign Key Constraint   A property that is created on a table column to establish a relationship between database columns. Values entered into a column that has a foreign key constraint defined on it must match the column values of the unique column in the other table involved in the relationship.

Format File   A file used in conjunction with BCP and BULK INSERT that describes the format of a datafile. Format files are useful when datafiles are consistently imported with custom row and field terminators.

Four-part Naming Convention   The way in which external linked servers are referenced within T-SQL. The format of the four-part naming convention is ServerName.DatabaseName.OwnerName.ObjectName.

Full Outer Join　A type of join that returns unmatching rows from both the left and right result sets involved in a table join. Full outer joins are sometimes useful in reporting, however they typically return too much data for a given query.

Heap　A table stored without any clustered index defined on it is known as a heap. A heap does not store its rows in any particular order, nor are the data pages in any particular order. It is recommended that every table have a clustered index defined on it to avoid heap structures in a database.

Heterogeneous Data　A term that refers to data stored on a number of different systems, in different formats.

Hierarchal Data　Data that forms a tree structure, with nested levels of parent and child records. An example of hierarchal data is tracking employees and supervisors.

Hint　An argument provided to a T-SQL operation that modifies the way the request is processed. Examples of hints include forcing a query to use a certain index, or manually specifying the type of lock that will be used for a query.

Horizontal Partition　The process of splitting a table horizontally for performance purposes. The newly created tables all contain the same columns, but only a subset of rows from the original table.

Identity Property　A property assigned to a table column in SQL Server that will automatically generate and increment a numeric value. The identity property is commonly used with surrogate keys.

Index Allocation Map (IAM)　A chain of pages that map the extents in a database file used by an index or heap. Index allocation maps create a chain of sorts that link extents together.

Index Clustered　A database object defined on a table that greatly speeds retrieval operations. In a clustered index, the leaf level of the B-Tree is the data itself, therefore the table rows are physically stored in the same order as the logical order of the indexed column.

Fragmentation   The normal process by which data pages no longer store data most efficiently due to data modification statements. Fragmentation can occur in both tables and indexes and increases the amount of pages that need to be read to satisfy a query. Fragmentation can be addressed by recreating the clustered index on a table.

Index Leaf Level   Indexes in SQL Server are stored as a B-Tree structure. The leaf level of the B-Tree is the final level, with no more descendant levels.

Index Non Clustered   A database object defined on a table that greatly speeds retrieval operations. In a non-clustered index, the table rows are not physically stored in the same order as the logical order of the indexed column.

Index Tuning Wizard   A utility provided with SQL Server 2000 that analyzes a workload and makes index recommendations. The workload is created using SQL Profiler.

Indexed View   A view in SQL Server whose result set is persisted in the database. This can speed up operations involving complex views that join and aggregate large amounts of data.

Index, Covering   An index that contains all of the columns involved in a specific query. In that case, all of the information needed is contained within the index so only the index, and not the table, needs to be scanned.

Information Schema View   A set of system supplied views in SQL Server that provide information from system tables. Information schema views are the preferred way to access information stored in the SQL Server system tables, as the system table structure can change from release to release of SQL Server.

Inner Join   A type of join that returns only the matching rows from the left and right result sets involved in a join. Also called an equi-join.

INSERT (DML)   The data modification language statement used to add new rows to a database table.

Instance   A distinct occurrence of SQL Server running on a computer. SQL Server 2000 can support multiple instances running on the same computer.

Intelligent Key   A key attribute of an entity that has actual business meaning, unlike a surrogate key that is typically an automatically generated numeric value.

Intent Lock   A lock placed on a resource at a higher lever prior to an actual lock being placed on the intended resource at a lower level. For instance, a process needs to place a shared lock on certain rows in a table. Prior to doing this it will place an intent lock on the table level to let other processes know they can't place locks on the table.

Internet Information Services (IIS)   Services that ship with Windows 2000 that provide for the administering and management of Web sites and other Internet functions such as FTP.

Job   A series of defined operations that are saved as a unit for scheduled execution by SQL Server Agent.

Left Outer Join   A type of join that returns the matching rows from the left and right result sets involved in a join, as well as any unmatching rows from the left result set.

Lineage   A term describing the way in which entities relate to one another with regard to relationships. Lineage expresses these relationships in the terms of family lines—parent, child, etc.

Linked Server   An OLE-DB datasource defined as a permanent connection in SQL Server. Once the datasource is established with the pertinent security information, the linked server can be referenced in queries as if it were a remote database table.

Log File   An operating system file that contains a record of modifications made to a database. Log files and Data files make up the physical storage of a SQL Server database.

Logins   The means by which users access a SQL Server. A login can either be an SQL Server login using standard security, or a Windows login that uses integrated security.

Logical Data Model (LDM)   A blueprint or prototype of a physical database. A logical data model contains entities and attributes, discovered through analysis, that are translated into the tables and columns of a physical database. The more complete and correct the definition of the logical data model, the more correct the structure of the physical database.

Master Database   The system database that records system information for each named and default instance of SQL Server. The master database keeps track of a great deal of information such as database object names, server logins, and locking information.

Merge Replication   Replication model where subscribers are permitted to make changes to the local data and, at a later time, merge the changes with the publisher. Merge replication provides the means for conflict resolution arising from merged publications.

Model Database   The system database that acts as a template for each user created database. Any changes made to the model database will be reflected in any new user created databases.

MSDB   The system database that records system information regarding SQL Server Agent. DTS packages can also be stored in MSDB.

Namespace   In XML documents, a way to uniquely identify elements on an enterprise-wide scale. An XML namespace consists of a uniform resource identifier, or URI.

Nesting   The concept of encapsulating objects or operations within themselves. For example, a subquery is considered a nested query, because it is contained within another query.

Non-key Attribute   Any attribute within an entity that is not a primary or alternate key within the entity. Non-key attributes provide descriptive information about entities.

Normal Form   Any of a set of rules that govern the structure of entities in a logical data model. The first, second, and third normal forms are the most important rules to follow when developing a logical data model.

Normalization   The process by which the normal forms are applied to a logical data model design. Normalization has the effect of minimizing redundant data in a data model.

NULL   Literally, an unknown value. NULL values are not the same as empty strings or zero values. Typically, it is a good idea to keep columns that permit NULL values to a minimum in the physical database.

Object Linking and Embedding (OLE-DB)   A component object model–based application interface used to access data stored in a variety of formats from text files and spreadsheets to a any number of relational database products.

Object Owner   The user account under which a database object has been created. Unless the object owner is DBO or the same user as the current connection, this value must be explicitly defined when referencing a database object

Online Analytical Processing (OLAP)   A class of data storage that uses multidimensional structures to provide quick access to historical data for analysis. OLAP typically operates against a data warehouse, which is a version of summary historical data.

Online Transaction Processing (OLTP)   A class of data storage that services any number of concurrent users in real time. An example of an OLTP system is an order entry system. Whereas OLAP is used to study trends and make business decisions, OLTP is used to service users and contains heavily updated data.

Open Database Connectivity (ODBC)   An application programming interface that provides access to a wide number of data sources. ODBC is able to communicate with any datasource for which an ODBC driver exists.

Ownership Chain   The concept of procedures, views, and functions that depend on other database objects with respect to ownership of each dependant object. For example, a view is owned by one user that references a table owned by the same user. An ownership chain is considered broken when different users own the object and object referenced.

Page   A unit of storage in SQL Server equal to 8k. Database space is allocated in pages.

Parameter   A user defined value that is passed to a procedure or function. For example, the system function DATEDIFF requires three parameters to be passed to it in order to determine the time difference between two dates.

Parallelism   The concept of SQL Server using more than one CPU to process an operation. The maximum amount of processors that SQL Server can use may be controlled by the 'max degree of parallelism' option.

Partitioned View   A view that merges horizontally partitioned data from several tables to produce a result set appearing as a single table. An example would be an orders table that has been horizontally portioned by sales region, reassembled using a partitioned view.

Pass-Through Query   A query that is submitted on a local server but processed on a remote server. OPENQUERY is an example of a way to submit a pass-through query.

Permission, Statement-level   Determines if a user has rights to issue a CREATE or BACKUP statement in T-SQL. Statement permissions are given using the GRANT data control language command.

Permission, Object-level   A property of a database object that allows or prohibits a user from performing an action against the object. For example, in order to retrieve rows from the Authors table in the Pubs database, a user must have SELECT permissions on the Authors table database object.

Permission, GRANT   The Data Control Language statement used to assign a user permissions to a database object, such as a table or view, or statement permissions.

Permission, DENY   The Data Control Language statement used to prevent a user from gaining a permission directly or indirectly through group or role membership.

Permission, REVOKE   The Data Control Language statement used to remove a previously granted or denied permission.

Platform Independence   The concept of a system developed without regard for the vendor products it will operate on. A logical data model is considered to be platform independent.

Portability   How easily an application that runs on a particular system can be reworked to operate on a different system. The main purpose of using ANSI-compliant SQL is to enhance the portability of an application.

Precision   With regards to numeric data, the total amount of digits stored in a column both to the left and right of the decimal point.

Predicate   In T-SQL, an expression in a WHERE clause that is used to test a condition, thereby limiting a result set. In XPATH, a predicate is also used to test a condition and limit the resulting XML output. Examples include IN, LIKE, and BETWEEN.

Primary Key Constraint   A characteristic assigned to a column or group of columns, indicating that the column(s) will serve as the primary key of the table. Primary key constraints prohibit duplicate as well as NULL column values.

Profiler   A tool in SQL Server 2000 that can be used to display, record, and replay events that occur in SQL Server.

Profiler Event   Specific SQL Server occurrences that can be monitored by the Profiler application. SQL Server 2000 includes many built-in events (for example, transaction-related events). Additionally, developers can create their own events in order to monitor application-specific information.

Profiler Event Class   A logical grouping of Profiler Events. For example, all security auditing events are grouped within the "Security Audit" event class.

Profiler Template   Files that store trace definitions. SQL Server 2000 includes several pre-defined Profiler templates, and database administrators can create their own for monitoring specific aspects of system performance.

Profiler Trace File   A file that stored information collected by SQL Profiler. The file can be opened with the SQL Profiler tool, or by using special Transact-SQL system functions.

Profiler Trace Table   A database table that stored SQL Profiler trace information.

Profiler Trace Definition   A set of parameters and settings that define what types of information Profiler will collect, and how this information will be stored.

Publisher   In replication, the server that maintains the data that is replicated to subscribers of the data. The publisher also keeps track of publication information, as well as tracking changes to published data.

Query Analyzer   A graphical tool provided with SQL Server 2000 that allows ad-hoc queries to be issued and analyzed. Query Analyzer is also used to execute T-SQL batches and scripts, as well as study query execution plans.

Query Optimizer   The part of SQL Server responsible for generating execution plans and choosing the lowest cost method for retrieving data. The Query Optimizer considers things such as available indexes and join types when developing an execution plan.

Query Governor   A setting in SQL Server that defines a maximum time limit, defined in seconds, that a query can take to finish. The Query Optimizer considers the estimated time a query will take to finish and will only execute it if the time estimated does not exceed the Query Governor limit.

Recompile Setting   One of a number of ways to force SQL Server to discard the cached execution plan for a stored procedure and develop a new plan. Recompiling is useful if new indexes are added that are not considered in the current execution plan, but might increase the performance of a stored procedure.

Recovery Model   Determines how data is backed up and how the transaction log is utilized within a database. The available recovery models are Simple, Full, and Bulk Logged.

Recovery Process   A process that occurs each time SQL Server is started, either from a proper shutdown or from a system crash or failure. During the recovery process, completed transactions are rolled forward and incomplete transactions are rolled back.

Redundant Array of Independent Disks (RAID)   A system of using multiple disk drives to provide performance increases and/or fault tolerance to a storage system. Several levels of RAID exist: RAID 1, for example, is a mirrored disk drive; while RAID 5 is a striped set of disks with parity, or fault tolerance.

Referential Actions   Declared in a logical data model, the way in which each relationship will handle referential integrity violations. Examples include restrict, set null, and cascade.

Referential Integrity   The interaction between foreign key values and their parent primary key values. Referential integrity ensures that a foreign key value is either NULL or references a valid primary key value.

Relational Database Management System (RDBMS)   A vendor-developed product that hosts a relational database. Examples include SQL Server 2000, Oracle, and DB2.

Relationship   In a logical data model, the means by which entities interact with one another. Attributes in one entity will typically relate to attributes in another entity, thus forming a relationship.

Replication Agents   A series of processes that carry out the moment-to-moment tasks involved in replication.

Result Set   The actual rows and column values returned by a SQL statement. A result set can be the contents of an entire table, or restricted by using clauses.

Return Code   An integer value returned by a stored procedure to indicate the success or failure of the procedure. Return codes are defined in the body of the procedure.

Right Outer Join   A type of join that returns the matching rows from the left and right result sets involved in a join, as well as any unmatching rows from the right result set.

Rollback   The process of undoing any data modifications performed by a transaction. Rollbacks are necessary to preserve data integrity in the event of a system failure.

ROOT Element   The topmost element in a well formed XML document. Only one root element is permitted, however it does not have to be named root.

Row   An instance of a record in a database table.

Row Terminator   In a datafile, the character that separates lines of data. The newline character is a common row terminator.

Roles, Fixed Database   A predefined logical grouping of user accounts within SQL Server that exists at the database level. An example of a fixed database role is db_datareader, which has SELECT permissions on all user defined tables in a database.

Roles, Fixed Server   A role that exists at the server level. SQL Server provides several predefined server roles for simplifying administration. For example, members of the sysadmin fixed server role can perform any activity in the SQL Server installation.

Role, Public   A special role that every user in a database is a member of. Users cannot be removed from the public role, and the public role cannot be dropped.

Roles, User-defined   A custom role created when no fixed role will serve a security need. User-defined roles are created at the database level and are assigned the appropriate permissions.

Role, Application   A special kind of role used with an application to establish a security context. Application roles contain no members; they are activated from within an application and the permissions assigned to the application role will override all other permissions for the duration of the connection.

Rule   Similar to a check constraint, a rule is a database object that defines allowable values for a column and may be bound to more than one column. Check constraints are preferred over rules, as they are ANSI-92 compliant.

Scale   In a numeric datatype, the number of digits to the right of the decimal point.

Scan Operations (Table and Index)   Operations that require the SQL Server query optimizer to perform physical scans of tables and indexes. This process can be significantly slower than seek operations, especially for large tables or indexes.

Seek Operations (Table and Index)   Operations that allow the SQL Server query optimizer to take advantage of clustered and non-clustered indexes. Using seek operations can be significantly faster than using scan operations to perform the same tasks.

Schema   A visual representation of the tables, columns, and relationships that make up a physical database. Database schemas can be created and viewed using the Enterprise Manager diagramming tool.

Schema Lock   A lock applied to a database table when the table is being modified by an ALTER or DROP statement.

Schema Binding   In order to create an index on a view, the view being indexed as well as any user defined functions within the view definition must be created using schema binding. This prevents any changes to the underlying table that might invalidate the view index.

SELECT (DML)   The Data Modification Language statement used to retrieve column values and rows from database tables.

Server Login   A Windows or SQL Server account used to gain access to a SQL Server. Using Windows authentication, a user's Windows account is used to establish a connection to the SQL Server.

Shared Lock   A lock that is acquired on data being read but not updated. Shared locks are compatible with one another, meaning that many transactions can read the data at the same time. However, all shared locks must be released in order to update data.

Snapshot Replication   A type of replication that publishes an entire copy of the data at a given point in time and does not monitor any changes to the published data.

SQL Extension   A vendor-specific extension to the ANSI SQL standard. Relational database products such as Microsoft SQL Server and Oracle have their own unique enhancements to ANSI SQL.

SQL Server Agent   A service that runs alongside the SQL Server service that is responsible for such tasks as starting and stopping jobs and firing alerts. The SQL Server agent is useful for administering day-to-day tasks.

SQL Server Authentication   An alternative way to Windows authentication for validating attempts to connect to a SQL Server. When using SQL Server authentication, a valid SQL Server login and password must be provided that exist separately from the user's Windows login.

SQL Server Process ID (SPID)   A unique integer assigned to a database connection by SQL Server. While a SPID is used to uniquely identify a connection to the server, it is not permanent.

Statement   A command within T-SQL. Examples of statements are SELECT, INSERT, UPDATE, and DELETE.

Statistics   Information stored by SQL Server regarding the distribution of values in a table column or index. The query optimizer uses table and index statistics to determine the best way to satisfy a query. Statistics can become out of date when column and index values change, creating less than optimal query plans generated by the optimizer. Statistics can be updated both automatically and manually.

Stored Procedure   A block of T-SQL statements stored as a persistent object on the database server. Stored procedures promote the reuse of code, centralized management of code, and query plan reuse.

Structured Query Language (SQL)   The standard language used to communicate with relational databases as defined by ANSI, with vendor-specific extensions. Microsoft's implementation of SQL is known as Transact SQL.

Subquery   A query that is nested within a DML statement or other subquery. Subqueries allow queries to reference values in other database tables.

Subscriber   In replication, a server that is defined to receive copies of published data.

Subset   A grouping of data within a result set. Subsets of data can be identified and manipulated using the GROUP BY clause of SQL.

System Monitor   A graphical interface provided with Windows 2000 that uses a series of counters to monitor the behavior of a server. System Monitor was previously known as Performance Monitor in Windows NT.

Summary Data   Data produced by applying aggregate functions to a result set. Summary data is a single value obtained by aggregating a set or subset of values from a result set. Examples include the sum or average of all values in a particular column within a result set.

Super Aggregation   Aggregate functions applied to previously aggregated values in a result set. Super aggregations can by produced using the WITH CUBE and WITH ROLLUP clauses together with the GROUP BY clause.

Surrogate Key   A key value of an entity created for the sole purpose of serving as the key value of an entity. Surrogate keys have no real world meaning; they are typically an auto incremented numeric value. SQL Server's IDENTITY property is commonly used in the physical database to maintain a surrogate primary key.

System Function   A block of code treated as a single unit that takes arguments and returns information about SQL Server. Examples of system functions include CAST and GETDATE.

System Table   Built-in tables within a database that store internal information needed by the database engine to maintain an instance of SQL Server. System tables store information about database objects, users, and settings, and should not be modified directly.

Table   An object within the physical database used to store columns and rows of data. Database tables are translated from the entities of a logical data model.

Table Scan   A data retrieval operation in which no indexes are used. The entire table is scanned to determine which rows qualify to be returned in a query.

TEMPDB   A system database in SQL Server that is used to store temporary tables and stored procedures. TEMPDB serves as a workspace for temporary storage operations.

Template File   An XML document that contains an XPATH or T-SQL query. Template files are used with the Template virtual name type in SQL Server's XML IIS integration, and eliminate the need to enter long, complex queries in the URL line.

Temporary Table   A table that is created within the TEMPDB database. Temporary tables are not permanent database objects and are typically used as workspaces for complex queries.

Trace Flag   A group of flags or settings that can be switched on within SQL Server to further diagnose problems or change certain behavior. For example, setting trace flag 1204 on will give a more detailed report regarding the chain of events leading to a deadlock.

Transact SQL (T-SQL)   Microsoft's implementation of the ANSI SQL standard. T-SQL has entry-level compliance with ANSI SQL, as well as many useful extensions specific to T-SQL.

Transaction   A block of T-SQL statements treated as a single unit of work within the database. Transactions are either completely committed or completely rolled back, ensuring data consistency in the physical database.

Transaction Isolation Level   The means used to control the locking behavior of a transaction. The default transaction isolation level is READ COMMITED, which uses shared locks to retrieve data from tables. This prevents a transaction from reading uncommitted data.

Transaction Log   A database file used by SQL Server to track changes to a database. The transaction log is used to ensure data consistency in the event of a server failure.

Transactional Replication   A type of replication where subscribers have the transactions that have been applied at the publisher applied to their own local copy of the data. Transactional replication begins with the subscriber receiving a snapshot of the data, then transactions are applied as they occur on the publisher.

Transitive Dependency   A situation in which a non key attribute of an entity is not dependant on the primary key of the entity directly, but depends on the primary key of the entity transitively, by means of another attribute in the entity.

Transitive dependencies are eliminated by ensuring that entities comply with the third normal form of logical database design.

Trigger   A special type of stored procedure that executes when data in a database table is modified. Triggers can be set to execute after a data modification, or perform operations before the modification occurs using an INSTEAD OF trigger.

Unicode   A way of storing data using extended character sets. Traditional non-Unicode datatypes can store data that uses a 256 character set. Unicode data allows for each character to use a roughly 65,000 character set and is useful when dealing with international alphabets.

Union Join   A horizontal join that appends two result sets together, forming a virtual result set that is the total of the two. Both tables involved in a union join must have similar structures.

Unique Constraint   A characteristic assigned to a column that prevents duplicate values from being entered into a column. Unique constraints are useful for enforcing the integrity of alternate keys in the physical database.

Uniform Resource Identifier (URI)   A unique identifier used to prefix element names in an XML document, allowing them to be identified globally.

Universal Resource Locator (URL)   A unique string of text that identifies a location on the Internet. A URL contains information regarding the network protocol being used and the host name of the target—for instance, http://www.Microsoft.com.

Universal Table   A special table that is built when creating XML output using the FOR XML EXPLICIT clause. Universal tables require a very strict syntax and column naming convention to ensure correct XML output.

Update Lock   A type of lock placed on a resource that indicates a transaction will be modifying data. Update locks ensure that other connections do not attempt to read or update the locked data.

UPDATE (DML)   The data modification language statement used to modify column values in a database table.

User-Defined Datatype   A custom datatype created that is based on the underlying datatypes provided with SQL Server 2000.

User-Defined Function (UDF)   A user-created named block of code stored as an object in a database that is treated as a single unit that takes arguments and returns values.

Variable   A named object in a block of T-SQL code that is assigned a value. T-SQL variables are prefixed with the @ character.

Vertical Partition   The process of splitting a table vertically for performance or space utilization purposes. The newly created tables all contain the same number of rows, but only a subset of columns from the original table.

View   A virtual table that is built using underlying SQL Server tables and stored as a database object. Views are a convenient way to hide the complexity of joining many tables to produce a result set.

Virtual Directory   A directory used with SQL Server's XML IIS integration that is associated with a SQL Server database and used with URL based querying.

Well-Formed XML Document   Any XML document that adheres to the standards of XML. For example, a well-formed XML document can only have one root level element.

Wildcard   Characters that are not taken literally used for pattern matching in conjunction with the LIKE keyword. The _ is an example of a wildcard that indicates and single character.

Windows Authentication   A way to validate attempts to connect to a SQL Server that uses a connections existing Windows login. When using Windows authentication, no separate login or password need be provided to connect to the SQL Server.

Extensible Markup Language (XML)   A standard way of marking up documents to create structured information. XML is an attempt to create standardized documents for sharing.

XML-Data Reduced Schema (XDR)   A view of an XML document that describes the structure of the elements and attributes of the document, used with SQL Server XML IIS integration.

XPATH   A query language that is used to retrieve information from XML documents in much the same way that T-SQL is used to retrieve information from database tables. Much like T-SQL, XPATH supports the use of predicates to filter the data returned from the document.

INDEX

References to figures and illustrations are in italics.

S

U

INTERNATIONAL CONTACT INFORMATION

AUSTRALIA
McGraw-Hill Book Company Australia Pty. Ltd.
TEL +61-2-9417-9899
FAX +61-2-9417-5687
http://www.mcgraw-hill.com.au
books-it_sydney@mcgraw-hill.com

CANADA
McGraw-Hill Ryerson Ltd.
TEL +905-430-5000
FAX +905-430-5020
http://www.mcgrawhill.ca

GREECE, MIDDLE EAST,
NORTHERN AFRICA
McGraw-Hill Hellas
TEL +30-1-656-0990-3-4
FAX +30-1-654-5525

MEXICO (Also serving Latin America)
McGraw-Hill Interamericana Editores S.A. de C.V.
TEL +525-117-1583
FAX +525-117-1589
http://www.mcgraw-hill.com.mx
fernando_castellanos@mcgraw-hill.com

SINGAPORE (Serving Asia)
McGraw-Hill Book Company
TEL +65-863-1580
FAX +65-862-3354
http://www.mcgraw-hill.com.sg
mghasia@mcgraw-hill.com

SOUTH AFRICA
McGraw-Hill South Africa
TEL +27-11-622-7512
FAX +27-11-622-9045
robyn_swanepoel@mcgraw-hill.com

UNITED KINGDOM & EUROPE
(Excluding Southern Europe)
McGraw-Hill Education Europe
TEL +44-1-628-502500
FAX +44-1-628-770224
http://www.mcgraw-hill.co.uk
computing_neurope@mcgraw-hill.com

ALL OTHER INQUIRIES Contact:
Osborne/McGraw-Hill
TEL +1-510-549-6600
FAX +1-510-883-7600
http://www.osborne.com
omg_international@mcgraw-hill.com

Custom Corporate Network Training

Train on Cutting Edge Technology
We can bring the best in skill-based training to your facility to create a real-world hands-on training experience. Global Knowledge has invested millions of dollars in network hardware and software to train our students on the same equipment they will work with on the job. Our relationships with vendors allow us to incorporate the latest equipment and platforms into your on-site labs.

Maximize Your Training Budget
Global Knowledge provides experienced instructors, comprehensive course materials, and all the networking equipment needed to deliver high quality training. You provide the students; we provide the knowledge.

Avoid Travel Expenses
On-site courses allow you to schedule technical training at your convenience, saving time, expense, and the opportunity cost of travel away from the workplace.

Discuss Confidential Topics
Private on-site training permits the open discussion of sensitive issues such as security, access, and network design. We can work with your existing network's proprietary files while demonstrating the latest technologies.

Customize Course Content
Global Knowledge can tailor your courses to include the technologies and the topics which have the greatest impact on your business. We can complement your internal training efforts or provide a total solution to your training needs.

Corporate Pass
The Corporate Pass Discount Program rewards our best network training customers with preferred pricing on public courses, discounts on multimedia training packages, and an array of career planning services.

Global Knowledge Training Lifecycle
Supporting the Dynamic and Specialized Training Requirements of Information Technology Professionals

- Define Profile
- Assess Skills
- Design Training
- Deliver Training
- Test Knowledge
- Update Profile
- Use New Skills

College Credit Recommendation Program
The American Council on Education's CREDIT program recommends 53 Global Knowledge courses for college credit. Now our network training can help you earn your college degree while you learn the technical skills needed for your job. When you attend an ACE-certified Global Knowledge course and pass the associated exam, you earn college credit recommendations for that course. Global Knowledge can establish a transcript record for you with ACE, which you can use to gain credit at a college or as a written record of your professional training that you can attach to your resume.

Registration Information

COURSE FEE: The fee covers course tuition, refreshments, and all course materials. Any parking expenses that may be incurred are not included. Payment or government training form must be received six business days prior to the course date. We will also accept Visa/MasterCard and American Express. For non-U.S. credit card users, charges will be in U.S. funds and will be converted by your credit card company. Checks drawn on Canadian banks in Canadian funds are acceptable.

COURSE SCHEDULE: Registration is at 8:00 a.m. on the first day. The program begins at 8:30 a.m. and concludes at 4:30 p.m. each day.

CANCELLATION POLICY: Cancellation and full refund will be allowed if written cancellation is received in our office at least six business days prior to the course start date. Registrants who do not attend the course or do not cancel more than six business days in advance are responsible for the full registration fee; you may transfer to a later date provided the course fee has been paid in full. Substitutions may be made at any time. If Global Knowledge must cancel a course for any reason, liability is limited to the registration fee only.

GLOBAL KNOWLEDGE: Global Knowledge programs are developed and presented by industry professionals with "real-world" experience. Designed to help professionals meet today's interconnectivity and interoperability challenges, most of our programs feature hands-on labs that incorporate state-of-the-art communication components and equipment.

ON-SITE TEAM TRAINING: Bring Global Knowledge's powerful training programs to your company. At Global Knowledge, we will custom design courses to meet your specific network requirements. Call 1 (919) 461-8686 for more information.

YOUR GUARANTEE: Global Knowledge believes its courses offer the best possible training in this field. If during the first day you are not satisfied and wish to withdraw from the course, simply notify the instructor, return all course materials, and receive a 100% refund.

In the US:

CALL: 1 (888) 762-4442

FAX: 1 (919) 469-7070

VISIT OUR WEBSITE:

www.globalknowledge.com

MAIL CHECK AND THIS FORM TO:

Global Knowledge

Suite 200

114 Edinburgh South

P.O. Box 1187

Cary, NC 27512

In Canada:

CALL: 1 (800) 465-2226

FAX: 1 (613) 567-3899

VISIT OUR WEBSITE:

www.globalknowledge.com.ca

MAIL CHECK AND THIS FORM TO:

Global Knowledge

Suite 1601

393 University Ave.

Toronto, ON M5G 1E6

REGISTRATION INFORMATION:

Course title _____

Course location _____ Course date _____

Name/title _____ Company _____

Name/title _____ Company _____

Name/title _____ Company _____

Address _____ Telephone _____ Fax _____

City _____ State/Province _____ Zip/Postal Code _____

Credit card _____ Card # _____ Expiration date _____

Signature _____

GET CERTIFIED WITH HELP FROM THE EXPERTS

MCDBA SQL Server™ 2000 Database Design Study Guide (Exam 70-229)

A COMPLETE STUDY PROGRAM BUILT UPON
PROVEN INSTRUCTIONAL METHODS

Expert advice on how to take a[...] [...]roblems and solutions

"Remember that views don't a[...]
(although you can use them in m[...]
use tables). Therefore, views have a minimal impact [...] [...]y not be match-
size of a database."

Step-by-step Certification Exercises fo[...]
skills most likely to be on the exam. T[...]
you to the instructional video animation t[...]
skill set on CD-ROM.

Special warnings that prepare you for tricky exam [...]

exam
Watch

"Sometimes they are unavoidable, but NULL v[...]
can be problematic in a database table. Carefully
consider any exam answers that suggest incorporat-
ing NULL values into a database structure."

MCDBA **On The Job Notes** present important lessons that help
you work more efficiently:

on the
Job

"Note that in cases where the inserted values refer-
ence other tables, the VALUES keyword is not speci-
fied. Specifying VALUES in such a situation will
result in a syntax error."

Two-Minute Drills at the end of every chapter quickly reinforce
your knowledge and ensure better retention of key concepts:

"Aggregate functions are most commonly used with
subsets of data. The GROUP BY clause allows for a
result set to be grouped into subsets. The HAVING
clause allows for the restricting of rows in a result
set based on aggregate values."

D. OPENX[...]
ment to r[...]

☑ **C** is the correct a[...] [...]d with the
sp_xml_preparedoc[...] [...]edure, which
creates a handle that O[...]n then reference.

☒ **A** is incorrect because OPENXML requires a document handle created by the sp_xml_preparedocu-
ment stored procedure as an argument, not the
XML document itself as variable. **B** is incorrect
because OPENXML can use any XML document
fragment that has only one top-level element. **D** is
also incorrect, as OPENXML uses an XPATH query
to determine which elements and attributes to
retrieve from the XML document.

DATE DUE

DEMCO, INC. 38-2931